MUSIC AND MORALS

MUSIC AND MORALS

H. R. HAWEIS

GYAN

Published by

GYAN

Gyan Publishing House
5, Ansari Road
Daryaganj, New Delhi-110002
Phone: 011-47034999, 9811692060
E-mail: books@gyanbooks.com

Distribution Network
gyanbooks.com
India, USA, Canada, UK, Australia

ISBN: 978-93-7447-338-2 (PB)

First Published, 1881

2nd Impression 2026

Printed at: Gyan Press, Delhi.

MUSIC AND MORALS
Author: H. R. HAWEIS

MUSIC AND MORALS

Yours ever
faithfully
H R Haweis.

MUSIC AND MORALS

BY THE

REV. H. R. HAWEIS, M.A.

1881

TO MY WIFE

WHOSE PEN HAS SAVED ME SO MUCH LABOUR,

AND TO WHOSE PENCIL I OWE

ALL THE ILLUSTRATIONS, FAC-SIMILES, AND DIAGRAMS IN THIS VOLUME,

I Dedicate

THESE STUDIES OF MY LEISURE HOURS.

CONTENTS.

First Book.

PHILOSOPHICAL.

Music, Emotion, and Morals.

	PAGE
The Fount of Colour	3
The Fount of Sound	4
Nature and Art	5
Music and other Arts	8
Emotions and Objects	10
Abstract Emotion	14
Analysis of Emotion	18
Connection between Music and Emotion	22
Dull Music	25
Objections	26
Connection between Music and Words	27
Sound-Art and Colour-Art	30
Music and the Age	34
Art and Morals	38
Morality Defined	40
Morality Applied	43
Music and Morality	46
Emotion and Morals	49
The Composer	51
Rise of Music	52
Realism and Sentimentalism	54
German, Italian, and French Schools	55
The Executive Musician	60
Soloists	65
Orchestral Players	72
Culture	79
Morality	81

PAGE
Longevity 91
The Listener 92
Planes of Emotion 95
Shakspeare and Raphael 98
Italian and German Sentiment 100
Patriotic Songs 102
Musical Perturbations 103
Memory 106
Musical Quotation 108
Women and Music 109
Dream-Life 111
Sacred Music.—The Oratorio 113
Congregational Singing 114
Slow Church 116
Choir Reformation 117
Use of Anthems and Voluntaries 118
Need of Artistic Unity 119

Second Book.

BIOGRAPHICAL.

From Ambrose to Handel.

First and Second Periods 125
Third Period 129
Carissimi, Italy 131
John Dunstable, England 132
Lulli, France 133
Purcell 134
Handel, Germany 136

Handel.

His Portraits 138
Childhood 140
Early Manhood 143
Italy 145
England 150
Second Visit to England 152
Handel and his Friends 154
Operas 161
Reverses 163

	PAGE
More Trials	165
Contemporary Composers	170
Music in England	175
Oratorios	178
Cabals	181
Handel at Oxford	183
More Operas and Cabals	184
A Funeral Anthem	187
Failure and Success	188
Saul and Israel in Egypt	190
Handel in Ireland	195
The Messiah	196
Samson and the Occasional Oratorio	207
Judas Maccabæus	209
Joshua, Solomon, Susannah, Theodora	210
Handel at Peace	213
A Visit to Master Hardcastle	215
The Last Act	219

GLUCK.

Portrait of Gluck	224
Rise of Gluck and State of Music in 1714	225
Gluck and Handel	227
Gluck's Style	228
The Opera a Defective Form of Art	229
Rise of the German Opera	232
Gluck in Paris	233
Gluckists and Piccinists	235
Old Age and Death	237
Estimate of his Character	238

HAYDN.

Likeness and Difference	241
Early Days	243
Metastasio and Porpora	246
Quartets	247
A Tempest	248
Symphonies	249
Prince Esterhazy	250
Work and Wife	251
Mozart	253

	PAGE
Haydn in England	255
The Creation and the Seasons	258
Characteristics	260

SCHUBERT.

Schubert and Chopin	264
Precocious Talent	265
Early Compositions	268
His Friends	271
His Appearance	273
Work and Romance	274
Beethoven	279
Last Days	281
His Compositions	282

CHOPIN.

Romantic and Classical Schools	290
First Years	292
His Manners	294
His Style	294
Paris	295
His Friends	296
Chopin and Madame Sand	300
England	302
Death	303
His Compositions	304

THE LETTERS OF MOZART.

Omissions Explained	307
Vivid Letters	308
Paris, Vienna, and Love	310
Haydn	312
Activity and Death	313

THE LETTERS OF BEETHOVEN.

Appearance	318
Childhood and only Loves	319
Deafness	321
Carl, the Young Rascal	323

	PAGE
His Generosity and Poverty	325
His Religion and his Art	327
Death	328

MENDELSSOHN.

Books about Mendelssohn	331
Characteristics	333
Temperament	335
Wife, Children, Death	336
Elijah.—Introduction	338
Entrance of the Prophet Elijah	339
Famine and Dearth	340
The Desert	342
The Sacrifice on Mount Carmel	343
The Storm on Mount Carmel—"Thanks be to God"	345
The Elijah and the Messiah	347
Exultation, and "Be not Afraid"	348
Jezebel	350
Elijah Forsaken and Comforted	352
Earthquake on Mount Horeb	355
Elijah is taken up into Heaven	358
A Perfect Close	361

Third Book.

INSTRUMENTAL.

VIOLINS.

Introduction	367
Origin of the Violin	369
Gasparo di Salo, Magini, and the Amatis	376
Stradiuarius	379
Violin-making	387
Conclusion	393

PIANOFORTES.

Origin of the Pianoforte	396
The Virginal	399
The Spinet	402

PAGE
The Pianoforte 403
Sebastien Bach 404
Mozart and Clementi 405
Erard, Broadwood, Collard, Pleyel 407

Bells.

Towers and Belfries 410
Bell-hunting 417
Antiquity of Bells 419
Use of Bells 422
Bell-founding in Belgium 424
Belgian Bell-Founders 429
Inscriptions 433
St. Paul's and Westminster Abbey 437
Big Ben 440
Our Belfries 446
Waste and Ruin 448
Remedies 451
Our Musical Country again 453
The Bells of Belgium 457
Bell Music 459
The Carillon 460
Carillonneurs 463
Matthias van den Gheyn 465
Van den Gheyn's Music 469
Van den Gheyn Redivivus 472
English Bell Works 475
Reform Needed 479

Fourth Book.

CRITICAL.

Music in England.

England not Musical 483
English Liberality 487
Seed and Soil 488
Mendelssohn in England 490
Growing Taste for Good Music 492
Mons. Jullien 493
His Followers 495

	PAGE
Musical Progress	496
Music Halls and Negro Melodies	498
String Quartets	501
The Musical Amateur	505
People who Play the Piano	506
Concerted Chamber Music	511
The People who Sing	515
The Quartet Party	519
The Scratch Quartet	521
Orchestral Societies	523
Vocal Associations	526
Harp, Bagpipes, Cornemuse, and Hurdy-Gurdy	529
The Organ-Grinder	532
Bands	538
The Brass without the Band	540
The Band without the Brass	541
The String Band	541
The String Band Dissolved	543
Miscellaneous Artists	544
Vocal Street Music	546
Ballad Singers, Male and Female	549
Blind Singers	550
Negro Melodists	550
CONCLUSION	553
APPENDIX	555

First Book.

PHILOSOPHICAL.

MUSIC, EMOTION, AND MORALS.

First Book.

MUSIC, EMOTION, AND MORALS.

I.

THE sun smiting through crystal drops shakes its white light into blue, and red, and yellow fire; and, as the beads of fresh-fallen rain tremble in the wind, we may watch the primary colours of the rainbow combined and recombined with wondrous alchemy into more subtle flame of emerald, purple, and orange. A cloud passes over the sky, and in a moment every tiny globe hangs before us, scintillant still, but pale and colourless, with its one quivering speck of crystalline light. Then we can see with quiet eyes the metallic lustre upon the wide blue wings of the Brazilian butterfly—the green dissolving into glitter of rubies upon the breast of the humming-bird—the long reaches of golden king-cups in June meadows, or opal tints upon wet shells and blown foam. Have we not looked into the great laboratories of light itself? Have we not seen the essential colours in the very moment of their evolution falling like shattered flame-flakes from the sun? Is it so strange to find them mingled bountifully with all created things, and made fast in every conceivable tint upon plume of bird and petal of flower?

The painter goes forth each day into a new Eden, and finds his palette already laid for him. He cannot choose but take the materials and follow the suggestions which Nature so freely gives him. He, too, can combine and recombine; can distribute his hues in concord and discord of colour; can associate them with definite images, or, making them the vehicles of poetic emotion, paint "the sunshine of sunshine, and the gloom of gloom."

The wailing of the wind at night, the hum of insect life, the nightingale's note, the scream of the eagle, the cries of animals, and, above all, the natural inflections of the human voice—such are the rough elements of music, multitudinous, incoherent, and formless. Earth, and sea, and air are full of these inarticulate voices; sound floats upward from populous cities to the Cloudland, and thunder rolls down its monotonous reply. Alone by the sea we may listen and hear a distinct and different tone each time the swelling wavelet breaks crisply at our feet; and when the wind with fitful and angry howl drives inland the foam of the breakers, the shriek of the retiring surge upon the shingles will often run through several descending semitones.

It would seem, then, that we have only to take the Colour and the Sound provided for us by Nature and transform them at once through the arts of Painting and Music into the interpreters of human thought and emotion. But, in reality, between music and painting there is fixed a great gulf of difference. Nature gives man the art of Painting, as it were, ready made. For him the sun sets and rises, and the summer glows, and the woods change so softly and slowly beneath his gaze, that he has time to chronicle every tint before it has passed away. All forms of beauty, from the supreme outline of the human body to the filmy speck of the minutest insect, are constantly limning themselves upon the retina of his eye until his sensitive brain is supplied with objects of enchanting loveliness, which he is at liberty to reproduce and recombine at will. Nature not only provides the painter with fair forms and rich colours, but she also teaches him the magical art of selection and arrangement. But what has she done for the musician? She has given him sound, not music. Nowhere does there fall upon his ear, as he walks through the wide world, such an arrangement of consecutive sounds as can be called a musical subject, or theme, or melody. Far less does he find anything which can be described as musical harmony. The thunder is not affecting because it is melodic, but because it is loud and elemental. The much-extolled note of the lark is only pleasant because associated with the little warbler, "the sightless song" in the depth of the blue sky, for when the lark's trill is so exactly imitated (as it can be with a whistle in a tumbler full of water) that it deceives the very birds themselves, it ceases to be in the least agreeable, just as the sound of the wind, which can also be well imitated by any one compressing his lips and moaning, ceases under such circumstances to be in the least romantic. The nightingale's song, when at its best, has the advantage of being a single and not unpleasantly loud whistle. That, too, can be imitated so as to defy detection. But once let the veil of night be withdrawn, and the human nightingale disclosed, and we shall probably all admit that his performance is dull, monotonous, and unmeaning. The cuckoo, who often sings a true third, and sometimes a sharp third or even a fourth, is the nearest approach to music in Nature; but this tuneful fowl gets less credit for his vocal powers than almost any other; and whilst he is screamed at and hunted from hedge to hedge by his own species as a very outlaw among birds, he is voted but a coarse and vulgar songster by man. At any rate, though some may admire his call as the herald note of spring, yet when "cuckoo cuckoo" is blown, as boys know how to blow, upon the hollow fists, no one except the cuckoo cares to listen to the strain for its own sweet sake. The cries of most large birds, such as the ostrich and peacock, are intolerably disagreeable. Nor are the voices of the animals, from the pig, the cat, and the donkey downwards, any better. We need not go so far as Mr. Darwin's Gibbon monkey to find an animal that sings several notes and occasionally hits an octave, for the same can be said of the domestic cat; but in neither case is there such an arrangement of notes as can be called Melody, or such a combination of notes as can be called Harmony. Poets from time immemorial have tried to throw dust in the eyes of mankind whenever they have touched upon this subject, but it is high time the truth should be told. The Harmonies of Nature are purely metaphorical. There is no music in Nature, neither melody nor harmony. Music is the creation of man. He does not reproduce in music any combination of sounds he has ever heard or could possibly hear in the natural world, as the painter transfers to his canvas the forms and tints he sees around him. No, the musician seizes the rough element of sound and compels it to work his will, and having with infinite pains subjugated and tamed it, he is rewarded by discovering in it the most direct and perfect medium in all Nature for the expression of his emotions.

The Painter's art lies upon the surface of the world; its secrets are whispered by the yellow corn-fields spotted with crimson fire, and the dappled purple of heather upon the hills; but the Musician's art lies beneath the surface. His rough material of Sound is like the dull diamond, earth-encrusted and buried in deep mines; it simply does not exist as a brilliant and a thing of priceless beauty, until it has been refined and made luminous by deliberate arrangement of glittering facets, set in splendour of chaste gold.

And then—what then, it will be asked, what does all this manipulation of sound end in? what is the value or dignity of this art of Music? We easily recognise the foundation of other arts. The art of Sculpture rests upon the fact that when man awakens to a sense of the beauty, power, or even grotesqueness of form, he is impelled by a creative instinct to reproduce, select, and combine its various qualities—firstly, that he may perpetuate the forms of fleeting beauty that he sees around him; and secondly, that he may impart to the ideal conceptions of his imagination an outward and concrete existence. We are not ashamed to derive the keenest satisfaction from the Niobe or the Antinous, for we see in these a perennial and dignified expression of human grace and pathos. And even when we turn to such painful and distorted figures as the Laocoon, although we may call them "debased art" according to our canons of taste, yet neither these nor any other specimens, however corrupt or weak, can affect the real dignity of sculpture itself. Similarly, the art of Painting rests upon a rational impulse to select and combine colours, chiefly in connection with intelligible forms and subjects of definite interest; and although painting is less definite in some respects, and less complete in others, than sculpture, yet its range is wider, its material infinitely more ductile, whilst its command of emotion through the vehicle of colour, and of ideas through variety of outline, gives it an importance and dignity which it would be difficult to overestimate. Even such an art as Legerdemain is capable of a satisfactory explanation; for it is the outward realization in one department, however narrow, of certain excellent qualities of the eye and hand. A Phidian sculpture, a picture by Titian, even a conjuring trick by Professor Frikell, can be accounted for and justified in a few words. But when we come to a Symphony by Beethoven, philosophy is dumb, or rides off upon a quibble about the scientific structure of music or its technical qualities, all true and interesting, no doubt, but still leaving untouched the great Art-problem of music—What is the rationale of its existence, and what the secret of its power over the soul?

Music, as distinguished from the various rude attempts of the past, is only about four hundred years old. Modern music, which is alone worthy of the name, is in fact the youngest of the arts, and stands at present in a correspondingly unfavourable position: for whilst it has been brought to the highest perfection, the secret of its power is almost wholly unexplored; and as long as this is the case, music must continue to be ranked last among the fine arts. But the day is at hand when the veil of the prophetess will be lifted. Already in Germany, the land of thought, music has been adopted as the national art—as painting was once in Italy, and sculpture in Greece. Already the names of Beethoven and Mozart are whispered through the civilized world in the same breath with those of Phidias and Michael Angelo, and the time is probably not far distant when music will stand revealed perchance as the mightiest of the arts, and certainly as the one art peculiarly representative of our modern world, with its intense life, complex civilization, and feverish self-consciousness.

It has often been said that music is the language of the emotions; but what there is in music to act upon emotion, or how it both expresses and excites it, sometimes compelling the mind to clothe the awakened emotion with definite ideas—at others, dispensing with ideas altogether—this has never yet been explained. With the cautiousness and humility of one who feels himself upon untrodden ground, I offer the following reflections as a contribution to the much-neglected study of Musical Psychology.

II.

WE cannot do better than start with the popular assertion that music is the language of the emotions. But before we attempt to show the points of contact between emotion and its art-medium, and before we can understand how it is that music finds itself on the same plane of action with the emotions, and so fitted to become at one time their minister expressing them, at another their master commanding them, it will be necessary to form a clear and almost concrete conception of the emotions themselves. Of course we can no more get to the root of that aspect of life exhibited in emotion, than we can get to the root of life itself in man, or beast, or vegetable. Life is only known by the sensations and appearances which accompany it—by its proximate, and not its ultimate causes. Speaking physically, then, what happens when a person is moved or excited? A certain quickening or slackening of the blood as it rushes through the heart, or what we call a hurried or enfeebled pulse, and a corresponding disarrangement of molecules in the brain. If it were not for these, acting through what we may call nerve-currents, we should not be capable, constituted as we are at present, of experiencing any emotion at all. The nature of our emotions may depend either upon the nature of external objects presented to the senses, or upon internal and unexplained processes connected with what we call our thoughts. Now, what most people are alive to is the existence of emotions in their more intense forms. Once in the course of the day, or two or three times during the month, they have been greatly moved or excited pleasurably or otherwise. But what few people realize is, that emotion is actually coextensive with consciousness. Physically this is the case, for there is no pause in the incessant disturbance and rearrangement of the cerebral molecules which are inseparably connected with the phenomena of human consciousness, and human consciousness itself is nothing but an uninterrupted concatenation of emotions, most of them so unimportant, so involved, and succeeding each other with such intense rapidity, that we take no note of them. Like distant lights in a dark night, only those of a certain brightness are visible to the naked eye. As a traveller in a railway-carriage sees the objects fly by him with a rapidity which lessens the impression that each is calculated to make by itself, but takes note of a cathedral or a regiment of soldiers, so the multitudinous objects and events that crowd upon us during the most uneventful day may indeed affect us consciously, and produce a great variety of feelings without once awakening the emphatic self-consciousness of a strong emotion.

It may be a relief to the reader if we ask him to pause at this stage of the proceedings, and analyze very roughly a few of the emotions which in a very short space of time he is in the habit of experiencing. It would require volumes to analyze properly the emotional history of a single hour, but the reality and continuity of such a history may be briefly indicated.

On first awakening we may all have experienced at times a puzzled kind of feeling. This is produced by the conflict between the conditions of the waking and the sleeping states. A feeling of doubt, as to whether we are really going to be hanged, as we just now dreamed, is succeeded by a sense of relief, passing quickly into a sense of humour, which in its turn is arrested by a sense of depression caused by the eye falling on a letter containing bad news received on the previous night. Then follows a train of speculation, resulting in an infinite series of little elations and depressions as we take a hopeful view of the concern or otherwise. A knock at the door brings a welcome distraction, and we leap up with an energy which is really the result of a complex state of feeling; that is to say, emotion of relief at getting rid of a disagreeable subject; emotion caused by a resolution to get dressed; emotion caused by anxiety to be in time for an engagement; emotion caused by a chilly feeling, which reminds us of a fire down-stairs, &c., &c. Upon opening the door and seizing the hot-water jug, we experience a sudden depression on finding the water barely tepid; but quick as thought the elation of anger succeeds as we rush to the bell-rope, which comes down beneath our too vigorous efforts, and again supplies us with a complex emotion; emotion of resentment against the servant, the cause of all the mischief; ditto against the carpenter who put up the bell-rope the day before; ditto against ourselves for angry haste; reflex feeling of resolve to be more careful next time; prospective feeling of annoyance at having to pay for putting up the rope again. It is perhaps needless to continue the analysis of that internal life which consists of such an infinite variety of important, trivial, and complex feelings. But before we consider how music deals with emotion, we must try and seize the fact that the history of each hour does not only consist of outward incidents, but that each one of these incidents and objects, as also every thought which flits through the mind, has its own accompanying emotion, or train of emotions, and that the whole of human life forms one vast emotional fabric, begun long before thought, and continued down to the feeblest pulse of second childhood.

Hitherto we have considered emotion in connection with definite images such as letters, bell-ropes, hot-water jugs: but it is quite a mistake to suppose that definite images, or even thoughts, are indispensable to the existence of emotion. We may be tempted to think that emotions derive all their importance and dignity from the thoughts with which they happen to be associated. The very reverse of this, however, is the case. Emotion is often weakened by association with thought, whereas thoughts are always strengthened by emotion. Indeed emotion is the very breath and life-blood of thought, which without it would remain but a pale and powerless shadow, incapable of asserting itself, or of exercising any kind of influence, good or bad. As the sun brings light and warmth to the visible world, as without it the whole realm of physical life would lie forlorn in one long midnight of cold paralysis, even so the solar orb of our emotions kindles each thought and endows each conception with fertile activity. What power can any thought have without emotion? When a man is exhausted with hunger and fatigue, you may pass through his mind the most striking thoughts of Shakspeare or the most thrilling images of Byron, but they will be without effect, because of the absence of emotional force in him.

On the other hand, the commonest object in nature, a wayside daisy,

> "The meanest flower that blows,"

seen a thousand times without the smallest emotion, may one day be seen with the poet's eye, and will suddenly be found to contain thoughts

> "Too deep for tears."

No doubt, granting a certain measure of sensibility, out of a definite thought an emotion of some sort will arise; it is equally true that out of an indefinite emotion corresponding thoughts will often arise. But there is this difference between Thought and Emotion —thought is dead without emotion, whereas emotion has a life of its own entirely independent of thought. Thoughts are but wandering spirits that depend for their vitality upon the magnetic currents of feeling.

The essential power of emotions over thoughts is recognised in the most popular forms of language. The thought of heaven as a *Place* is sufficiently powerless, however much we may deck it out with apocalyptical splendours; but we speak of the *State* of the Blessed as of a certain emotional condition of joy, and are perfectly satisfied to rest in that definition as the profoundest of all realities, although we may not be able to illustrate it by one definite thought, or associate it with any one distinct image. But further, when viewed through the lenses of more abstract reflection, all definite thoughts and distinct images are seen more clearly still to be but the helps and crutches to something beyond them—something which may hereafter become in its turn definite and distinct, leading us on to yet another dimness and yet another Revelation. Once raise a thought to its highest power, and it not only is accompanied by the strongest emotion, but, strange to say, actually passes out of the condition of a thought altogether into the condition of an emotion, just as hard metal raised to a sufficient power of heat evaporates into the most subtle and attenuated gases. The pious Roman Catholic kneeling before the crucifix passes through successive emotional stages, from the gross representation of a tortured human body to the ideal form of a risen and glorified Saviour, until at length to the devotee, whose adoring eyes are still fixed upon the wooden crucifix, nothing remains but the emotion of a presence, felt but not understood, in which he seems to live, and move, and have his being. That is the moment, he will tell you, of his highest life, the seventh heaven has been reached, more intensely real than any scene of earth: but it is wholly internal, a kingdom within, the fulness of life, and yet to the common senses impalpable, without form and void. The same phenomena are presented to us by every fine actor; we feel that his art culminates, not in the rounded period, nor even in the loud roar and violent gesticulation of excited passion, but in the breathless silence of intense feeling, as he stands apart and allows the impotency of exhausted symbols, the quivering lip and the glazed eye, to express for him the crisis of inarticulate emotion.

But, it will be urged, in each case we start from something definite; in the latter we start from the incidents of the play. That provides us with a key to the emotion. Exactly so. But what I am maintaining is, not that emotion does not accompany definite thought, but simply that thought, in proportion to its intensity, has a tendency to pass into a region of abstract emotion independent and self-sufficing.

In the same way Poetry, which, as Mr. J. S. Mill observes, is nothing but "thought coloured by strong emotion, expressed in metre, and overheard," is constantly composed of words which will hardly bear analysis, as simple vehicles for the expression of definite thoughts, but which may be justified as attempts to express the quickening of an idea, or the evaporation of thought in emotion. Nothing is more common than to hear a person say, "A truly exquisite poem; but what on earth does it mean?" A search for definite thoughts may very likely be in vain. What the poem really means is a certain succession or arrangement of feelings, in which emotion is everything, and the ideas only helps and crutches. This result is often obtained by what stupid people call extravagance of language or confusion of imagery, and by what Mr. R. H. Hutton has happily termed "the physical atmosphere of words." J. M. W. Turner's vagueness and extravagance, so much complained of by common folk, is another example of the transformation of thoughts into emotion. Mr. Ruskin has observed that Turner painted the *souls* of pictures. Even Turner's opponents will agree that in many of his pictures most of the distinct images have evaporated; while others perceive that these have only vanished to make way for emotions of transcendent force and beauty.

It seems to us evident, then, that the tendency of emotion in all its higher stages is to leave in abeyance definite thoughts and images—is it equally certain that it occupies an independent region, and can start without them? A very little reflection will probably convince us that we may be in a state of emotional depression, or otherwise—what we call in good spirits or in bad spirits—without being able to assign any reason, or to trace the mood in any way to any one thought or combination of ideas. A thought may, indeed, flash upon the depressed spirit, and dissipate in an instant our depression—or the fit of depression may pass away of itself by mere force of reaction. Sensitive temperaments are peculiarly liable to such "ups and downs;" but we shall find, if we examine our experiences, that although the emotional region is constantly traversed by thoughts of every possible description, it has a life of its own, and is distinct from them even as water is distinct from the various reflections that float across its surface.

So far we have merely attempted to show the connection which exists between Thoughts and Emotions; and during the process we have affirmed the independent existence of an emotional region, in which there takes place a never-ceasing play and endless succession of emotions, simple and complex. But in order to show the ground of contact between music and emotion, it will be necessary to put emotion itself into the crucible of thought, and express its properties by symbols.

We shall then subject Sound, as manipulated by the art of music, to the same kind of analysis; and if we find that Sound contains exactly the same properties as emotion, we shall not only have established points of resemblance between the two, but we shall have actually reached the common ground, or kind of border-land, upon which internal emotion becomes wedded to external. sound, and realizes for itself that kind of concrete existence which it is the proper function and glory of art to bestow upon human thought and feeling. If we now attempt to analyze a simple emotion we shall find that it invariably possesses one or more of the following properties; complex emotions possess them all.

I. ELATION AND DEPRESSION.—When a man is suffering from intense thirst in a sandy desert the emotional fount within him is at a low ebb, A; but, on catching sight of a pool of water not far off, he instantly becomes highly elated, and, forgetting his fatigue, he hastens forward upon a new platform of feeling, B. On arriving at the water he finds it too salt to drink, and his emotion from the highest elation sinks at once to the deepest depression, C.

II. VELOCITY.—At this crisis our traveller sees a man with a water-skin coming towards him, and his hopes instantly rise, D; and, running up to him, he relates how his hopes have been suddenly raised, and as suddenly cast down, at B and C respectively; but long before his words have expressed or even begun to express his meaning he has in a moment of time, ⟵ x, in fact spontaneously with the utmost mental velocity, repassed through the emotions of elation and depression, A B C, which may at first have lasted some time, but are now traversed in one sudden flash of reflex consciousness.

III. Intensity.—As he drinks the sparkling water, we may safely affirm that his emotion increases in intensity up to the point where his thirst becomes quenched, and that every drop that he takes after that is accompanied by less and less pungent or intense feeling.

IV. Variety.—Up to this time his emotion has been comparatively simple; but a suffering companion now arrives, and as he hands to him the grateful cup his emotion becomes complex, that is to say, he experiences a variety of emotions simultaneously. First, the emotion of contentment at having quenched his own thirst; second, gratitude to the man who supplied him with water—an emotion probably in abeyance until he had quenched his thirst; third, joy at seeing his friend participating in his own relief.

V. Form.—If the reader will now glance over this simple narrative once more by the aid of the accompanying diagrams, he will see that both the simple and the complex emotions above described have what,

EMOTIONAL SYMBOLS.

Fig. 1.

I. Elation and Depression .

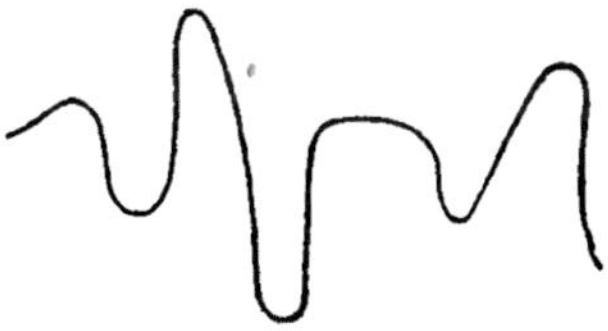

Fig. 2.

II. Velocity x

Fig. 3.

III. Intensity . . . . . .

Fig. 4.

IV. Variety . . . .

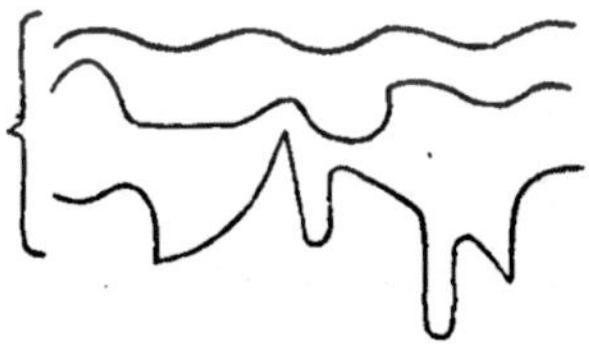

V. Form :—(See Fig. 5.)

EMOTIONAL DIAGRAM OF THE MAN IN THE DESERT.

Fig. 5.

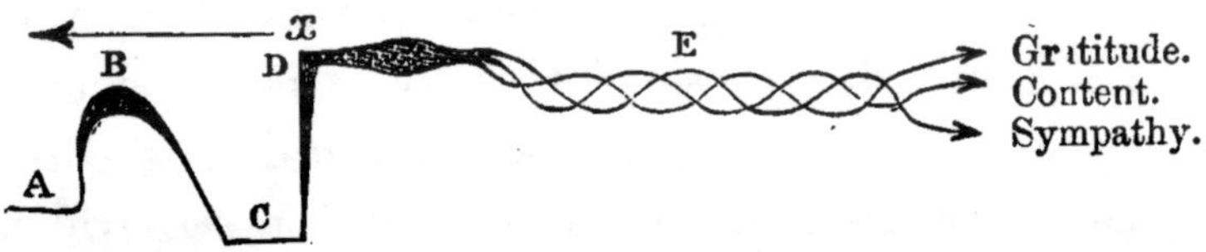

A. Thirst.
B. Expectation.
C. Disappointment.

X. Mental repetition of A B C.
D. Satisfaction.
E. Complex feeling.

for want of a better term, we may call *form, i.e.* they succeed each other in one order rather than another, and are at length combined with a definite purpose in certain fixed proportions.

Now although I have, in order to lighten the burden of metaphysics, tacked on a story to the above emotional diagram, I wish to remind the reader that it needs none, and that it is capable of indicating the progression and the qualities of emotion without the aid of a single definite idea. It must also be observed that although I have expressed by symbols the properties of emotion, simple and complex, no art-medium of emotion has as yet been arrived at; nothing but barren symbols are before us, incapable of awakening any feeling at all, however well they may suffice to indicate its nature and properties. We have now to discover some set of symbols capable of bringing these emotional properties into direct communication with sound, and Music will then emerge, like a new Venus from a sea of confused murmur, and announce herself as the royal Art-medium of Emotion.

The reader will perceive in a moment that musical notation is the symbolism required, for it is capable not only of indicating all the properties of emotion, but of connecting these with every variety and combination of sound. That every musical note corresponds to a fixed sound may be called a self-evident proposition. I hasten further to point out that the art of music is an arrangement or manipulation of sounds, which clearly reveals to us the fact that sound possesses all the properties of emotion, and is, for this reason, admirably calculated to provide it with its true and universal language.

In order to realize this we had better at once compare our analysis of Emotion with the following brief analysis of Sound, as it comes before us in the art of musical notation.

I. Elation and Depression.—The modern musical scale consists of seven notes, or an octave of eight, with their accompanying semi-tones. The human voice, or a violin, will, in addition, express every gradation of sound between each note; thus from C to C, ascending or descending, we can get any possible degree of Elation or Depression.

II. Velocity.—This property is expressed by the employment of notes indicating the durations of the different sounds, *e.g.* minims, quavers, crotchets, &c. Also by terms such as *adagio*, *allegro*, &c., which do not indicate any change in the relative value of the notes, but raise or lower the Velocity of the whole movement.

III. Intensity.—Between *ppp* and *fff* lie the various degrees of intensity which may be given to a single note. Intensity can also be produced by accumulating a multitude of notes simultaneously either in unisons, octaves, or concords, while the words *crescendo* and *diminuendo*, or certain marks, denote the gradual increase or decrease of Intensity.

IV. Variety.—We have only to think of the

simplest duet or trio to realize how perfectly music possesses this powerful property of complex emotion; and we have only to glance at a score of Beethoven's or Spohr's to see how almost any emotion, however complex, is susceptible of musical expression.

V. Form.—Nothing is more common than to hear it said that Mozart is a great master of form; that Beethoven's form is at times obscure, and so forth. Of course what is meant is, that in the arrangement and development of the musical phrases, there is a greater or less fitness of proportion producing an effect of unity or incoherence, as the case may be. But the idea of musical form can be made intelligible to any one who will take the trouble to glance at so simple a melody as the "Blue Bells of Scotland." That air consists of four phrases, each of which is divided into an elation and depression. The first two phrases are repeated: the third and fourth occur in the middle: and the first two phrases recur at the close. We might express the form numerically in this way:—

The Blue Bells of Scotland.

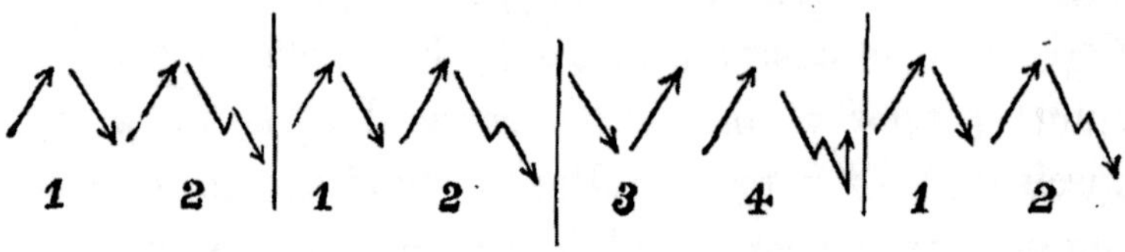

Thus music appears visibly to the eye to possess all the essential properties of emotion. May we not therefore say that the secret of its power consists in this, that it alone is capable of giving to the simplest, the subtlest, and the most complex emotions alike, that full and satisfactory expression through sound which hitherto it has been found impossible to give to many of them in any other way?

When alluding to the succession of emotions through which we pass hour after hour, I called attention to the fact that most of them were so unimportant as hardly to be worth the name of emotion, that yet so long as consciousness lasts we must be in some emotional state or other. This consideration may help us to understand the nature of a good deal of dull music which is, in fact, the expression of what may be called neutral emotion. How strange it seems to some people that composers should think it worth while to write down page after page which is devoid of interest! But if we lived more in the composer's world, our wonder would cease. We should soon feel with him that our neutral states called for musical expression as well as the higher Intensities and Velocities of Elation and Depression. Music does not cover a little excited bit of life, but the whole of life; and the mind trained to the disciplined expression of emotion in music, takes delight in long trains of quiet emotion, conscientiously worked out by what some may call diffuse and dull music. There is a quantity of music—of Schubert, for instance—which seems hardly written for the public at all. It is the expression of unimportant and uninteresting successions of emotion, whose only merit consists in their being true to life; and until we have learnt to think of every moment of our lives as being a fit subject for music, we shall never understand the Sound-reveries of Tone Poets who were in the habit of regarding the whole of their inner life as melodic and symphonic, and setting vast portions of it to music, quite regardless of what the world at large was likely to say or think about it.

And here let me pause to say that I am perfectly aware of the objections that may be urged against my analysis of emotion and music into five properties. I shall be told that my explanation is inadequate; that it is impossible to analyze a great many emotions at all; that music is often in the same way incapable of being cut up into the above-named five properties. My answer is, that it is only possible to indicate very roughly by words and symbols the bare outlines and coarsest forms of the general laws and properties of emotion. At the bottom of some historical engraving containing the portraits of a number of eminent personages, we may have sometimes noticed a row of heads in outline sketched, without colour, shadow, or expression, yet docketed with the names of the eminent personages above; so we have sketched in the bare outlines of emotion. They lie before us dumb and passionless. They are no more than skeleton likenesses of what cannot be given in mere black and white. But it would be possible to show by diagrams much more clearly the enormous detail and intricacy of musical phraseology covered in our diagram by one meagre line up and down, and expressed in such words as elation and depression; I might show that an elation can consist of any length, and might contain within itself an infinite number of subordinate elations and depressions, involving different measures of velocity and intensity, and as complicated in form and variety as those gossamer webs we meet with on misty commons about sunrise. The eye gathers some notion of the capacities of sound for the expression of the most labyrinthine and complex emotion, by looking at a full orchestral score, or trying to follow the minute inflexions made by the *bâton* of a fine conductor. Such things no words can convey. Language is given us to indicate the existence of a vast number of truths which can only be fully realized by other and more subtle modes of expression.

As emotion exists independently of Thought, so also does Music. But Music may be appropriately wedded to Thought. It is a mistake to suppose that the music itself always gains by being associated with words, or definite ideas of any sort. The words often gain a good deal, but the music is just as good without them. I do not mean to deny that images and thoughts are capable of exciting the deepest emotions; but they are inadequate to express the emotions they excite. Music is more adequate; and hence will often seize an emotion that may have been excited by an image, and partially expressed by words

—will deepen its expression, and, by so doing, will excite a still deeper emotion. That is how words gain by being set to music. But to set words to music—as in Oratorio or Opera, or any kind of song—is in fact to mix two arts together. On the whole, a striking effect may be produced; but in reality it is at the expense of the purity of each art. Poetry is a great art; so is music: but as a medium for emotion, each is greater alone than in company, although various good ends are obtained by linking the two together, providing that the words are kept in subordination to the greater expression-medium of music. Even then they are apt to hinder the development of the music. What an amount of feeble recitative and incoherent choral writing do we not owe to the clumsy endeavours of even good composers to wed music to words! How often is the poet hampered by the composer, and the composer by the poet! And yet when we remember such operas as *Don Giovanni*, and such oratorios as the *Elijah*, and note how instinctively the composer has treated the leading emotions, without being hampered by the words and the sentences of the libretto, we are bound to admit that the objections to the mixed art may be to a great extent overcome, whilst its advantages are obvious. Words, situations, and ideas are very useful to the composer, and still more so to his audience; for a story, or the bare suggestion of some situation, provides a good skeleton form, and serves to awaken trains of emotion, which music is all powerful to deepen; and whilst the words are being declaimed, the music has already passed into depths of feeling beyond the control of words. Let any one look at the four parts of a chorus, and see the kind of subordinate use made of the words. After the first glance, no one thinks much about the words: they come in more as incidents of vocalisation than of thought, and are piled up often without sense, and repeated by the different voices *pêle-mêle.* And yet the first sentence of such choruses as "Rex Tremendæ," in the *Requiem,* or "The night is departing," in the *Lobgesang,* is an immense assistance to the hearer, striking the keynote to the emotions which music alone can fully express. On the other hand, when we turn to the pure art, and inquire what good could any words do to a symphony of Beethoven, it must be answered, less and less good just in proportion as the symphony itself is musically appreciated. Even an opera is largely independent of words, and depends for its success not upon the poetry of the libretto, or even the scenery or the plot, but upon its emotional range —*i.e.* upon the region which is dominated by the musical element. Has the reader never witnessed with satisfaction a fine opera, the words of which he could not understand, and whose plot he was entirely unable to follow? Has he never seen a musician, in estimating a new song, run through it rapidly on the piano, and then turn back to the beginning to see what the words were all about? We may be sure long before he has read the words he will have estimated the value of the song. The words were good to set the composer's emotions a-going. They are interesting to his audience exactly in proportion to its ignorance of, and indifference to, music. Persons who know and care little about music, are always very particular about the words of a song. They want to know what it all means—the words will tell them of course. They are naturally glad to find something they can understand; yet all the while the open secret which they will never read lies in the music, not the words. The title, "Songs without Words," which Mendelssohn has given to his six books of musical idylls, is full of delicate raillery, aimed good-humouredly enough at the non-musical world. "A 'song without words!' What an idea! How can such a song be possible?" cries one. "What more perfect song could be imagined?" exclaims another. If we are to have words to songs, let us subordinate the thought to the emotion. The best words to music are those which contain the fewest number of thoughts, and the greatest number of emotions. Such are the shorter poems of Goethe, of Heine, of Byron, and, as a consequence, it is notorious that Beethoven, Schubert, Mendelssohn, and Schumann between them have, with pardonable avidity, set to music almost all these precious lyrics.

The only possible rival to Sound as a vehicle for pure emotion is Colour, but up to the present time no art has been invented which stands in exactly the same relation to colour as music does to sound. No one who has ever attentively watched a sunset, can fail to have noticed that colour, as well as sound, possesses all the five qualities which belong to emotion: the passing of dark tints into bright ones corresponds to Elation and Depression. The palpitations of light and mobility of hues give Velocity, poorness or richness of the same colour constitutes its Intensity, the presence of more than one colour gives Variety, whilst Form is determined by the various degrees of space occupied by the different colours. Yet there exists no colour-art as a language of pure emotion. The art of painting has hitherto always been dependent upon definite ideas, faces, cliffs, clouds, incidents. Present by the engraver's art a Sir Joshua Reynolds, or even a Turner, and although the spectator has no notion of the *colouring* of the original, he gets some notion of the work because the colour was an accessory—most important, no doubt, but still an accessory—not an essential of the artist's thought. But to present a symphony without sound, or without the notes or symbols which, through the eye, convey to the ear sound, is impossible, because sound, heard or conceived, is not the accessory, but the essential, of the composer's work. The composer's art makes sound into a language of pure emotion. The painter's art uses colour only as the accessory of emotion. No method has yet been discovered of arranging colour by itself for the eye, as the musician's art arranges sound for the ear. We have no colour pictures depending solely upon colour as we have symphonies depending solely upon sound. In Turner's works we find the nearest approach; but even he, by the necessary limitation of his art, is without the property of velocity. The canvas does not change to the eye—all that is, is presented simultaneously as in one complex chord, and thus the charm of velocity, which is so great a property in emotion, and which might belong to a colour-art, is denied to the painter. Colour now stands in the same kind of relation to the painter's art as Sound amongst the Greeks did to the art of the gymnast. But just as we speak of the classic age as a time long before the era of real music, so by-and-by posterity may allude to the present age as an age before the colour-art was known—an age in which colour had not yet been developed into a language of pure emotion, but simply used as an accessory to drawing, as music was once to bodily exercise and rhythmic recitation. And here I will express my conviction that a Colour-art exactly analogous to the Sound-art of music is possible, and is amongst the arts which have to be traversed in the future, as Sculpture, Architecture, Painting, and Music have been in the past. Nor do I see why it should not equal any of these in the splendour of its results and variety of its applications. Had we but a system of colour-notation which would as intensely and instantaneously connect itself with every possible tint, and possess the power of combining colours before the mind's eye, as a page of music combines sounds through the eye to the mind's ear—had we but instruments, or some appropriate art-mechanism for rendering such colour-notation into real waves of colour before the bodily eye, we should then have actually realized a new art, the extent and grandeur of whose developments it is simply impossible to estimate. The reader, whose eye is passionately responsive to colour, may gain some faint anticipation of the Colour-art of the future, if he will try to recall the kind of impression made upon him by the exquisite tints painted upon the dark curtain of the night at a display of fireworks. I select fireworks as an illustration in preference to the most gorgeous sunset, because I am not speaking of Nature, but Art—that is to say, something into the composition of which the mind of man has entered, and whose very meaning depends upon its bearing the evidences of human design; and I select pyrotechny, instead of painting of any kind, because in it we get the important emotional property of velocity, necessarily absent from fixed colouring.

At such a display as I have mentioned, we are, in fact, present at the most astonishing revelations of Light and Colour. The effects produced are indeed often associated with vulgar patterns, loud noises, and the most coarse and stupid contrasts. Sometimes the combinations are felicitous for a moment, and by the merest chance. But usually they are chaotic, incoherent, discordant, and supportable only owing to the splendour of the materials employed. But what a majestic Symphony might not be played with such orchestral blazes of incomparable hues! what delicate melodies composed of single floating lights, changing and melting from one slow intensity to another through the dark, until some tender dawn of opal from below might perchance receive the last fluttering pulse of ruby flame, and prepare the eye for some new passage of exquisite colour! Why should we not go down to the Palace of the People and assist at a real Colour-prelude or Symphony, as we now go down to hear a work by Mozart or Mendelssohn? But the Colour-art must first be constituted, its symbols and phraseology discovered, its instruments invented, and its composers born. Up to that time, music will have no rival as an Art-medium of emotion.

III.

Modern Music is the last great legacy which Rome has left to the world. It is also remarkable as a distinct product of modern civilization. Christianity ended by producing that peculiar passion for self-analysis, that rage for the anatomy of emotion, and that reverence for the individual soul which was almost entirely unknown to the ancient world. The life of the Greek was exceedingly simple and objective. His art represented the physical beauty in which he delighted; but the faces of his statues were usually without emotion. His poetry was the expression of strong rather than subtle feeling. He delighted in dramas with but few characters, and with hardly any plot. He could have but little need of music to express his emotions, for they could be adequately rendered by sculpture and recitation. Ancient Rome, in its best times, had no sympathy with any kind of art; to conquer and to make laws for the conquered was her peculiar mission. Still less than Greece could she stand in need of a special language for her emotions, which were of a simple, austere, and practical character, and found in the daily duties of the citizen-life a sufficient outlet of expression. Christianity, by dwelling especially upon the sanctity of the individual life, deepened the channels of natural feeling, and unfolded capacities of emotion which strove in vain for any articulate expression. But Christianity had to pass through several stages before she met with Modern Music. The active missionary spirit had first to subside and be replaced by the otiose and contemplative mood, before the need of any elaborate Art-medium of expression could make itself felt in Christendom. Unrest is fatal to Art. It was in the peaceful seclusion of monastic life that a new tonal system and a sound method of instruction first arose. From being intensely objective and practical, the genius of Christianity became intensely meditative and introspective and mystical. The Roman monks may thus be said to have created modern music. The devotee, relieved from poverty and delivered from persecution, had time to examine what was going on within him, to chronicle the different emotional atmospheres of his ecstasy, to note the elations and depressions of the religious life, the velocity of its aspirations, the intensity of its enthusiasms, the complex struggle for ever raging between the spirit and the flesh, and the ever-changing proportions and forms assumed by one and the other. Out of these experiences at length arose the desire for art-expression. Gothic architecture supplied one form, and the Italian schools of painting another; but already the key-note of a more perfect emotional language had been struck, which was destined to supply an unparalleled mode of utterance both for the Church and the World. Such a language would be valuable exactly in proportion to the complexity of thought and feeling to be expressed and the desire for its expression. The fusion of the Church and the World at the time of the Reformation was at once the type and the starting-point of those mixed and powerful influences which characterize what we call Modern Civilization, and it is remarkable that the sceptre of music should have passed from fallen Rome to free Germany just at the time when Rome showed herself most incompetent to understand and cope with the rising Spirit of the New Age, which Germany may almost be said to have created.

If we were now asked roughly to define what we mean by the Spirit of the Age, we should say the genius of the nineteenth century is analytic. There is hardly anything on earth which Goethe—the very incarnation of modern culture—has not done something towards analyzing. Scientific research has taken possession of the unexplored regions of the physical world. Kant and Hegel have endeavoured to define the limits of pure reason. Swedenborg and his followers the Spiritualists have striven to give law and system to the most abnormal states of human consciousness. There is not an aspect of nature, or complication of character, or contrast of thought and feeling, which has not been delineated by modern novelists and painted by modern artists, whilst the national poets of Europe, whether we think of Goethe, Heine, Lamartine, De Muset, or our own living poets—Tennyson, Browning, and Swinburne—have all shown the strongest disposition to probe and explore the hidden mysteries of thought and feeling, to arrange and re-arrange the insoluble problems of life, which never seemed so insoluble as now, to present facts with all their by-play, to trace emotion through all its intricate windings, and describe the variations of the soul's temperature from its most fiery heats down to its most glacial intensities.

If I were asked to select two poems most characteristic of the emotional tendencies of this age, I should select the "In Memoriam" and the "Ring and the Book"—for in both these works the introspective tendency and the restless endeavour to present, with minute fidelity, an immense crowd of feelings with something like a symphonic unity of effect, culminate. Art, literature, and science are all redundant with the same analytical and emotional tendencies. Is it wonderful that such an age should be the very age in which music, at once an analytical Science and a pure Art-medium of Emotion, has, with a rapidity like that of sculpture in Greece or painting in Italy, suddenly reached its highest perfection? Music is pre-eminently the art of the nineteenth century, because it is in a supreme manner responsive to the emotional wants, the mixed aspirations and the passionate self-consciousness of The Age.

IV.

But if Music stands in such definite and important relations to The Age, it becomes highly desirable to know whether Music has any definite connection with Morality, and, if so, what that connection really is? Of course, this question is part of a much wider subject; viz., The general connection between Art and Morals. We must often have heard people anxiously inquiring, "Must good art be moral? may it be un-moral?" or perhaps the problem is more often stated thus: "Is the object of Art to produce Pleasure or to promote Morality?" To this general question, the best answer is, "Art should do both." But before we can discuss the subject at all, another question has to be answered, namely, what is the origin of Art? Without attempting any exhaustive research, we may remind the reader that all The Arts arise out of a certain instinct, which impels man to make an appeal to the senses by expressing his thoughts and emotions in some external form. When his thoughts and emotions happen to be worthily directed towards great subjects, his Art will have dignity; when, in addition to being happily and wisely selected, what he aims at is represented with fidelity and skill, his Art will have æsthetic worth; and when its general tendency is good, his Art may be called moral. It is quite clear from this that Morality is a quality which Art may or may not possess; it does not, except in a very secondary sense, belong to its constitution. The Morality depends upon the Artist, not upon the Art. If a man is a good man, the tendency of his work will probably be moral; and if a bad man, it will most likely be the reverse; but you may have a work of Art at one and the same time æsthetically good and morally bad. Provided there be intelligent selection, fidelity, and skill, although the subject be presented in a manner disastrous to morals, the Art will be in a sense good. Even then we may say that its goodness depends upon the moral qualities of patience, industry, and truthfulness; but we cannot call it moral Art, because these qualities have been used without regard to, or in defiance of, Morality. Those who are content to value Art merely for its power of representing the imaginations of a man's heart through the senses, are perfectly entitled to say that Art need not aim at promoting morals; that it is in its nature an un-moral thing, and of course it is so in the same sense in which a drug given one day as a poison and another day as a medicine is in itself perfectly un-moral. The morality lies in the administration, and comes from a quality which belongs not to the drug, but to the agent who administers it. In like manner the morality of an artist's work depends upon the good intention of the artist, as displayed in the general effect which the expression of his thoughts and emotions is calculated to produce. Thus while it is a great mistake to confuse the nature and constitution of Art with its effects and possible tendencies by asking such inconsequent questions as whether it is meant to produce Pleasure or to promote Morality, it seems to us a still graver mistake to ignore the fact that the region of Art has everywhere points of contact with the region of Morals, and that its dignity and helpfulness to man depend not only upon a propitious selection and happy execution, but also upon the manifest aims and objects of the work itself.

But what do we mean by the Region of Morals? When a man is placed at the Equator and told to travel North or South, his first question will be, which is the North Pole and which is the South Pole? and unless he makes up his mind on this preliminary question he cannot tell whether his steps are leading him right or wrong. And before we begin to speculate about the good and evil tendencies of art, we must in like manner be able to point to the poles of Good and Evil themselves. Of course people will dispute endlessly about the application of principles, just as people may select different roads to get to the North and South, but the poles and their general whereabouts must be assumed before any kind of certain progress can be made.

I must here ask the reader to give his assent to some

general principles. I must induce him to admit, for instance, that moral health consists in a certain activity combined with the relative subordination of all his faculties,—in a self-control not checking development, but assisting it, enabling him at once to prevent any disastrous violence through the rebellion of the senses, whilst giving fair play to those too often pampered menials. And above all, I must ask him to condemn as immoral the deliberate cultivation of unbalanced emotions merely for the sake of producing pleasure. Our rough scheme of morals, or our general idea of right and wrong, will moreover insist upon the healthful activity of each individual *according to his special gifts and capacities*, directed in such a way as to respect and promote the healthful activity of society in general. This may be thought a sufficiently vague statement of morals, but it is quite definite enough for our present purpose, and will be found to cover most cases in point. I will venture to call special attention to the assertion that moral health is consistent with development *according to special gifts and capacities*. It will not do to make moral health consist only in the equal development of all a man's faculties; he may be fitted to excel in some one direction; we must admit the principle of speciality in Human Nature, and if a man be born to excel in eloquence, we must, if necessary, let him off his arithmetic; or if he is to be a good engineer, we must excuse him his arts and literature, if needful. Will that be healthy development? Well, it may be on the whole, considering the limits and imperfections of our present state, the best kind of development of which he is capable; for it is morally more healthful to arrive at perfection in one department than to enjoy a puny mediocrity, or even an inferior excellence in several, and Nature herself guides us to this conclusion by signally endowing men with special faculties. For this reason our notion of moral health should include a special development of the individual according to his gifts. But as a man is not an unit, but a member of society, his activity has to be judged, not only with a reference to himself, but also with reference to his fellows; and here the word *healthful* supplies us with a keynote, for what is really morally healthful for the individual will be found as a general rule healthful to society at large. The man, for instance, whose art is chiefly devoted to the delineation of love under its most self-indulgent and least ennobling aspects must be called an immoral artist, not because he paints the soft side of love, which is legitimately entitled to have a soft side to it, but because he dwells exclusively and obtrusively, for the mere sake of producing pleasure, upon that side of love which, when unrestrained and exaggerated, is of all others most calculated to injure the moral health, both of the individual and of society at large. No doubt everything may be represented in art, and when once a subject has been chosen, nothing is gained by a timorous holding back of anything which adds to its power as a faithful representation of the artist's conception. But the morality of the work must depend upon the way in which the conception, as presented, is calculated to affect the moral health of society. Now in attempting to judge the ethical value of a work of art, we must, as I have said, have a general notion of what we mean by good and evil; then we shall have to look at the work itself, not with reference merely to the actual good and evil expressed by it, but to the proportions in which the two are mixed, and above all to the kind of sympathy with which they are intended to be viewed.

In some of the Gothic cathedrals we may have noticed strange figures hiding in nooks and corners, or obtrusively claiming attention as waterspouts. Some of them are revolting enough, but they are not to be severed from their connection with the whole building. *That* is the work of art—these are but the details, and only some of the details. How many statues are there in all those niches?—let us say a thousand. You shall find seventy pure Virgins praying in long robes, and forty Monks and Apostles and Bishops, and Angels in choirs, and Archangels standing high and alone upon lofty façade and pinnacle and tower; and round the corner of the roof shall be two devils prowling, or a hideous-looking villain in great pain, or (as in Chester Cathedral) there may be a proportion—a very small proportion—of obscene figures, hard, and true, and pitiless. "What scandalous subjects for church decoration!" some may exclaim; yet the whole impression produced is a profoundly moral one. The sculptor has given you the life he saw; but he has given it from a really high stand-point, and all is moral, because all is in healthy proportion. There is degradation, but there is also divine beauty; there is passionate and despairing sin, but there is also calmness and victory; there are devils, but they are infinitely outnumbered by angels; there lurks the blur of human depravity, but as we pass out beneath groups of long-robed saints in prayer, the thought of sin fades out before a dream of divine purity and peace. We can see what the artist loved and what he taught; that is the right test, and we may take any man's work as a whole, and apply that test fearlessly. If we would know whether a work of art is moral or not, let us ask such questions as these:—Does the artist show that his sympathies lie with an unwholesome preponderance of horrible, degraded, or of simply pleasurable, as distinct from healthy, emotions? Is he for whipping the jaded senses to their work, or merely for rejoicing in the highest activity of their healthful exercise? Does he love what is good whilst acknowledging the existence of evil, or does he delight in what is evil, and merely introduce what is good for the vicious sake of trampling upon it?

How differently may the same subject involving human sin be treated! Given, for instance, the history of a crime; one man will represent a bad action as so pleasurable and attractive as to make us forget its criminality, whilst another, without flinching from descriptive fidelity, will mix his proportions of good and evil, and distribute his sympathies in such a manner as to deprive us of all satisfaction in contemplating the wrong, and inspire us with a wholesome horror of the crime involved. I need only refer to the catastrophe in Lord Lytton's "Alice, or the Mysteries," and in George Eliot's "Adam Bede," as illustrations of the profoundly immoral and moral treatment of the same subject. The morbid taste which French and Belgian painters exhibit for scenes of bloodshed and murder is another instance of the way in which art becomes immoral by stimulating an unwholesome appetite for horrors. Holbein's "Christ in the Tomb" is dreadful enough, but there is this difference between that picture and such a picture as the two decapitated corpses of Counts Egmont and Horn, by Louis Gallait —the German masterpiece reflects the profound impression made upon the painter by his sacred theme, while the other is simply a disgusting sop cast forth to a demoralized and bloodthirsty Parisian populace.

The best art is like Shakspeare's art, and Titian's art, always true to the great glad aboriginal instincts of our nature, severely faithful to its foibles, never representing disease in the guise of health, never rejoicing in the exercise of morbid fancy, many-sided without being unbalanced, tender without weakness, and forcible without ever losing the fine sense of proportion. Nothing can be falser than to suppose that morality is served by representing facts other than they are; no emasculated picture of life can be moral—it may be meaningless, and it is sure to be false. No ; we must stand upon the holy hill with hands uplifted like those of Moses, and see the battle of Good against Evil with a deep and inexhaustible sympathy for righteousness, and a sense of triumph and victory in our hearts. The highest service that art can accomplish for man is to become at once the voice of his nobler aspirations, and the steady disciplinarian of his emotions, and it is with this mission, rather than with any æsthetic perfection, that we are at present concerned.

I proceed to ask how Music, which I have shown to be the special Art-medium of Emotion, is capable, in common with all the other arts, of exercising by itself moral and immoral functions.

V.

WHEN music becomes a mixed art—that is to say, when it is wedded to words, and associated with definite ideas—when it is made the accompaniment of scenes which in themselves are calculated to work powerfully for good or evil upon the emotions—then it is as easy to see how music is a moral or an immoral agent as it is to decide upon the tendency of a picture or a poem. The song is patriotic, or languishing, or comic, and in each case the music is used not as a primary agent to originate, but as a powerful secondary agent to deepen and intensify the emotion already awakened by the words of the song or the operatic situation. But how can a piece of music, like a picture, be in itself moral, immoral, sublime or degraded, trivial or dignified? Must it not entirely depend for such qualities as these upon the definite thoughts and images with which it happens to be associated? I will answer this question by reminding the reader of another. Does emotion itself always need definite thoughts and images before it can become healthful or harmful—in other words, moral or immoral? I have endeavoured, Book First, II., pp. 14-22, to show that there was a region of abstract emotion in human nature constantly indeed traversed by definite thoughts, but not dependent upon them for its existence—that this region of emotion consisted of infinite varieties of mental temperature—that upon these temperatures or atmospheres of the soul depended the degree, and often the kind of actions of which at different moments we were capable, and that quite apart from definite ideas, the emotional region might be dull, apathetic, eager, brooding, severe, resolute, impulsive, &c., but that each one of these states might exist and pass without culminating in any kind of action, or being clothed with any appropriate set of ideas. But if thus much be granted, who will deny that the experience of such Soul-atmospheres must leave a definite impress upon the character? For example, the experience of sustained languor without an effort at acquiring a more vigorous impulse, will be deleterious; excitement passing into calmness — vague fear or discomfort giving place to deep and satisfied feelings of peace or a sense of exhaustion, followed by recreation and revival of power—such will be beneficial, productive, on the whole, of a hopeful and encouraging temper of mind; and it is just as possible to classify these various atmospheric states of mind as wholesome or the reverse, as it is to classify the various appropriate thoughts and images to which they may be attached. Of course, in a thousand instances, they are actually so attached, for as thought is always seeking emotion, so is emotion always seeking thought, and the atmospheres of the soul may be said to be constantly penetrated by crowds of appropriate thoughts, which take their peculiar colouring and intensity only upon entering the magic precincts of emotion. But if, as we have maintained, music has the power of actually creating and manipulating these mental atmospheres, what vast capacities for good or evil must music possess! For what troops of pleasurable, stimulating, or enervating ideas and fancies is good dance music responsible, by providing all these with the emotional atmospheres which invite their presence, and by intensifying the situation! The strains of martial music as a military band passes by are capable of rousing something like a spirited and energetic emotion for a moment at least in the breast of the tamest auditor, and the Bible itself pays a tribute to the emotional effect and power of changing the soul's atmosphere possessed by even such a primitive instrument as David's harp—"When the evil spirit from God was upon Saul, then David took an harp, and played with his hand. So Saul was refreshed, and was well, and the evil spirit departed from him." (1 Sam. xvi. 23.) Poor George III. in his fits of melancholy madness was deeply sensible of the power of music to create atmospheres of peace, and restore something like harmony to the "sweet bells" of the spirit "jangled out of tune." I have no doubt whatever that the acknowledged influence of music over the insane might be far more extensively used—indeed, if applied judiciously to a disorganized mind, it might be as powerful an agent as galvanism in restoring healthy and pleasurable activity to the emotional regions. Who can deny, then, if such a mysterious command as this is possessed by music over the realm of abstract emotion, that music itself must be held responsible for the manner in which it deals with that realm, and the kind of succession, proportion, and degrees of the various emotional atmospheres it has the power of generating?

I pause for a moment to meet the objection often brought against the exercise of emotion apart from action. Everything, it may be said, music included, which excites an emotion not destined to culminate in action, has a weakening and enervating effect upon character. This is true when an emotion is roused which has for its object the performance of a duty. We may derive pleasure from a glowing appeal to help the suffering—we may listen with excitement to the details of the suffering we are called upon to alleviate, —yet, if we do no more, the emotion will indeed have enervated us. But to be affected by a drama, a novel, or poem, which points to no immediate duty of action in us, need not enervate—it may be a healthy exercise or discipline of emotion; we may be the better for it, we may be the more likely to act rightly when the opportunity occurs for having felt rightly when there was no immediate call for action. We ought not to be afraid of our emotions because they may not be instantly called upon to inspire action. Depend upon it, a man is better for his formless aspirations after good, and the more powerful and disciplined the emotions become through constant exercise, the better it will be for us. It is better to feel sometimes without action, than to act often without feeling. The unpardonable sin is to allow feeling to supersede action when the time for action as the fruit of feeling has arrived. This is the barren sin of Sentimentalism.

In considering practically the Good and Evil of music as it comes before us in its highly-developed modern form, we shall naturally have to refer to the three classes of people most concerned:—the COMPOSER, the EXECUTIVE MUSICIAN, the LISTENER.

VI.

THE COMPOSER lives in a world apart, into which only those who have the golden key are admitted. The golden key is not the sense of hearing, but what is called an "Ear for Music." Even then half the treasures of the composer's world may be as dead letters to the vulgar or untrained, just as a village school-boy who can read fluently might roam, with an unappreciative gape, through the library of the British Museum. The composer's world is the world of emotion, full of delicate elations and depressions, which, like the hum of minute insects, hardly arrest the uncultivated ear—full of melodious thunder, and rolling waters, and the voice of the south wind—without charm for the many who pass by. Full of intensity, like the incessant blaze of Eastern lightning—full of velocity, like the trailing fire of the falling stars—full of variety, like woodlands smitten by the breath of autumn, or the waste of many colours changing and iridescent upon a sunset sea. The emotions which such images are calculated to arouse in the hearts of those who are prepared to entertain them, the composer, who has studied well the secrets of his art, can excite through the medium of sound alone; formless emotions are his friends. Intimately do the spirits of the air, called into existence by the pulsing vibrations of melody and harmony, converse with him. They are the familiars that he can send forth speeding to all hearts with messages too subtle for words,—sometimes sparkling with irresistible mirth, at others wild with terror and despair, or filled with the sweet whispers of imperishable consolation. All this, and far more than any words can utter, was to be done, and has been done for man, by music. But not suddenly, or at once and altogether, as the first rude attempts, still extant and familiar to most of us in the shape of Gregorian chants, live to attest.

As the early violin-makers, by long lives of solitary toil and intense thought, slowly discovered the perfect lines and exquisite proportions which make the violins of Stradiuarius the wonder of the world; as the various schools of painting in Italy brought to light, one by one, those elements of form, colour, and chiaroscuro which are found united, with incomparable richness and grace, in the master-pieces of Raphael, Tintoret, and Titian—so did the great maestros of the sixteenth century begin to arrange the rudiments of musical sound in combinations, not merely correct according to the narrow code of melody and harmony suggested by a few leading properties of vibration and the natural divisions of the scale, but in studied and sympathetic relations adapted to the ever-changing, complex, and subtle emotions of the heart. About the time that Italian painting reached its acme of splendour, the dawn of modern music—that form of art which was destined to succeed painting, as painting had succeeded architecture—had already begun. Palestrina, to whom we owe modern melody, and whose harmonies enchanted even Mozart and Mendelssohn, when they first heard them in the Pope's chapel at Rome, was born in 1524, nine years after the death of Raphael. In two hundred and fifty years from that date, the delights of melody, the depths and resources of harmony had been explored. The powers of the human voice, the capacities of stringed instruments, every important variety of wind instrument, the modern organ, and the pianoforte, had been discovered. Music could no longer be called a *terra incognita*. When Mozart died, all its great mines, as far as we can see, had at least been opened. We are not aware that any important instrument has been invented since his day, or that any new form of musical composition has made its appearance. Innumerable improvements in the instrumental department have been introduced, and doubtless the forms of Symphony, Cantata, Opera, and Cabinet music, bequeathed to us by the great masters of the eighteenth century, have been strangely elaborated by Beethoven, Mendelssohn, and Schumann, and are even now undergoing startling modifications in the hands of Wagner and his disciples. It is not for us to say in what direction the rich veins of ore will be found still further to extend, or what undiscovered gems may yet lie in the rivers, or be embedded in the mountain ranges of the musical cosmos. But we may safely affirm that for all purposes of inquiry into the rationale or into the moral properties of music, we are at this moment as much in possession of the full and sufficient facts as we ever shall be; and therefore we see no reason why inquiries, to which every other Art has been fully and satisfactorily subjected, should be any longer deferred in the case of Music.

The difference between "tweedle-dum and tweedle-dee" has always been a subject of profound mystery to the unmusical world; but the musical world is undoubtedly right in feeling strongly upon the subject, though unhappily often wrong when trying to give its reasons. It is quite impossible for any one, who has thoughtfully and sympathetically studied the different schools of music, not to feel that one style and conception of the art is nobler than another. That certain methods of using musical sound are affected, or extravagant, or fatiguing, or incoherent, whilst others are dignified, natural, or really pathetic, arranging and expressing the emotions in a true order, representing no vamped-up passion, but passion as it is, with its elations, depressions, intensities, velocities, varieties, and infinitely fine inflexions of form. Between the spirit of the musical Sentimentalist and the musical Realist there is eternal war. The contest may rage under different captains. At one time it is the mighty Gluck, who opposes the ballad-mongering Piccini; at another, it is the giant Handel *versus* the melodramatic Bononcini; or it is Mozart against all France and Italy; or Beethoven against Rossini; or Wagner against the world. In each case the points at issue are, or are supposed by the belligerents to be, substantially the same. False emotion, or abused emotion, or frivolous emotion, *versus* true feeling, disciplined feeling, or sublime feeling. Musicians perhaps cannot always explain how music is capable of the above radical distinctions—granted. I am concerned just now with this remarkable fact—the distinction exists in their minds. They arrange the German, the Italian, French, and the Franco-German schools in a certain order of musical merit and importance; there is a fair general agreement about what this order should be; and, perhaps without knowing why, an enlightened musician would no more compare Rossini to Beethoven, or Gounod to Mozart, than a literary critic would speak of Thomas Moore in the same breath with Shakspeare, or place Boucicault by the side of Schiller.

The reason of the superiority of the modern German school from Gluck to Schumann, over the French and Italian, we believe to be a real and substantial one; although, owing to the extraordinary nature of the connection between sound and emotion, it is far more easy to feel than to explain the distinction between a noble and an ignoble school of music. This difference, however, we believe consists entirely in the view taken of the emotions and the order and spirit in which they are evoked and manipulated by the composer's magical art. Towards the close of the seventeenth century, in Italy, music began to feel its great powers as an emotional medium. The great musical works were then nearly all of a sacred character, and devoted to the service of the Roman Catholic churches. The art was still firmly held in the trammels of strict fugue and severe counterpoint; the solemn and startling process of musical discovery was nevertheless in rapid progress. The composers seemed a little overawed by the novel effects they were daily producing, and the still powerful devotion to the Catholic religion hallowed their emotions, and gave to their Masses a severity and purity quite unknown to the Italian music of the nineteenth century. We cannot now stop to inquire whether it was the rapid decline of the Papal Power, and consequently of the Roman Catholic faith, which caused the degradation of Italian music; or whether, when sound came to be understood as a most subtle and ravishing minister to pleasure, the temptation to use it simply as the slave of the senses proved too great for a politically-degraded people, whose religion had become half an indolent superstition and half a still more indolent scepticism; certain it is that about the time of Giambattista Pergolese, who died in 1736, the high culture of music passed from Italy to Germany, which latter country was destined presently to see the rise and astonishing progress of Symphony and modern Oratorio, whilst Italy devoted itself henceforth to that brilliant bathos of art known as the "Italian Opera."

We cannot deny to Italy the gift of sweet and enchanting melody. Rossini has also shown himself a master of the very limited effects of harmony which it suited his purpose to cultivate. Then why is not Rossini as good as Beethoven? Absurd as the question sounds to a musician, it is not an unreasonable one when coming from the general public, and the only answer we can find is this. Not to mention the enormous resources in the study and cultivation of harmony which the Italians, from want of inclination or ability, neglect, the German music is higher than the Italian because it is a truer expression, and a more disciplined expression, of the emotions. To follow a movement of Beethoven is, in the first place, a bracing exercise of the intellect. The emotions evoked, whilst assuming a double degree of importance by association with the analytical faculty, do not become enervated, because in the masterful grip of the great composer we are conducted through a cycle of naturally progressive feeling, which always ends by leaving the mind recreated, balanced, and ennobled by the exercise. In Beethoven all is restrained, nothing morbid which is not almost instantly corrected, nothing luxurious which is not finally raised into the clear atmosphere of wholesome and brisk activity, or some corrective mood of peaceful self-mastery, or even playfulness. And the emotions thus roused are not the vamped-up feelings of a jaded appetite, or the false, inconsequent spasms of the sentimentalist. They are such as we have experienced in high moods or passionately sad ones, or in the night, in summer-time, or by the sea; at all events, they are unfolded before us, not with the want of perspective, or violent frenzy of a bad dream, but with true gradations in natural succession, and tempered with all the middle tints that go to make up the truth of life. Hence the different nature of the emotional exercise gone through in listening to typical German and typical Italian music. The Italian makes us sentimentalise, the German makes us feel. The sentiment of the one gives the emotional conception of artificial suffering or joy, the natural feeling of the other gives us the emotional conception which belongs to real suffering or joy. The one is stagey—smells of the oil and the rouge pot—the other is real, earnest, natural, and reproduces with irresistible force the deepest emotional experiences of our lives. It is not good to be constantly dissolved in a state of love-melancholy, full of the languor of passion without its real spirit—but that is what Italian music aims at. Again, the violent crises of emotion should come in their right places—like spots of primary colour with wastes of grey between them. There are no middle tints in Italian music; the listeners are subjected to shock after shock of emotion—half a dozen smashing surprises, and twenty or thirty spasms and languors in each scene, until at last we become like children who thrust their hands again and again into water charged with electricity, just on purpose to feel the thrill and the relapse. But that is not healthy emotion—it does not recreate the feelings; it kindles artificial feelings, and makes reality tasteless.

Now whenever feeling is not disciplined, it becomes weak, diseased, and unnatural. It is because German music takes emotion fairly in hand, disciplines it, expresses its depressions in order to remove them, renders with terrible accuracy even its insanity and incoherence in order to give relief through such expression, and restore calm, flinches not from the tender and the passionate, stoops to pity, and becomes a very angel in sorrow;—it is because German music has probed the humanities and sounded the depths of our nature—taught us how to bring the emotional region, not only into the highest activity, but also under the highest control—that we place German music in the first rank, and allow no names to stand before Gluck, Bach, Handel, Haydn, Mozart, Beethoven, Schubert, Spohr, Mendelssohn, and Schumann.

It would not be difficult to show in great detail the essentially voluptuous character of Italian music, the essentially frivolous and sentimental character of French music, and the essentially moral, many-sided, and philosophical character of German music; but I hasten to pass on to the Executive Musician, merely qualifying the above remarks with this general caution—Let not the reader suppose that in the schools of music that take rank after the German School, there is nothing worthy and beautiful to be found. Rossini, and even Verdi, are manifestly full of extraordinary merit; the veteran Auber was a real musical giant; and M. Gounod is surely a very remarkable genius. Nor must we forget that before the rise of German music there were in England such composers as Tallis, Gibbons, and Purcell. What I have said above on the three national Schools of European music applies to the general tendencies of each *as a School*, and is not intended to condemn in the productions of individual composers much that is, and that deserves to be, the admiration of the civilized world.

VII.

WHAT possible moral influence can an EXECUTIVE MUSICIAN either receive or distribute through his Art? First let us inquire what he is, with reference to his Art. The Player, like the Composer, is passive. The one is possessed by the inspirations of his own genius, the other by the inspirations of a genius not his own. The Player, like the Composer, is active. The one exerts himself to put his conceptions into a communicable form; the other charges himself with the office of conveying them, through that form, to the world. The composing and executive faculties are quite distinct. A great composer is often an ineffective player, whilst many a leading player, with all the requisite knowledge and study, is incapable of composing good music. The same is true of the Drama. The great actors are seldom great dramatists; neither Garrick nor any of the Keans or Kembles have been famous authors. The great dramatic authors, in their turn, have usually been but mediocre before the footlights. Shakspeare himself, if we may trust tradition, was not more than respectable in his great parts. The originative faculty is usually considered more heaven-born, and it is certainly far more rare than the executive gift. Few women have hitherto possessed the first, numbers have attained the highest rank in the second. We have had peerless actresses, but no female dramatists of mark. Music has an unlimited number of notable syrens and lady instrumentalists, but not one original female composer has yet made her appearance. The ladies of the period, even in England, no doubt write drawing-room ballads, and their friends sing them; but the typical English ballad—we do not speak of really fine old tunes, or the good work of Mr. Sullivan, and a few other true English musicians—can hardly be called a musical composition, even when warbled in bad English by a Patti. But however high we may place the composer (and if we regard him as the recreator and disciplinarian of the emotions we shall place him very high), the person who stands between the composer and the audience has a vast and direct power of which we are bound to give some account.

And here I notice the double function of music as an executive art; not only is it a means of revealing a certain order or succession of emotion in the composer's mind, but it provides each player with a powerful medium of self-revelation. There are many different ways of playing the same piece of music; the conscientious player will no doubt begin by carefully studying the movement, noting any *p*'s or *f*'s, &c., which the composer may have vouchsafed to give us as hints of his meaning; and having tried to master the emotional unity of the piece, he will then—bearing a few prominent *p's* and *f's* in his mind—trust to a certain infection of impulse to carry him through its execution. But as the music develops beneath his fingers, what opportunities there are for the expression of his own individuality; what little refinements, what subtle points, what imperceptible artifices for riveting choice turns in the composition upon the ear of the listener! The great composers seem to cast off all egotism when they lay down their pens. They are the generous and sympathetic friends of those who interpret them; they will give them all reasonable license. "The music," each master seems to say, "is yours and mine; if you would discover and share my impulse through it, I would also discover and share yours in it. I will bring the gem and you shall bring the light, and together we will set before the world the raptures and mysteries of sound, wrought through the golden art of music into immortal Tone Poems."

But although music is given to the player as a sort of private property, the player must no doubt respect the general outline and balance of emotion discoverable upon a careful study of his sonata or solo; but he was intended to interpret its details for himself, to express through the unalterable elations and depressions involved in the structure of the music the various and subtle degrees of intensity of which he may be at the time capable. He may give inflections of his own, delicate treatments in different measures of velocity, often unperceived by the many, but none the less of infinite importance and meaning to the intelligent hearer.

In different hands, the same piece will sound quite differently. Then music has no fixed significance of its own, and is merely the plaything of caprice, and the vague and doubtful echo of emotion? Not so. Every piece of music worthy of the name has a fixed progression and completeness of emotion, but within its outlines it also possesses an elastic quality and a power of expressional variety which helps it to combine and cling about each new executant as though made for him alone. The player thus discovers in his music not only the emotional scheme and conception of the composer, but also congenial elements, which he appropriates after his own fashion, and which constitute that striking bond of momentary sympathy which exists so strangely between fine singers or soloists and their audiences. But may I here observe, that substantially there is far less difference than is generally supposed between the "readings" of eminent players. Between M. Charles Hallé's and Madame Schumann's readings of the Moonlight Sonata, for instance (and we select these eminent artists as the opposite poles of the musical temperament), there is the same kind of difference as we might notice between Miss Glyn's and Mrs. Kemble's readings of a scene in Shakspeare, or between Mr. Phelps's and M. Fechter's impersonations of Hamlet. Difference of minute inflections and variety of inflections—difference of degrees in the intensity or velocity of the emotion traversed; but substantially each would be found to preserve the same general appreciation of the way in which the different sections are intended to march. Here and there a dispute would arise; but, in fact, the good reader or actor does exactly what the performer ought to do. In the first place, he carefully studies the meaning of his author; and in the second, he allows his own individuality free play, in flowing period and subtle rendering within the elastic limits always characteristic of a highly emotional work of art. The best executive musician, then, is he who has thoroughly mastered his composer's thought, and who, in expressing that thought to others, allows his own individuality to pierce freely, as every man must do who has not only learned by rote, but really assimilated what he comes forward to reproduce. To the above definition of what an executant should be, every other description of what executants are can be easily referred. Executants are of six kinds:—

1. Those who study the composer, and also express themselves.
2. Those who express themselves, without regard to the composer.
3. Those who express the composer, without regard to themselves.
4. Those who caricature both.
5. Those who express other people's views of the composition.
6. The dullards, who express nothing.

It would be very tempting to dilate upon these six classes. We can only at present afford to enumerate them, and pass on.

The life of a successful singer or an illustrious instrumentalist is full of peril—peril to virtue, peril to art, peril to society; and this not owing at all to the exigencies of the executive gift in itself, but entirely owing to the conditions imposed upon the artist from without. There need be nothing in the life-work of a great Prima-donna to demoralize any more than in the life-work of any other gifted and industrious woman. There are great operas which are calculated to ennoble whilst they delight; there are songs which stir within us the finest impulses; there are characters to be impersonated on the operatic stage which not only do not shock decency, but tend to promote the highest and most generous sentiment. There are many others of an un-moral description, perfectly harmless, and calculated to produce the utmost enjoyment. Given a right selection of songs—given a course of operas dealing, if you will, with a certain amount of crime and a fair instalment of horrors, but so constructed as to be effective in result without being immoral in tendency (and the greatest works of Shakspeare and Beethoven satisfy both these conditions); given to the singer good remuneration, and, above all, sufficient repose; given some choice of congenial subjects; given a sphere of wholesome activity, and, lastly, given a recognised and an honourable social position, and all special peril to personal virtue immediately ceases. It is nonsense to say that a certain physical exhaustion which must accompany any highly-sustained effort of mind or body is specially deleterious in the case of a musician. Exertion need not produce disease. People were intended to exert themselves. Does the Parliamentary orator speak for four hours without fatigue? Does the medical man see one hundred patients in the course of the morning without severe mental tension? Does a judge deliver his charges without a similar effort? Does the author compose without highly-wrought and sustained attention, practised advisedly, and without necessary injury to his brain, or stomach, or moral equilibrium? Let us settle it in our minds, there is nothing demoralising in deliberately and for a definite art-purpose, putting oneself or others through the experience of a highly-strung series of emotions. It is even a good and healthy function of art to raise our feelings at times to their highest pitch of intensity. It is part of a right system of discipline, calculated to bring the emotions into high condition and healthy activity, and to keep them in a good state of repair. The body is intended and fitted to bear at times an extreme tension of its muscles. The professional athlete knows this, and when he is rubbed down and rolled up in his hot blanket after violent exercise, he is not alarmed at feeling himself going off into a profound sleep through sheer exhaustion, for he knows that such systematic exertion and exhaustion must be undergone in order to raise his physique to its highest state of health and power. Well, the laws which regulate the life and health of the emotions are exactly similar; and these laws prescribe steady exercise, rest, recreation, and sometimes extreme tension. In itself, we repeat, the habitual exercise and discipline of the emotions, as, for example, in music or acting, is not the ruin of, but the very condition of, moral health. It is the kind of strain imposed upon our musical artists not by their art, but by the struggle for existence, and by the thoughtless, extravagant, indolent, and often immoral demands of a public that has little musical education, and that little bad, which hurries nine-tenths of all our gifted executants to a premature grave. The cantatrice should be allowed to unfold her aspirations in noble music; but she has the misfortune to have half an octave more than other singers, and so bad and flimsy songs must be chosen, or noble songs must be spoiled, for the sake of an upper C, E, or G. The public go mad, not about the superb trio in *William Tell* (for example), but for the one bar in which the tenor has to come out with a high chest-note. Can anything be more sadly indicative of the low musical feeling of the British public than the way in which Mademoiselle Carlotta Patti was run after for her head-notes, and Herr Wachtel for his chest-notes? These excessive calisthenic and gymnastic explosions are the degradation of taste and the ruin of many an incomparable voice. Again:

has a musician no private taste, no feeling, no love for good music? Possibly he may have; but what is he to do? Composers pay him to sing their trash; publishers bribe even good composers to write the kind of stuff the public have been fooled into applauding. That is one, and not the only, chronic complaint from which Music in England is suffering at present.

There are hundreds of magnificent songs of Schubert, of Beethoven, and Schumann; but these composers, who had but few bank-notes to spare during their lifetime, have unfortunately left no money to pay singers after their death. The public do not hear numbers of the best songs that exist. One or two perhaps emerge. "Adelaide" for ever! and what other song by Beethoven does a certain eminent Tenor habitually sing? And what songs does he generally sing, and why? There are a good many first-rate English ballads. Thanks to the enterprise of a few bold and conscientious singers, we occasionally hear some of them. But are the English ballads most commonly sung at concerts selected for their merit? Why are they sung? The truth had better be told; they are sung because they are paid for, and they are clapped and puffed by people who ought to know better; and who do know better, but who are paid to pocket their conscience, and applaud what they know to be meaningless trash. How are singers to fulfil the first simple duty they owe to their art, and sing good music, when there is a conspiracy to make them stoop to the humiliation of their noble gifts, or starve? Once more: there is the peril of over-wrought powers. When the mind, through excessive artistic excitement, "like a jarred pendulum, retains only its motion, not its power," then absolute repose is wanted. All may have been within the bounds of healthful though intense excitation; it is not *that* we complain of—not the excitement of singing and playing, but the want of rest which follows it. After (let us say) an opera of M. Wagner, where the screeching has been intense, and the crises almost constant for some hours, the Prima-donna must have rest; no stormy rehearsal next morning, no fatiguing opera the next night. One or two great sustained efforts during the week are sufficient. But let any one glance at the programme which a favourite singer is expected to carry out day and night, at opera and concert, during the season. No flesh and blood can stand such an ordeal. Chronic exhaustion begins to set in; and exhaustion is not met by rest, but by stimulants—it must be so; and then more exhaustion is met by more stimulants, and what becomes of healthy emotional activity and emotional discipline? Mind and body are unhinged. The artist's health suffers, the artist's voice suffers, and probably becomes extinct in a few years. Hence we cannot blame popular singers for asking enormous sums so long as they have a note left in their voices. It is the public that makes them abuse their priceless gifts for gold. It is the public who are content to demand the sacrifice of fresh, girlish constitutions, and the shattering of young, manly frames, and the general wreck of mind, and sometimes of morals, through over-fatigue and over-excitement, and unhealthy conditions of activity.

But, be it observed, the perils above alluded to, and others which cannot here be discussed in detail, are not inseparable from the vocation of a public singer or solo instrumentalist. The vocation is simply honourable: it might and ought to be always noble in its use and exercise. How many esteemed and high-minded musicians are there who resist the perils which I have mentioned? Thank God there are many, and we trust every year there will be more and more as Music in England becomes more and more appreciated. Let music be recognised here as in Germany, as a thing of Reason and a thing of Morals as well as a thing of Beauty and Emotion, and the public will cease to look upon musicians as mere purveyors of Pleasure. We should not encourage singers to wear themselves out; should not clamour for incessant *encores*, which utterly ruin the balance of a sustained work of art, and we should remember that the gifted persons who delight us, are made of flesh and blood like ourselves, that they have human hearts, and passions, and trials, and are often exposed, when very young and at a great disadvantage, to temptations not easily resisted even under favourable circumstances. And those who love music should make allowance for those who devote themselves to music, and not tempt them to make money by the degradation of art to the ruin of their own moral sense and the destruction of the public taste.

I honour the musical profession; but I declare that musical taste in England is degraded and kept low by jealousy and time-serving, and that musical criticism is so gagged, and prejudiced, and corrupt, that those whose business it is to see that right principles prevail, seem too often led by their interest rather than their duty. When it comes to judging a new composer, the truth is not told, or only half told; when a new player is allowed to appear, his success depends not upon his merits, but upon his friends; and whilst it is, of course, impossible entirely to quell first-class merit, second-class merit is constantly ignored, and many sound English musicians are often compelled to stand aside and see their places taken by young quacks or foreigners inferior to themselves. No one wishes to deny the supreme merit of artists like M. Joachim or Madame Schumann, and none but the interested or the envious can grudge them their distinguished popularity; but in England, when a foreigner and an English artist are of equal merit, the English artist ought to receive at least an equal share of support from the public and the press. But he never does; and why? because the employers of musical talent in this country pander to the appetite for everything that is foreign; because they keep down the development of English talent in order to gain an easy reputation in accordance with established prejudices by constantly bringing over players and singers from abroad whose chief merits seem to consist in long hair and a very imperfect acquaintance with the English language. It is difficult for a musician, especially an English musician, in England to be at once true to his own interests and to the interests of his art; it is difficult for him to be true to his conscience in the exercise of his profession; but he may receive some small comfort from the reflection that this last difficulty at least is one which he shares with every man in every profession, and that, at all events, it is not a difficulty inherent in his art, neither is it altogether insurmountable.

I am not writing a dissertation upon "Music in England," and although I have allowed myself in this place to take a sidelong glance at that important subject, I am not bound here to discuss English musicians in particular, whether composers or players. Much might be said about musical taste in the provinces, our system of pianoforte instruction, which is in fact that branch of the musical profession to which a large majority of our musicians owe their incomes; our organists, and our orchestral players, and choral singers. To follow out such a programme in detail would lead me beyond my present limits. I am dealing simply with the general moral tendencies of executive art, and as that divides itself naturally into solo playing and cabinet playing, such as the playing of quartet music, and orchestral playing, or the performance of full instrumental scores, a few words upon the Morals of the Orchestra may not be out of place. As I shall elsewhere speak of cabinet music, and as from the quasi-solo position of cabinet players a good deal which has been said about solo-players applies to them, I shall not here dwell upon them, but pass at once to the Orchestral Player.

The orchestral player, if he knows his business, will deny himself the luxury of expressing too much of himself, yet is he not therefore a machine. Through the medium of the conductor, whose inspiration trickles to him by a kind of magnetism from that electric wand, he, too, realizes the music in its double capacity of expressing the composer's thought and the conductor's private reading or expression of that thought. But the Conductor is now in the place of the Soloist: his instrument is the orchestra, but that instrument is not a machine. You may imagine, if you please, a number of instruments worked by machinery; they may play a movement accurately with all its *p's* and *f's*, but that will not be an orchestral rendering of the work. It will be like the grinding of a barrel-organ, and that is all—no life, no emotion, no mind. Catgut, wooden tubes, hammering of calf-skins, and fatal explosion of serpents, all this you shall accomplish with cunning mechanism, more than this you shall not. Therefore the mind and the heart and the skill of a man shall be required in every member of an orchestra. To the eye of an uninitiated spectator that uniform drawing up and down of bows all in the same direction and all at once—that simultaneous blare of horns, trumpets, and flute-notes sounded instantly at the call of the magic wand, may seem like human mechanism, but it is not, it is sympathy. The individuality of each player may indeed be merged in a larger and more comprehensive unity of thought and feeling; but it is a unity with which he is in electric accord, and to which he brings spontaneously the faculties of personal appreciation and individual skill.

Let no one say that orchestral work is beneath the dignity of a good musical artist. The very delays and vexations of rehearsal often unfold new turns and critical points in a great work which might otherwise pass unnoticed. The position and use of the other instruments is better realized by one who is playing in the orchestra than by any one else. The fact of the drums being close behind you will sometimes rivet your attention, unpleasantly perhaps, upon the way in which but two notes are made to produce the illusive but beautiful effect of several repeating the leading subject, as in the opening movement of Mendelssohn's *Lobgesang*. The tenor close beside you forces a phrase upon your ear, the ghost of which, or a fragment of which, may be just suggested again by a distant flute a line or two further on. You cannot miss the author's intention. Of course it is not impossible, but it is not easy for any one who has not played a violin or some other prominent instrument in such works as Beethoven's C minor, or Pastoral Symphony, and played it often, to realize the reasons why certain passages are given to the tenors rather than to the violoncellos, why some notes are reinforced by the double-bass whilst some are left to the violoncellos; why the rhythmic beat of the drum is broken here or completed there. A great deal no doubt can be done by reading a full score without an orchestra. Some kind, and a very good kind of appreciation may be formed of an orchestral work from a pianoforte score, especially if it be arranged for four hands. For perfect enjoyment again let a person study his score at home, and then taking his seat in a favourable position, not too near the orchestra, with his score marked for reference at certain points rather than for steady perusal, let him concentrate his mind upon the emotional development of the work with a full and foregone appreciation of its intellectual form. But still if you really want to discover the technical mysteries of the orchestration you must get inside and look more closely at the astonishing works; nay, you must become one of the works, you must take an instrument and plod away in the orchestra yourself. When you have tried that, you will begin to understand why so few people succeed in writing well for an orchestra. How easy it is to mistake a tenor for a 'cello effect, or to give a phrase to the clarionet when the texture or consistency of the harmony would be best consulted by the thinner, sweeter, but equally incisive oboe.

There is therefore in the orchestra incessant work for the player's mind; and as he is also greatly privileged in constantly assisting in the production of masterpieces, what opportunities for the culture and discipline of the emotional regions of the soul are his! When he opens his part of the "Italian Symphony," or plunges into the "Fidelio," what a magnificent panorama of emotion opens out before him! But it is no unreal spectacle. Like Ulysses, who was a part of all he saw, he is a part of all he hears; shall not something of the spirit and power of the great composers with whose works he is constantly identifying himself, pass into him as the reward of his enthusiasm, his docility, and his self-immolation?

It may be said that we are taking an ideal view of orchestral playing. No doubt we are dealing with the essence of the thing itself—not as it is, but as it should be. Practically as it is, the vocation of the orchestral player has many drawbacks. The weary repetition of what he knows for the sake of other players who do not know their parts, the constant thwarting of the gifted players by the stolid ones, and the tension of long and harrowing rehearsals under conductors who do not know their own minds, or who cannot impart what they do know to the players, or who are so irritable, cantankerous, and at the same time so vexatiously exacting, as to destroy every particle of pleasure or sympathy with their work in the breasts of the executants at the very moment when these qualities are most indispensable to the execution of the music. Then there is the cheerless musical wear and tear of regular orchestral life. The pantomime music, not in moderation and once in a way, but every night all through a protracted season; for we are afraid to say how long the pantomime goes on after the departure of that inveterate bore, Old Father Christmas.

Then really excellent players are occasionally subjected to the demoniac influences of that rhythmic purgatory known as the Quadrille Band; or the humbler violinists are to be met with, accompanied by a harp and cornet-à-piston, making what is commonly understood to be music for the dancers in "marble halls," or anywhere else, it matters little enough to them. Shall we blame them if they look upon such work as mere mechanical grind—as the omnibus-horse looks upon his journey to the city and home again—a performance inevitable, indeed, but highly objectionable, and not to be borne save for the sake of the feed at the end? Then we must not forget the low salaries of many orchestral players, the small prospect of a slow rise, and the still smaller chance of ever becoming leaders in any orchestra worth leading. Or again, the weariness and disgust of your efficient men at seeing themselves kept out of their right places by old, incompetent players.

On the Continent, wise provisions are made, and retiring pensions provided by Government, or there are special societies for superannuated musicians. Every man in the orchestra knows that he will have to retire when his hand begins to lose its cunning; in his old age he is honourably supported, as he deserves to be, and his place is filled up by an efficient substitute. Art does not suffer, the public does not suffer, the interests of music are not jobbed, and no one is the worse. But in England the Government treats music with a supercilious smile, and with the most undisguised stinginess; as who should say, "A fig for your Bands and Bear-gardens!" And the Prime Minister would as soon think of granting pensions to superannuated musicians as of giving an annual banquet in Westminster Hall to the industrious fraternity of the Metropolitan Organ-grinders.

It is quite impossible to say at what age a man gets past his work, but the conductor of every orchestra knows very well who it is that mars the whole; and it is quite notorious that whatever inferiority there is in our leading orchestras in comparison with leading continental orchestras, is chiefly owing to the fact that a conductor in England cannot very easily get rid of men who have grown infirm in their places, and who would have retired long ago from any foreign orchestra as a matter of course.

It would be foolish to underrate the value of veteran experience and steadiness, but it must be remembered that the muscles will stiffen, and the ear and eye will grow dull, and that many a man whose brain is still active, may become through mere want of flexibility and feebleness of nerve, unfit for efficient work in the orchestra. We repeat emphatically, it is impossible, with so many still splendid old players before the public, to say when age means infirmity; and when we think of the prodigies of military valour, forensic ability, literary and artistic power which we have witnessed within the last few years; when we recollect that Lord Brougham, Lord Lyndhurst, and Lord Palmerston, have but lately passed away; that Thomas Carlyle is still with us; that M. Victor Hugo but lately published one of the most stirring and eloquent apostrophes to Liberty; that Sir E. Landseer painted down to an advanced age; that M. Auber still composed operas in extreme old age; that General Garibaldi is still ready (1871) to draw the sword; that even the Pope feels equal to an Œcumenical Council; and that the aged monarch of Prussia, in company with the still more aged Von Moltke, has just been leading his troops to victory against what all Europe supposed to be the greatest military nation in the world—when we remember a few of such facts, it is not too much to say that the nineteenth century is emphatically the triumphant Era of Old Age.

That musicians are commonly devoid of culture is an assertion only half true. The culture of ideas they may or may not possess—the culture of emotion the true musician has in a degree incomparably greater than the self-satisfied *flaneurs*, who talk the common slang about culture, can believe or understand. On the other hand, there are classes of musicians, as there are classes of lawyers, and classes of painters. There are pettifoggers, for whom no job is too dishonourable, and there are law lords and incorruptible judges of the realm ; there are sign-board manufacturers, and servile tricksters, and copyists, who may call themselves painters, and there are Wattses and Holman Hunts ; and so there are drunken fiddlers and Joachims, low ballad-writers and Mendelssohns. Still, it must be admitted that an ordinary musician is likely to be less cultured in the common acceptation of the term than a good painter, and probably, as a rule, the executive musicians, as a class of thoughtful and well-read men, rank below the Artist-world ; and for this reason :— They have not so much time for reading and thinking. A pianoforte teacher gives lessons all day long ; an orchestral player must practise incessantly ; so must the solo player. It may be replied, so must the artist paint incessantly. True ; but practising on an instrument to keep the fingers well "in," or to master difficult passages, is almost entirely mechanical, and painting is not.

The practice of musical mechanism is not intellectual —it does not nourish the brain or feed the heart, it does not even leave the mind at liberty to think— it chokes everything but its own development, and that is mere physical development. But as the painter works on, every stroke of the brush is not only a mechanical action, but a thought or an emotion; and there is no reason why the emotions he experiences should not clothe themselves with definite trains of definite ideas—they are nearly certain to do so—he will think when he paints alone; he can also converse whilst painting; all his manual labour is inseparably connected with intellectual, imaginative, or emotional processes. The musician's strict exercise, which, after all, takes up a great deal of his time, admits of very little intellect, imagination, or emotion. It requires industry, perception, and nerve; in short, because it is more mechanical it is therefore less refining and elevating. And this is the worst that can be said concerning the Intellectual effects of his essential training upon the Executive Musician.

Of course good people who think music and the drama necessarily wicked, must be respected, but cannot be reasoned with. However, it is hardly fair not to recognise in society an under-current of belief to the effect that executive musicians are less distinguished for morality than their neighbours. The belief may not be quite unfounded, but it is, nevertheless, most unfair. Inspect closely any class of persons, and attention to morals will not appear to be one of its strong points. But some classes fail more publicly than others. The executive musician is always before the world, and as a consequence his private life is more frequently and rudely handled than other people's. Yet it cannot be denied that he has fewer outward inducements to be moral, and more temptations to be the reverse, than falls to the lot of men in other professions. One of his disadvantages consists in the comparative indifference of the public to his morals. There have been cases in England of great solo players excluded from public engagements owing to a momentary sentiment of indignant virtue on the part of the Public, and received back to favour only a few months after some more than usually glaring violation of morals. Others have left this moral country hurriedly, and under a cloud, and been rapturously welcomed back to London in the following season. So long as the *virtuoso* plays well the Public seems willing to condone his offences more easily than those of any other professional man, and for this obvious reason—it feels no direct interest in his morality. An intemperate doctor may poison you, a dishonest lawyer may cheat you; but a musician may be both intemperate and dishonest, and yet may play superbly, which means that apart from morality he may have a fine perception of the functions of musical sound, and a delicate executive gift in expressing the subtle atmospheres of the soul.

That intemperance will end by impairing his powers, that even whilst occasionally stimulating them to high achievements it will destroy the fine balance and natural healthy force of the emotions themselves; this can hardly be doubted; and, indeed, within the last few years we have seen lamentable cases in point. That dishonesty will make the musician sadly indifferent to the interests of art when opposed to his own, that he will be unscrupulous in the use of his gifts, and unconscientious in music as in other things, this we might fairly expect, and it is, unhappily, a matter of daily notoriety; but the Public who hears what he can do, does not much trouble itself with what he might do; and it is just this apathy which destroys one very common incentive to external morality by removing the pressure put upon a man from without to lead a respectable life. What is here said of the male portion of the musical community is equally true of the female portion. As a rule, women have been far more valued by society for their personal virtue than for their gifts; and as an eminent writer has observed, society condones in men certain offences which it deems almost unpardonable in women, because it values men, and needs them for their intellectual, imaginative, or administrative powers quite independently of their morals; but when women come before the world as possessed of gifts which cause them to be valued apart from their virtue, like the sterner sex, society shows a disposition to extend to them the same weak indulgence it gives so freely and so selfishly to men.

Again, the unhealthy conditions of work alluded to above oppose special and often very great obstacles to virtue; but to say that executive musical art has a tendency to demoralize, or that, taking everything into consideration, executive musicians as a class are worse than other people, is either the assertion of one who knows nothing at all about them or their art, or who, knowing them, is guilty of pronouncing a cruel and unjust libel upon both. Together with a sprinkling of very distinguished vocalists and instrumentalists from other countries, a large number of very low-class foreigners, with foreign habits and very foreign morals, have unhappily taken up their abode in England. They announce themselves as professors of music, and it is to be feared that people of limited information and intelligence are in the habit of sometimes visiting the irregularities of these unwelcome strangers upon the whole of the musical profession. In defence of music in general, and to the honour of English musicians in particular, be it said that whoever will think of the most prominent English singers and players now before the public will have to recall the names of a number of distinguished men and women who have led laborious and honourable lives, and who are justly entitled to the esteem and affection of an ever-widening circle of friends.

But if we turn for a moment from the world of Executants to the world of Composers, one fact must strike us—that not only were the great composers as a rule not addicted to the excesses which some would have us believe almost inseparable from a musical temperament, but they appear to have been singularly free from them. Without asserting that every portion of a man's work is always a true index of his character, it is, nevertheless, noteworthy that so many great composers have been men whose emotions were so severely disciplined, and whose lives were so well regulated, that they stand out as examples not only of steady and indefatigable workers, but also of high-minded moral and even religious men. Nor is it true that the constant emotional excitement of a composer's life is certain to impair his health and bring him to an early grave. His profession, rightly exercised, does not lead to the unbalanced excitement of sensuous emotions, which is certainly highly prejudicial to both moral and physical health—but to the orderly education and discipline of emotion, which is a very different thing. This consideration may help to explain not only the settled principle and moral impulse, but also the longevity of so many great composers. The early Italian masters became great chiefly through their sacred music, and whilst it must not be supposed that the fact of composing for the church makes a man holy, we cannot deny to these men as a class a great deal of exalted and often mystical religious fervour. Unhappily, this quality does not seem to be inconsistent with an occasional laxity of morals which cannot be too much deplored; but in judging the men we must think of the age in which they lived, the temptations to which they were exposed, and the loose state of morals which in Italy, Germany, and France seems at certain epochs to have been all but universal. We shall then see that the composers were no worse than their neighbours, and we shall be surprised to find how often they actually rose superior to the moral level of their age and country.

Alessandro Scarlatti, who was born in Sicily in 1659, was one of the most industrious composers that ever lived. He discharged for many years the functions of Royal Chapel Master at Naples; but his chief claim to the esteem and affections of the Neapolitans consisted in his gratuitous and indefatigable labours as music-master in a large charity school known under the name of "Jesus Christ's Poor of Loretto." He was universally respected.

Marcello, born at Venice, 1686, underwent what some persons would call a regular conversion. As he was hearing mass in the Church of the Holy Apostles, the pavement gave way, and let him through into the vault beneath. This sudden meeting with the Dead seems to have made a lasting impression upon him, and he is said to have abandoned from that time forth his somewhat free habits for a more strict style of living. His greatest works are the "Psalmi" and "Laudi Spirituali;" and his monument at the Church of S. Joseph at Brescia, subscribed to by all the poets and musicians of the age, bears the inscription, "Benedicto Marcello, patricio Veneto, piissimo philologo."

The gentle Lalande, born in 1657, was much respected by the dissolute courtiers of Louis XIV. He was naturally of a religious temperament, nor does he seem to have been spoiled by the corruption of the Parisian court. He was twice married, and had two beautiful daughters, both of whom died: and one of the few pious sentiments recorded of the

Grand Monarque, who had just lost his own son, the Dauphin, was addressed to the bereaved composer: "*You* have lost two daughters full of merit; *I* have lost Monseigneur." Then, pointing to the sky, the king added: "Lalande, we must learn submission to the will of God."

GLUCK, born in 1714, was the most severe and conscientious of men in his own vocation. He first conceived the germs of those ideas which under Mozart were destined to blossom into the classical school of German opera. Notwithstanding his immense popularity, he made few friends, but those few respected him. Incessant labour at length shattered his naturally robust constitution, and in his declining years he was unfortunately somewhat addicted to drinking; yet, no one remembering what Paris was in the time of the Gluckists and Piccinists, Marmontel, D'Alembert, and Marie Antoinette, can deny that Gluck, in his best days, gave a good example to the dissolute capital, of moderation and self-respect.

Of dear old SEBASTIEN BACH, born at Eisenach, 1685, let us merely say that he was a good husband, father, and friend; in the words of his friend Kittl, "he was an excellent man."

HANDEL, born in 1685, need not found his claim to religion on the number and sublimity of his sacred compositions alone. He lived so long amongst us that we know he was a good man. He was brought up as a Lutheran Protestant, and in an age of bitter sectarianism has often been charged with lukewarmness for refusing to define accurately his religious opinions, and still more for refusing to excommunicate Roman Catholics, Jews, Turks, infidels, and heretics; but his honour was unblemished, his personal purity (a matter in the eyes of the religious world apparently of less consequence than theological opinions) was always absolutely unquestioned, and his genuine piety is fully attested by his affectionate biographer Hawkins.

HAYDN, born in 1732, was naturally of a most happy and equable disposition. For many years he bore with great patience and fortitude the society of a most uncongenial wife; and although in the decline of life, after a friendly separation had been effected, and a liberal allowance settled upon the partner of his sorrows, his relations with a certain Mademoiselle Boselli are said to have been more than Platonic, this accusation has never been proved; and certainly no words would be less fit to describe his habits of life at any time than "excess" or "intemperance." Whatever may have been his weaknesses, it is certain that Papa Haydn to the end retained a lively sense of religion, and it is interesting and characteristic of this great and simple man to know that he never began writing without inscribing his compositions with the words "In nomine Domini," and that whenever he found it difficult to compose, he would resort to his rosary in prayer—a practice which he declared was always accompanied with the happiest results. He was a man without ambition, and without jealousy, simply devoted to his art, quite uncovetous; and, until comparatively late in life, equally unconscious of his own immense merit and widespread fame.

CHERUBINI, born at Florence in 1760, for many years commanded the respect and admiration of the French public by his steady and conscientious labours at the Conservatoire at Paris.

SPOHR, born at Brunswick, 1784, and MEYERBEER, born at Berlin, 1794, were both distinguished for their abstemious and laborious lives. The name of neither is associated with excesses of any kind—both were personally respected and beloved by a large circle of friends.

MOZART, born in 1756, at Salzburg, was a man of the most singularly well-balanced character. His natural dispositions seemed all good, his affectional instincts all healthy, and his religious life earnest and practical. The following passage out of one of his letters to his father, in 1782, will give a better idea of the man's rare simplicity and religious feeling than pages of eulogy :—

> "Previous to our marriage we had for some time past attended mass together, as well as confessed and taken the Holy Communion, and I found that I never prayed so fervently nor confessed so piously as by her side, and she felt the same. In short, we are made for each other; and God, who orders all things, will not forsake us."

BEETHOVEN, born at Bonn, 1770, was equally great in his intellect and his affections. How deep and tender was that noble heart, those know who have read his letters to his abandoned nephew whom he commits so earnestly to "God's holy keeping." There is no stain upon his life. His integrity was spotless;

his purity unblemished; his generosity boundless; his affections deep and lasting; his piety simple and sincere. "To-day happens to be Sunday," he writes to a friend in the most unaffected way, "so I will quote you something out of the Bible—'See that ye love one another.'" Beethoven was not only severely moral and deeply religious, but he has this further claim to the admiration and respect of the musical world, that his ideal of art was the highest, and that he was true to his ideal—utterly and disinterestedly true to the end.

Of MENDELSSOHN, born at Hamburg in 1809, it is difficult even yet to speak without emotion. Many are still alive who knew him and loved him. That keen piercing intellect, flashing with the summer lightning of sensibility and wit, that full, generous heart, that great and child-like simplicity of manners, that sweet humanity, and absolute devotion to all that was true and noble, coupled with an instinctive shrinking from all that was mean; that fierce scorn of a lie, that strong hatred of hypocrisy, that gentle, unassuming goodness—all this, and more than this, they knew who knew Mendelssohn. Those volumes of priceless letters, and that life of him which some day must be written, will make him beloved and honoured for ever by generations yet unborn. Like Beethoven, he had the highest conception of the dignity of art and the moral responsibility of the artist. In this age of mercenary musical manufacture and art degradation, Mendelssohn towers above his contemporaries like a moral lighthouse in the midst of a dark and troubled sea. His light always shone strong and pure. The winds of heaven were about his head, and the "STILL SMALL VOICE" was in his heart. In a lying generation he was true, and in an adulterous generation he was pure—and not popularity nor gain could tempt him to sully the pages of his spotless inspiration with one meretricious effect or one impure association. Of *Fra Diavolo* he writes: "In this opera a young girl divests herself of her garments and sings a song to the effect that next day at this time she will be married. All this produces effect, but I have no music for such things. I consider it ignoble. So if the present epoch exacts this style and considers it indispensable, then I will write oratorios." These are the words of the greatest master of musical form since Mozart, and also of the most popular composer who ever lived. We commend them to the attention of the artistic and musical circles in England.

The notion that the pursuit of music, owing to its exciting character, is prejudicial to health and longevity, gathers small weight from facts. Great composers as a rule have been remarkably healthy and long-lived. Scarlatti was 66 when he died; Lalande, 76; Palestrina, 70; Handel, 74; Bach, 65; Marcello, 53; Gluck, 73; Piccini, 72; Haydn, 77; Paisiello, 75; Cherubini, 82; Beethoven, 57; Spohr, 75; Meyerbeer, 70; Rossini, 78; and Monsieur Auber still composed, and was in the enjoyment of excellent health, at the advanced age of 88. On the other hand, Purcell died at the early age of 37; Pergolesi at 26; Mozart at 35; Bellini at 33; Schubert at 31; Mendelssohn at 38; Chopin at 39.

We fear that, from causes already referred to, the health and longevity of executive musicians as a class might bear a somewhat less satisfactory scrutiny; but we must again repeat that such a result would be owing not to tendencies inherent in the executive art itself, so much as to the unfair and sometimes pitiless conditions which have been too often imposed by society upon the Executive Musician.

VIII.

Like the sound of bells at night, breaking the silence only to lead the spirit into deeper peace. Like a leaden cloud at morn, rising in grey twilight to hang as a golden mist before the furnace of the sun. Like the dull, deep pain of one who sits in an empty room, watching the shadows of the firelight, full of memories. Like the plaint of souls that are wasted with sighing: like pæans of exalted praise: like sudden songs from the open gates of paradise—so is Music.

Like one who stands in the midst of a hot and terrible battle, drunk with the fiery smoke, and hearing the roar of cannon in a trance: like one who sees the thick fog creep along the shore, and gathers his cloak about him as the dank wind strikes a thin rain upon his face: like one who finds himself in a long cathedral aisle, and hears the pealing organ, and sees a kneeling crowd smitten with fringes of coloured light: like one who from a precipice leaps out upon the warm mid-summer air towards the peaceful valleys below, and, feeling himself buoyed up with wings that suddenly fail him, wakens in great despair from his wild dream—so is he who can listen and understand.

No such scenes need be actually present to the LISTENER; yet the emotions which might accompany them, music enables him to realize. To him belongs a threefold privilege. He hears the composer's conception, he feels the player's or conductor's individuality, and he brings to both the peculiar temperature or what I may call the harmonic level of his own soul. Ask him to describe his feelings, and he will seek some such imagery as I have used above. And there can be no great objection to this, so long as such an expression of feeling passes for what it is worth, and no more. No music—except imitative music (which is rather noise than music) or music acting through association—has in itself power to suggest scenes to the mind's eye. When we seek to explain our musical emotions, we look about for images calculated to excite similar emotions, and strive to convey through these images to others the effect produced by music upon ourselves. The method is, no doubt, sufficiently clumsy and inadequate; but it helps to make clear some things in connection with our musical impressions which might otherwise puzzle us.

Perhaps the great puzzle of all is why, if music has any meaning, different people suppose different things to be shadowed forth by the same piece. The answer is, because Music expresses Emotion. Now, as I have shown, the same emotion may take very different forms, or express itself by very different images, according to circumstances.

When the fire-irons are thrown down, a sleeper may start from his slumbers under the impression that he is in Strasburg during the late siege, and that a shell has just burst into his room; or that he finds himself up in the Westminster belfry when Big Ben strikes the hour; or that a great rock has rolled from a precipitous cliff into the sea, threatening to crush him; or the dreamer will raise his hand in fright to ward off an impending blow which seems to descend upon his skull. Here, then, are a number of distinct images which might be connected with the same emotion. If, then, in sleep, the Emotional Region is so ready to assimilate appropriate ideas, no wonder if it retain this property when the mind is in full and wakeful activity. Mr. Grewgious's emotions afford a fine example of this. One and the same energetic feeling finds vent in two separate and equally forcible ideas in the following remarkable passage:—

"'I will!' cried Mr. Grewgious. 'Damn him!
'Confound his politics,
Frustrate his knavish tricks,
On thee his hopes to fix—
Damn him again.'

After this most extraordinary outburst, Mr. Grewgious, quite beside himself, plunged about the room to all *appearance undecided whether he was in a fit of loyal enthusiasm, or combative denunciation.*"—("Edwin Drood," p. 156.)

Emotion aroused by music, in like manner, clothes itself in different draperies of ideas. Six different people, hearing the same piece of music, will give you six different accounts of it. Yet between all their explanations there will be a certain kind of emotional congruity, quite enough to persuade us that they have been under a fixed influence and the same influence. But here we are constrained to push this question well home. Is music, after all, in any sense a fixed influence? Is it really expressive of the same emotion to different people? Yes, music is the same; but people are not. People think and feel on different planes of thought and feeling.

There are different Planes of Emotion. If your character is base, the plane of your emotion will be low. If your character is noble, the plane of your emotion will be high. Every emotion is capable of being expressed in both planes. For example, what is craven fear in a low plane becomes a reverent awe when expressed in a high plane. Mean and gnawing spite in a low plane becomes an emotion of bitter and just vengeance in a high one; and low desire is raised to the power of pure and burning love. The question for the listener then is, What are his planes of thought and feeling—in other words, what is the character of his musical mediumship? Music will give him whatever he is capable of receiving. The same strain will kindle the same emotion with its elations, depressions, velocities, intensities, &c., in the plane of awe and in the plane of fear. The mind habitually at home in meanness and spite will yield its emotions in that plane to combinations of music which, to a nobler spirit, suggest the higher longings for a retributive justice. He whose ideas of Love are merely sensual will travel contentedly along a correspondingly grovelling plane of emotion, whilst the very same music will kindle in another the noble self-abandonment of a lofty and purifying Passion.

This surely explains how very easy it is to put different words to the same song. Some of Handel's melodies which had done duty as love songs in operas, have since been made the vehicles for religious aspiration and prayer. The supplicating love song, "Cara sposa amante cara," in *Rinaldo*, raised from the plane of a lover's adoration to the high level of devotional longing, becomes the sacred air, "Hear my crying." The exalting strain of earth, "To the triumph of our fury," is raised to the high plane of a devotional pæan in "Praise ye Jehovah which dwelleth in Zion." We wish for the honour of music, and for the honour of Handel, it could be said that he was always equally conscientious in choosing words of higher or lower congruity to the feeling of the music; but, like so many great composers, he seems to have been often indifferent to his words, under the conviction that the music was all-powerful to convey the right emotional expression, whatever the words might say to the contrary. But the difficulties with which composers have to deal in setting several verses to the same piece of melody are often very great, and if we attempt, like Wagner, to make every bar—almost every note—correspond to a word, we may almost say that such difficulties can only be surmounted by the sacrifice of melody and the destruction of musical form. We must be content if the words selected help to set the mind going in a certain plane of emotion. We may then hope to find them true enough in the main, although quite unreasonable when pressed in detail.

Poor Weber, in Agatha's song in *Der Freischütz*, has the first verse thus:—

> "Softly sighs the voice of evening
> Stealing through yon willow groves."

And in the next his English translator has adapted the same peaceful melody to the words—

> "O, what terrors fill my bosom!
> Where, my Rudolph, dost thou roam?"

But even then the two verses are quite near enough to the general emotion expressed by their music; for the last two lines of the first verse are—

> "While the stars, like guardian spirits,
> Set their nightly watch above,"

and the last two lines of the second verse, which begins with the highly perturbed sentiment above quoted, stand thus:—

> **"Oh, may Heaven's protection shelter
> Him my heart must ever love!"**

Of course, in speaking of high and low planes of emotion, I have here assumed what I have tried to establish in this First Book, II. pp. 14-18 : that Emotions, although traversed by Ideas, are not merely states of sensation produced by one idea, or any number of ideas, but enjoy an independent existence and a special character of their own, which give them a moral dignity, and enable them to place themselves at the disposal of ideas congenial to their various planes.

But I think at this point an objector may fairly say, After all, then, music does not determine what you call the Plane of our Emotions—has nothing to do with either a high or low plane of Love, for instance—but merely lends itself to each individual, and is willing to express the force, feebleness, or complexity of his emotions in any plane in which they may happen to lie at the time. No doubt the moral effect of music largely depends upon the moral state of the listener ; but so does the moral effect of painting, and everything else. Show me what a man is, and I will show you the kind of influences he is likely to assimilate. I will show how what to others shall be harmless, shall to him be as poison—how he will select from what he sees and hears everything that is congenial to his disposition, and leave the rest ; in this sense all the arts will give him back the reflection of himself—he will "see himself in all he sees ;" it does not, therefore, follow that there will be nothing else to see. A work of art may really be calculated to create a very high level of emotion; yet a man may be so base that, owing to a refusal on his part to see, or a wilful distortion of what he sees, or a wanton selection of only such suggestions as coincide with what is base in him, the work of art may produce nothing but an emotion worked out on the level of his own baseness. To the pure all things are pure; but the vicious will find in the most guileless innocence only one more incentive to vice. The noblest themes may also be approached through licentious avenues. But what should we say of a man who read through Shakspeare and selected only the coarse passages for his meditation, viewing all the others as in some way connected with them, but existing only for their sakes? We should say not Shakspeare is a low teacher, but the man who receives such an impression from Shakspeare is a low man. What should we say of one who accepted the "Fornarina" of the Barberini as the true type of Raphael's art, and viewed all his Madonnas from that ignoble stand-point? We should say, of course, the man's own mind was to blame for the deplorable nature of his impressions. There was that in the art of Raphael, there is that in the teaching of Shakspeare, which is not only capable of, but infinitely more conducive to, a high than to a low state of feeling. And we do not hesitate to say exactly the same of music. It is, more than any other art, ready to mould itself about our emotions; but it is undeniable that music, however we may wrest it to express our own level of feeling, has its own proper and distinct levels, which it should be our business to discover and appropriate, if we wish to understand or rightly to estimate a composer's work. And this is so true, that at times the music itself opposes the greatest obstacles to any attempts on our part to twist it into accordance with our private levels of feeling.

The modern Italian music is so imbued with the languid sentimentalism in which that nation has until lately been sunk, that, however vigorous we may feel, we grow insensibly languid and sentimental in either hearing or singing it. On the other hand, you cannot sentimentalize Beethoven's music; you cannot make it a vehicle for permanently morbid trains of emotion. When it deals with the emotions of Love, for instance, it deals with them on the high planes of pure and strong passion. Beethoven is the "true and tender North" Italy is the "fierce and fickle South." The Italians know this, and that is why the Italians dislike Beethoven. They cannot make his music express emotion down to their level, and so they do not sing him or play him. Nothing is more ludicrous than to hear a fashionable Italian pianist attempt a sonata of Beethoven. Exaggerated pathos has to be pumped into the quiet phrases, hectic explosions must be let off where nothing but a grave *forte* is required, and the repose of the whole is broken up by an uneasy effervescence which shows that the player is like a fish on shore—excited and bewildered, but quite out of his element.

The emotional plane of Italy is one thing, and that of Germany is another. Your clown may put on the monk's cowl, but he forgets to wipe off the paint, and by-and-by, in spite of his costume, he will grin and throw his somersault as usual. Let any one who doubts that music is really capable of pitching a high plane for the emotions to work in, recall Beethoven's love-song "Adelaide." No modern Italian master could have written that song. No one can suppose the melody to be expressive of languid sentimentality. We are thrilled; we are not dissolved, we are moved, yet without losing our self-control; and we are too much in earnest to be the mere sport of our emotions. They sweep with flame and thunder through the soul, leaving its atmosphere purified and sweetened by the storm. Let us now think of any popular Italian love-song, *e.g.* "Si fossi un Angelo del Paradiso non potere vivere di te diviso." Most of our readers may have heard this song by Marras, and it is a very typical one. The emotions are all upon a low plane. The kind of man who could so express his love is an artificial sentimentalist, his feeling is at once exaggerated and extravagant, but not deep; and we have a shrewd idea that the whole thing is poured out by a sham lover, in the presence of some person of doubtful character, by the light of an artificial moon. Without doing absolute violence to the obvious intention of Beethoven, you cannot sentimentalize "Adelaide," whereas it is impossible to do anything else with such a song as "Si fossi un Angelo." If the reader admits the justice of the above remarks, he can hardly refuse to believe that music not only expresses the various qualities of emotion, but has also the power—subject, no doubt, to perturbing influences—of determining the level of emotion, or what may be termed the moral atmosphere of feeling.

And now it is a very noteworthy thing, as bearing upon the life of a Nation, that whatever the spirit which pervades its music happens to be,—whether that spirit be languid and erotic, as in Italy; or frivolous, graceful, noisy, and, at times, blustering, as in France,—the music of patriotic tunes and national anthems is invariably earnest and dignified. The tune known as Garibaldi's Hymn, which raged like a fever throughout Italy during the revolution, is so fresh and buoyant and manly in its cheerful vigour and determination, that it fails to suggest a single characteristic of modern Italian music, save only that exemplary one of clear and facile melody. The time for Love-languor is past; the sun of Liberty has dawned, the breeze is on the mountain, the bugle sounds the *reveillé*, and the youth of Italy, active, alert, hopeful, and confident, march cheerfully to the deliverance of their beautiful but enslaved country. In the Marseillaise there is an almost sombre severity, wholly unlike the frivolous superficial grace and sentimental pathos of the ordinary French school. The men who sing it are not playing at war, like fools; nor are they mere children, delighting in its outward pomp and circumstance. They trudge on, footsore and weary, knowing all the horror and the pain that is in store for them, and still willing to conquer and to die. That is the spirit of the Marseillaise; and in it, as in Garibaldi's Hymn, the seriousness of the crisis has called forth the finest qualities of both the French and Italian characters, and banished for a time what is languishing in the one and frivolous in the other. I need hardly allude here to the Austrian and Russian hymns, or to our own national anthem, as there has never been any question about the musical merit, dignity, and earnestness of these.

Philosophers have often been at a loss to explain the secret of the strange power which patriotic tunes seem to exercise over the people, and especially over the armies of nations. Historians have been contented simply to record the fact; but the mystery is at an end if we are willing to attribute to music the power which I have claimed for it, of pitching high the plane of the emotions, and driving them home with the most efficacious and incomparable energy.

The laws which regulate the effect of music upon the listener are subject to many strange perturbations. Unless we admit this to be the case, and try to detect the operation of certain irregular influences, we shall be at a loss to understand why, if music really has its own planes as well as progressions of emotion, gay music should make us sad, and solemn music should sometimes provoke a smile. Musical perturbations are sometimes due to the singer, player, or conductor,—sometimes to the listener. Madame Lind-Goldschmidt had, or let us rather say has, the power of perturbing a trivial melody of any kind almost to any extent. A magical prolongation of single notes here and there, until the vulgarity of the rhythm be broken—a pause, a little *appogiatura,* even a smile—and the original melody, such as we may know it to be, is changed and sublimated into the high expression of a high individuality. Ernst, certainly the most romantic player we have had since Paganini, possessed the same marvellous quality of perturbing almost everything he played until it became absolutely nothing but a melodic expression of his own wild mood. Those who remember the way in which he was wont to play one of his great solos on Hungarian airs, with orchestral accompaniments, will remember the profound meditation, almost coma, into which he seemed to fall in the middle of one of those slow and measured melodies —losing the sense of time and rhythm—allowing, as it were, his own soul to float out upon the waves of melody, which swelled and shook with sensitive thrills, holding the audience breathless, until, in the utter stillness of the room, it was impossible to tell when the notes actually ceased to vibrate. Such players as he must be classed under the head of "Those who express themselves through the music," just as such players as Joachim belong emphatically to the class of those who invariably express the composer's thought, not their own. It is hardly necessary to allude to the manner of any living conductors, to establish the fact that immense powers of perturbation are in the hands of orchestral conductors. We had no idea that Mendelssohn's Hymn of Praise could be made to sound positively trivial until it was our misfortune to hear it under the auspices of a thoroughly sentimental and incompetent conductor.

But the perturbations in the natural effect of the music which come from the listener are even more numerous and perplexing. They proceed chiefly from association and memory. If one is by the death-bed of a friend, and a band passes in the street playing a cheerful tune, that tune will sound even more sadly than a really mournful air, which might serve at once to express and to relieve the deep heaviness of the heart. An unhappy girl, out of her mind for the loss of her lover, singing a merry song to herself in a madhouse, will make the joyous melody sound sad enough—sad as the raptures of an imprisoned skylark hanging caged in the London streets. On the other hand, a grave tune may, in like manner, be fairly perturbed out of all sobriety; and, as we have shown it is possible to pass from gay to grave in the lunatic asylum, so we may pass from grave to gay, in spite of our best intentions, upon hearing some well-known psalm-tune intoned through the nose by an ancient schoolmaster in a country church, where the service resembles nothing so much as a pitched battle between the clergyman and the clerk in the presence of a silent congregation, and where the said schoolmaster is, for some unintelligible reason, occasionally permitted to interrupt the duel with an extraordinary succession of sounds supposed to represent the 119th Psalm. In this case, however grave the melody may really be in itself, it will be undeniably perturbed by an unfortunate association of ideas at the moment when it reaches the ears of the judicious hearer.

The strangest phenomena of all connected with musical perturbation are to be found in alliance with memory: but musical sound is only one of many mediums which connect us vividly with the past. Scents have a remarkable power of recalling past scenes. Who has not got memories connected with otto of roses or the perfume of violets? The peculiar combination of odours to be met with only in a steamboat cabin will recall to some many a disastrous passage across the British Channel. To a Londoner, the smell of a tan-yard or tallow manufactory, will certainly be associated with those lines of railway running out of London over the roofs of serried houses overlooking certain odorous yards,—instantly he may remember his holding his nose, or seizing the window-strap to pull up the window of the railway-carriage. The odour of tar calls up many a watering-place in summer—we are on the pier in an instant, with some little child, perchance now grown up or dead—the fishing-smack lies alongside lazily, smoke issuing from a pot at the stern, a sailor sits with a pipe in his mouth, throwing vegetable parings into the black kettle for the nondescript midday meal—the hot sea beneath a blazing sun lies almost stagnant, waiting for the turn of the tide, the white cliffs glimmer along the coast—and all this flashes for a moment before the mind's eye as we chance to pass over a piece of asphalte pavement, newly laid down, and smelling faintly of pitch.

The sight of a faded flower pressed in a book, brings back, with a little shock of feeling, the hand that gathered it, or the distant hills upon which it once bloomed years ago. The touch of satin or velvet, or fine hair, is also capable of reviving the recollection of scenes and places and persons. But for freshness and suddenness and power over memory all the senses must yield to the sense of hearing. Memory is the great perturber of musical meaning. When memory is concerned, music is no longer itself, it ceases to have any proper plane of feeling; it surrenders itself wholly, with all its rights, to memory, to be the patient, stern, and terrible exponent of that recording angel. What is it? Only a few trivial bars of an old pianoforte piece—"Murmures du Rhone," or "Pluie des Perles." The drawing-room window is open, the children are playing on the lawn, the warm morning air is charged with the scent of lilac blossom. Then the ring at the bell, the confusion in the hall, the girl at the piano stops, the door opens, and one is lifted in dying or dead. Years, years ago! but passing through the streets, a bar or two of the "Murmures du Rhone" brings the whole scene up before the girl, now no longer a girl, but a middle-aged woman, looking back to one fatal summer morning. The enthusiastic old men, who invariably turned up in force whenever poor Madame Grisi was advertised to sing in her last days, seemed always deeply affected. Yet it could hardly be at what they actually heard—no, the few notes recalled the most superb soprano of the age in her best days; recalled, also, the scenes of youth for ever faded out, and the lights of youth quenched in the grey mists of the dull declining years. It was worth any money to hear even the hollow echo of a voice which had power to bring back, if only for a moment, the "tender grace of a day that was dead."

Composers, by re-treating, quoting, or paraphrasing well-known airs and harmonic sequences, might have made much more use of memory and association than they have. Schumann has shown us what might be done in this way by the amazing effect produced in his song "The Two Grenadiers," by the introduction of the "Marseillaise." The words of this wonderful little song of Heinrich Heine's are intended, like the music, to express that peculiar type of character in the French army called into existence by the genius of the first Napoleon.

The disastrous campaign in Russia is over. The

great Emperor has been taken captive. Two French grenadiers, wearied, dispirited, one of them suffering from a deadly wound, approach the German frontier. The same desolate feeling has taken possession of both, and the veterans are moved to tears as they think over the humiliation of France, and the defeat of their Emperor, who is dearer to them than life itself. Then up speaks the wounded warrior to his companion. "Friend, when I am dead, bury me in my native France, with my cross of honour on my breast, and my musket in my hand, and lay my good sword by my side." Up to this point the melody has been in the minor key. A slow, dreary, dirge-like stave; but as the old soldier declares his belief that he will rise once more and fight when he hears the Emperor walk over his grave amid the tramp of horsemen and the roar of cannon, the minor breaks into a truly ghostly form of the "Marseillaise." It rolls forth in the major key, but is not carried through, and is brought to an abrupt close with five solemn bars of chords in *adagio*, upon which the smoke of the battle seems to sweep into the distance as the vision of the phantom host fades out upon the wide plain, with its lonely green mounds and mouldering wooden crosses.

The emotional force in women is usually stronger, and always more delicate, than in men. Their constitutions are like those fine violins which vibrate to the lightest touch. Women are the great listeners, not only to eloquence, but also to music. The wind has swept many an Æolian lyre, but never such a sensitive harp as a woman's soul. In listening to music, her face is often lighted up with tenderness, with mirth, or with the simple expansiveness of intense pleasure. Her attitude changes unconsciously with the truest, because the most natural, dramatic feeling. At times she is shaken and melts into tears, as the flowers stand and shake when the wind blows upon them and the drops of rain fall off. The woman's temperament is naturally artistic, not in a creative, but in a receptive, sense. A woman seldom writes good music, never great music: and, strange to say, many of the best singers have been incapable of giving even a good musical reading to the songs in which they have been most famous. It was rumoured that Madame Grisi had to be taught all her songs, and became great by her wonderful power of appropriating suggestions of pathos and expression which she was incapable of originating herself. Madame Malibran had a great dash of original genius, and seldom sang a song twice in the same way. Most women reflect with astonishing ease, and it has often been remarked that they have more perception than thought, more passion than judgment, more generosity than justice, and more religious sentiment than moral taste.

Many a woman, though capable of so much, is frequently called upon in the best years of her life to do but little, but at all times society imposes upon her a strict reticence as to her real feelings. What is she to do with the weary hours, with the days full of the intolerable sunshine, and the nights full of the pitiless stars? Her village duties or town visits are done. Perchance neither have any attractions for her. She has read till her head aches; but all the reading leads to nothing. She has worked till her fingers ache; but what is the work good for when it is done? To set women to do the things which some people suppose are the only things fit for them to do, is often like setting the steam-hammer to knock pins into a board. The skilful and ingenious operation leaves them dissatisfied or listless, or makes them, by a kind of reaction, frivolous, wicked, and exaggerated caricatures of what God intended them to be. Some outlet is wanted. Control is good, but at a certain point control becomes something very much like paralysis. The steam-hammer, as it contemplates the everlasting pin's head, cannot help feeling that if some day, when the steam was on, it might give one good smashing blow, it would feel all the better for it. To women—and how many thousands are there in our placid modern drawing-rooms!—who feel like this, music comes with a power of relief and a gentle grace of ministration little short of supernatural.

That girl who sings to herself her favourite songs of Schubert, Mendelssohn, or Schumann, sings more than a song: it is her own plaint of suffering floating away on the wings of melody. That poor lonely little sorrower, hardly more than a child, who sits dreaming at her piano, whilst her fingers, caressing the deliciously cool ivory keys, glide through a weird *nocturne* of Chopin, is playing no mere study or set piece. Ah, what heavy burden seems lifted up, and borne away in the dusk? Her eyes are half closed—her heart is far away; she dreams a dream as the long, yellow light fades in the west, and the wet vine-leaves tremble outside to the nestling birds; the angel of music has come down; she has poured into his ear the tale which she will confide to no one else, and the "restless, unsatisfied longing" has passed; for one sweet moment the cup of life seems full—she raises it to her trembling lips. What if it is only a dream—a dream of comfort sent by music? Who will say she is not the better for it? She has been taken away from the commonplaceness and dulness of life—from the old books in the study, and the familiar faces in the school-room, and the people in the streets; she has been alone with herself, but not fretting or brooding—alone with herself and the minstrel spirit. Blessed recreation, that brings back freshness to the tired life and buoyancy to the heavy heart! Happy rain of tears and stormy wind of sighs sweeping the sky clear, and showing once more the deep blue heaven of the soul beyond! Let no one say that the moral effects of music are small or insignificant. That domestic and long-suffering instrument, the cottage piano, has probably done more to sweeten existence and bring peace and happiness to families in general, and to young women in particular, than all the homilies on the domestic virtues ever yet penned.

IX.

THE social effects of music would be a very interesting subject of discussion; but they lie a little outside the purpose of our present book. In writing on a subject so extremely fertile as music, it is almost impossible not to diverge at times into pleasant byways and unexplored paths. I have now only space for a few remarks on the moral effects of sacred music upon the listener. Those who attend the performances of the Sacred Harmonic Society at Exeter Hall and the other great musical festivals in England, need not be told that almost all the greatest composers have found, in the sacred cantata or oratorio, a form of art capable of expressing the noblest progressions of the religious sentiment in the highest planes of emotion. Those who have been familiar with the Bible from childhood are apt to grow insensible to the majestic beauty of its style, to the frequently inspired level of its ideas, and the subtle charm of its diction. Some day they may chance suddenly to read a passage of it in French or German, and the simple novelty of form will wonderfully arrest their attention and kindle their emotion. But this is nothing compared with the effect which is produced by arranging the magnificent episodes of Scripture in a dramatic—not operatic—form, and translating their emotional significance into the universal language of music. In the oratorio, unlike the opera, there is nothing absurd or *outré*. The fact of

Elijah standing before us in a well-trimmed moustache and clean kid gloves does not in the least shock our sense of propriety, because no impersonation is attempted. The singers are there, not to personate character, but to help us to realize the force and procession of certain emotions through which the characters in the sacred drama are supposed to pass. By doing this, and no more, we attempt the possible, and succeed. A good deal depends upon the libretto. Mendelssohn was himself ever a loving and reverent student of the Bible. He selected and arranged in great measure the words of his own oratorios; and so admirably has he entered into the spirit of his work, that it is difficult to listen to the *Elijah* or *St. Paul*, with the words before us, without each time receiving some new impression of the depth and sublimity of those characters, whose figures at this distance of time stand out prominently among all the prophets of the Old and New Testaments. I have written so much elsewhere upon oratorios, that I willingly, without further preamble, pass on to congregational singing.

In all times men and women have shown a strong disposition to express their praises and lamentations by what for some better term may be called a kind of howling or wailing. This method may not be thought very musical or hymn-like. Nevertheless, all such vocal expressions are actual attempts to utter deep feeling through appropriate channels of sound. When properly disciplined and elaborated, that mode of utterance becomes devotional and congregational singing. The Lollards, who according to some took their name from *lullen*, "to sing," found in hymn tunes and chants a great medium for expressing the rush of a new religious life upon their spirits, and within the last hundred years the Methodist hymns have served a like purpose. No doubt upon entering a chapel where the congregation were singing, heart and soul, some easily-learned and well-known hymn, the hearer was liable to be caught by the devotional impetuosity thus expressed through musical sound; and, indeed, no greater bond of worship could be devised than hymn tunes suited to the capacities and tastes of the people. Mr. Ward Beecher, in his own peculiar vein, has lately preached a very eloquent sermon to his congregation upon this subject, and we need make no apology for presenting our readers with the following extract to the point:—

"Singing is that natural method by which thoughts are reduced to feeling, more easily, more surely, and more universally than by any other. You are conscious when you go to an earnest meeting, for instance, that, while hymns are being sung and you listen to them, your heart is, as it were, loosened, and there comes out of those hymns to you a realization of the truth such as you never had before. There is a pleading element, there is a sense of humiliation of heart, there is a poignant realization of sin and its guiltiness, there is a yearning for a brighter life in a hymn which you do not find in your closet; and, in singing, you come into sympathy with the truth as you perhaps never do under the preaching of a discourse. There is a provision made in singing for the development of almost every phase of Christian experience. Singing also has a wonderful effect upon those feelings which we wish to restrain. All are not alike susceptible; but all are susceptible to some extent. I speak with emphasis on this point, because I am peculiarly sensitive to singing, and because I owe so much to it. How many times have I come into the church on Sunday morning, jaded and somewhat desponding, saddened, at any rate,—and before the organ voluntary was completed, undergone a change as great as though I had been taken out of January and been plumped down in the middle of May, with spring blossoms on every hand! How many, many times have I been lifted out of a depressed state of mind into a cheerful mood by the singing before I began to preach! How often, in looking forward to the Friday-night meeting, has my prevailing thought been, not of what I was going to say, but of the hymns that would be sung! My prayer-meeting consists largely of the singing of hymns which are full of prayings, and my predominant thought in connection with our Friday-night gatherings is, 'Oh, that sweet, joyful singing!'"

As faith in the great evangelical movement cooled, the hearty congregational singing also began to die down in the Church of England, and in fashionable chapels the voices of the people were represented by a few careless professional ladies and gentlemen, who showed themselves off to considerable advantage in a private box, situated in the west gallery, in front of the organ. There the ladies were wont to fan themselves and flirt during the prayers, and there the gentlemen "made up" their "little books," or sat yawning through the sermon. The congregation being mostly asleep, and the clergyman also somewhat comatose, it seemed for some time unlikely that the above odious performance would give way to anything a shade less irreverent; when lo! the great High Church movement in a very few years pulled the wheezy organs out of their dingy nooks, and swept half the old musical boxes in the land from our churches, concert singers and all.

Then arose the age of white surplices, and new hymn tunes, and decent versicles and anthems. In short, a cathedral service soon became fashionable all over England, not in High churches only, but even in Low and Broad churches. Whatever we may think of their doctrines, the High Church party have stood up for the æsthetic element in devotion, and by introducing a respectable amount of ritual, with good music, they have shown us how it was possible to be emotional without being vulgar. The charge brought against the High Church singing is that it is uncongregational, and this is held to be a fatal objection, especially to anthems. The objection is only one more proof of how much the English people have still to learn concerning the real functions of music. There is a grace of hearing, as well as a grace of singing; there is a passive, as well as an active, side of worship. In every congregation there must be some who cannot join even in the simplest tune. Some are too old, some have no voices, others have no ear for music; but it would be a great mistake to suppose that all who are thus reduced to the state of listeners get nothing at all out of the singing. If we take note of old and devout worshippers as some familiar hymn is being sung, we shall see their faces lighten up and their heads move in unconscious sympathy, and we shall know that although their lips are silent, they are singing in the spirit. One day noticing a very poor and aged woman in tears during the service, I spoke to her at the close, and inquired the cause of her grief. "Oh, sir," she replied, "that blessed, blessed song in the middle of the prayers!" She could say no more; but she was alluding to an anthem by Sir Sterndale Bennett—"O Lord, thou hast searched me out."

The function of anthems is no doubt quite different from that of psalms or hymns. It is greatly to be wished that the congregation would never attempt to join in the anthem—not even in the chorus, strong as the temptation may sometimes be. Above all, let not people with musical ears sing fancy parts to their own edification and the great distress of their fellow-worshippers. The strength of the congregation during the anthem is emphatically to sit, or at all events to stand, still. They need lose nothing by their silence, for, rightly understood, it may be quite as blessed a thing to allow music to flow into the soul as to pour forth actively songs of praise. This is hardly a popular view of the subject. In every church where an anthem is sung, the majority of the congregation seems to belong to one of two classes—those who look upon the anthem as an unwarrantable interloper, and those who regard it simply in the light of a show-off for the choir. Need we observe that neither of these two views is the correct one?

The worshipper has for some time been engaged in the service of active prayer and praise, when there comes "in choirs and places where they sing" a pause, and "Here followeth the anthem." The active phase of devotion is exchanged for the passive at the moment when the powers of congregational attention begin to fail, and physical energy is waxing a little faint. The emotions which we have just been connecting in prayer with solemn, perhaps even harrowing, thoughts—the feelings we have been labouring to express, with a certain strained and fatiguing mental effort—in short, all burdensome activity is suddenly suspended, and the spirit, raised into the atmosphere of devotion, remains passive, in order that it may be recruited, by having its weight of feeling lifted up and its emotion expressed for it, through music in harmony with its inner consciousness. It is as though a traveller grown weary in a winter's walk were suddenly to be lifted up and borne along upon wings without word or action of his own, what time the land grew warm with sunlight, the air scented with flowers and full of angel voices. When the times of refreshing are past he finds himself again upon the earth; but all his fatigue has vanished, and he is now able to go on his journey with renewed life and "compassed about with songs of rejoicing." When the hearing of voluntaries and anthems is thus regarded as part of the needful solace and recreation of the religious life, we shall, no doubt, find music much more widely and intelligently used in our churches than it is at present.

Musically speaking, there is as yet in the Reformed Churches nothing approaching the grandeur of the great Roman Catholic Masses, where we have a mind like that of Mozart or Beethoven steadily working out, in strains of incomparable depth and pathos, a great connected series of thoughts, embodying all the varied phases of religious emotion. Indeed, the notion that a religious service may be wrought out with the force and majesty of a great work of art, having its various parts welded into a powerful and satisfactory unity by the agency of music, is a conception which has evidently not yet reached this isle of the Protestant Gentiles. Yet no religious service can with impunity violate, in however small a degree, the great laws of beauty, fitness, and order which are involved in the conception of a Mass; nor is it impossible, without making the music incessant throughout the service, to arrange our own liturgy in such an order, and so to incorporate the musical element, as to sustain the attention of the congregation, and produce a unity of effect, far greater than is at present at all usual. In some High churches we find a glimmering of what a musical service might and ought to be; but what with unbending mediævalism and rigid ecclesiastical prejudices, we must not hope for anything like a good type of congregational service from that quarter. On the other hand, anything more disjointed and slovenly than the ordinary brown-coloured sort of church service still prevalent in most country churches and London chapels can hardly be conceived. Have people no ears —do they not care what is piped and what is harped—is their attention never exhausted—have they no idea of the strain which the human mind is constructed to bear—that they can listen for an hour to a nasal droning of the prayers, interlarded here with a chant, the very memory of which makes one yawn, and there with some hymn tune, sung at a pace compared to which *adagio* might be called fast? There is a hopeless want of decision and energy in the ordinary conduct of our church prayers. We do not want rapidity so much as a definite conception of the emotional fabric of the whole; and here is the point where music might come to our assistance, by defining the pauses and divisions which the life and interest of the whole service demands. Every orator, every singer, every soloist, and every conductor will readily understand what I mean. He who arranges a religious service, if he wishes it to secure the attention and minister to the edification of the people, should place himself somewhat in the position of an orchestral conductor; it is his business to arrange every detail of the proceedings. The exact moment at which the opening hymn is sung, the general impulse and feeling of the hymn should be impressed upon the choir; the organist should enter into the spirit of the music, and understand its place and function in the service; he should be always on the watch; there should be no *unintentional* delays in giving out the hymns—no unsettled pauses before the hymn is commenced; the hymns, responses, canticles, anthems, and voluntaries should succeed one another in such a succession and style as to relieve one another, each fitting into its place at the nick of time, never dragging, never jolting, not baulking the attention, or executed in so aimless a manner as to allow the congregation to grow listless. But to accomplish all this, or a tithe of it, there must be true art feeling and true religious feeling and true musical taste: and although we are inclined to admit that the English are on the whole a Religious People, we arrive at the sad conviction that, however improving and improvable, the English are not, as a nation, an artistic people, *and the English are not a Musical People.*

END OF THE FIRST BOOK.

Second Book.

BIOGRAPHICAL.

HANDEL, GLUCK, HAYDN, SCHUBERT,
CHOPIN, MOZART, BEETHOVEN,
AND MENDELSSOHN.

Second Book.

FROM

AMBROSE TO HANDEL.

I.

WE sometimes hear music called the universal language. That will be true some day. Civilized music must ultimately triumph over every other kind of music, because it is based upon natural principles discovered once and for ever, and capable of being universally applied and understood. But at present to speak of music, ancient and modern, savage and scientific, as a universal language, is only true in a limited sense. There is probably no nation upon earth so devoid of tonal sensibility as to be quite callous to the attraction, or even fascination, of sounds produced artificially with a view to excite or to relieve emotion. If we like to call any such medley of sounds music, of course we are at liberty to do so. The rudest howl of the savage as he dances round his bonfire, in the pages of "Robinson Crusoe" or elsewhere, the wildest monody of the Eastern donkey-driver, or the most exasperating scrape of a Japanese fiddle, is essentially a kind of music.

Sound, as an emotional vehicle, is universal—in the same way that speech is universal. But if we mean by universal that every kind of music possesses the property of being everywhere equally intelligible, that is simply not the case. The Indian who sits down to yell for two hours and beat the *tom-tom* may possibly soothe the savage mind, but he drives the European mad. Mr. Hullah, to whose excellent lectures we are indebted for much of the following essay, tells us of an Arabian artist whose conception of the scale on his *eoud*, or lute, was not only different from ours, but who refused to tolerate the order of tones and semi-tones adopted in our *major* and *minor*. The music of the savage is not as our music, neither do we delight in the music of the past—by which I mean the music of the ancients and the music of the middle ages. The monuments, the paintings, the literature of the past are still eloquent. We still admire Westminster Abbey, Notre Dame de Chartres, or the frescoes at Padua. We are still warmed by the rough geniality of Chaucer, and the lines of Petrarch and Dante are woven like golden threads into the fabric of our conversation and literature; but when we are asked to sit down with these worthies and hear a little music, we cannot pretend to be very anxious to do so—there might have been a certain charm about the wild inspirations of the *trouvères*, but not sufficient to atone for the want of form and the fixed tonality of modern melody—whilst at church the monks would treat you to a kind of harmony, consisting of one *bourdon* in the bass, and a few consecutive fifths and octaves to relieve the ear! So bad must have been these effects that many writers have maintained that the art of reading the old music is lost, and that sharps, flats, and rhythm were really used long before they were indicated in the notation.

Nor is the music of the old world more satisfactory. We may, indeed, trace music from India to Egypt, from Egypt to Judæa, from Judæa to Greece; but the pre-Grecian period is utterly barren, and the Grecian period, with its better understood octave and monotone notation, is dulness itself. The attempts of the old world, B.C., ingenious and complicated as some of them were, may be safely dismissed as clumsy and unsuccessful; they are not worth the study that has been bestowed upon them. Mr. Hullah reckons the First Period of music from 370 A.D. to 1400. Until about the year 700 A.D. people did not even stumble in the right direction, and not until 1400 was that glorious vista opened up, at whose distant extremity sat the crowned genius of Modern Music presiding over the immortal tone-poetry of the sixteenth, seventeenth, eighteenth, and nineteenth centuries. However, it would be unfair, even in the most cursory sketch, not to notice the attempts made by St. Ambrose of Milan (elected 374) to adapt a few of the Greek scales for the use of the Church. Much of his work was afterwards undone by the stupidity of his followers, until Gregory the Great (elected 590) revived what could be found of the Ambrosian system, added four new scales, and issued an antiphonary, or authorised book of ecclesiastical music.

The monk Hucbald of St. Armand, diocese of Tournay, who died in 932, has collected and systematized the best music current in his day. The harmony then admired must have resembled the mixture-stop of our organs played alone. Guido of Arezzo (1020) and Franco of Cologne (about 1200—some writers place him much earlier) are the only other names worth mentioning at this early period. The labours of the first culminated in the rise of descant, *i.e.* the combination of sounds of unequal length, or "music in which two or more sounds succeed each other while one equal to them in length was sustained" (*Hullah*); the labours of Franco may be connected with a better system of musical notation, the introduction of sharps and flats, and the *cantus mensurabilis*, or division of music into bars. Both were voluminous authors; to the first, Guido, undoubtedly belongs the honour of popularizing the study of music, by the invention of a simple method of instruction. In his day there were very few organs, and a great dearth of other instruments. Thus the music-master had the greatest difficulty in directing the voice and forming the musical ear; and, indeed, apart from his immediate presence, little practice or progress could be made by the pupil. Guido used a simple instrument, called a monochord, which had letters written on a finger-board corresponding to definite notes—the said notes being produced by shifting a movable bridge up and down the letters, just as the finger is shifted up and down the frets of a guitar. No doubt, also, Guido taught all that was then known of the art, and formulated a great deal which he is erroneously supposed to have invented.

The Second Period (1400—1600) is marked towards its close by a definite system of "tonality," or arrangement of the scale. The name of Josquin des Pres may be connected with its rise and progress, while France and Belgium divide between them the honours of its early development. About the end of the sixteenth century the Gallo-Belgian was completely absorbed into the Italian school, and as Josquin des Pres is the foundation, so Palestrina is the crown of the Second Period.

The Third Period (1600—1750), or the *transition*, bridges over the great gulf between the second and fourth periods, or between the ancient and the modern music.

The Third or Transition Period begins with the close of the sixteenth century. The old *tonality* was the great obstacle to all progress. A scale of notes arranged on a simple and uniform system was the remedy. The old masters would begin a scale anywhere in the series, without writing flats or sharps to make the semitones fall in the same places, whatever the key or mode. The change from such a system to our simple *major* and *minor*, with its uniform arrangement of accidentals, was immense. This, and the consequent discovery of the *perfect cadence*, made the radical difference between the old and the new music. No man is responsible for these startling innovations, but most of them are attributed to Monteverde (born 1565). At all events it is certain that about this time the world got very tired of the old forms. And no wonder; for a scientific movement in music was worked out like an equation in algebra, and was necessarily devoid of either life or expression. The wild strains of the wandering minstrels, on the other hand, were full of feeling, but had no consistency or method. In short, as Mr. Hullah well expresses it, "the scholastic music had no art, the popular music no science."

The glory of the Transition Period is the marriage of Art with Science. Science, grim and ecclesiastical, peeped forth from his severe cloister and beheld the wild and beautiful creature singing her roundelays, captivating the hearts of the people, who followed her in crowds—detained by princes to sing the story of crusades and the triumphs of love—all the while knowing nothing and caring nothing for the modes "*authentic*" and "*plagal*," but striking the harp or mandoline to the wild and irregular rhythm of fancy or passion; and Science, greatly shocked, withdrew itself from so frivolous a spectacle, just as the monks of the day lived apart from a bad world. But presently the grave face looked out once more, opened a window—a door—stepped forth and mingled with the crowd, just as the preaching friars came forth, until the line between the secular and the religious began slowly to fade. The stern heart of Science was smitten by the enchantress, popular Art, and conceived the daring plan of wooing and winning her for himself. It was a long process; it took nearly two hundred and fifty years. Science was so dull and prejudiced; Art was so impatient, and wild, and careless. But the first advances of Science were favoured by that wondrous spring-tide which followed the winter of the middle ages—the *Renaissance*. Emerging from the cold cell into the warm air and sunlight of a new world, Science relaxed, cast his theories to the winds, sighed for natural Art, and raved incoherently about the "musical declamation of the Greeks." Here, then, was the first point of sympathy. Wild enthusiasm and impatience of forms was, for one moment, common to Science and Art, and that was the moment of their betrothal. Immediately afterwards, with Carissimi, Science recovered the lost equilibrium, but Art was captivated by the strong spirit, and the perfect marriage was now only a matter of time.

Carissimi (born 1582, according to Mattheson, died 1672) was the very type of The Transition. He might have seen Palestrina, and he lived to hear Corelli. The germs of every style of music known since, arose during his long and eventful lifetime. He witnessed the bloom and gradual decay of the madrigal in England and Germany; the birth and adolescence of the musical drama in France, under Lulli; the invention of the oratorio in the oratory of San Philippo Neri, at Rome; and lastly, the rise and progress of instrumental music as an independent branch of the art. About 1659, Francisco Pistocchi established his great school of Italian singing at Bologna. "Before this," says an old writer, "they used to howl like wolves." He was followed, twenty years later, by Scarlatti, at Naples, and this improvement in vocal operatic music made corresponding demands upon the orchestra. Between 1650 and 1750 flourished the schools of the great violin makers near Cremona, the Amatis, the Guarnerii, and Stradiuarius, and with them rose at once the dignity and importance of instrumental music. Overtures, sonatas, quartets began to be written in vast quantities, and the way was thus rapidly paved for the later developments of the modern symphony. Germany, meanwhile, though far from original, had not been idle. Deriving her inspiration copiously from Italy, she became, during the seventeenth century, the land of organs and organists, and at the beginning of the eighteenth showed signs of independent thought, and began to encourage native effort in such men as Zachau and Keiser.

But we must now glance, for a moment, at the place which England holds in the rise and progress of music. The gloomy period of the old tonality, *i.e.* before 1600, is relieved in this country by the lustre of one great name,—John Dunstable. His fame was prodigious, and yet his own age could hardly have understood him. He had misgivings about the prevalent system of timeless music, strange anticipations of coming harmonies, and he is even said to have invented *counterpoint*. But towards the close of the Second Period (1500—1600) was born a real English school,—a school, no doubt, which took largely from others, and, owing perhaps to our insular position, gave little in return, but a school which could boast of Tallis, Farrant, Byrd, and Bevin in church music; Morley, Ward, Wilbye, and Weelkes in the madrigal; Bull equally great as an executant and a composer; Dowland, the friend of Shakspeare, in the part-song; and, last in the catalogue, but first in in every style of composition, Orlando Gibbons. Then comes a blank. The old traditions were fairly used up; and the echoes of the new music, with which France and Italy were ringing, had not yet reached us. The civil wars seemed to paralyze our musical invention and extinguish our enthusiasm. In Germany, during the Thirty Years' War, organs and organists abounded, and composers were busy absorbing all the new influences. In England, under similar circumstances, music got old and dull; few composed or played, and fewer cared to listen.

In 1660, Pelham Humphreys, a chorister boy in the Royal choir of His Majesty Charles II., went to Paris. There he fell in with the new opera school of Lulli. He immediately placed himself under the great French composer; and the result was, that Master Humphreys returned in a few years "an absolute Monsieur, disparaging everything and everybody's skill but his own." (*Pepys's Diary.*) The astonished gentlemen of the King's band then got their first peep into the new world. Humphreys told them that, besides playing old rubbish, they could keep neither time nor tune; and as for the King's musical director, he promised to "give him a lift out of his place, for that he (Master Humphreys) and the King understood each other, and were mighty thick." In truth, "that brisk and airy prince" was charmed with the new style; and Pepys describes him nodding his royal head, and beating time in chapel with the greatest zest.

The songs of Lulli, founded on Carissimi, and the anthems of Humphreys, founded on Lulli, must indeed, as Mr. Hullah observes, have come upon English ears like a revelation, and startled the lovers of Gibbons, Lawes, and Jenkins, as much as Mozart's "Idomeneo" surprised the operatic world, or Beethoven's "Eroica" the lovers of the older symphonies. Humphreys died in 1674, at the early age of twenty-seven; but his direct influence may be traced in Wise, Blow, and Henry Purcell.

Purcell, born 1658, is distinguished by some of those rare qualities peculiar to genius of the highest order. He sympathized with and drank freely into the spirit of his age, but was not, like Humphreys, absorbed by it. His music stands as it were nicely balanced between the past and the future. He felt his relations to the one by sympathy, and to the other by a kind of almost prophetic intuition. In his day, "that grave and solemn manner of music by Byrd, Tallis, &c.," was in sad disrepute,—the King liked cheerful airs he could hum and beat time to. Purcell satisfied him fully, and yet we cannot listen to his music without being struck sometimes by a certain old flow of rhythm and harmony, which we feel could only have been derived from a deep study of the schools of Henry VIII. and Elizabeth. As in reading Tennyson we are sometimes affected with a strange sense of George Herbert and Milton, so in listening to Purcell there steals over us a memory of the olden time,—like a kindly ghost that rises and floats by with a sweet and solemn smile.

It is a pity that Purcell should have stooped occasionally to musical imitation. The passion for expressing words in notes, founded, as we believe, on a puerile and mistaken view of the sphere and legitimate functions of music, reaches the ridiculous in him. For instance, he has to set the words, "They that go down to the sea in ships," and proceeds to perform that operation musically by taking the bass down a couple of octaves, and leaving him drowned at the lower *D.* The same unhappy bass is soon after "carried up to heaven" on a high dotted crotchet. Other composers have been fond of similar devices. Handel's "plagues" are full of them; Haydn's "Creation" rejoices in "a long and sinuous worm" of the earth, earthy; the illusion of Beethoven's "Pastoral" vanishes with the appearance of a real cuckoo; and even Mendelssohn must disturb with what can hardly be anything but a live donkey the enchantment of "A Midsummer Night's Dream!" But with all abatements, the music of Purcell, which after two hundred years has still the power to charm, bears a signal witness to the force and originality of his genius. Purcell died in his thirty-eighth year, 1696.

Handel came to England in 1710. The year 1706 is the turning-point in his musical history. In that year he visited Naples, and met Scarlatti, Porpora, and Corelli. It was to him a period of rapid assimilation. With one stride he reached the front rank, and felt that henceforth no musician alive could teach him anything. He died in 1759, aged seventy-four. There can be no doubt that Handel, by his single might, greatly advanced music in all its branches; but his action is far more remarkable on vocal than on instrumental music. Modern instrumental music is simply the most extraordinary art-development which the world has ever seen. It can only be compared to the perfection reached so suddenly, after a certain point, by the Greek drama. But the stride from Corelli to Beethoven was too great even for the giant Handel; and yet the men who completed that stride were Handel's contemporaries. Handel was forty-seven when Haydn was born, and Mozart was in his third year when Handel died. Musically, how many centuries does Handel seem to us behind modern music! yet we can all but join hands with him; and the musical enthusiast is filled with a certain awe when he thinks that men are still alive (1871) who may have listened to Mozart, and conversed with the venerable Haydn.

HANDEL.

Born 1685, Died 1759.

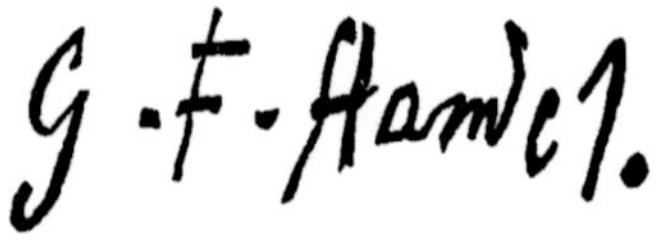

II.

IT may sound like an anachronism to call Handel a contemporary; and yet he seems so constantly present with us, that at times we can hardly believe that he has passed away. We are surrounded by his effigies; no living face is more familiar—no modern minstrel more beloved than he who has now lain quietly in the great Abbey for some one hundred and ten years.

A few hours after death, the sculptor Roubiliac took a cast of his face: that dead face made alive again, and wrought into imperishable marble, is indeed the very face of Handel. There, towering above his tomb, towering, too, above the passing generations of men, he seems to accept their homage benignly, like a god, whilst he himself stands wrapt from the "fickle and the frail," and "moulded in colossal calm."

The frequenters of Exeter Hall are familiar with another figure of him clothed in a long robe, with the legs crossed, and holding a lyre in his hand. A marble bust of the same date (1738) is at the Foundling Hospital. The head is shaven and crowned with a sort of turban cap; the face is irascible and highly characteristic. Casts of this bust have been multiplied through the land, and can be easily obtained.

The original of what is perhaps the best known of all (1758) is in the Queen's private apartments at Windsor. The little china bust sold at all music shops is a fair copy; on either side of the face falls down a voluminous wig elaborately wrought. The sculptor seems to have felt he could no more dare to treat that wig lightly than some other persons whom we shall have to refer to by-and-by.

There are more than fifty known pictures of Handel, and the best of them happens to be also the best known. It is by T. Hudson, signed "1756 A," at Gopsall, the seat of his remarkable friend, Charles Jennens. Handel is seated in full gorgeous costume of the period, with sword, shot-silk breeches, and coat gorge de pigeon, embroidered with gold. The face is noble in its repose; a touch of kindly benevolence plays about the finely-shaped mouth; every trace of angry emotion seems to have died out; yet the lines of age that are somewhat marked do not rob the countenance of its strength. The great master wears the mellow dignity of years without weakness or austerity.

In that wonderful collection of pictures lately exhibited at the South Kensington Museum, the often-recurring face and figure of Handel—young, middle-aged, and old—life-size, full figure, head and shoulders, standing up, and sitting down—filled us with the sense of one who had left a deep and yet bewildering impression upon his own age. The portraits were not only different in look, but even in features. The same face has been subjected to the minute photographic treatment of Denner, and the robust handling of Wolfand, who makes the composer fat, rosy, and in excellent condition. There are few collectors of prints who have not a lithograph, woodcut, or line engraving of him. He is exposed in every second-hand print-shop, still hangs on the walls of many old nook-and-corner houses in London, or lies buried in unnumbered portfolios throughout England.

With such memories fresh in our minds, and with the melodious thunders of the great Festival constantly ringing in our ears, let us attempt to trace once more the history of Handel's life, and hang another wreath upon the monument of his imperishable fame.

Händel or Handel (George Frederic) was born at Halle, on the Saale, in the duchy of Magdeburg,

Lower Saxony. The date on his tomb in Westminster Abbey is a mistake (Feb. 23, 1684); his real birthday is Feb. 23, 1685. Germany was not then the great musical country which it has since become, and was chiefly engaged in cultivating at second-hand the flowers of Italian music, which grew pale enough beneath those alien skies. The Italian maestro might be looked upon with some respect, but the native artist was not yet considered a prophet in his own country. Even eighty years later Mozart and Haydn were treated like lacqueys. "Music," remarked Handel's father, about a hundred and seventy years ago, "is an elegant art and fine amusement, but as an occupation it hath little dignity, having for its object nothing better than mere entertainment and pleasure."

No wonder the boy Handel, who, from his earliest childhood, seems to have been passionately fond of sweet sounds, encountered opposition and disappointment in his early musical endeavours. He was to go to no concerts, not even to a public school, for fear he should learn the gamut. He must be taught Latin at home, and become a good doctor, like his father; and leave the divine art to Italian fiddlers and French mountebanks. But up in a little garret the child of seven years, perhaps with the connivance of his nurse or his mother, had hidden a dumb spinet—even at night the faint tinkling could not be heard down below—and in stolen hours, without assistance of any kind, we are told the boy taught himself to play.

By-and-by Father Handel has a mind to visit another son in the service of the Duke of Saxe-Weissenfels, and little George runs after the carriage, and begs so hard to go, that at last he is taken to the ducal palace. But he soon turns out to be an *enfant terrible* to his poor old father. He is caught playing the chapel organ, and is brought up before the duke, trembling more, no doubt, at his father than at the duke, who has heard him, and now pats him on the back with "bravo!" Then, turning to his enraged and afflicted parent, he tells him that his son is a genius, and must not be snubbed any more. The boy's fear is now exchanged for the wildest delight, and the father's rage is quickly followed by astonishment. Handel would often tell the story in after years; and he never forgot the duke, the kindest, because the earliest of his benefactors.

From this moment fortune seemed to smile upon him, and his early career exhibits a combination of circumstances wonderfully favourable to the orderly development of his genius. Severe training, patronage, and encouragement, ardent friendship, the constant society of the first composers, wholesome rivalry, and regular orchestral practice—all seem to be suddenly poured upon him out of Fortune's great Horn of Plenty. As the favourite pupil of the great Halle organist, Zachau, he analyzes at the outset very nearly the whole existing mass of German and Italian music, and is set to write a cantata or motet once a week. At last the good Zachau has not the conscience to put him through any more fugues; tells him with kindly pride that he already knows more than his master, and advises him to go to Berlin, and study the opera school, under the auspices of the Elector of Brandenburg. Attilio Ariosti and Bononcini were then the favourite composers. The first received Handel with open arms; but the second scowled at him from the beginning, and determining to put the conceited boy's powers to the test, composed an elaborate piece, which he challenged him to play at sight. Handel played it off like any other piece, and from that hour Bononcini, who had a bad disposition, but excellent brains, treated the boy with the hatred of a rival, but with the respect due to an equal.

Dr. Handel's failing health brought George Frederic back to Halle. In 1697 the old man died, leaving his family ill provided for, and young Handel was thus driven into a course of immediate, though somewhat dry industry. He descended into the ranks, and became an occasional second violin *ripieno* at the Hamburg opera-house. As he played little, and badly, the band soon began to sneer at an artist who could hardly earn his salt; but one day the harpsichordist (the principal person in the orchestra) being absent, Handel, then about nineteen, laid his fiddle aside, sat down in the maestro's place, and finished by conducting the rehearsal with such ability, that the whole orchestra broke into loud applause. About this time Handel received an offer of marriage. He might be organist of Lubeck if he would take the daughter of the retiring organist along with the organ. He went down with his friend Mattheson, and Mattheson appears to have been offered the same terms. Something, however, did not suit—whether it was the organ, or the daughter, or the salary, we are not told; but both the young men returned in single blessedness to Hamburg.

Handel was never married; and perhaps he felt it would be neither wise nor generous to accept as a gift what he had not asked for, and did not want. The rivals in unrequited affection were also rivals in music: both Mattheson and Handel composed operas for the Hamburg opera. They had not come to blows over love, but what love could not do, music did, and the two, who had probably laughed heartily together at the maid of Lubeck, found themselves soon after with drawn swords in front of the theatre, surrounded by a circle of friends and admirers. They fought, as young men will fight in Germany to this day, for the merest trifles. Mattheson's rapier struck Handel on the bosom, but the point shivered on a great brass button; a distinguished councillor of the town then stepped in, and gravely declaring that the claims of honour were satisfied, called on the combatants to desist, and "on the 30th of the same month," writes Mattheson, "I had the pleasure of having Handel to dine with me, and we were better friends than ever."

The mind of genius in its early stages is habitually

gloomy, and dark tales of crime and sorrow often possess irresistible attractions for the happiest and most innocent of men. Shakspeare early painted the tragedy of Lucrece, and the death of Adonis; Schiller first made his mark with "The Robbers;" Goethe with the "Sorrows of Werther;" Schubert, when a mere boy, wrote the "Parricide" and a "Corpse Fantasia." We shall, therefore, not be surprised to learn that Handel's first opera, *Almira*, turns on the misfortunes of a dethroned queen; whilst his second, *Nero*, is, as the prospectus briefly explains, intended to show how "Love" is "obtained by Blood and Murder."

Handel, not content with manufacturing Italian operas in Germany, had, in common with every other musician of that day, a strong desire to visit Italy itself, the great seat of musical learning. With singular independence, he refused the offers of Prince Gaston de' Medici to send him; but by working hard with his pupils he soon got together money enough to go at his own expense. In the month of July, 1706, being twenty-one years old, he first entered Florence.

In that beautiful city, where the flowers seem to come so early and linger so late, the German musician stayed, under the auspices of the Grand Duke, until Christmas. Equal to Venice as a great centre of art revival in Italy, with its strange octagonal dome, its matchless Giotto campanile of black and white marble, its bronze doors, its ducal palazzo, and rich memories of Giovanni, or Angelico da Fiesole—second only to Rome in its passion for the revival of learning, and second to no city in poetic fame—Florence was, indeed, a fit residence for the re-creator of all music. Remembering the vivid impression which the first aspect of Italy left upon the minds of Mozart and Mendelssohn, we cannot but regret that Handel's life at Florence is a simple blank to us. He composed the opera of *Roderigo*, for which he obtained one hundred sequins, and left for Venice, where he came in for the thick of the Carnival. Here, too, we would fain know what impression the city in the sea made upon him. The marble palaces, not yet ruined by the hand of decay, the façades, the domes, and the porticos, still retaining a certain splendour long after the bloom of the Renaissance had passed away—the shrines decorated with the spiritual heads of Bellini—the staircases and ceilings plastered all over by Tintoret—the cool plash of the oars in the still lagunes—the sound of a guitar at night in the dark water-streets—the sights and sounds, and, above all, the silences peculiar to Venice, must have exerted a powerful influence over a mind upon which nothing was thrown away.

Whatever effect Venice had upon Handel, it is certain that Handel took Venice by storm. "Il caro Sassone," the dear Saxon, came upon a formidable rival in the person of Domenico Scarlatti, the first harpsichord player in Italy, and the two met frequently in the brilliant saloons of the Venetian aristocracy. One night during the Carnival, Handel, being masked, seated himself at the harpsichord and began playing. The Masques took little notice until Scarlatti, entering, arrested their attention. The great Italian was soon struck as his ear caught the sound of the harpsichord, and making his way across the room, he shouted, "It is either the devil or the Saxon!" It was not the devil; and let it be written for the learning of all other Saxons and Italians, that Handel and Scarlatti were ever afterwards honourable rivals and fast friends. In a later contest at Rome the superiority of Handel on the harpsichord was thought doubtful, but he remained the unchallenged monarch of the organ. Handel always spoke of Scarlatti with admiration; and Scarlatti, whenever he was complimented on his own playing, used to pronounce Handel's name, and cross himself.

To satisfy the Venetian public, Handel composed in three weeks the opera of *Agrippina*, which made furor even in that emporium of connoisseurs, and gained for its composer the above-mentioned title, "Il caro Sassone." Having seen Summer in Florence, and the Carnival in Venice, it was natural that he should hurry on to be in time for the great Easter celebrations in the Eternal City.

Rome in those days was still a power, and though shorn of much strength, she remained the greatest ecclesiastical force in Europe. Let us hope that the Pope's retinue was not quite so shabby as it is now, and that the cardinals' dingy old coaches were gilded and painted a little more frequently. Probably they were; for although the Pope himself was comparatively poor, some of the cardinals had managed to amass enormous wealth. Cardinal Ottoboni, Handel's great friend at Rome, was something of a pluralist, and lived above all sumptuary laws. He advanced to the purple a mere stripling of twenty-two, and he died forty years later the possessor of five abbeys in Venice, and three more in France (which last were alone worth 56,000 livres). He was Dean of the Sacred College, Bishop of Velletri and Ostia, Protector of France, Archpriest of St. John Lateran, besides being an official of the Inquisition. Unlike some of his compeers, he was not a mere voluptuary, but was the friend of the people. He kept for them hospitals, surgeries, was princely in the distribution of alms, patronized men of science and art, and entertained the public with comedies, operas, puppet-shows, oratorios, and academics.

Under the auspices of such a man, Handel wrote the *Resurrection* and the *Triumph of Time and Truth* (1708-9). This last was composed in honour of the great cardinal himself, whose bandmaster was none other than Corelli, who gave an orchestral performance in his house once a week.

At this early period of his composition, Handel began insensibly to part company with the old Italian traditions, although not until he had abandoned entirely the false forms of opera was it possible for him to carry out the changes in choral and orchestral music with which his name is for ever associated. In the

Triumph of Time the dead level of melody and recitative is definitely abandoned, and we find there, in addition to the usual chorus at the end, a striking innovation in the shape of two long vocal quartets. The MS. of the *Resurrection* contains an unusual number of wind instruments, although it may be doubted, for this very reason, whether it was ever performed in Italy with the full orchestra.

Bidding adieu to the pomps and splendours of Rome, Handel now went southwards, and chose the Bay of Naples for his second summer in Italy; and no doubt amongst the vine-clad hills that rise above that delightful city he encountered the scenes, and came upon the types of rugged men, gentle swains, and Neapolitan women, which provided him with the *mise en scène* and *dramatis personæ* of *Aci, Galatea e Polifemo* (1708).

This Italian serenata differs from the English cantata of *Acis and Galatea*, although, when the latter was brought out in 1732, it contained several Italian airs, and the Sicilienne "Non sempre no crudele" of *Polifemo*, which, although quite distinct from "O, ruddier than the cherry," is excellent rough singing for a *basso* giant. Whilst in this romantic and pastoral vein, he composed a number of songs on the model of the French canzonets, which became fashionable all over Europe. Then touching, as it were, cautiously the fringes of Catholicism, he composed a few sacred pieces for the Mass; but this kind of thing was never much to his taste. Handel brought from the land of the Reformation all the instincts of a stern Lutheran. He seems to have revolted from shams of all kinds. No wonder, then, if he found it impossible to clothe with a religious sentiment, dogmas which his common sense repudiated, and which his section of the Church denounced. Passing back slowly through Rome, Florence, Venice, there seemed to him less and less inducement to linger anywhere. The composer of Halle was made of sterner stuff than the maestros of Italy, and probably began to be dimly conscious of the fact that his methods of work and his mission were essentially different from theirs.

In the autumn of 1709 he arrived in Hanover; and it was at the court of George of Brunswick (afterwards King of England) that he fell in with certain English noblemen, who invited him over to see them. Although he was retained in the service of the Elector, at a salary of £300 a year, he obtained leave from that liberal prince to visit England; and after once more greeting his old master Zachau, and embracing his aged mother at Halle, he prepared to cross that untried and treacherous ocean on which poor Papa Haydn (who was to be born only twenty-three years afterwards) was destined to be so terribly tossed about, before he arrived here on a similar mission. Both found London mad for Italian music; but, whilst Haydn was able, through the advance of taste, to impose his own style in the symphony, Handel, less fortunate, had to fall in with the prevalent taste, and toil through many years of Italian opera-manufacturing before he could gain a hearing for his real creations in oratorio music.

What the public adored was opera "after the Italian model"—what they tolerated was "English singing between the acts by Doggett;" and Handel proved fully equal to the occasion. His first opera, *Rinaldo*, was brought out at a theatre which stood on the site of the present Haymarket. It proved an immense success. Nearly the whole of it was arranged for the harpsichord, and thrummed incessantly throughout the kingdom. The march was adopted by the band of the Life Guards, and died hard about the beginning of this century. It has since been revived in the gardens at the Crystal Palace. One air has at least survived, and by virtue of a certain undefined quality, inherent only in the highest works of art, seems to have defied with success the developments of modern music and the changes of taste. Like Stradella's divine "I miei Sospiri," like Gluck's "Che faro," Handel's "Lascia ch' io pianga" is still listened to with profound interest and genuine emotion. Handel considered it one of his best airs. Walsh published the whole opera, and is said to have made a profit of £1,500 out of the sale. When Handel, who, it was said (apparently without much foundation), had been but shabbily paid, was told of this, he accosted the publisher in the following characteristic manner:—"My friend, next time you shall compose the opera, and I will sell it." It is probable that Walsh, who published many of Handel's works in after years, took the hint.

But the Elector's Chapel-master could no longer be spared. He returned to Hanover in about six months, and settled down to compose all sorts of trifles for the court dilettanti. After the stir and excitement of London, that dull and pompous little court must have been terribly monotonous. Chapel-master Handel soon escaped back to England, and in 1712 he brought out an ode for Queen Anne's birthday. In 1713, to celebrate the peace of Utrecht, appeared two more works, that must always be listened to with interest—the famous *Te Deum* and *Jubilate.* They were played then with a full band and organ, and not a little startled people who were unaccustomed to hear sacred music with such an accompaniment. The queen granted the composer a pension of £200 a year, and he seems to have immediately forgotten all about Elector George and his stupid court. But the day of reckoning was not far off, and the truant Chapel-master soon found himself in an awkward position. When good Queen Anne died, Elector George took possession of the empty throne as George I. of England, and Handel was forbidden to appear before his old patron, who was naturally very angry with him.

But the atmosphere of London was charged with Handel. People sang him in the streets, and he came floating in at the windows; the band played him in the Palace Yard; his name filled the opera-house, and was inscribed on numberless music books, programmes, and newspapers—nay, at last, the first violinist of the day insisted on having Handel into the king's ante-chamber to accompany some sonatas. It was obvious that terms must be made with so irrepressible a person. One day as the king went down the river in his state barge, a boat came after him, playing new and delightful "water music." But one man could have written such music, and the king knew it; he called for Handel, who could now have no temptation to run away, and sealed his pardon with a new pension of £200 a year. The day on which the king and Handel were reconciled was a day of feasting and joy. Houses on both sides of the river were brilliantly illuminated. As they came back, numbers of boats, filled with spectators, put off to meet the royal barge, and cannons continued to fire salutes until after nightfall.

The "water music" may be said to be steadily written down to the requirements of the age. The author seems to say to himself all the way through, "Let us be popular, or we are nothing." Within the stiff periods, which seemed so charming and so spontaneous to our forefathers, and which are so tedious to us, there is no doubt a considerable play of fancy. And had there been more originality, the music would, doubtless, have had a less immediate success.

Soon after, the opera of *Amadigi* made its appearance, and with it came that infallible symptom of dramatic decline—minute attention to stage fittings and gorgeous scenery; and we fear it must be confessed that these accessories, and not Handel's music, began to be relied on for success. Melancholy stress is laid on the "new clothes, and scenes, and novel variety of dancing;" and among other things, attention was called "particularly to the fountain," which, like the "pump" property belonging to another illustrious company of players, was real, and had to be lugged in on all occasions. The music certainly attempted some novel effects, and in the accompaniment to one cavatina, the experiment first tried in the *Resurrection* in Rome, 1708, of making the violins all play in octaves, was repeated in London, 1715.

Handel at this time moved in good society. Rival factions had not yet been organized to crush him. Lord Burlington was glad to have him at his mansion, which was then considered out of town. When the king twitted this nobleman good-humouredly for living out at what we may call the St. John's Wood of the period, his lordship replied that he liked his "house in the middle of the fields," for he was fond of solitude, and was placed where none could build near. The beadle of the Burlington arcade, much like a superannuated relic of his lordship's household, had not then come into existence. For years the noisy stream of life has flowed along Piccadilly, close past the portico of the once secluded "house in the fields."

It is strange now to think of the people with whom Handel must daily have rubbed elbows, without knowing that their names and his would in a century be famous. Yonder heavy, ragged-looking youth, standing at the corner of Regent Street, with a slight and rather more refined-looking companion, is the obscure

Samuel Johnson, quite unknown to fame. He is walking with Richard Savage. As Signor Handel, "the composer of Italian music," passes by, Savage becomes excited, and nudges his friend, who takes only a languid interest in the foreigner. Johnson did not care for music; of many noises he considered it the least disagreeable.

Towards Charing Cross comes, in shovel hat and cossack, the renowned ecclesiastic Dean Swift. He has just nodded patronizingly to Bononcini in the Strand, and suddenly meets Handel, who cuts him dead. Nothing disconcerted, the dean moves on, muttering his famous epigram:—

> "Some say that Signor Bononcini,
> Compared to Handel, is a ninny;
> Whilst others vow that to him Handel
> Is hardly fit to hold a candle.
> Strange that such difference should be
> 'Twixt tweedle-dum and tweedle-dee."

As Handel enters the "Turk's Head," at the corner of Regent Street, a noble coach and four drives up. It is the Duke of Chandos, who is inquiring for Mr. Pope. Presently a deformed little man, in an iron-grey suit, and with a face as keen as a razor, hobbles out, makes a low bow to the burly Handel, who, helping him into the chariot, gets in after him, and they drive off together to Cannons, the duke's mansion at Edgware. There they may meet Mr. Addison, the poet Gay, and the witty Arbuthnot, who have been asked to luncheon. The last number of the *Spectator* lies on the table, and a brisk discussion soon arises between Pope and Addison, concerning the merits of the Italian opera, in which Pope would have the better if he only knew a little more about music, and could keep his temper. Arbuthnot sides with Pope in favour of Mr. Handel's operas; the duke endeavours to keep the peace. Handel probably uses his favourite exclamation: "Vat de tevil I care!" and consumes the *recherché* wines and rare viands with undiminished gusto.

The magnificent, or the grand duke, as he was called, had built himself a palace for £230,000. He had a private chapel, and appointed Handel organist in the room of the celebrated Dr. Pepusch, who retired with excellent grace before one manifestly his superior. On week-days the duke and duchess entertained all the wits and grandees in town, and on Sundays the Edgware Road was thronged with the gay equipages of those who went to worship at the ducal chapel and hear Mr. Handel play on the organ.

The Edgware Road was a pleasant country drive, but parts of it were so solitary that highwaymen were much to be feared. The duke was himself attacked on one occasion; and those who could afford it, never travelled so far out of town without armed retainers. Cannons was the pride of the neighbourhood, and the duke—of whom Pope wrote,

"Thus gracious Chandos is beloved at sight"—

was as popular as he was wealthy. But his name is

made still more illustrious by the Chandos anthems. They were all written at Cannons between 1718 and 1720, and number in all eleven overtures, thirty-two solos, six duets, a trio, quartet, and forty-seven choruses. Some of the above are real masterpieces; but, with the exception of "The waves of the sea rage horribly," and "Who is God but the Lord?" few of them are ever heard now. And yet these anthems were most significant in the variety of the choruses and in the range of the accompaniments; and it was then, no doubt, that Handel was feeling his way towards the great and immortal sphere of his oratorio music. Indeed, his first oratorio of *Esther* was composed at Cannons, as also the *Acis and Galatea.*

But what has become of the noble duke and his mansion? The little chapel, now Whitchurch, at Edgware, alone survives. Handel's organ is still there; and Mr. Julius Plummer, of honourable memory, fixed this plate upon it in 1750:—

HANDEL WAS ORGANIST OF THIS CHURCH
FROM MDCCXVIII. TO MDCCXXI.
AND COMPOSED THE ORATORIO OF ESTHER
ON THIS ORGAN.

The castle has been pulled down, and the plough has prepared the site for cultivation. In the prophetic words of Pope,—

"Another age has seen the golden ear
Embrown the slope and nod on the parterre;
Deep harvests bury all his pride has plann'd,
And laughing Ceres reassumes the land."

But Handel had other associates, and we must now visit Thomas Britton, the coalheaver of Clerkenwell Green. As he stands at the door of his stable, with his dustman's hat on, a coarse blouse, and a kerchief tied round his neck like a rope, who should drive up but the beautiful Duchess of Queensberry—not to order coals, forsooth, but to visit Mr. Britton. Laying down his pipe, he receives her like one accustomed to mix with "the quality," and pushing open a rickety wooden door, discloses a narrow staircase. This leads up to a long, low room, built over the stable. As the lovely duchess trips laughingly up the stairs after her strange host, sounds of a chamber organ and stringed instruments reach them, and as they enter the imperfectly-lighted apartment, they perceive that Mr. Handel is at the organ, helping the others to tune up.

There is Mr. Banister, the first Englishman who distinguished himself on the violin: he gave concerts of his own at Whitefriars, near the Temple back-gate, fitted up a room over the "George Tavern," with seats and tables—charge, "one shilling admission and call for what you please;" but he was always glad to play gratis for his friend the coal-heaver, in whose den he met with the last musical novelties, and the best society in town. Then there is Sir Roger l'Estrange, gentleman, in close converse with the excise officer, Henry Needler; and Robe, a justice of the peace, is telling the last bit of scandal about Madame Cuzzoni to John Hughes, who wrote the "Siege of Damascus," once favourably known in the literary world, but now forgotten. And there is Mr. Woolaston, the painter, who, when Britton has sat down with his viol de gamba, and got to work on a trio of Hasse or a saraband by Galuppi, will take out his pencil and make a rough sketch of him, to be afterwards worked into one of his famous pictures (for he painted two portraits of his singular friend).

Amongst other friends that are crowding into the long room to listen to a particularly favourite trio of Corelli's, or to hear Mr. Handel play his original piece now known as the "Harmonious Blacksmith,"—that favourite *morceau* from the "Suites de pièces pour le Clavecin," which, like Stephen Heller's "Nuits Blanches," or "Wanderstunden," was soon reprinted in France, Switzerland, Holland, and Germany,—amongst other distinguished guests, we notice Henry Symonds, Abiel Wichello, and Obadiah Shuttleworth. The little form of Pope is probably not far from the fair Queensberry or her Grace of Chandos; and later in the evening, the celebrated Dr. Pepusch will look in with that wag Colley Cibber, whose jokes he will in vain endeavour to prevent from exploding in the middle of some favourite gavotte by Hasse.

But the gentleman with a full, good-natured face, the carefully-powdered wig, the maroon-coloured coat, who enters on tiptoe, is evidently of importance in the present circle. Britton motions him to a seat, and Handel makes room for him close to the organ. It is Mr. Charles Jennens, the amateur poet, who wrote many of Handel's librettos for him, and arranged the words for the *Messiah*. He lived in Great Ormond Street, in such magnificence that the neighbours called him "Soliman the Magnificent." Later in life he had a controversy with Samuel Johnson about Shakspeare, but the world which has since learnt to love the dear doctor, has forgotten the magnate of Great Ormond Street; and even at that time it was commonly allowed that the dictionary-maker had the best of the argument.

It is hard to leave that goodly company of wits, poets, musicians, and philosophers, when we have once drawn aside the curtain and taken a peep at their faces. We follow them about from one great dingy house to another—some of their houses are still standing. They have deep wainscoted walls and narrow windows and backyards, with perhaps a superannuated fig-tree, and a classic fountain dripping over some Cupid with a large sham cockle-shell. All is dreary enough and changed—the place is probably a hospital or an attorney's chambers now—but the old tenants come back to us in imagination as we stand at the door or sit down in the dining-room. Whilst the vision lasts we long to have more details; but scene after scene rises only to vanish too rapidly from the mind's eye. We have hardly time to master the trains and puffs, the frills and the patches of the ladies; to note the set of the nodding wigs, the glitter of colour in plush and satin, the clinking swords of the cavaliers, the rumble of the heavy coaches and four, the shouts of the link-boys and torch-bearers, the swearing of the tall footmen who wait outside in the ill-lighted streets with those snug sedan-chairs: they are there, but only, like Mr. Pepper's ghosts, behind glass; the voices sound hollow and distant, the magic light is flashed upon them for a moment, presently it fades out, and they are gone.

In 1720, Handel, being at the time the organist at Cannons, was engaged by a society of noblemen, including his Grace of Chandos, to compose operas for the Royal Academy of Music at the Haymarket, and the *Postboy* soon afterwards announces "the most celebrated opera *Radamistus*, by Mr. Handell." Of this opera, "Ombra Cara," which Handel considered one of the finest airs he had ever written, may still be occasionally heard. The work was fairly successful, and was followed, in 1721, by *Muzio Scævola*, to which we shall return presently.

In 1721, *Floridante* also appeared. It was this opera which called forth the remark from Dr. Burney, "I am convinced that his slow airs are as much superior to those of his contemporaries as the others are in spirit and science." *Otho*, which appeared in 1723, was generally considered the flower of his dramatic works. Like Mozart's *Don Juan*, Weber's *Freischütz*, Rossini's *Tell*, Meyerbeer's *Prophète*, and Gounod's *Faust*, it was a work composed of one long string of gems, and each air became in its turn a favourite throughout the land. Pepusch, who could never quite forget that he had been the best organist in England before the arrival of Handel, remarked of "Affanni del pensier," "That great bear was certainly inspired when he wrote that song." The celebrated Madame Cuzzoni came out in it. On the second night the tickets rose to four guineas each, and the Cuzzoni was paid £2,000 for the season.

In the same year *Flavio* and *Giulio Cesare* were produced. The first is celebrated for the "Dona Pace" (the first scenic quintet ever composed). The second is for ever associated with poor George III. It was revived in 1787 in order to attract him to the theatre to hear some of Handel's music, of which he was passionately fond. "Da Tempesta" and "Alma del gran Pompeo" are still much esteemed by connoisseurs. In 1725 *Rodelinda* was received with enthusiasm; the public going so far as to adopt in society the costume worn by the favourite prima donna.

Between 1726 and 1727 appeared *Scipio, Siroe*, and *Ptolemy*, of which little can now be said. The principal airs were popular at the time, and published in the favourite form of harpsichord pieces, in which some of them are still extant; and many more have been worked up by subsequent composers until their phrases have passed into modern music, and now live over again unrecognised in the works of many a contemporary composer, and, perhaps, suspected least of all by the composer himself. We remember our astonishment at discovering M. Jullien's once celebrated "Bridal Waltz" in a trio of Corelli; it is notorious that "Where the Bee Sucks," by Dr. Arne, is taken from a movement in *Rinaldo;* and we doubt not that a further study of the old masters would bring to light similar cases. Thus the soil of music is ever growing rich with the dead leaves of the past, and what appears to us the new life in forest and glade is, after all, but the old life under a new form.

But a change was at hand. In 1720 this Royal Academy of noblemen had subscribed £50,000 to get up the Italian opera, and they had engaged Mr. Handel to compose. The first operas, as we have seen, made furor; the singers were the finest in the world, the audience of the very grandest description. Opera after opera rolled from Mr. Handel's facile pen. But as time went on sinister rumours got afloat. It was said the funds were not coming in. It is quite certain they were going out. In two years the committee of management had spent £15,000; the wits and critics were beginning to abuse Mr. Handel, and laugh at his supporters. The appeals for money became urgent. The libretto to *Ptolemy* even announces that they were "in the last extremity." Some of his warm supporters began to cool; either they could not or would not pay. Threats at last caused an open breach. Many forsook the opera-house; the rest got up a ball to pay the expenses, and invitations were issued to improper characters. The proceedings were declared by legal authority to be "an offence to his Majesty's virtuous subjects;" the opera itself "a nursery of lewdness, extravagance, and immorality." It ended by the whole thing being put a stop to by order of the king; and poor Handel, who had nothing to do with the ball, and never got the money, found himself defiled without having touched the pitch. To make matters worse, an opposition house started up. The *Beggars' Opera*, with music by Dr. Pepusch, who stole some of it from Handel, was brought out at the Lincoln's Inn Fields Theatre, and the fickle public, suffering under a surfeit of *Julius Cæsar*, *Cyrus*, and all the *Ptolemies*, went off in crowds to enjoy a little low life with the burglar Macheath and Polly. Rich was the name of the manager, and Gay that of the poet; and the people who nightly greeted the smiling manager and called loudly for the needy poet, remarked that the *Beggars' Opera* had made Gay rich and Rich gay.

Handel, who either could not or would not see that a change had taken place in the public taste, gathered up the remnant of his fortune, and making arrangements with Heidegger, proprietor of the Haymarket, prepared to make another serious attack on the musical world in the character of an operatic composer. He made up his various quarrels with the singers and managers, got together his scattered orchestra, and finally went off in person to Italy for reinforcements. His energy was undiminished; he was in his finest musical vein, and prepared to pour forth opera after opera upon a public whose ears and eyes seemed closed.

In 1729 *Lothario* was produced. *Parthenope* followed in 1731. Both fell flat. The wonderful voice of Senesino carried *Porus* through fifteen representations in 1731, then *Rinaldo* was revived with "new cloathes," but the public had heard the music, and did not care for the "cloathes;" and when *Ætius* appeared in the following year, they grumbled at the old clothes, and did not care for the new music. A faint flicker of interest was shown in *Sosarme*, produced in the same year, but the audience steadily dropped off; and *Orlando* (1733), although the scenery was admitted to be "extraordinary fine and magnificent," died without a struggle in an empty house.

True originality has usually the same battle to fight with conventional tastes, stupidity, or ignorance. The Duke of Wellington, in the Peninsula, contending for his own measures with a distant Government; Nelson disobeying orders at Copenhagen; Jenner trying to persuade people to be vaccinated; or the Liberal politicians of our own age labouring for years to pass Liberal measures; are only instances in other spheres of action of what is constantly going on in the world of Art.

It would be interesting to inquire in such cases how far circumstances control men and their measures, and how far men and their measures were influenced by circumstances. In some cases we seem to have very nearly a balance of power. Handel's operatic career is a case in point. It would be curious to study how far the very music and instrumentation were dictated to him at times by the tyranny, necessity, or solicitation of circumstance. One of the airs allotted to Polifemo was certainly written for an exceptional voice, for it contains a range of two octaves and five notes. *Semiramis, Caius Fabricius,* and *Arbaces,* played in 1734, are simply *pasticcio* operas, composed of all sorts of airs, in which each singer has the opportunity of singing his own *bravura* songs. Some of them are Italian, others German, and these fragmentary songs are all strung together by a recitative, which is the only new part of the opera. It would not be difficult to find curious hints and suggestions in the writings of other composers which point to a similar pressure or peculiarity of circumstance. The soprano part of Mozart's *Flauto Magico*, especially the great aria with the staccato passages, was written for a special voice.

The only reason why Schubert did not write more symphonies was the difficulty of getting them played. It has been remarked in the notices in the Crystal Palace Saturday programmes that Beethoven's relations with the instruments of his orchestras, and especially with the horn, are often suggestive. In the B flat symphony there is only one flute instead of two. Of Mozart's G minor symphony there are two versions, one with clarionets and one without. It is well known that the opening to *William Tell* overture was written for a celebrated violoncello at Vienna, whilst there can be little doubt that Handel wrote many of his finest airs for particular voices.

But it is refreshing to learn that the voices had occasionally to bend to the genius of the composer or the imperious will of the man. When Carestini, the celebrated *evirato*, sent back the air, "Verdi Prati," Handel was furious, and rushing into the trembling Italian's house, shook the music in his face with, "You tog! don't I know better as yourself vat you shall sing? If you vill not sing all de song vat I give you, I vill not pay you ein stiver!" Carestini afterwards found that Handel was right. "Verdi Prati" was one of his *grands succès*. When, in a similar spirit of ill-timed revolt, the famous Cuzzoni declined to sing "Falsa Immagine" at the rehearsal, Handel, who had been waxing hot at sundry signs of insubordination, exploded at last. He flew at the wretched woman, and seizing her arm, shook her like a rat. "Ah! I always knew you were a fery tevil," he cried; "and I shall now let you know that I am Beelzebub, de prince of de tevils!" and dragging her to the open window, was just on the point of pitching her into the street, when, in every sense of the word, she recanted. Although Handel sometimes gained his point in this way, yet his violence occasionally laid him open to the ridicule and contempt of small minds.

Persons have been known to appreciate that indescribable mixture of sound produced by the preparatory tuning of an orchestra with the organ, even more than the performance itself. Handel was not of this opinion. After he was once at his desk, woe betide the belated fiddle that scraped a fifth, or the inexperienced flute that attempted the least "tootle." Some of us may have witnessed the despair of a professional conductor at the endless and insatiable tuning of an amateur orchestra. Others may have watched the calm distraction of an accompanyist at having to play through "Vaga Luna" to some one not more than half a semitone flat. Others may have seen the expression on the master's face when in some pause the drum comes in with a confident, but perfectly uncalled-for "rataplan;" but these incidents are trivial compared with the scene which it is now our painful duty to describe.

It was a grand night at the Opera. The Prince of Wales had arrived in good time, remembering how Handel had been annoyed sometimes at his coming in late. The instruments, supposed to be in perfect tune, were lying ready, and the performers entered. Alas! a wag had crept in before them, and put every one of the stringed instruments out of tune. Handel enters; and now all the bows are raised together, and at the given beat they all start off *con spirito.* The effect must have been as if every one of the performers had been musically tumbling down-stairs. The unhappy maestro rushes wildly from his place, kicks to pieces the first double bass that opposes him, and seizing a kettledrum, throws it violently at the leader of the band. The effort sends his full-bottomed wig flying, but he does not heed it; and, rushing bareheaded to the footlights, he stands for a few moments amid the roars of the house, snorting with rage, and choked with passion.

The Prince, although highly amused, soon thought

this kind of entertainment had lasted long enough, and, going down in person, he besought Handel to be calm, and with much difficulty prevailed on him to resume his wig and his opera.

Like Burleigh's nod, Handel's wig seems to have been a sure guide to Handel's temper. "When things went well at the oratorio," writes Burney, "it had a certain nod or vibration which manifested his pleasure and satisfaction. Without it, nice observers were certain that he was out of humour." The ominous sign always appeared if, when Handel was conducting the Prince of Wales's concerts, any of the ladies-in-waiting talked instead of listening. "Hush! hush!" the Princess would say; "don't you see Handel is in a passion?"

But it must be added that Handel, who knew his own hastiness, was often willing to apologize; and on one occasion, after roundly scolding Burney, then a mere lad, for what turned out to be an error of Smith, the copyist, he instantly made the *amende honorable.* "I peg your pardon; I am a very odd tog; Meister Schmidt is to plame."

Handel paid his singers what in those days were considered enormous prices. Senesino and Carestini had each £1,200 for the season; and on one occasion, as we have seen, the Cuzzoni got £2,000. Towards the close of what may be called his operatic period, most of the singers, and almost all the nobles, forsook Handel, and supported the greatest singer of the age, Farinelli, at the rival house in Lincoln's Inn Fields.

But before we proceed further, we will give the reader a glance at some of the composers with whom Handel came into immediate contact, and with whose genius, effrontery, or cabals he was forced to contend.

To GLUCK I have devoted a separate notice. He crossed Handel's path late, and was but slightly connected with him.

Of DOMENICO SCARLATTI, who died 1757, we shall not say much more here. He was the real creator of the advanced harpsichord school of the period, as much as Mendelssohn was of the advanced pianoforte school of the present day. But his range, like that of Chopin, was limited, and he wrote little besides harpsichord music. Those who care to examine some of his allegros in $\frac{12}{8}$ time will be surprised to find the prototypes of many of the *tarantelles* written in such profusion for the modern pianoforte. His father, the celebrated Alessandro Scarlatti, was the greater of the two. He wrote a hundred and fifteen operas, besides an immense mass of sacred music.

Of all Handel's rivals BONONCINI was certainly the most formidable. He came to England about 1720, with ARIOSTI, a composer of merit. When something or other in the tone and spirit of Handel's music (not then recognised as the high peculiar tone of the German school) made people feel that he was quite different from the beloved Italians, factions began to form themselves, and the Handelists, backed by the Prince of Wales, ranged themselves against the Bononcinists, supported by the Duke of Marlborough and most of the nobility. A whole chorus of popular writers rehearsed the sublime merits of the Italian school, whilst Pope, Arbuthnot, and a few others, stood by Handel.

Exactly the same drama repeated itself with a different *mise en scène*, and other actors, about thirty years later. Paris was then the seat of war: Gluck was the German hero, supported by Marie Antoinette; Piccini fought for Italy, under the meretricious banners of the Du Barry; l'Abbé Arnault plied his dignified pen for Gluck, whilst Marmontel answered with daring and unscrupulous sarcasm for Piccini. Even before the open breach the parallel holds good—for as Gluck and Piccini were each engaged to compose an opera (*Iphigenia*) on the same subject, so Bononcini, Ariosti, and Handel where associated together in the composition of *Muzio Scævola;* and, moreover, as Gluck was clearly victorious, so was Handel. Here, however, the parallel ceases. Gluck left Paris in possession of the Italian opera; Bononcini, to our honour be it said, left London in possession of German oratorio.

Between two giants like Handel and Bononcini, poor Ariosti seems to have been crushed to pieces. Originally he had been a Dominican monk. His temperament was gentle; he loved music, and wrote compositions much admired in his own country; but he should never have met either the Achilles or Hector of his day. His feeble light, that would have illumined a smaller sphere with a mild and gentle lustre, paled at once before the mighty sun of Handel, and the continuous blaze of Bononcini's fireworks. His Act of *Muzio Scævolo* (1721) was voted the worst—a decision in which he fully acquiesced. In 1730 it was not worth while to compose any more; his place was filled; the public would hardly listen to his performances on the viol de gamba—an instrument which he himself had introduced into England in 1716. A humble-minded and inoffensive man, as graceful as a woman, and nearly as timid, he lapsed into silence and poverty, and died neglected, but not before he had been forgotten.

The career in England of the brilliant, but arrogant Bononcini, came to a fitting end in 1733. A certain madrigal of his was discovered to be note for note the composition of a Signor LOTTI in Italy. Lotti was communicated with by the Royal Academy of Music. The matter was made public, and Bononcini, not caring to plead guilty, left the country, never to return, amidst the jubilations of the Handelists. The defeated maestro travelled through Europe, still pouring out from his astonishingly facile brain things new and old, and at last fell into the hands of an impostor, who professed to have discovered the philosopher's stone. He died soon afterwards in obscurity and solitude, having outlived his popularity, and lost his character.

Not the least of Handel's rivals was PORPORA, or as Handel used to call him, "old Borbora." Without the romantic fire of Bononcini, the grace of Ariosti, or the originality of Handel, he represented the high and dry Italian school. He was a great singing-master, a learned contrapuntist, famous throughout Italy. He was invited over in 1733 by the Italian faction in London, under the patronage of Marlborough and Lord Cooper. His opera of *Ariadne* was brought out at Lincoln's Inn Fields, and was a great success. But when later on he had the audacity to oppose to Handel's oratorios his own *David*, his failure was conspicuous, and he was candid enough to admit his great rival's superiority in sacred music. He thought no one's operas equal to his own. He wrote fifty of them; and had the distinguished honour when an old man of teaching young HAYDN, who in return cleaned his boots and powdered his wig for him.

Amongst other Italians who were as thorns in Handel's side, we may mention HASSE, a man of real genius, whose chamber music is still esteemed by amateurs. ARRIGONI came over with Porpora, and helped to supply the Italian programmes at Lincoln's Inn Fields Theatre.

We must not forget to mention one or two other celebrities—Dr. PEPUSCH, the Prussian, and Dr. GREENE, the Englishman. Pepusch held the first place in England before the arrival of Handel, and made a distinct sphere for himself even when Handel and the Italian composers were in their glory. His *Beggars' Opera* killed everything at the time, and still keeps possession of the stage. Pepusch may be said to have understood the merits of the English ballad. They are not considerable; but whenever the public taste gets jaded with Italian syrup or German solids, English ballads have ever been found useful as a kind of fillip. Pepusch was a learned, but not a very original composer, and his skill in arranging and adapting, especially the popular songs of the day, was greater than his skill in creating. He had the sense to bow before Handel, and the grace to subscribe to his works.

Dr. Boyce, Dr. Arne, and Dr. Greene were all composers of the day: no lover of cathedral music is ignorant of their names; and many of Boyce's anthems have become regular items in the week's services. Boyce was incomparably the greatest, Arne was more graceful than powerful, whilst the name of Greene is usually more respected than loved by the frequenters of choral services. His relations with Handel and Bononcini are hardly creditable to him. He seems to have flattered each in turn. He upheld Bononcini in the great madrigal controversy, and appears to have wearied Handel by his repeated visits. The great Saxon easily saw through the flatteries of a man who was in reality an ambitious rival, and joked about him, not always in the best taste. When he was told that Greene was giving concerts at the "Devil Tavern," near Temple Bar, "Ah!" he exclaimed, "mein poor friend Toctor Greene—so he is gone to de Tevil!"

On one occasion we are told that Greene had left a new solo anthem of his with Handel, who good-naturedly asked him to breakfast the next morning. The great German was most affable, and discoursed on every possible subject, but all Greene's attempts to lead the conversation round to the anthem proved futile. At last, growing desperate, he interrupted his host's flowing talk with,—

"But my anthem, sir—how do you like my anthem?"

"Oh, your anthem? Vell, sir, I did tink it wanted air."

"Wanted air, sir?"

"Yes, sare—air—so I did hang it out of de vindow!"

It must be noticed how entirely English music was swamped by German and Italian masters. It is an unwelcome fact to many, but it must not be overlooked. Much offence has been taken at the phrase, "The English are not a musical people." That phrase interpreted to mean "the English do not care for music," or "they cannot be got to like good music," or "they do not make good executive artists," is certainly untrue, and we should never use it in any of the above senses; but if a musical nation means a nation with a musical tradition and school of its own—a nation not only in possession of old popular melodies, whose origin it is always difficult and sometimes impossible to trace, but also possessing a development of the musical art distinct in character from that of all other nations, and subject to the inspiration of national genius—then we fear that England can scarcely yet be said to have established her claim to be called a musical nation. It is hardly possible not to see that the facts of history bear out the assertion. As the religion of England was Roman up to the time of Henry VIII., church music in England, that came along with Rome's ecclesiastical system, drew its chief inspiration from Italy. In so far as there was a popular movement running side by side with the ecclesiastical, it is still more easy to trace that popular movement to the trouveres and troubadours of Provence, who wandered all over Europe, and whose very names betray their foreign origin. If, however, we admit that Tallis and Farrant and Byrd founded an English school, and that Morley, Ward, and Weelkes, in their madrigals (observe, the very word *madrigal* is an Italian one), and Orlando Gibbons, continued the good work—it remains to be explained why Humphreys deliberately chose the French school in the reign of Charles II.—a school of music which was enthusiastically received in England—and why Purcell (died 1695), original, prolific, and above all eclectic, had no followers at all. The fact is, the so-called English school had not life enough to survive the paralysis of the civil wars, nor memory enough to continue its own tradition; and France and Italy alternately or jointly contended for the honour of carrying off the musical prizes in England, until Germany, like a very David, arose and slew both the lion and the bear.

We do not observe, then, from looking back, that England has had a great musical past; what we do see is a constant taking root, and springing up, and withering, a certain appetite, succeeded by nausea and repose. With the growing passion for good, in other words, for wholesome food, this state of things may perhaps cease. Once, we know, she was distinguished among the nations for her commercial apathy. That apathy has passed away. There was a time before even Germany had developed her musical genius. Italy and France were long the leading composers of the world. That time has passed away, and England herself may even now be about to rise and claim a position among musical nations. Meanwhile, let us be just to the patrons of music in England. It is the fashion to say that native talent was crushed by the Hanoverian Georges, who showed favour only to German musicians. But this is not the case. On the contrary, native talent was for long protected in England. Italian music was not preferred to English until the two met in a fair fight, and Italy won. Nor was Germany installed supreme until she had beaten Italian opera out of the field with German oratorio.

For many years great efforts were made to encourage English talent. As late as George II.'s reign only an Englishman could hold the place of king's organist. Almost every English composer of any note was a Doctor of Music, and installed in some place of honour and emolument. The cathedral choirs were superintended by Englishmen; nor was there any effort made to suppress the ballads they wrote, or to keep their operas off the stage. The *Beggars' Opera* was full of English songs, and Pepusch, who, although a Prussian, was a naturalized English subject, collected and arranged large quantities of them. But England originated nothing, or next to nothing. Pistocchi invented the singing school; the Amatis, Stradiuarius, and his followers, lay at the foundation of modern instrumental music. It is to Italy again we have to turn for the opera: whilst Handel gave us the highest form of the oratorio, and Haydn may be fairly said to have created the symphony.

But to return to Handel. We left him playing *Orlando* to empty houses in 1733. But an event had already occurred which was destined ultimately to turn the tide in his favour, and which struck the key-note of his immortality. We know that the MS. of Walter Scott's "Waverley" was laid aside for many years; so was the MS. of Handel's first oratorio, *Esther*. It was composed as early as 1720 for the Duke of Chandos at Cannons. Eleven years afterwards (1731) Bernard Gates, Royal Chapel-master of St. James's, got it up in private with his choir. Its fame soon spread, and a society called the Philharmonic, as also the Academy of Music, produced it on a larger scale under the direction of Gates. Handel seems to have thoroughly revised it himself, and in 1732 we read that "*Hester*, an English oratorio, was performed six times, and very full."

To us it is tolerably clear that there was something in the form as well as in the subjects of oratorio music especially appropriate to the genius of Handel; and yet such were the force of habit and the tyranny of fashion, that it was not until 1741—twenty-one years after the composition of *Esther*—that Handel definitely, upon repeated failures, abandoned the composition of Italian operas.

Without seeing these works represented it may be difficult to decide why they failed. One thing is certain, that the better the music the less did it suit the operatic tastes of the age. The most popular parts were the most puerile. Compare the silly, but celebrated, march in *Rinaldo* (1711) with the splendid, but little known, march in *Scipio* (1726). Perhaps the singers did not follow the development of his genius, and got tired of him as he marched on with colossal strides towards the music of the future. We know that Cuzzoni and Carestini both refused to sing some of his finest airs. Perhaps the public grew tired of the singers. At all events, Farinelli, the greatest of them, left England in 1737 rather than sing to an audience of five-and-thirty pounds. But the best reason is indicated by Colley Cibber, and explains why Italian opera could never satisfy the requirements of the great German composer, or be anything more than an artificial luxury with the English people :—"The truth is, that this kind of entertainment is entirely sensual."

As Handel's instincts ripened his intellect also developed. Perhaps he may have felt that dramatic action and musical emotion were two things that ought not to be mixed up together by making actors sing; and assuredly in the cantata and oratorio he attained a more satisfactory and philosophical form by presenting a drama to the mind, clothed with musical emotion, but not confounded with dramatic action. Incidents can be acted, and incidents can be described in song; but incidents cannot be sung except in the way of description, simply because music does not express *acts*, but the emotions which underlie action. Probably Handel did not explain his reasons for abandoning Italian opera thus; but the fact that his operas are forgotten, whilst *Acis and Galatea* and the *Messiah* remain, shows that in these last he had hit upon a form sufficiently philosophical to outlive all the operas of the day, and one which they did not possess.

From 1732 to 1740 he presents the familiar spectacle of a man of genius struggling with the tendencies of his age—half sailing, half drifting, but gaining strength with every passage of conflict. In those twelve memorable years he composed sixteen operas and five oratorios. After 1740 he composed no operas, and from 1741 to 1751 he composed eleven oratorios, beginning with the *Messiah* and ending with *Jephtha*. The success of the long-neglected *Esther* induced Handel to compose *Deborah* in 1733, and the success of *Deborah* awoke all the dogs that had gone to sleep during the failure of his operas and the decline of his popularity.

"The rise and progress of Mr. Handel," writes one paper, "are too well known for me to relate. Let it suffice to say that he has grown so insolent upon the sudden and undeserved increase of both, that he thinks that nothing ought to oppose his imperious and extravagant will." We are then treated to a description of "the thing called an oratorio," and informed that "the fairest breasts were fired with indignation against this new imposition."

The Italian faction opposed him with close and serried ranks, and all the malcontents, from whatever cause, deserted from Handel's camp and joined Bononcini. It does not appear that opposition improved a temperament naturally hot, and there can be little doubt that as Handel went on in life he lost friends and made enemies. He quarrelled with the celebrated Senesino, who, of course, joined his rival; and many of the nobles who were accustomed to treat musicians like servants, and even to cane them, were so taken aback at the great German's haughty and overbearing demeanour, that they decided in favour of the astute and servile Italian, who lived in Lady Godolphin's house in the enjoyment of a large pension.

No slander was spared. Handel was a swindler, he was a false friend, a glutton, a drunkard, a raving idiot, a profane fellow, to whom not even Holy Writ was sacred. The very idea of setting *Deborah* to music scandalized deeply the pietists, who applauded loudly the operas of Bononcini and the canzonets of Arrigoni.

Rolli satirized him, and Goupy caricatured him; his person was voted ridiculous, and his innovations monstrous. People complained of the loud effects produced by his new brass instruments, his heavy choruses, and his numberless violins. We are accustomed to think of Handel's orchestra as poor; but, in fact, with the exception of the clarionet, cornet-à-piston, and ophicleide, it comprised all the instruments now used, and several extinct ones besides,—*i.e.* violetta marina, theorbo, lute, &c. He also wrote for serpents, although few could then play them; and we are told of a bassoon sixteen feet high, which only one man could play; this was called a grand double bassoon (contrafagotto), and was made by Mr. Stanesby, the Distin of the period.

Under these circumstances we are not surprised to find Bold Briareus with a hundred hands abused and laughed at. Fielding, in "Tom Jones," has the following amusing hit at the taste of the period:—"It was Mr. Western's custom every afternoon, as soon as he was drunk, to hear his daughter play on the harpsichord; for he was a great lover of music, and, perhaps, had he lived in town, might have passed for a connoisseur, for he always excepted against the finest compositions of Mr. Handel." Even his friends complained that he "tore their ears to pieces," and one writes: "I expected his house to be blown down with his artificial wind; at another time the sea overflowed its banks and swallowed us up. But beyond everything, his thunder was most intolerable; I shall never get the horrid rumbling out of my head."

So much had it become the fashion to criticize the new effects, that some years later Mr. Sheridan makes one of his characters let off a pistol simply to shock the audience, and makes him say in a stage whisper to the gallery, "This hint, gentlemen, I took from Handel."

In 1733, *Esther* and *Deborah*, together with *Floridante* (1723) and *Orlando* (1732), were the chief attractions at the Haymarket. On July 5th of that year we find "one Handell, a foreigner (who, they say, was born at Hanover), was desired to come to Oxford to perform in music." The same writer goes on to say "that Handel, with his lowsy crew, a great number of foreign fiddlers, had a performance for his own benefit in the theatre. N.B.—His book (not worth 1*d.*) he sells for 1*s.*" The grave Dons seemed rather perplexed at the whole performance. "This," says one, "is an innovation," but most people paid their 5*s.*, and went to "try how a little fiddling would sit upon them;" and so great was the crush to get in that, "notwithstanding the barbarous and inhuman combination of such a parcel of unconscionable scamps, he disposed of most of his tickets."

Before "Handel and his lowsy crew" left Oxford, the victory was won. *Athalia* was received "with vast applause by an audience of 3,700 persons." Some of his university admirers, who appear to have thought then as now that any university honour was of priceless value, urged Handel to accept the degree of Doctor of Music, for which he would, of course, have to pay a small fee. We can understand the good Dons opening their eyes at his characteristic reply: "Vat te tevil I trow my money away for dat vich the blockhead vish? I no vant!"

When Handel opened the Haymarket in the autumn of the same year (1733), he did so as manager on his own account. His recent successes seem to have inspired him with confidence, and he was slow to believe that the public had done with his Italian operas. He made great efforts to write in a popular style. The *Ariadne* (1733) was avowedly written to outbid the Italian composers, and regain the favour of the faithless nobles. He plied them alternately with quality and quantity, and in the following year produced several patchwork operas, into which many favourite Italian airs were introduced to please either the singers or the public. Then comes an allegorical poem, *Parnasso in Festa* (1734). After which we have a relapse into instrumental music, *e.g.* the Hautboy concertos (1734), which are more like symphonies than concertos; and, above all, the famous "*six fugues or voluntaries,*" (1735)—a species of composition in which Handel must own his superior in Sebastien Bach. Then we have a ballet written for a French danseuse newly arrived. Gods in the clouds and out of the clouds were to appear—Jupiter with plenty of thunder, and actually "two Cupids." What could be more attractive? The Cupids and the danseuse had to be lugged into the *Ariodante* (1735); after which, in the same year, was composed and produced *Alcina*, which contained thirty-two airs, one duet, and no less than four little choruses. Then comes, as it were, a sudden revulsion of feeling. Opera is once more abandoned, and *Athaliah*, with parts of *Esther* and *Deborah*, is advertised.

But notwithstanding all his efforts, the Italian opposition at Lincoln's Inn Theatre grew stronger every day. Almost all the good singers had joined Porpora, Arrigoni, and Bononcini. Farinelli, whom the fashionable world raved about; Cuzzoni, whose very dresses were copied by the court ladies; Senesino, whose departure for Italy cast a gloom over the London season; Montagnana, considered by some the most finished artist that Italy ever produced—all sang at the opposition house against Bold Briareus, in order to crush him entirely. The nobles sent for the celebrated Hasse; but the great man, with becoming modesty, exclaimed, "Oh! then Handel is dead?" and on being told he was yet alive, refused indignantly to go over in opposition to one so much his superior. It is strange to notice how, partly by the progress of his genius, and partly by the force of circumstances, Handel was being drifted out of Italian opera at the very moment when he tried to tighten his grasp on it.

The free introduction of choral and instrumental music into opera offended the singers and retarded the action of the drama in the eyes of the audience. Yet it was by these unpopular characteristics that the public mind was being trained to understand a species of composition which, from the first, seems to have proved attractive under the form of the cantata and the oratorio.

It was in 1736 that Carestini, the only great Italian singer who had stood by Handel, left for Italy, and with his departure all further operas at the Haymarket became impossible. It was in that year also that Handel, once more left to follow the bent of his own genius, revived *Acis* and *Esther*, and composed the music to *Alexander's Feast*. However, in April, 1736, the Italian singer Conti was got over, and another Italian opera was tried—*Atalanta.*

The piece was in honour of the Prince of Wales, on the occasion of his marriage with a princess of Saxe-Gotha; and was followed, in the same month, by a light wedding anthem, written down to their Royal Highnesses' taste. But the flicker of popularity which attended these two works came too late to restore the fortunes of a lost game, and although Handel stood out stoutly to the last, he must have been aware of the impending ruin. In 1737 *Arminius* appeared. Burney says, "It had few captivating airs." At any rate, it failed. *Justin* (1738) followed, and although it is acknowledged to be one of Handel's most agreeable compositions, it had but five representations. The master was getting worn and depressed with exertion, disappointment, and failure. The public seemed tired of everything. The Italian singers had not only deserted the Haymarket, but were again beginning to leave the country.

In eight years Handel had dissipated a fortune of

£10,000 on Italian opera, and on the fall of *Berenice* he was forced to suspend payment, and closed the theatre.

The rival house lasted but a few months longer. Its pride and success had been, after all, the pride of party spirit and the vamped-up success of a clique; and when Handel gave in, the game seemed hardly worth the candle—the candle having cost the Duchess of Marlborough and her friends as nearly as possible £12,000.

In April, 1737, the daily papers announced that Mr. Handel, who had been indisposed with rheumatism, was recovering. In October we read in the *Daily Post* that Mr. Handel, "the composer of Italian music, was hourly expected from Aix, greatly recovered in health." All sorts of rumours had been afloat. Handel had left the country, some said mad—others dying—all knew in debt. But the iron frame with the iron will lasted out. Handel did not return from Aix-la-Chapelle, like Mozart from Baden, to write his own Requiem, but some one's else.

Queen Caroline's failing health had long been the talk of town—and it was commonly said that anxiety and weariness of spirit were rapidly hastening her to the grave.

When the last hour had struck, Handel was called in to make music for the king's sorrow, and the Funeral Anthem was performed in Henry VII.'s chapel in the presence of an immense concourse of people. The whole of this magnificent anthem was afterwards introduced into the oratorio of *Saul* as an elegy on the death of Saul and Jonathan—and the whole of it is, on second thoughts, crossed out in the MS. of that oratorio.

With an inexplicable tenacity of purpose, Handel instantly resumed the composition of opera music which had only just now ruined him, and *Faramondo* was immediately produced, with La Francesina and the famous Cafarelli Duca di Santo Dorato, who thought himself the greatest singer in the world, and wrote outside his chateau in Italy, "Amphion Thebas, Ego Domum." *Faramondo* failed. On the 25th of February, 1728, came *Alexander Severus*, a Pasticcio of favourite airs—that failed. Two months afterwards *Xerxes*, with a comic man in it, failed. The work does not flow easily, in spite of the comedy, and the scored and blotted MS. attests to this day the agitations of a mind ill at ease and fevered with anxiety. In fact, the house was empty—the band grumbled—the singers were not paid—and somewhere about March of the same year one Signor Strada threatened to arrest Handel for debt. At this crisis his friends induced him to give a great benefit concert, which brought him in—some said—£1,500, and which enabled him to pay many of his debts.

In his adversity he was not without consolations. His creditors believed in his sterling integrity, and were, as a rule, very patient with him. The king paid him well for his work, and at a time when the nobles forsook him, his royal patron went steadily to all the oratorios. George II. taught the youthful Prince of Wales, afterwards George III., to love his music. Southey tells us that Handel asked the boy, then quite a child, who was listening very earnestly to his playing, if he liked the music, and when the little prince expressed his delight—"A good boy! a good boy!" cried Handel; "you shall protect my fame when I am dead." Little did the young prince know how much he would require in later years all the solaces that can be derived from art and light literature to soothe him in the lucid intervals of his lonely aberration. Sir Walter Scott's novels and Handel's music proved the chief resources of his old age.

There were many besides the king who never for a moment despaired of Handel; amongst them were Gay, Arbuthnot, Hughes, Colley Cibber, Pope, Fielding, Hogarth, and Smollett. These were the men who kept their fingers on the pulse of the age—they gauged Handel accurately, and they were not wrong. At a time when others jeered at his oratorios, these men wrote them up—when the tide of fine society ebbed, and left Handel high and dry on the boards of a deserted theatre, they occupied the pit—when he gave his benefit concert they bought the tickets, and when his operas failed they immediately subscribed and had them engraved.

And it is curious to notice how true the really popular instinct was to Handel. It was the nobles, not the people, who refused to hear his oratorios and complained of his instrumentation; but when for a time he was forced to abandon opera, and to devote himself to oratorio and cabinet music, the tide of adverse fortune received an instant check. His attention being drawn off opera, he poured forth organ concertos and pieces for stringed instruments, which rapidly spread through the kingdom. About this time he seems to have grown very popular as a player, and whenever an oratorio was performed, he gave what were called "entertainments" on the organ. It was soon found that Mr. Handel's music was good bait for the holiday makers of the period as well as for the men of genius. The proprietor of Vauxhall was so impressed with Handel's usefulness in bringing grist to his mill, that he had his music constantly played there, and erected a statue to the great man at his own expense. The manager of the Marylebone Gardens also set up a band and played the people in with similar effect. Handel himself was sometimes to be seen there with a friend. "Come, Mr. Fountayne," said he one day, "let us sit down and listen to this piece; I want to know your opinion of it." The old clergyman (for such he was) sat down and listened for a time, and at last turning round impatiently, said, "It's not worth listening to—it's very poor stuff." "You are right, Mr. Fountayne," said Handel, "it *is* very poor stuff: I thought so when I finished it!"

The years 1737-8-9 were years of prodigious activity. The oratorio of *Saul* was produced and repeated five times. The overture is not entirely unknown by the public of to-day, and is full of grace and delicacy. The chorus, "à Carillons," "Welcome, welcome, mighty King," should be more frequently heard. The parts of Jonathan and David are full of tender pathos, and the scene between the king and the witch of Endor is all the more dramatic for not being coupled with action. To this day no dirge is complete without the "Dead March," which is especially important, from a musical point of view, as being one of the few intensely sad and solemn symphonies written in a major key. In the same year *Alexander's Feast* was twice played; an early oratorio, *Il Trionfo del Tempo,* was revived (1737); and last and most notable fact of all, the *Israel in Egypt* was composed in the incredibly short space of twenty-seven days. The *Israel in Egypt* (1738) hardly survived three representations. It was certainly the least popular oratorio yet produced. *Saul* was preferred to it, and about this time Signor Piantanida, the great fiddler, arriving from Italy, was preferred to both. The *Israel* was produced but nine times in Handel's lifetime. Each time it had to be cooked—sometimes by cutting out choruses and putting in airs, at others by leaving out both. No book of extracts from it was published, and the score remained unedited in 1759, the year of Handel's death.

With the exception of a brief and disastrous return to Italian opera in 1740, *Imeneo* and *Deidamia*, Handel now definitely renounced the stage which had witnessed the triumph of his youthful powers and the failure of his mature genius. He was now fifty-five years old, and had entered, after many a long and weary contest, upon his last and greatest creative period. His genius culminates in the *Israel;* elsewhere he has produced longer recitatives and more pathetic arias, nowhere has he written finer tenor songs than "The Enemy saith," or finer duets than "The Lord is a man of war;" and there is not in the history of music an example of choruses piled up like so many Ossas on Pelions in such majestic strength, and hurled in open defiance at a public whose ears were itching for Italian love lays and English ballads.

In these twenty-eight colossal choruses we perceive at once a reaction against and a triumph over the tastes of the age. The wonder is, not that the *Israel* was unpopular, but that it should have been tolerated; but Handel, whilst he appears to have been for years driven by the public, had been, in reality, driving them. His earliest oratorio, *Il Trionfo del Tempo*, had but two choruses—into his operas more and more were introduced, with disastrous consequences—but when at the zenith of his strength he produced a work which consisted almost entirely of these unpopular peculiarities, the public treated him with respect, and actually sat out three performances in one season!

But the choruses themselves were not without a popular fibre, and probably they were saved by the very qualities which are now least esteemed. The notion that music should be imitative (except in a very secondary sense) is rapidly losing ground. The function of music is to kindle emotion, not to raise images. No doubt images, when raised, have the power of kindling emotions, but music can do it without them, and better than they can. When, then, music seeks first to raise an image in the mind, that through the image emotion may be kindled, it is abdicating its proper authority in committing its own special business to an inferior agent. However, since no one wishes to re-write the "Hailstone Chorus," we may admit that a skilful compromise between images and emotions may be made by music. But then it becomes more than ever necessary to ask how far music may suggest images without injury to its own peculiar function as an emotional agent. And the answer seems to be this: laying aside the whole subject of association and memory in music, we may say that the effect of music as the language of the emotions is in proportion to the unimpeded beauty of its expression. Therefore no tempting imitation must impede that expression, or render it less musical—the image, if introduced at all, must be absorbed naturally by the music, and woven into the very texture of the work. This, we may fairly say, has been done in the fire and hail, which run along the ground in the "Hailstone Chorus." It was possible to imitate the running and rattling of hail, and it has been done, but without controlling the free and beautiful expression, or disturbing the essential development of the chorus.

When we come to the frogs leaping, the image begins to get the upper hand, and the emotional force is instantly diminished, and necessarily so. For images derive their significance from the emotion with which you are prepared to clothe them; and if, as is certainly the case, they ever create emotion by themselves, it is only because the mind at some previous time has invested them with the emotion, which it subsequently draws from them. But images in themselves are passionless symbols, and that mysterious movement of life which we call emotion is the only heat and glory of them. To appeal, then, from sound which touches directly the very springs of emotion to images which only affect us when they are touched by those very springs, is like appealing from the sun itself to a pool of water in which we may have once seen it reflected.

But Handel's finest effects are not imitations, although they have been called so; they are analogies, or musical counterparts. It is obvious that a thing like darkness, which is simply the negation of light, is not imitable by any sound—yet the emotion of darkness that may be felt is very intensely produced by means of that wonderful sound analogue beginning, "He sent a thick darkness." We have another fine sound analogue in *Joshua*, where the sun standing still is represented by a long-drawn-out note. But we repeat that analogy is not imitation; and if we wish to compare musical analogy with musical imitation we cannot do better than pass from Handel's "darkness" in the *Israel*, and "light" in the *Joshua*, to Beethoven's real "cuckoo" in the *Pastoral Symphony*, and Mendelssohn's live donkey in the *Midsummer Night's Dream*.

It was clear that henceforth neither praise nor blame could turn Handel out of his course. He was not popular at this time with the musical world ; his operas had been quenched for good, and the first surprise of his oratorio music over, his greatest works failed to bring him in much money; his enemies tore down his handbills, and his finest cantatas, such as *L'Allegro* and *Il Penseroso,* were voted tedious. But we find no more undignified catering for popular taste; no more writing in the Italian style ; no more ballets ; no more silly and emasculated operas. The eagle has finally left the small birds chattering on the tree tops, and has soared once for all into the higher region.

Handel continued to compose with the greatest industry, but he was getting very tired of London, and was beginning to turn his eyes from an ungrateful English public towards Ireland.

Handel was very fond of the Irish, and this truly musical people had long been devoted to him. The Duke of Devonshire, Lord-Lieutenant, had asked him over, and an influential society of amateurs in Dublin requested him to come and compose music for a festival in aid of "poor and distressed prisoners for debt" in the Marshalsea of Dublin.

There was nothing to keep him in London, and the Dublin papers announce that on the "18th of November, 1741, Dr. Handel arrived here in the packet-boat from Holyhead ; a gentleman universally known by his excellent composition in all kinds of music."

From the moment of his arrival Handel's house in Abbey Street, near Liffey Street, became the resort of all the professors and amateurs in Dublin. No time was lost in producing selections from the splendid repertory of music which the German composer had brought over with him. One after another his principal works were unfolded to an admiring audience in the New Music Hall, Fishamble Street. The crush was so great to hear the *Allegro* and *Penseroso* that the doors had to be closed, and a handbill put up to say that no more money could be taken, and the papers declared there never had been such a scene. Handel gave twelve performances at incredibly short intervals, comprising almost all his finest and chiefly his latest works. In these concerts the *Acis* and *Alexander's Feast* held the most prominent places. But the lustre even of these compositions was about to pale before the *Messiah*, as the mere vestibule is forgotten when we stand at last by the sacred shrine of the inner temple.

At midday of the 13th April, 1742, the great hall in Fishamble Street was densely crowded with an enthusiastic audience. Mr. Handel's new oratorio, the *Messiah*, composed in England especially for Dublin, was to be performed for the first time. Mrs. Cibber, Mrs. Avolio, and Mr. Dubourg were the chief singers, and, following the example of Handel, they gave their services gratuitously; for by a remarkable and perhaps not wholly undesigned coincidence the first performance of the *Messiah* literally proclaimed deliverance to the captives, for it was, as we have said, for the benefit and enlargement of poor distressed prisoners for debt in the several prisons in the city of Dublin.

The newspapers and the critics, the poets and the tattlers, exhausted every trope and figure in their praise of the new oratorio. A reverend gentleman in the audience is recorded to have so far forgotten himself, or his Bible, as to exclaim, at the close of one of Mrs. Cibber's airs, "Woman, for this be all thy sins forgiven thee;" whilst another enthusiast observed in terms even more poetical and scarcely less secular, that—

> "To harmony like *his* celestial power was given,
> To exalt the soul from earth and make of hell a heaven."

The penny-a-liners wrote that "words were wanting to express the exquisite delight that it afforded," &c., &c.; and, lastly, to their honour be it recorded, the ladies of the period consented to leave their hoops at home in order that an additional one hundred listeners might be got into the room. The proceeds amounted to about £400, and the event may truly be regarded as the greatest in Handel's life. Years of misconception, partial neglect, and bitter rivalry were forgotten in that hour of triumph. A few months before, the equally great oratorio of *Israel* had been but coldly received in England—it had been reserved for the Irish people without hesitation to set their seal of enthusiastic approval upon an oratorio which, to this day, is considered by the majority of the English people the greatest oratorio that was ever written.

Works of the highest genius should not be compared.

The *Messiah* has surely earned for itself the right of being judged by itself, as a great whole, without reference to any other great whole. So has the *Israel*, and so, we may add, has the *Elijah*.

When generations have been melted into tears, or raised to religious fervour—when courses of sermons have been preached, volumes of criticisms been written about, and thousands of afflicted and poor people supported by the oratorio of the *Messiah*—it becomes exceedingly difficult to say anything new. Yet no notice of Handel, however sketchy, should be written without some special tribute of reverence to this sublime treatment of a sublime subject. Bach, Graun, Beethoven, Spohr, Rossini, and, it may be added, Mendelssohn, and later still Mr. Henry Leslie, have all composed on the same theme. But no one in completeness, in range of effect, in elevation and variety of conception, has ever approached Handel's music upon this particular subject.

The orchestral prelude, fairly overstepping the mannerisms of the period, opens with a series of chords which, in their abrupt and deliberate shocks of startling harmony, immediately arrest the attention, and inspire the hearer with a certain majestic anticipation. This strange *grave* soon breaks into the short fugue, which, in its simple and clear severity, prepares the mind with an almost ascetic tone for the sustained act of devotional contemplation about to follow.

Upon this temper of devout expectation the words, "Comfort ye my people," fall like a refreshing day-spring from on high. The soul seeking for God has but just withdrawn itself from an evil and a suffering world to wait in faith, when at the hour of that world's greatest need—in the moment of a resignation almost stoical—a glimpse of the blue heaven is seen, and the voice of prophecy rolls forth, "Thus saith the Lord!" Immediately the heat and stir of human interest is once more kindled, and the Deliverer seems very near. With a merry noise of joyful encouragement, each man finds some work to do—these in levelling the mountains, those in bridging the vales with viaducts, for the King of Glory to pass over. We hear a vast multitude, not of slaves, but of freemen, singing at their work, "Every valley shall be exalted," and suddenly breaking from monologue into chorus, their lips send forth the one thought that possesses them, "The glory of the Lord—the glory of the Lord shall be revealed."

But the exceeding light will surely blind them; they are so weak with sin, and He is of purer eyes than to behold iniquity. "Who may abide the day of his coming?"—a terror seems to seize them. The voice scales up to a high pitch, and dwells with a kind of awful suspense and fascination on the word "appeareth." The first burst of joyful activity over, their sinful hearts quail before the thought of the mighty and spotless King. But do they indeed desire Him? Would they rather have his severity than their own sin? Then He Himself will fit them for his presence. "He shall purify them," and help them to "offer unto Him an offering of righteousness."

Therefore, with hearts docile and teachable, waiting for the Messiah, they eagerly listen to the words of the Seer, "Behold, a virgin shall conceive." Is it indeed so? What a different message from the one they expected, and yet how reassuring! All their fears are at once calmed. He was to be humble as well as mighty. He was to be one of them, and yet in some mysterious way exalted above them all. The image of a King coming with pomp and majesty is now withdrawn, and in its place we have simply a Virgin and a Child.

But at that moment, whilst a chorus of those who accept this strange and unexpected revelation with the utmost joy and confidence, believing that, in spite of appearances, "the government shall be upon his shoulders," the first ominous forebodings of the impending catastrophe may be noticed in the recitative and aria, dwelling on the gross darkness of the people at large, and forcibly reminding us of "the light which shone in the darkness, and the darkness which comprehended it not."

Then comes one of those pauses so common in the works of the great dramatists, where the mind has been led up to the threshold of certain startling events, and is called upon to recreate itself for a moment before entering upon a train of the most exciting interest and rapid action.

We are upon the hill-sides around Bethlehem; the delicious pastoral symphony makes us aware of a land of flocks and herds. It is towards evening; the flocks of sheep are being gathered by the shepherds, and are winding slowly towards the wells before settling down on the mountain slopes for the night. The melody breathes peace as the shadows lengthen with the setting sun; at length we seem to hear the faint tinkle of the last bells die away in the distance, and then all is still. The flocks are resting, the shepherds are watching beside them in the darkness, when lo! the angel of the Lord comes upon them, and in an instant the bright light gleams out upon the green and glittering sward; the gloom is suddenly broken up with tints of heavenly colour, and the night is filled with music. The accompaniment to the recitative "And lo!" gives the sensation of the mustering from afar of the angels; and by the time we come to the angelic chorus, "Glory to God," which is exquisitely written, chiefly in treble, and is ringing with pure melody, the whole air seems full of visions—myriads of flame-like faces, sublime and tender, such as Fra Angelico loved to paint, are around us, the distance is thronged with them, the air vibrates with the pulsation of their innumerable wings as they chant to each other, with the voices of another world, the hymn of glory; and then, just as the shepherds are beginning to realize their own ecstasy, the light fades, the sound seems to ascend and be lost among the stars, and all is again dark on the hill-sides of Bethlehem. But the light was evermore in the shepherds' eyes, and the sound of the angels' voices in their ears, and with images culled from their own gentle calling, they returned bringing a message of joy to Sion, and proclaiming in snatches of that very melody they had heard by night the advent of One "who should feed his flock like a shepherd, and carry the lambs in his bosom."

The second part, which is occupied with the sufferings and exaltation of Christ, the spread and final triumph of the Gospel, opens with what is probably the finest piece of choral declamation in existence. "Behold the Lamb of God!" now sounds through the world, and each time, as the august cry sinks, it is taken up again and again until the whole land is ringing with the announcement.

It is curious to observe how, in obedience to the prevalent theology of the day, the teaching of Jesus is suppressed, and only his more conspicuous sufferings and death are dwelt upon.

We are now brought close to a Messiah very different from the popular conception at the beginning of the first part; and instead of a triumphant King, one appears who, "without form or comeliness," treads the path of suffering, and is made acquainted with grief. A heavy shame and sorrow seems to pervade the next few pieces, as of some beloved disciple who stands aside comprehending in part the nature of the tragic spectacle before him, and a prey to all its desolating influences. The flood-gates of feeling are at length loosed, and, after the air, "He was despised and rejected of men," written singularly enough in the major key, three choruses are poured forth in succession. The first two, "Surely He hath borne our griefs," and "With his stripes we are healed," bringing before us the willing victim and the propitiation for sin, and the third, "All we like sheep have gone astray," representing with marvellous fidelity the constant and hopeless wanderings of the sheep. It was this hopeless disorder that had to be atoned for, these hopeless wanderers that had to be reclaimed. The Shepherd of Israel could alone seek and save that which was lost. He would not shrink from the necessary suffering; He would endure scorn and solitude and agony; He was the Good Shepherd who laid down his life for the sheep. Then we are shown the outside world laughing Him to scorn, and the vulgar rabble shooting out their tongues and mocking Him in harsh and abrupt staves of ribald irony—"He trusted in God that He would deliver Him!" till at last the disciple who stands by can bear the sight no longer, and, as he hears the Saviour cry out, "Eloi, Eloi, lama sabachthani!" he himself turns away, overcome with misery, exclaiming, "Thy rebuke hath broken his heart!"

The first feeling at the sight of the dead Christ upon the cross is one of simple and blank despair. He who should have redeemed Israel — upon whose shoulders the government was to rest—the Mighty Counsellor, the Prince of Peace—He was no victorious monarch—only a crucified man! "He was cut off out of the land of the living." But this train of thought is soon arrested, and we are carried rapidly forward through death and the grave, until, ascending from those depths with the now glorified Saviour, we rise higher and higher towards the blinding splendours of the heavenly courts. A shout of triumph bursts forth as the everlasting gates roll asunder, and throngs of angels with the bright seraphim stream forth to meet the King. The sky itself seems to throb with the thrilling cry, "He is the King of Glory!" and just as we begin to feel that we have been whirled along with the prodigious power of the sound until we have almost forgotten our own powers of endurance, and are made sensible that we can no longer bear the strain of excitement, the abrupt dead pause falls, and then, with a last, long, shattering cry "of glory," the mighty pæan swoons away into the echoless silence.

After such a climax we are not surprised to find the next three pieces deficient in interest; this may even be intentional. The great artist knows when the eye requires rest, and lays on his middle tints, until our emotion has been subdued, and we are ready to contemplate with calmness the progress of the Gospel in the world.

Something like a second pastoral now follows—the Lord Christ speaks from heaven, and sends forth shepherds to feed his lambs—"How beautiful are their feet!" and then the mind is absorbed by the stir and enterprise of missionary labour until the chorus, "Their sound is gone out into all lands," is felt to be as powerfully descriptive as the going astray of the sheep themselves. In another moment the shepherds have become warrior-pilgrims, the nations rage furiously together, but their bows are broken asunder—the rod of iron smites them, and God Himself declares for the soldiers of the Cross. The battle-scene in its turn vanishes, and the final triumph of good over evil is anticipated by a daring and indomitable effort of faith; for a moment all heaven is opened; we are caught up in the clouds, and hear from the vast multitude which no man can number the hallelujahs of those that chime "after the chiming of the eternal spheres."

The "Hallelujah Chorus" stands alone. It is not easy to speak of it. It appears to have the same overpowering effect upon learned and unlearned; it is felt and understood by all. The thought is absolutely simple, so is the expression; two or three massive phrases growing out of each other, or rather, rising one after another, in reiterated bursts of glory, a piece of divine melody in the middle, succeeded by the last clause of the triumphal shout, "And He shall reign for ever and ever," which is taken up rapturously by the flaming choirs of the immortals, and hurled from side to side, until at last the energies of heaven itself seem spent, and the mighty strain itself dies away before "the Great White Throne, and Him that sitteth thereon."

Such are the leading ideas and sensations of this chorus. But perhaps Handel's own words are the only ones fit to describe this shout of inspired praise—"I did think I did see all heaven before me, and the great God Himself!"

That two such choruses as "Lift up your heads" and the "Hallelujah" should be placed not far from each other in one and the same part without prejudice to either, is in itself a marvel; but the greater marvel is, that after the "Hallelujah" Handel should be able to recover himself and carry his audience through a third part. Mendelssohn has done something similar in the *Elijah*, after the great choruses "Thanks be to God" and "Be not afraid," and the scene of the fiery chariot, with which an inferior man would certainly have culminated. He has shown that he could refresh and recreate the heart with less tremendous but not less elevating emotions until his hearers are fairly restored to their self-possession, and finally left in a calm and almost severely meditative frame of mind by the last chorus.

The third part of the *Messiah* is purely theological, yet the interest does not flag. When the history of the first two parts has been told, there is left to the world a body of Christian truth than which nothing can be more consolatory and sublime. "I know that my Redeemer liveth" belongs to a type of melody that is never likely to grow old nor pass away. The two doctrinal quartets, "Since by man came death," and "As in Adam all die," have never been surpassed; whilst in sweetness and solemn force "The trumpet shall sound" will probably retain its popularity as long as there is a silver-toned trumpet in existence.

The oratorio closes with two choruses, of which

the first, "Worthy is the Lamb," is by far the most florid. The last is the measured and severe "Amen" chorus.

It is a fitting and dignified close to so exciting, and at the same time majestic, a work. All emotion has now been spent, and the mind, like the still heaving waves of the sea after a storm, is left to rock itself slowly into deep and perfect peace. Thus the oratorio opens with the hope of "comfort," and ends with the full calm joy of attainment. One feeling now fills the Christian disciple through and through, and one word only is found sufficient to express it—it is the glorious "Amen" of the final chorus.

On his return from Ireland in 1742, Handel immediately prepared a new oratorio—*Samson*—for the following Lent season; and this, together with the *Messiah*, then heard for the first time in London, was intended to form the staple of twelve performances. Whether many people went to hear them or not is doubtful; the papers have not a word of comment on that season. It is to be feared that the fashionable world in London had made up its mind not to care for Mr. Handel. One Lady Brown, a lady of fashion, gave large tea-parties whenever his music was advertised; there were regular sets made up at Lady Godolphin's to play cards on those nights; one Mr. Russell, a comic man, was hired to sing at the great houses; a few went to hear a new Italian opera, the *Caduta di Giganti*, by a young man just arrived from abroad named Gluck; and Horace Walpole had the impudence to say of Handel (who had excellent singers), that "he had hired all the goddesses from farces, and singers of roast-beef,* from between the acts of both theatres, with a man with one note in his voice, and a girl with never a one, and so they sang, and made brave Hallelujahs!"

In 1745, poor Handel, deserted by the paying world, struggled through fifteen performances of his finest oratorios, but the effort cost him dear. He was unable to discharge his debts, and for the second time in his life was forced to suspend payment as a complete bankrupt. Luckily his health did not give way, and with indomitable energy he sat down to compose the first two acts of the *Occasional Oratorio*, the third act of which, though containing many new pieces, is of the nature of a pasticcio. Henceforth he determined to enter into no engagement with subscribers for so many performances per season, but to give concerts when he chose, and to throw himself rather upon the general public, who, as it had no share in the luxuries and follies of the nobles, felt little enough sympathy with their musical tastes and prejudices. Although constantly persecuted by a frivolous and effeminate clique, Handel never appealed in vain to the people at large. In a short time he had discharged his unfulfilled obligations to subscribers, by issuing free tickets for some Lent performances, and had also laid

* In allusion to the "Roast Beef of Old England," a popular song of the period.

by sufficient to pay off most of his debts. This was in 1746.

In the following year, the third of his great masterpieces, the *Judas Maccabæus*, appeared. It was composed in thirty days, between the 9th of July and the 11th of August, and was produced at Covent Garden on the 1st of April, 1747.

Justice is usually discovered to be on the winning side, and after the victory of Culloden, Prince William, Duke of Cumberland, not too popular in some quarters, had to be greeted as the Judas Maccabæus of the age. The application was not obvious, but it served Handel's turn. The first part opens with the celebrated chorus, "Mourn, ye afflicted;" but grief for the departed hero who had roused the Jews to resist the oppression of Antiochus Epiphanes soon vanished before the fair promise of his noble son Judas. The "pious orgies" for the father over, "Arm, arm, ye brave!" is the war-cry of the son, and the rest of the part is occupied with appropriate meditations on, and preparations for, the war, until at length they go to battle with the chorus, "Hear us, O Lord." The second part celebrates the victories of Judas Maccabæus, and contains one of the best known of Handel's songs, "Sound an alarm!" It concludes with one of the freest and most original of his choruses, "We never will bow down." The last part celebrates the return of Judas after re-establishing the liberties of his country, and winds up with the national thanksgiving. "O Lovely Peace" is one of the freshest soprano duets ever written, and "See the Conquering Hero comes," which originally belonged to *Joshua*, is perhaps the most widely popular of all Handel's compositions.

The *Messiah* excepted, no oratorio is more often performed in England than *Judas Maccabæus.* In many respects it is not so difficult to get through passably, and is consequently a great favourite with amateur choirs; although not too long, it readily admits of being shortened, and in provincial towns is seldom heard in its entirety. It contains much repetition of sentiment, and yet little that we can afford to lose: it is one of the very finest works of his most mature period. The *Morning Herald* of the 19th of February, 1852, indulged in the following sapient criticisms, which we cannot do better than quote:—"The airs of *Judas Maccabæus*, like those of many other works of Handel, are occasionally feeble and insipid; but two or three of them are exactly the reverse, and in the hands of singers of ability become both important and interesting." *O patria! O mores!*

In 1747 appeared *Joshua.* The graceful air, "Hark, 'tis the linnet," still never fails to please. Haydn observed of the chorus, "The nations tremble," that only one inspired author ever did, or ever would, pen so sublime a composition. The amount of recitative makes the oratorio heavy as a whole. In 1748, Handel being then in his sixty-fourth year, wrote the oratorio of *Solomon;* between the 5th of May and the 19th of June the oratorio of *Susannah;* between the 11th of July and the 24th of August, towards the close of the same year, he prepared the Firework Music, which was played at night before the king's palace in the Green Park. Let us hope that his love of noise was for once fully gratified. The music ended with the explosion of a hundred and one brass cannons, seventy-one six-pounders, twenty twelve-pounders, and ten twenty-four pounders. There was no lack of hunting-horns, haut-boys, bassoons, kettle-drums, and side-drums, besides bass-viols innumerable. Every one seems to have been delighted; and when the magnificent Doric Temple, under the superintendence of that great pyrotechnist the Chevalier Servardoni, went off with a terrific bang, it was thought success could go no further, and the king's library was very nearly burnt down. When in 1749 the Firework Music was repeated at the Vauxhall Gardens by a band of a hundred musicians, twelve thousand persons are said to have attended. There was such a stoppage on London Bridge that no carriage could pass for three hours, and the receipts were set down at the fabulous sum of £5,700.

In 1749 Handel produced one of his least popular oratorios, *Theodora.* It was a great favourite with him, and he used to say that the chorus, "He saw the Lovely Youth," was finer than anything in the *Messiah.* The public were not of this opinion, and he was glad to give away tickets to any professors who applied for them. When the *Messiah* was again produced, two of these gentlemen who had neglected *Theodora* applied for admission. "Oh! your sarvant, meine Herren!" exclaimed the indignant composer. "You are tamnable dainty! You would not go to *Teodora*—dere was room enough to tance dere when dat was perform." When Handel heard that an enthusiast had offered to make himself responsible for all the boxes the next time the despised oratorio should be given—"He is a fool," said he; "the Jews will not come to it as to *Judas Maccabæus*, because it is a Christian story; and the ladies will not come, because it is a virtuous one."

It is difficult to believe that virtue itself, under so attractive a form, could fail to charm. "Angels ever bright and fair" is probably the highest flight of melody that even Handel ever reached.

But the long struggle was drawing to a close, and the battle was nearly won, as the great ship floated out of the storm into the calm sunset waters. Handel had turned from the nobles to the people, and the people had welcomed him throughout the length and breadth of the land. An aristocratic reaction soon began to take place—it was found necessary to produce pasticcio operas by the lately-neglected composer, and to republish numbers of airs as harpsichord pieces which in their original connection had found small favour. Publishers vied with each other in producing works with Mr. Handel's name, and there is reason to fear that unscrupulous persons manufactured music by Handel as freely as Italian artists are in the habit of attaching the name of Domenichino to their dull and smoky daubs. By the time Handel had reached his sixty-seventh year the merits of rival factions were pretty generally understood, and the last ten years of his life were passed in comparative tranquillity.

No voice was now raised to proclaim the superior charms of Bononcini—no rival composer sent for to ruin the great sacred writer with Italian rubbish—no foreign fiddler announced to supersede Mr. Handel's entertainments on the organ—nor any comic man to grin the *Israel* or the *Judas Maccabæus* out of court. The closing years of the great master's life witnessed a general drawing together of adverse parties and reconcilement of private quarrels. Handel at last found his way to an elevation from which no one thought of dislodging him.

It is pleasant, before the last sad short act of his life, to bring him before us as he appeared at this time to those who knew him best, and loved him most. His life of alternate contemplation, industry, and excitement, from beginning to end, is unstained by any suspicion of dishonesty or licentiousness. A few indistinct rumours of unsuccessful love affairs in very early life (unsuccessful on the part of the ladies) reach us; and we hear no more of women, nor of any need of their love experienced by Handel. He lived for the most part very quietly in the house now numbered 57, Brook Street, Hanover Square, and let the charmers of this world go their way. Of no man was it ever truer than of

Handel, that he was wedded to his art. His recreations were few and simple. Occasionally he would stroll into St. Paul's Cathedral, and amuse himself with ineffectual attempts to play the people out; then taking sculls, or when in better circumstances indulging himself in oars, he would be rowed towards the village of Charing, along the banks of the Thames whose waters were then somewhat more transparent than they are now. Not far from his favourite organ at St. Paul's there was a favourite tavern called the "Queen's Head." Thither he often resorted at nightfall, and smoked his pipe and drank his beer, with three others,—Goupy, the painter; Hunter, the scarlet dyer; and John Christopher Smith, his secretary. There was an old harpsichord in the tavern, and he would often sit thrumming away to himself and a few musical connoisseurs, who were content to drop in and spend their time over papers, porter, silence, and applause. These were the times of Handel's social exhilaration; and although we have no reason to believe that he indulged in excesses, we have abundant evidence that he despised not conviviality. Surrounded by a circle of familiars, his conversation flowed freely, and sparkled with satire and fun of all kinds. He spoke English, like some Italians, with great fluency and infinite satisfaction to himself, but with a strong accent, and the construction of his sentences was sometimes German, sometimes Italian. He was often passionate, but never ill-natured; no man ever had more rivals, or was less jealous of them. Although he had numerous acquaintances, he had few friends; and during the last years of his life steadily declined the invitations of the nobles, whose patronage might twice have saved him from ruin, but whose flattery he could now afford to dispense with. His friend Goupy, whose caricatures, although often levelled against himself, never seemed to have offended him, would frequently accompany him to picture-galleries, in which he took the most vivid interest, and it is more than likely that his operas owe as much to the classical inspirations of Poussin and Duval, or the Pastorals of Watteau, as his sacred music undoubtedly does to the great sacred painters of Italy. In his latter years he was a regular attendant at St. George's, Hanover Square, and it was noticed by one who records the fact with affectionate emotion, that on such occasions he appeared to be deeply absorbed by his devotions.

Let us look once more at this noble and portly figure sauntering along with the peculiar rocking motion common to those whose legs are a little bowed; let us note the somewhat heavy but expressive face gathering freshness from the morning air, moved at times with a frown like a thunder-cloud, or with a smile like the sun that bursts from behind it. The general impression is the right one. There was a man of inflexible integrity, of solid genius and sterling benevolence; a man fitted to cope with the puerilities of fashion, singularly generous to foes, singularly faithful to friends. So, unconscious of the approaching shadow that was to dim the brightness of his last days, with a light heart which comes of a conscience void of offence towards God or man, we may picture to ourselves good Father Handel as he rocks along this morning towards Paper Buildings to see his friend Master Hardcastle, and crave his hospitality for breakfast.

It happened to be the very day on which a competition was to take place for the post of organist to the Temple Church, and Zachary Hardcastle had bidden his old friends, Colley Cibber, Dr. Pepusch, and Dr. Arne, be with him to a dish of coffee and a roll at nine o'clock, in order that they might all go together to hear the contest.

"Vat, mein dear friend Hardcastle!" exclaimed Handel, breaking in upon the party; "vat! and Mr. Golley Cibber, too! and Toctor Bepusch as vell! Vell, dat is gomical. And how vags the vorld mit you, mein dears? Bray, bray let me sit down a moment!" Pepusch took the great man's hat, Colley Cibber took his stick, and old Zachary Hardcastle wheeled round his reading-chair, which was somewhat about the dimensions of that in which kings and queens are crowned, and then the great man sat him down. "Vell, I thank you, gentlemens. Now I am at mein ease vonce more. 'Bon my vord dat is a bicture of a ham! and I have brought along mit me a nodable abbetite."

"You do me great honour, Mr. Handel," said the host. "I take this early visit as a great kindness. It is ten minutes past nine. Shall we wait more for Dr. Arne?"

"Let us give him another five minutes," says Colley Cibber; "he is too great a genius to keep time."

"Let us put it to the vote," says Pepusch, smiling. "Who holds up hands?"

"I will zecond your motion wid all mein heart," says Handel. "I will hold up mein feeble hands for my old friend Gustos" (Arne's name was Augustine), "for I know not who I would wait for over and above mein old rival, Master Dom" (meaning Thomas Pepusch); "only, by your bermission, I vill take a snag of your ham and a slice of French roll, or a modicum of chicken; for, to dell you the honest fact, I am all but famished, for I laid me down on my billow in bed the last night mitout mein supper, at the instance of mein physician, for which I am not altogether inglined to extend mein fast no longer." At this moment Arne's footstep being heard outside—"Bresto! be quick!" roared Handel, "fifteen minutes of dime is bretty well for an *ad libitum.*"

Arne enters, a chair is placed, and they soon fall to. "So, sir, I presume you are come to witness the trial of skill at the old round church? I understand that the amateurs expect a pretty round contest," said Arne.

"Gontest!" echoed Handel, laying down his knife and fork; "no doubt; your amateurs have a passion for gontest. Not what it was in our remembrance. Hey, mein friend? Ha, ha, ha!"

"No, sir; I am happy to say those days of envy,

bickering, and party feeling are gone and past. To be sure, we had enough of such disgraceful warfare. It lasted too long."

"Why, yes, it tid last too long. It bereft me of my poor limbs; it tid bereave me of that vot is de most blessed gift of Him vat made us, and not we ourselves" (in allusion to the paralysis and mental alienation of 1737). "And for vat? Vy, for nodings in the world bote the bleasure and bastime of them who, having no wit, nor no want, set at loggerheads men as live by their wits, to worry and destroy von anodere as wild beasts in the Golloseum in the dimes of the Romans."

"I hope, sir," said Dr. Pepusch, who had evidently been sitting on thorns, "you do not include me among those who did injustice to your talents?"

"Nod at all, nod at all; God forbid! I am a great admirer of the airs of the *Peggars' Obera*, and every professional gentleman must do his best for to live. Put why play the Peggar yourself, Toctor, and adapt old ballad humstrum, ven, as a man of science, you could gompose original airs of your own? Here is mein vriend, Gustus Arne, who has made a road for himself for to drive along his own genius to the Demple of Fame." Then, turning to our illustrious Arne, "Mein vriend, you and I must meet togedere sometimes before it is long, and hold a tede-a-tede of old days vat is gone. Oh! it is gomical, now dat it is all gone by. Do not you remember as it was almost only of yesterday dat she-devil Cuzzoni and dat odere precious daughter of iniquity, Beelzepup's spoilt child, the bretty-faced Faustine? Oh, the mad rage vat I have to answer for! vat with von and the other of these fine ladies' airs and graces! Again, do you not remember dat upstart buppy, Senesino, and de goxcomb, Farinelli? Next, again, mein somedime notable rival, Master Bononcini and old Borbora? All at var mit me, and all at var mit demselves; such a gonfusion of rivalships, and double-facedness, and hypogrisy, and malice, vot would make a gomical subject for a boem in rhymes, or a biece for the stage, as I hopes to be saved!" *

In 1751, whilst composing *Jephtha*, Handel was attacked with that peculiar blindness produced by *gutta serena*. Between January and August this, his last oratorio, was nevertheless completed; again and again with indomitable ardour he seized his pen, and in the growing dimness traced the last choruses with his own hand. The same year the *Messiah* was twice performed for the Foundling Hospital, Handel presiding at the organ.

In 1752 he was couched for the third and last time, and at first he was tempted to believe that his sight was returning; but the darkness soon settled down upon him, and towards the close of the year he became quite blind.

Beethoven standing deaf in the middle of his

* A clever fiction quoted by V. Schœlcher from *Somerset House Gazette*, 1823.

orchestra; Handel turning his sightless eyes towards the sun; it is not easy to think upon either without emotion. The great master presided at the organ to the last, but it is said that he could never hear the pathetic air allotted to blind Samson, in the oratorio of that name, without being visibly affected; we quote Milton's well-known lines in preference to the garbled version in the libretto of Samson:—

> "O dark, dark, dark, amid the blaze of noon,
> Irrecoverably dark, total eclipse
> Without all hope of day!
> O first created Beam, and thou great Word,
> 'Let there be light,' and light was over all;
> Why am I thus bereaved thy prime decree?
> The sun to me is dark . . . . ."

When Handel became conscious that his blindness was incurable, he was perfectly resigned, and seemed to know that his end was not far off. With the exception of "Zion now her head shall raise," and "Tune your harps," dictated to Smith for the *Judas Maccabæus*, and some portion of the *Triumph of Time* (1757), he almost ceased to compose, but not to play; and he was as active as ever in organizing the performances of his oratorios. The last years of his life were also the most lucrative. He often drove home at night in a coach quite heavy with bags of silver and gold. But the bags of silver and gold were not unfrequently transferred to some charitable institution. Sometimes it was the Society for Poor Musicians, at others the Sons of the Clergy, and very often the Foundling Hospital.

His friends noticed that after his blindness, instead of becoming soured, impatient, or irritable, he grew gentle and subdued. He desired now to be at peace with all men, showed himself more than ever anxious to assist poor and suffering people by the performance of his music, and looked forward to his departure without anxiety or dismay. Latterly his thoughts constantly turned upon the subject, and he was heard to express a wish that "he might breathe his last on Good Friday; in hopes," he said, "of meeting his good God, his sweet Lord and Saviour, on the day of his resurrection."

On the 6th of April, 1759, at Covent Garden, Handel, being in his seventy-fifth year, conducted the oratorio of the *Messiah* for the last time. The same night he was seized with a deadly faintness, and, calling for his will whilst in the full possession of his reason, he added a codicil. On Good Friday, April 13th, it being the anniversary of the first performance of the *Messiah*, the *Public Advertiser* has this short announcement:—"Yesterday morning died G. F. Handel, Esq." This is, according to Schœlcher, incorrect; and he proceeds to affirm on the alleged testimony of Dr. Warren, the physician who attended him, that Handel died late on Good Friday night. The question is exhausted in Husk's Preface to the Handel Festival of 1868, from which it appears that the 14th is after all the right date. He had always longed to rest in the old Abbey amongst the people who had made room for him in their homes and hearts.

We have all read the simple inscription beneath his monument:—

GEORGE FREDERIC HANDEL, Esquire,

BORN FEBRUARY XXIII. MDCLXXXIV.

DIED ON GOOD FRIDAY, APRIL XIV. MDCCLIX.

GLUCK.

Born 1714, Died 1787.

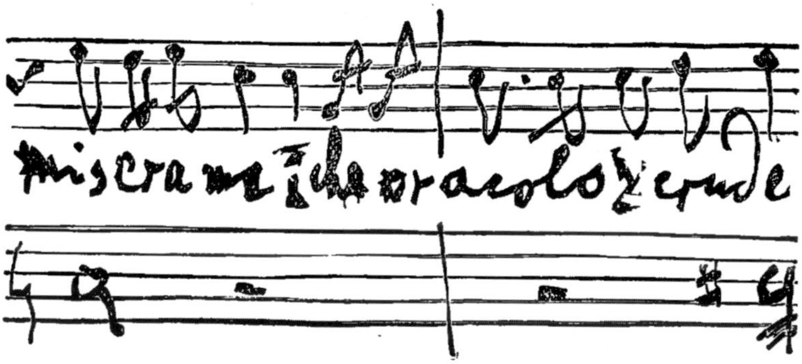

III.

I SHALL now proceed to notice in succession two men who exercised a vast influence over the course and progress of modern music in the eighteenth century—GLUCK and HAYDN: Gluck, if not the founder of the modern opera, certainly the founder of the German opera; Haydn, if not the founder of the modern orchestra, certainly the founder of the modern quartet and symphony.

As we turn over the well-known batch of letters, recently translated by Lady Wallace, the ghost of Christoph Gluck looks out from the pages, and gradually assumes more and more the semblance of flesh and blood. His portrait, finely painted by Duplessis, and of which a miserable travestie is affixed to the above-named volume, explains the man and many of his abrupt and exultant utterances: he is looking straight out of the canvas with wide and eager eyes,—his nostril a little distended, as of one eager to reply,—his mouth shut, but evidently on the point of hastily opening. The noble brow and pronounced temples carry off the large development of the cheek-bone, and slightly heavy, though firm and expressive nose. The attitude is one of noble and expectant repose, but has in it all the suggestion of resolute and even fiery action. "Madame," said he, drawing himself up to his full height, and addressing Marie Antoinette, then Dauphiness, who inquired after his opera of *Armida*, "Madame, il est bientôt fini, et vraiment ce sera superbe!"

These words might be written at the foot of Duplessis' picture; they evidently express one of Gluck's most characteristic moods. His life seems to have been illumined and buoyed up by the indomitable sense of his own power. He exults in his music: like a giant refreshed with wine, he rejoices in his strength. A wretched French writer has lately mistaken this for vanity. It is the vanity of the eagle as he wheels above the horde of small birds, and rejoices to be alone with the sun. "I have written," he says, "the music of my *Armida* in a manner which will prevent its soon growing old." If ordinary men are permitted to be conscious of life, why should we grudge to genius the consciousness of its own immortality?

Christoph Willibald Ritter von Gluck was the son of a gamekeeper in the service of Prince Lobkowitz, and was born at Weidenwang, in the Upper Palatinate, on July 2, 1714. The shadow of Italy still lay far and wide over the fields of German music. Bach and Handel, it is true, had created a national school of sacred music; but then, and long afterwards, Italy was popular with the masses. Handel, in common with Gluck, and even Mozart in his early days, wrote operas for the people in the Italian style.

Orchestral music, as such, was not as yet in high repute. Indeed, the orchestra was usually eked out with a harpsichord, and the conductor alternately strummed away on the keys and beat time on the back of his instrument to a few violins, basses, a flute, a drum, oboes, and trumpets.

Cabinet instrumental music had only reached as far as trios; and although Corelli and Hasse were both a good deal played in Germany, yet, until the string quartet came into fashion, the combination most favourable to the progress of cabinet music was wanting.

Choir singing and organ-playing were far more advanced, and it was to this department that Gluck, in common with most other young musicians, had to look for a maintenance. From the first, the musical training of Gluck was happily varied and comprehensive. At the age of eighteen he emerged from the Jesuit college of Kommotau, where he had received a good education, and been taught to sing, and to play the organ, the violin, and the harpsichord. Prague was at that time famous for musical discernment; and its connoisseurs, who a few years later rejoiced in the title of Mozart's favourite public, were the first to recognise and to support Gluck. But they supported him as they supported dozens of others. They only saw in him an excellent violin-player, a steady chorister, and a fair organist, in all which capacities he figured at the Polish convent of St. Agnes. Probably there was nothing more to see. He was groping about in the dark himself, and had not even begun to break into the track of his future glory. In 1736, after giving a few concerts in the neighbourhood, he decided upon finishing his musical education at Vienna under the guidance of such masters as Caldara, Fux, and the brothers Conti. Up to this time the attention of Gluck had been impartially divided between Italian and German influences; but Prince Lobkowitz, who remembered his old gamekeeper, and took a kindly interest in his son, introduced Christoph to the Italian Prince, Melzi, whose usual residence was at Milan; and when that nobleman went back, Gluck was easily prevailed upon to accompany him to Italy. He soon became the devoted pupil of the well-known Italian composer and organist, Sammartini. The first age, even of genius, is more imitative and receptive than original or independent, and Gluck began to pour forth Italian operas to Italian audiences. In four years he had produced eight, every one of which may safely be forgotten. They were all successful, and success then, as now, proved a ready passport. What was good enough for Italy was good enough for London, and to London was Gluck, now aged twenty-two, summoned by the managers of the Haymarket theatre.

Here he fell in with Handel, who, after listening to one of his operas, the *Caduta di Giganti*, merely observed that the author knew no more of counterpoint than his cook. This may have been true enough, but the remark was hardly appreciative. Great men do not always look at genius with prophetic eyes. Weber failed to see the merits of Schubert. Goethe, sixty of whose songs he set to music, took no notice of him. Spohr never fairly appreciated Mendelssohn. We must not wonder if the author of the *Messiah* failed to see, in such feeble glimmer of transalpine melody as may be found in the *Artamene*, the rising sun of *Orpheus and Eurydice*.

Thus it was from Handel, no unfitting Mentor, that Gluck received the first blow which led to his happy disenchantment with the Italian opera. There must be something wrong; henceforth he would not go on composing opera after opera on the same model. Perhaps the model itself might be a wrong one. What was the model? A story, told as much as possible by a series of songs; dramatic declamation in recitative much neglected; orchestral accompaniment still more so; and, worst of all, the character and the style of the song music itself not necessarily in keeping with the words. Any taking tune seems to have done for almost any words; a little scraping and strumming by way of accompaniments, which nobody was supposed to attend to, and *l'opéra, le voilà!*

The discovery of these defects, now so patent to all the world, was the second and last blow which ruined the credit of Italy with Gluck, and it happened on this wise. His operas had hitherto not pleased in England. He now determined to please. *Pyramus and Thisbe* was to be the triumph. He chose the best bits out of all his most successful operas, and this *omnium gatherum* was to be the music of *Pyramus and Thisbe.* The opera was a miserable failure. The experiment was too glaring, although it was after all nothing but a *reductio ad absurdum* of the Italian method.

Gluck perceived henceforth the necessity for a more exact and rigid correspondence between the drama and the music. It never occurred to him to abandon the form of opera altogether as a form of art which was false, because it used music to express not only the emotion which accompanies action, but action itself; but he thought, and thought rightly, that the opera might be improved philosophically, by at least making the music always express emotions in harmony with the dramatic action, instead of any emotion in connection with any action.

Shortly afterwards, passing through Paris, Gluck heard for the first time the French operas of Rameau; he received a new element, and one sadly wanting to the Italian opera,—the dramatic declamation of recitative. This was the one element that France contributed to the formation of the opera as now existing. We observe, therefore, three sources from which this composer derived the elements of his own system. His early training in Italy determined the importance which he ever afterwards attached to pure melody. His subsequent acquaintance with France taught him the value of dramatic declamation. Germany gave him harmony, a more careful study of the orchestra, and that philosophical spirit which enabled him to lay the foundation of the distinctive German opera.

We have often expressed an opinion that opera is a defective form of art. That music can only represent the emotions of a drama, and not its incidents, is a truth enunciated alike by Gluck the first, and Richard Wagner the latest, of the German opera writers. Gluck writes, "My purpose was to restrict music to its true office, that of ministering to the *expression* of the poetry without interrupting the action."

Wagner, in extolling legendary subjects as best fitted for the opera, observes that "music does not stop at the exterior incidents, but expresses the underlying emotion." Yet neither of these writers seems to perceive that his admission is fatal to the very existence of the opera. We may fairly ask Gluck,

"Must not music, when sung by the person acting, always interrupt the spontaneity of the action?" And we may say to Wagner, "The music at the opera, in so far as it is acted, loses its power of expressing the emotion of an action by becoming itself the action," or, as he says, "stopping at the exterior incident." The sun is distinct from the planets which it illumines. The sphere of musical emotion is equally distinct from that of dramatic action. The two spheres may have important mutual relations, but they must not be confounded.

A situation *can* be expressed by action and language; the emotion of the situation *can* be expressed by music; but music *cannot* express a situation, and we must not try to make it do so by making the actor sing. People do *not* go about the world singing incidents; people do *not* wail out melodious strains in the midst of consumptive agonies.

But it may be asked, in reply to these remarks, "If the opera is a false form of art, because men do not sing off, as they do on, the stage, is not the whole drama false in art, since men do not speak and act off, as they do on, the stage?" No. The drama is not false in art, because words and actions are fitted to express situations, do actually enter into all situations; it is for the dramatist to represent and combine them in the most forcible and natural manner which the necessary limits of his art will allow. Even in the case of soliloquy no radical violence is done to nature, since people do really sometimes think aloud: besides, it is universally admitted that language and action are the fit exponents of thought and incident, whilst it must not be for a moment conceded that music can express definite thoughts or incidents, but only the emotions which accompany these. The fallacy that music expresses incidents or any definite thought whatever lies at the root of all the nonsense that is talked about this tune meaning the sea, and the moon, Vesuvius, or the scarlet fever.

Nor, to return to the drama, is undue violence done to the mind by years being supposed to have elapsed between the acts of a play, as it is not attempted in any way to represent the passage of those years before the public. That is left to the imagination, and no exception can be taken to the representation of that which is not represented. In *Macbeth*, as produced some time ago by Mr. Phelps, no man could take exception to the manner in which the ghost of Banquo was represented, because the ghost never appeared at all. It was left to the imagination of the audience. The dramatist leaves the years to the imagination of the audience. If they do not conceive them aright, it is no business of his.

We submit, then, that the drama and the opera have separate foundations, or rather, the one has a foundation which the other lacks. It is perfectly fair in all forms of art to leave to the imagination what cannot be expressed, but it is perfectly false in any form of art to try and make a power—like music, for instance—express what it is incapable of expressing.

But it is time to return to Gluck. Disconcerted by the failure of *Pyramus and Thisbe,* perhaps with Handel's music fresh in his mind, and strongly impressed with the importance of copious recitative and plenty of declamation, after the manner of the French, he entered upon his transition period. From *Telemacco* (1750) to *Il Rè Pastore,* produced at Vienna, 1756, we may notice a continuous development in the direction of the new German opera style. Between 1756 and 1762 he appears, like a man struggling with the apprehension of new ideas, to have tried various experiments. We cannot regard his comic operas as anything but tentative; they bear witness more to his versatile activity than to his judgment. The *Pilgrims of Mecca* might indeed have established the fame of a lesser composer, but it is little better than waste from the author of *Orpheus and Eurydice.*

The time now drew nigh for that fortunate conjunction of circumstances upon which genius itself is obliged to wait. In 1762 Gluck at last met the man capable of understanding him, and of producing a libretto after his own heart. This man was Calzabigi, the writer of *Orpheus and Eurydice, Alceste,* and other librettos belonging to Gluck's finest period. The *Orpheus* and *Alceste* were produced at Vienna with that amount of success which the author's name could by this time command. But Gluck, with his strong feeling for dramatic declamation, was dissatisfied with the German actors and with the German stage, and turned his eyes toward Paris. His overtures were gladly met by the directors of the French opera, and the event proved their discernment.

The success of Gluck at Paris has to be accounted for. Although Paris has generally admitted the results of German music, as it has in due time appropriated the results of German philosophy, it has seldom been forward to acknowledge any new development of either. German composers have usually found themselves specially miserable in Paris; Mozart, Beethoven, Schumann, Wagner, have each in their day been snuffed out by the Parisian public, and only enjoyed a tardy recognition when it could no longer be withheld. Yet both Gluck and Haydn were from the first *fêted* and admired by at least important sections of the French musical world.

How can this be explained in the case of Gluck? We must remember, in the first place, that Gluck hoisted no opposition flag. Of the deep lines which have been since drawn, and rightly drawn, between German, Italian, and French music, hardly a trace at this time existed.

Modern music was not sufficiently developed for each nation to appropriate its own speciality; and what existed of music was cosmopolitan rather than national. So little conscious was Gluck of founding a school, that he writes innocently to his old pupil, Marie Antoinette:—

"It has been no pretension of mine, though some have reproached me with it, to come here to give lessons to the French in their own language. I thought that I might attempt with French words the new style of music that I have adopted in my three last *Italian* (*s c*) operas. I see with satisfaction that the language of nature is the universal language."

Hence we observe that he had the singular good fortune of entering Paris under the auspices of the Dauphiness Marie Antoinette, and without a thought of rivalry, but simply with the *naïve* intention of improving the French music; and this pacific garb, no doubt, greatly conduced to his courteous reception.

The political revolution was also favourable to a revolution in art. The old fabric of the French monarchy was ready to crumble. The Encyclopædists had set up a ferment of new ideas throughout the country, which not only pointed to an abuse, but had a remedy to propose. The signs of the times were not hard to read, yet no one seemed to read them. There was something in the very air which told of imminent change. None escaped the subtle influence. The doomed palace itself was full of it. And the courtiers, in listening to Rousseau's *Devin du Village*, in admiring a return to nature, in craving for ideals as far as possible removed from the effete civilization of their own age and country, in applauding the classical but revolutionary operas of Gluck, were like children playing with the sparks that were destined presently to burn the house down.

Meanwhile Gluck had it all his own way. Armed with a French libretto by Du Rollet, protected by the mantle of royalty, and filled unconsciously, like so many others, with the revolutionary spirit, he produced his opera of *Iphigenia in Aulis.* The orchestra, as orchestras will, tittered over his scores, and grumbled at the instrumentation, but ended by playing them, and playing them well. The audience, as audiences will, acted philosopher on the first night, but applauded vigorously on the second. The Abbé Arnault, a great leader of taste, is said to have exclaimed, "With such music one might found a new religion." The orchestral effects of the *Iphigenia* were found somewhat difficult to understand at times, but deemed vastly learned by the connoisseurs; whilst the apostrophe sung by Agamemnon to the Creator of Light, as also the celebrated phrase, "I hear within my breast the cry of nature," were considered quite sublime by the general public.

It was the midsummer of 1774. The Parisians, then as now, were in the habit of flying from the white heat of the city to the cool retreats of their suburban villas, but the opera-house still continued to be crammed nightly. Gluck was called the Hercules of music. Admirers dogged his footsteps in the streets. His appearance at public assemblies was the sign for loud acclamations. And a few privileged ones were admitted to the rehearsal of his new opera *Alceste,* to see him conduct in his night-cap and dressing-gown.

But the enemy was not far off. The musicians who had grumbled at his scores, the old school who had been shocked, and the second-rate composers who had been shelved, were only biding their time to organize an open attack. The Italian Piccini was pitted against Gluck. There were powerful leaders on both sides, and the chances at one time seemed about equal. Marie Antoinette (Gluckist) was influential, but so was Madame du Barri (Piccinist), the king's mistress; l'Abbé Arnault (Gluckist) was sarcastic, but Marmontel (Piccinist) was witty; Du Rollet was diplomatic, but La Harpe was eloquent; and the storm burst thus upon the unsuspecting Gluck. During his absence from Paris, he learned that Piccini had been commissioned to compose music for the same opera (*Roland*) upon which he himself was engaged. Gluck tore up his unfinished score in a rage, and declared open war upon the Italian school. The boards of the opera became the scene of hot contentions, and the rival partisans abused and bullied each other like schoolboys. "I know some one," says Gluck, "who will give dinners and suppers to three-fourths of Paris, to gain proselytes for M. Piccini. Marmontel, who tells stories so well, will tell one more to explain to the whole kingdom the exclusive merits of M. Piccini." "The famous Gluck," wrote La Harpe, "may puff his own compositions, but he cannot prevent them from boring us to death." And the wags of Paris, who looked on and thought of the difference between tweedle-dum and tweedle-dee, named the street in which Gluck lived, "Rue du Grand Hurleur," whilst Piccini's and Marmontel's *quartiers* were nicknamed respectively, "Rue des Petits Chants" and "Rue des Mauvaises Paroles." But pleasant and exciting as all this must have been, it had its inconveniences. Piccini was very well, but Paris could not afford to lose Gluck, and Gluck declined at first to compose as Piccini's rival. At this crisis, a bright idea occurred to Berton, the new opera director: could not the rival *maestros* be induced to compose an opera jointly? He asked them both to dinner, and *inter pocula* all seemed to go well. But it was only the convivial lull that was to precede a post-prandial storm. It was arranged that each should compose an opera of his own on the subject of Iphigenia in Tauris. In 1779 Gluck produced his second *Iphigenia* first, and Piccini was so conscious of its superior excellence, that he shut his own opera up in a portfolio, which was not opened until two years later, when the Italian *Iphegenia* was brought out, and fell quite flat. *Væ victis!* The Italian school seemed fairly vanquished; but even now Fortune was turning her capricious wheel. Four months afterwards Gluck produced his *Echo and Narcissus*, which, to the consternation of the Gluckists, fell as flat as Piccini's *Iphigenia*.

He was offered many consolations, and Marie Antoinette besought him eagerly to stay and retrieve the position which seemed for the moment lost; but he was getting old and fretful; all his life long he had been the spoilt child of Fortune, and he was less able than most men to bear any reverses. He had amassed considerable wealth, and in 1780 left Paris for Vienna; but he does not appear to have been happy in his old age. Nervous maladies, long kept off by dint of sheer excitement and incessant labour, seemed now to grow upon him rapidly. He had always been fond of wine, but at a time when his system was least able to bear it, he began to substitute brandy. The very thought of action after his recent failure in Paris filled him with disgust. He did nothing, but his inactivity was not repose, and the fire which had been a shining light for so many years, now in its smouldering embers seemed to waste and consume him inwardly. His wife, who was ever on the watch, succeeded in keeping stimulants away from the poor old man for weeks together; but one day a friend came to dine. After dinner, coffee was handed round, and liqueurs were placed upon the table. The temptation was too strong. Gluck seized the bottle of brandy, and before his wife could stop him he had drained its contents. That night he fell down in a fit of apoplexy, and he died November 25th, 1787, aged seventy-three.

Gluck has been hardly handled by his French critics. To be a successful German musician in France is no doubt a crime; a hot temper is perhaps another; but when we read that Gluck was consumedly vain, full of a malevolent egotism, that he seized every occasion to injure his rivals, that he was the enemy of rising or foreign merit, that he tried to stifle Mozart and to sneer down Piccini, we require an explanation. Some of us may be consoled by the reflection that these assertions—coming from M. Felix Clement, whose book is more distinguished for bulk than benevolence, for screams and commonplaces than for criticism or candour—are unfounded.

The vanity of Gluck consisted in the consciousness of his own superiority. His malevolent egotism was merely the ebullition of a hasty temper stung into self-assertion by detraction and abuse. When party spirit ran so high at Paris between Gluckists and Piccinists, without imputing to either malevolent egotism, we might expect to find the rivals themselves not always calm and measured in their language. But, in truth, Gluck was a single-minded man, devoted to music and generous to other musicians. In his sixty-fourth year he writes, not to his own supporters, but to "the friends of music in Paris"—Paris, the stormy scene of his first contentions with the Italian factions; Paris, the witness of his early triumphs, and his late discomfiture; Paris, the place where he is said to have shown nothing but malevolent egotism:—

"M. Gluck is very sensible of the politeness of Messieurs les amateurs and M. Cambini. He has the honour to assure these gentlemen that it will give him much pleasure to hear the performance of M. Cambini's scene from *Armida* [the subject of one of his own operas]. It would be indeed tyranny in music to seek to prevent authors from bringing forward their productions. M. Gluck enters into rivalry with no one, and it will always give him pleasure to listen to music better than his own. The progress of art ought alone to be considered."

An old broken-down man, he sat in a box and applauded the young Mozart's new symphonies. He extolled Mozart's music in Viennese circles, and asked him and his wife to dinner; and Mozart speaks of him everywhere in his letters in terms of reverence and affection. It is said that he was fond of money, and he was, no doubt, in his later years unhappily addicted to wine; but his purse-strings were often loosed for the needy, and many of his detractors were fed at his hospitable board. Under trying circumstances, he always maintained the dignity and independence of his art; and the favourite of princes and courtiers, he knew how to enlist sympathy without truckling to power.

M. Felix Clement is facetious on the subject of the intemperance which marked the failing years of a man whose nerves had been shattered by hard work and the excitement inseparable from his vocation. We prefer to recall one who, in the midst of an immoral court, remained comparatively pure, and who, in an age of flippant atheism, retained to the last his trust in God and his reverence for religion.

HAYDN.

Born 1732, Died 1809.

IV.

GLUCK and Haydn worked parallel to each other. We are not aware that they ever met. Both carried out great reforms—Gluck in the sphere of opera, Haydn in symphonic and instrumental music. Both were adored in foreign countries—whilst Gluck was known in England and worshipped in France, Haydn was known in France and worshipped in England. Both, however, were recognised and admired in Germany; both were generous in their recognition of others; both were the friends of Mozart; both knew how to be popular with princes without forfeiting the respect of equals; both could compose for the people without pandering to what was vicious or ignorant in their tastes; both began as "poor devils" (to use Haydn's phrase), and lived to enjoy an easy competence; and both descended to the grave, after long, laborious lives, heavy with years and honours,—Gluck dying, 1787, at the age of seventy-three; Haydn, 1809, at seventy-seven.

We may thus draw an outward parallel between the founder of the German opera and the inventor of the German symphony; but the parallel belongs more to the career than to the character, to the work than to the person, of the composers. As we turn from that eager, restless, ambitious face by Duplessis, to the placid, easy-going, and contented profile by Dance, the contrast between Chevalier Gluck and "Papa Haydn," as Mozart loved to call him, is complete.

The face of Haydn is remarkable quite as much for what it does not as for what it does express. No ambition, no avarice, no impatience, very little excitability, no malice. On the other hand, it indicates a placid flow of even health, an exceeding good-humour, combined with a vivacity which seems to say, "I must lose my temper sometimes, but I cannot lose it for long;" a geniality which it took much to disturb, and a digestion which it took more to impair; a power of work steady and uninterrupted; a healthy devotional feeling; a strong sense of humour; a capacity for the enjoyment of all the world's good things, without any morbid craving for irregular indulgence; affections warm, but not intense; a presence accepted and beloved; a mind contented almost anywhere, attaching supreme importance to one, and one thing only—the composing of music—and pursuing this object with the steady instinct of one who believed himself to have come into the world for this purpose alone;—such was Francis-Joseph Haydn, born on the 31st of March, 1732, at Rohrau, a little village about thirty miles from Vienna, on the confines of Austria and Hungary.

The father, Matthias Haydn, coachmaker and parish clerk, had married a domestic servant, in the household of one Count Harrach. He was fond of the harp, and after the day's work he delighted to sing and play whilst Frau Haydn sat busily knitting, and joined in occasionally, after the manner of German Fraus. Joseph, when about five years old, began to assist on these occasions with two pieces of stick, grinding away in perfect time, like any real fiddler. These wooden performances were not thrown away, for one day a Hamburg schoolmaster named Franck happened to see the child thus earnestly employed, and ascertaining that he had a good voice, took him off to Hamburg, and promised to educate him, to the great delight of the honest coachmaker.

Franck seems to have taught him well, although he

knocked him about a good deal; but the boy was a merry and industrious little fellow, and did not mind, providing he was allowed to transfer the blows in play-hours to a big drum, on which he practised incessantly. When he was about nine years old, Reuter, the *Capellmeister* of St. Stephen's, Vienna, happened to be dining with Franck, and Joseph was produced as a musical prodigy. Franck had taught him to sing, and all that his master knew, he could do. At the close of his song the delighted Reuter cried "Bravo! But, my little man, how is it you cannot shake?" "How can you expect me to shake when Herr Franck himself cannot?" replied the *enfant terrible*. "Come here, then;" and drawing the child to him, he showed him how to manage his breath, and then make the necessary vibrations in his throat once or twice, and the boy caught the trick and began shaking like a practised singer. The *Capellmeister* had found a new star for his cathedral choir, and Haydn was carried off in triumph to Vienna. Here he gained instruction in singing, and an acquaintance with sacred music; but it was no part of Reuter's plan to teach him the theory of music. At the age of thirteen he tried to compose a mass, at which his master merely laughed; indeed, Haydn was wholly uninstructed in composition, and no doubt the mass was poor stuff. But genius was not to be daunted; money was hoarded up, the "Gradus ad Parnassum" and the "Parfait Maître de Chapelle," by Mattheson, were purchased, and with these two dull and verbose dampers to enthusiasm the lad set to work to discover the science of harmony. We have no means of knowing what progress he made; we only know that he worked away for eight years. At the end of that time his voice broke, and he was turned away by Reuter on quite a frivolous pretext. Some say the master was afraid of finding a rival in the pupil, but we think this improbable, as at this time there is no proof that Haydn had arrived at any special excellence in composition, but Reuter was a selfish, and, in Haydn's case, a disappointed man. From the first he had desired to perpetuate, by the usual means, the fine soprano of his pupil, and thus retain him in his service for ever. Happily this project was firmly withstood by the parents; and Reuter, who was no doubt annoyed, kept the boy as long as he could sing; and when his voice broke, not caring to trouble himself with any further connection, picked a quarrel with him, and turned him out. But the chorister's sweet voice was known to many who came to worship at the cathedral of St. Stephen, and when Keller, the barber, heard that Haydn was a homeless wanderer, he came forward and offered him free board and lodging.

In a little upper room, with a little worm-eaten harpsichord, Haydn pursued his studies; and downstairs he dressed and powdered away at the wigs. Unhappily, there was something besides wigs downstairs—there was Anne Keller, the barber's daughter, to whom, in a luckless hour, he promised marriage, and of whom more presently.

By-and-by things began to improve. He played the violin in one church, the organ in another, and got a few pupils. Vienna was not the city to allow a good musician to starve, and Haydn soon found those who could appreciate and help him. He left Keller, took a small attic in a large house, and, as luck would have it, in the state apartments of that very house lived the great *poeta Cesareo,* or, as we should say, poet-laureate of the day—Metastasio. Through the poet Haydn's good fortune began: he introduced him to the Venetian ambassador's mistress, a rare musical enthusiast; and in her circle he met the famous Italian singing-master, Porpora, then a very crusty old gentleman, who appears to have occupied at Vienna the same post of musical dictator and privileged censor which Rossini for so many years held in Paris.

The relations between Haydn and the Porpora were sufficiently amusing. Madame Sand, in "Consuelo," has sketched them in her own incomparable way. Of course Porpora could have nothing to say to so lowly a personage as Joseph Haydn. But he was always meeting him. They even lived in the same house for some time, for they both accompanied the ambassador to the Manensdorf baths for the season. However, Haydn had found his man in the Porpora, and was not slow to take his cue. He wanted instruction: no one in Italy or Germany could give it better than Porpora; so he cleaned Porpora's boots, trimmed his wig to perfection, brushed his coat, ran his errands, and was his very humble and devoted servant. Before such attention as this the old man at last gave way. Haydn became the master's constant companion, disciple, and accompanyist; and the benefits which he derived in return were soon manifested in the increased saleableness of his compositions.

At the age of eighteen Haydn composed his first stringed quartet. It consists of a number of short movements, and does not differ materially from other cabinet music of the period, save in being written for four instruments. Let any one take up the famous eighty-four quartets, and trace the growth of the master's mind, and he will be astonished how slow, and yet how steady, is the development. Nothing hurried—no torch blown by the wind—but a lamp, well guarded from gusts and currents, slowly consuming an abundant supply of oil. It is not till we get past the No. 50's that all traces of the earlier school begin to disappear; the movements become fewer, but longer, and yet quite symphonic in their development, until we break upon such perfect gems as 63; whilst in 77, 78, 81, the master reaches that perfect form and freedom of harmony which is observed in the quartets of Mozart and Beethoven.

As quartets, Haydn's have never been surpassed. Mozart has been more rich, Beethoven more obscure and sublime, Spohr more mellifluous and chromatic, Schubert more diffuse and luxuriant, Mendelssohn more orchestral and passionate: but none have excelled Haydn in completeness of form, in fine perception of the capacities of the four instruments, in delicate distribution of parts to each, and in effects always legitimate—often tender, playful, and pathetic—sometimes even sublime.

At night the young minstrel, accompanied by two friends, used to wander about the streets of Vienna by moonlight, and serenade with trios of his composition his friends and patrons.

One night he happened to stop under the window of Bernardone Curtz, the director of the theatre. Down rushed the director in a state of great excitement.

"Who are you?" he shrieked.

"Joseph Haydn."

"Whose music is it?"

"Mine!"

"The deuce it is! at your age, too!"

"Why, I must begin with something."

"Come along up-stairs."

And the enthusiastic director collared his prize, and was soon deep in explaining the mysteries of a libretto entitled "The Devil on Two Sticks." Haydn must write music for it according to Curtz's directions. It was no easy task; the music was to represent all sorts of things—catastrophes, fiascos, tempests. The tempest brought Haydn to his wits' end, for neither he nor Curtz had ever witnessed a sea-storm.

Haydn sat at the piano banging away in despair: behind him stood the director fuming, and raving, and explaining what he did not understand to Haydn, who did not understand him. At last, in a state of distraction, the pianist, opening wide his arms and raising them aloft, brought down his fists simultaneously on the two extremities of the key-board, and then drawing them rapidly together till they met, made a clean sweep of all the notes.

"Bravo! bravo! that's it—that's the tempest!" cried Curtz; and jumping wildly about, he finally threw his arms round the magician who had called the spirits from the vasty deep, and afterwards paid him one hundred and thirty florins for the music—storm at sea included.

In 1759, at the age of twenty-eight, Haydn composed his first symphony, and thus struck the second key-note of his originality. To have fixed the form of the quartet and the symphony was to lay deep the foundations of all future cabinet and orchestral music. Of the one hundred and eighteen symphonies comparatively few are now played, but probably we have all heard the best. The twelve composed for Salomon in the haste of creative power, but in the full maturity of his genius, are constantly heard side by side with the amazing efforts of Mozart and Beethoven in the same department, and do not suffer by the comparison because they are related to them, as the sweet and simple forms of early Gothic are to the gorgeous flamboyant creations of a later period.

Haydn's last symphonies stand related to his earlier ones as the last quartets to the earlier. In both at first the form is struck, but the work is stiff and formal; latterly the outline is the same, but it is filled in with perfect grace and freedom. There is Mozart's easy fertility of thought, but not Mozart's luxurious imagination; there is Beethoven's power of laying hold of his subject—indeed, Haydn's grip is quite masterful in the allegros, and the expression of his slow movements is at all times clear and delicious —but the heights and the depths, together with the obscurities of the later master, are absent. Ravished at all times with what was beautiful, sublime, or pathetic in others, he himself lived in a work-a-day world; a world of common smiles and tears; a world of beautiful women and gifted men; of woods, and mountains, and rivers; of fishing and hunting; of genial acclamation, and generous endeavour, simple devotion, and constant, joyous, irreproachable labour and love.

Soon after his first symphony he had the good fortune to attract the attention of a man whose family has since become intimately associated with musical genius in Germany: this was old Prince Esterhazy.

"What! you don't mean to say that little blackamoor" (alluding to Haydn's brown complexion and small stature) "composed that symphony?"

"Surely, prince!" replied the director Friedburg, beckoning to Joseph Haydn, who advanced towards the orchestra.

"Little Moor," says the old gentleman, "you shall enter my service. I am Prince Esterhazy. What's your name?"

"Haydn."

"Ah! I've heard of you. Get along, and dress yourself like a *Capellmeister.* Clap on a new coat, and mind your wig is curled. You're too short; you shall have red heels; but they shall be high, that your stature may correspond with your merit."

We may not approve of the old prince's tone, but in those days musicians were not the confidential advisers of kings, like Herr Wagner; rich bankers' sons, like Meyerbeer; private gentlemen, like Mendelssohn; and members of the Imperial Parliament, like Verdi; but only "poor devils," like Haydn. Let these things be well weighed, and let England remember that as she has had to follow Germany in philosophy and theology, so must she sooner or later in her estimation of the musical profession.

Haydn now went to live at Eisenstadt, in the Esterhazy household, and received a salary of 400 florins. The old prince died a year afterwards, and Haydn continued in the service of his successor, Nicolas Esterhazy, at an increased salary of 700 florins, which was afterwards raised to 1,000 florins per annum. Nothing more uninteresting than the dull routine of a small German court, and nothing less eventful than the life of Haydn between 1760 and 1790 can be imagined. He continued the close friend and companion of Prince Nicolas, and death alone was able to dissolve, after a commerce of thirty years, the fair bond between him and his Mæcenas. Every morning a new composition was laid upon the prince's breakfast-table, generally something for his favourite instrument, the baryton, a kind of violoncello. One hundred and fifty of these pieces, we believe, are extant. His work was regular and uninterrupted, his recreations were calm and healthful, occasional journeys to Vienna, months and months passed at the prince's country seat, mountain rambles, hunting, fishing, open-air concerts, musical evenings, and friendly intercourse, and Haydn lived contented, laborious, and perfectly unambitious.

There was but one cloud in his sky—that was his wife. The promise made to the hair-dresser's daughter in a rash moment was fulfilled in what some may think a moment still more rash. Haydn could have been happy with most women, but there are limits to the endurance of a man, however amiable; and Haydn found those limits exceeded in the person of Anne Keller. His temperament was easy and cheerful; hers difficult and dismal. His religion turned on the love of God; hers on the fear of the devil. Her devotion was excessive, but her piety small; and she passed easily from mass to mischief-making, or from beads to broils. We are told that the tongue is a little fire, but it proved too hot for Haydn. He found that the incessant nagging of a quarrelsome partner was ruining his life-work, and the world has probably long pardoned him for refusing to sacrifice his time and genius to the caprices of a silly and ill-tempered woman. He did what was probably best for both. He gave her a fair trial, and then separated himself from her, making her a liberal allowance; and thus permitting her to enjoy the fruits of his labour, without destroying his peace of mind or robbing the world of his genius.

In the retirement of the prince's family, between 1760 and 1790, an incredible number, and amongst them some of his most famous works, were produced. We may note several of the later quartets, six symphonies written for Paris, and the famous last seven words written for Cadiz.

The labour of thirty years had not been thrown away. Haydn appears to have been very unconscious of the immense reputation which he had been acquiring all through France, Spain, and England, and was probably never more astonished in his life when a stranger burst into his room, only a few days after the death of his beloved patron, Prince Nicolas, and said abruptly—"I am Salomon from London, and am come to carry you off with me; we will strike a bargain to-morrow." There was no bond now sufficiently strong to keep him in Germany. He was getting on in life, although still hale and hearty; and now, at the age of sixty, he prepared to cross the sea on that journey to London so famous in the annals of music. Yet were there dear friends to part from. Dr. Leopold von Genzinger, the prince's physician; and the charming Frau von Genzinger, to whom so many of his letters are addressed, who made him such good tea and coffee, and sent him such excellent cream. Then there were Dittersdorf and Albrechtsberger; and, lastly, Mozart. These would fain have kept him. "Oh, papa!" said Mozart, who had already travelled so much and knew everything, "you have had no education for the wide, wide world, and you speak too few languages." "Oh, my language," replied the papa with a smile, "is understood all over the world."

December 15, 1790, was the day fixed for his departure. Mozart could not tear himself away, nor was he able to repress the tears that rose as he said in words so sadly prophetic—"We shall now doubtless take our last farewell." They dined together indeed for the last time. Both were deeply affected, but neither could have dreamed how very soon one of them, and that the youngest, was to be taken away. A year after we read in Haydn's diary, "Mozart died December 5, 1791." Nothing could exceed Haydn's admiration for Mozart. In 1787 he thus writes:—

"I only wish I could impress upon every friend of music, and on great men in particular, the same deep musical sympathy and profound appreciation which I myself feel for Mozart's inimitable music; then nations would vie with each other to possess such a jewel within their frontiers. It enrages me to think that the unparalleled Mozart is not yet engaged at any imperial court! Forgive my excitement; I love the man so dearly."

His wife must needs write to worry him in England by saying that Mozart had taken to running him down. "I cannot believe it," cried Haydn; "if true, I will forgive him." As late as 1807 the conversation turning one day on Mozart, Haydn burst into tears; but recovering himself—"Forgive me," he said; "I must ever, ever weep at the name of my Mozart."

On his way to England, Haydn was introduced to Beethoven, then twenty. Beethoven actually had a lesson or two from him, and Haydn was exceedingly anxious to claim him as a pupil. Beethoven, upon hearing this many years afterwards, said characteristically and no doubt truly—"Certainly I had a lesson from Haydn, but I was not his pupil; I never learned anything from him."

"By four o'clock we had come twenty-two miles. The large vessel stood out to sea five hours longer, till the tide carried it into the harbour. I remained on deck during the whole passage, in order to gaze my fill at that huge monster, the ocean." Haydn was soon safely but, according to his moderate German notions, expensively housed at 18, Great Pulteney Street, London. He was to give twenty concerts in the year, and receive £50 for each. The novelty of the concerts was to consist in the new symphonies which Haydn was to conduct in person, seated at the piano. His fame had long preceded him, and his reception everywhere delighted him. "I could dine out every day of the week," he writes. At concerts and public meetings his arrival was the sign for enthusiastic applause; and how, in the midst of Lord Mayors' feasts, royal visits, and general starring, he managed to have composed and produced the Salomon Symphonies and countless other works written in London, is a question we cannot attempt to solve.

But Haydn was hundred-handed, and had, moreover, eyes and ears for everything. He tells us how he enjoyed himself at the civic feast in company with William Pitt, the Lord Chancellor, and the Duke of Lids (Leeds). He says, after dinner, the highest nobility—*i.e.* the Lord Mayor and his wife (!)—were seated on a throne. In another room the gentlemen, as usual, drank freely the whole night; and the songs, and the crazy uproar, and smashing of glasses, were very great. The oil-lamps smelt terribly, and the dinner cost £6,000. He went down to stay with the Prince of Wales (George IV.), and Sir Joshua Reynolds painted his portrait. The prince played the violoncello not badly, and charmed Haydn by his affability. "He is the handsomest man on God's earth. He has an extraordinary love for music, and a great deal of feeling; but very little money." From the palace he passed to the laboratory, and was introduced to Dr. Herschel, in whom he was delighted to find an old oboë player. The big telescope astonished him, so did the astronomer. "He often sits out of doors in the most intense cold for five or six hours at a time."

From these and other dissipations Haydn had constantly to hasten back to direct his concerts at the Hanover Square Rooms, and before he left England he produced at the Haymarket the first six symphonies of the twelve composed for Salomon. The public was enthusiastic; but so much orchestral music was both a novelty and a trial; it is even possible that people may have gone to sleep in the middle of some of the adagios. The well-known "Surprise Symphony" is, in that case, Haydn's answer to such culpable inattention. The slow movement, it will be remembered, begins in the most *piano* and unobtrusive manner, and by about the time the audience should be nodding, a sudden explosive *fortissimo*, as Haydn remarked, "makes the ladies jump!" In amateur orchestras it is not unusual for some enthusiast to let off a pistol behind the stage to give tone to the drum, but it has been generally thought unnecessary to paint the lily in this manner.

The evenings at the Haymarket were triumphs that it was not easy to rival. In the public prints we read:—

> "It is truly wonderful what sublime and august thoughts this master weaves into his works. Passages often occur which it is impossible to listen to without becoming excited—we are carried away by admiration, and are forced to applaud with hand and mouth. The Frenchmen here cannot restrain their transports in soft adagios; they will clap their hands in loud applause, and thus mar the effect."

To stem this tide of popularity the Italian faction had recourse to Giardini; and to beat the German on his own ground, his own pupil, Pleyel, was got over to conduct rival concerts. At first Haydn writes, "He behaves himself with great modesty;" but, later, we read, "Pleyel's presumption is everywhere criticized;" yet he adds, "I go to all his concerts and applaud him, for I love him."

Very different were the social amenities which passed between Papa Haydn and the Italian Giardini. "I won't know the German hound!" cries the excited Italian. "I attended his concert at Ranelagh," says Haydn; "he played the fiddle like a hog!"

In a year and a half (July, 1792) Haydn was back at Vienna, conducting his new symphonies, which had not yet been heard in Germany. In 1794 he returned to the large circle of his friends in England, and in the course of another year and a half produced the remaining six symphonies promised to Salomon. In May, 1795, Haydn took his benefit at the Haymarket. He directed the whole of his twelve symphonies, and pocketing 12,000 florins, returned to Germany, August 15, 1795.

The eighteenth century was closing in, dark with storms, and the wave of revolution had burst in all its fury over France, casting its bloody spray upon the surrounding nations. From his little cottage near Vienna, Haydn watched the course of events. Like many other princes of art, he was no politician, but his affection for his country lay deep, and his loyalty to the Emperor Francis was warm; the hymn, "God save the Emperor," so exquisitely treated in the seventy-seventh quartet, remained his favourite melody; it seemed to have acquired a certain sacredness in his eyes in an age when kings were beheaded and their crowns tossed to a rabble. But his own world, the world of art, remained untouched by political convulsions. In 1795 he commenced, and in 1798 he finished the cantata or oratorio called the *Creation*. It very soon went the round of Germany, and passed to England; and it was the *Creation* that the First Consul was hastening to hear at the Opera on the memorable 24th of January, 1801, when he was stopped by an attempt at assassination.

In 1800 Haydn had finished another great work, "The Seasons," founded on Thomson's poem. In 1802 his two last quartets appeared. A third he was forced to leave unfinished; in it he introduced a phrase which latterly he was fond of writing on his visiting card:—

> "Hin ist alle meine Kraft,
> Alt und schwach bin ich!"

He was now seventy years old, and seldom left his room. On summer days he would linger in the garden. Friends came to see him, and found him often in a profound melancholy. He tells us, however, that God frequently revived his courage; indeed, his whole life is marked by a touching and simple faith, which did not forsake him in his old age. He considered his art a religious thing, and constantly wrote at the beginning of his works, "In nomine Domini," or "Soli Deo gloria;" and at the end, "Laus Deo."

In 1809 Vienna was bombarded by the French. A round-shot fell into his garden. He seemed to be in no alarm, but on May 25 he requested to be led to his piano, and three times over he played the "Hymn to the Emperor," with an emotion that fairly overcame both himself and those who heard him. He was to play no more; and being helped back to his couch, he lay down in extreme exhaustion to wait for the end. Five days afterwards, May 26, 1809, died Francis-Joseph Haydn, aged seventy-seven. He lies buried in the cemetery of Gumpfendorf, Vienna.

The number of Haydn's compositions is nearly estimated at eight hundred, comprising cantatas, symphonies, oratorios, masses, concertos, trios, quartets, sonatas, minuets, &c.; twenty-two operas, of which eight are German, and fourteen Italian. But the great father of symphony is not to be judged by his operas any more than the great father of oratorio.

The world has often been tantalized by the spectacle of genius without industry, or industry without genius, but in Haydn genius and industry were happily married.

> "Ego nec studium sine divite vena
> Nec rude quid possit video ingenium."

In early years he worked sixteen, and sometimes eighteen, hours a day, and latterly never less than five; and the work was not desultory, but very direct. No man had a clearer notion of what he meant to do, and no man carried out his programme more rigidly. He was equal to Schubert in the rich flow of his musical ideas, but superior to him in arrangement and selection. He could be grave and playful; serious, and sometimes sublime, but seldom romantic. In him there is nothing artificial, nothing abnormal; his tenderness is all real, and his gaiety quite natural; nor is the balance of symmetry anywhere sacrificed to passion or to power. The abundance of his ideas never tempted him to neglect the fit elaboration of any. He applied himself without distraction to his thought until it became clear to himself. He would often compose, and then recompose on a given theme, until the perfect expression had been found. We remember, some years ago, one of the finest classical scholars at Cambridge, who was in the habit of making miserable work of his Greek-construing during class-time. Few of his pupils could understand what he was about; to the inexperienced freshman it sounded like the bungling of a schoolboy. The sentence was rendered over and over again, and at the close probably not a word retained its original position. Whilst the novices scribbled and scratched out, the older hands waited calmly for the last perfect form. The process was fatiguing, but amply repaid the toil. Poets have been known to spend days over a line which may afterwards have been destined to sparkle for ever

"On the stretched forefinger of all time."

Like good construing or good poetry, good music demands the most unremitting toil. No doubt the artist attains at length a certain direct and accurate power of expression. We know that many of Turner's pictures were dashed off without an after-touch. Whilst Macaulay's manuscripts are almost illegibly interlined and corrected, many of Walter Scott's novels are written almost without an erasure; but such facility combined with accuracy is, after all, only the work of a mind rendered both facile and accurate by long practice.

Haydn is valuable in the history of art, not only as a brilliant, but also as a complete artist. Perhaps, with the exception of Goethe and Wordsworth, there is no equally remarkable instance of a man who was so permitted to work out all that was in him. His life was a rounded whole. There was no broken light about it; it orbed slowly with a mild, unclouded lustre into a perfect star. Time was gentle with him, and Death was kind, for both waited upon his genius until all was won. Mozart was taken away at an age when new and dazzling effects had not ceased to flash through his brain: at the very moment when his harmonies began to have a prophetic ring of the nineteenth century, it was decreed that he should not see its dawn. Beethoven himself had but just entered upon an unknown "sea whose margin seemed to fade for ever and for ever as he moved;" but good old Haydn had come into port over a calm sea, and after a prosperous voyage. The laurel wreath was this time woven about silver locks; the gathered-in harvest was ripe and golden.

SCHUBERT.

Born 1797, Died 1828.

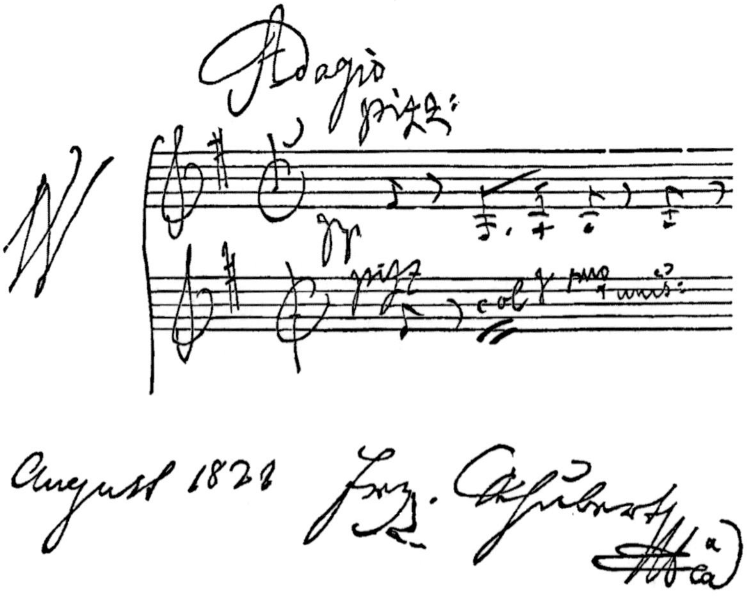

V.

IN passing from the great gods of music to those other delightful tone-poets and singers whose works the world will not willingly let die, we could scarcely find any names more dear to the heart of the true musician than those of FRANZ SCHUBERT and FREDERIC CHOPIN.

Schubert, the prince of lyrists—Chopin, the most romantic of pianoforte writers, Schubert rich with an inexhaustible fancy—Chopin perfect with an exquisite finish, each reaching a supreme excellence in his own department, whilst one narrowly escaped being greatest in all—both occupied intensely with their own meditations, and admitting into them but little of the outer world—both too indifferent to the public taste to become immediately popular, but too remarkable to remain long unknown—both exhibiting in their lives and in their music striking resemblances and still more forcible contrasts—both now so widely admired and beloved in this country—so advanced and novel, that although Schubert has been in his grave for forty-two years and Chopin for twenty-two, yet to us they seem to have died but yesterday—these men partners in the common sufferings of genius, and together crowned with immortality in death, may well claim from us again and again the tribute of memory to their lives, and of homage to their inspiration.

In the parish of Lichtenthal, Vienna, the inhabitants are fond of pointing out a house commonly known by the sign of the "Red Crab," which, in addition to that intelligent and interesting symbol, bears the decoration of a small grey marble tablet, with the inscription—"Franz Schubert's Geburtshaus." On the right hand is a sculptured lyre, on the left, a wreath, with the date of the composer's birth, January 31, 1797.

Franz Schubert was the youngest son of Franz and Elizabeth Schubert; he had eighteen brothers and sisters, few of whom lived very long. His father was a poor schoolmaster, who, having little else to bestow upon his children, took care to give them a good education. "When he was five years old," his father writes, "I prepared him for elementary instruction, and at six I sent him to school; he was always one of the first amongst his fellow-students." As in the case of Mozart and Mendelssohn, the ruling passion was early manifested, and nature seemed to feel that a career so soon to be closed by untimely death must be begun with the tottering steps and early lisp of childhood. From the first, Schubert entered upon music as a prince enters upon his own dominions. What others toiled for he won almost without an effort. Melody flowed from him like perfume from a rose, harmony was the native atmosphere he breathed. Like Handel and Beethoven, he retained no master for long, and soon learned to do without the assistance of any. His father began to teach him music, but found that he had somehow mastered the rudiments for himself. Holzer, the Lichtenthal choir master, took him in hand, but observed that "whenever he wanted to teach him anything, he knew it already;" and some years afterwards Salieri,* who considered himself superior to Mozart, admitted that his pupil Schubert was a born genius, and could do whatever he chose. At the age

* *Salieri*, born 1750, died 1825, now chiefly remembered as the person to whom Beethoven dedicated three sonatas.

of eleven Schubert was a good singer, and also an accomplished violinist; the composing mania soon afterwards set in, and at thirteen his consumption of music paper was something enormous. Overtures, symphonies, quartets, and vocal pieces were always forthcoming, and enjoyed the advantage of being performed every evening at the concerts of the "Convict" * school, where he was now being educated—Schubert regarding this as by far the most important part of the day's work. At times music had to be pursued under difficulties, *Adagios* had to be written between the pauses of grammar and mathematics, and *Prestos* finished off when the master's back was turned. Movements had to be practised, under some discouragements, during the hours of relaxation. "On one occasion," writes a friend, "I represented the audience: there was no fire, and the room was frightfully cold!" At the age of eleven, he had been admitted as chorister into the Imperial choir, then under the direction of Salieri, where he remained until 1813, when his voice broke. There can be no doubt that Salieri, the avowed rival of Mozart, and as narrow and jealous a man as ever lived, was very fond of Schubert, and exercised an important influence over his studies; and yet it would be impossible to conceive of two minds musically less congenial. Salieri was devoted to Italian tradition, and was never even familiar with the German language, although he had lived in Germany for fifty years.

* A sort of free grammar school, where poor students were boarded gratuitously.

Schubert was the apostle of German romanticism, and almost the founder of the German ballad, as distinct from the French and Italian Romance. Schubert thought Beethoven a great composer — Salieri considered him a very much overrated man; Schubert worshipped Mozart, Salieri did not appreciate him. It was evident that persons holding such dissimilar views would not long remain in the relation of master and pupil, and one day, after a bitter dispute over a Mass of Schubert's, out of which Salieri had struck all the passages which savoured of Haydn or Mozart, the recalcitrant pupil refused to have anything more to do with such a man as a teacher. It is pleasing, however, to find that this difference of opinion was not followed by any personal estrangement; and whilst Schubert always remained grateful to Salieri, Salieri watched with affectionate interest the rapid progress of his favourite pupil.

The boyish life of Schubert was not marked by any peculiarities apart from his devotion to music. He was light-hearted, disposed to make the best of his scanty income, a dutiful and obedient son, fond of society, and of all kinds of amusement. We find nothing to account for the lugubrious titles which belong to so many of his early works, and which seem to fall across the spring-time of his life like the prophetic shadows of coming sorrow and disappointment. Between the ages of eleven and sixteen his compositions were "A Complaint," "Hagar's Lament," "The

Parricide," and "A Corpse Fantasia!" He left the "Convict Academy" in his seventeenth year (1813), and returning to his father's house, engaged himself vigorously in the tuition of little boys. The next three years were passed in this delightful occupation, but the continuous stream of his music never ceased, and 1815 is marked as the most prolific year of his life. It witnessed the production of more than a hundred songs, half-a-dozen operas and operettas, several symphonic pieces, church music, chamber music, &c., &c. It is remarkable that at this early period he wrote some of his finest songs, and that whilst many of his larger works at that time, and for some years afterwards, continued to bear a strong resemblance to Mozart, some of these ballads are like no one but himself at his very best. Such are the "Mignon Songs," 1815, and the "Songs from Ossian."

Early in 1816, Schubert produced the most popular of all his works, "The Erl King." It was composed characteristically enough, in the true Schubertian fashion. One afternoon Schubert was alone in the little room allotted to him in his father's house, and happening to take up a volume of Goethe's poems, he read the "Erl King." The rushing sound of the wind and the terrors of the enchanted forest were instantly changed for him into realities. Every line of the poem seemed to flow into strange unearthly music as he read, and seizing a pen, he dashed down the song nearly as it is, in just the time necessary for the mechanical writing.

The song so hastily composed was destined to have a remarkable future. It was sung some years after by Vogl at Vienna, and produced a great sensation. The timid publishers, who had hitherto declined to publish Schubert's compositions, now began to think him a young man of some talent, and Diabelli was induced to engrave and sell the song. Schubert got little enough, but in a few months the publishers made over £80 by it, and have since realized thousands.—A few hours before his death, and when he was quite blind, Jean Paul desired to have it sung to him. Two years before Goethe's death (1830), and two years after Schubert's, Madame Schröder Devrient was passing through Weimar, and sang some songs to the aged poet; amongst them was the "Erl King." Goethe was deeply affected, and taking Schröder's head between both his hands, he kissed her forehead, and added, "A thousand thanks for this grand artistic performance: I heard the composition once before, and it did not please me, but when it is given like this, the whole becomes a living picture!" The startling effect produced by Madame Viardot in this song may still be fresh in the memory of some of our readers.

In 1816, Schubert applied for a small musical appointment at Laibach, under Government. The salary was only £20 a year; but although now a rising young man, and highly recommended by Salieri, he proved unsuccessful. However, he was not destined to struggle much longer with the trials of the pedagogue's vocation, and soon afterwards he consented to take up his abode in the house of his friend Schober. Schubert soon gathered about him a small but congenial circle of friends, and from the very scanty biographical materials before us, we are able to catch some glimpses of them.

Schober was several years his friend's senior, and lived a quiet bachelor life with his widowed mother. He was not especially musical himself, but passionately attached to art in all its forms, and when unable to give, was all the more ready to receive. Schober was a poet, but his great merit will always consist in having recognised and assisted Schubert in the days of his obscurity, and the one poem by which he will be longest remembered, is the poem inscribed on his friend's coffin, beginning,—

> "Der Friede sei mit dir, du engelreine Seele!"
>
> "All bliss be thine, thou pure angelic soul!"

Gahy was a close friend of Schubert's, especially towards the close of his short life. He was a first-rate pianist, and with him Schubert studied Beethoven's symphonies, arranged for four hands, which could then so seldom be heard, besides immense quantities of his own fantasies, marches, and endless pianoforte movements.

At once the most singular and the most intimate of Schubert's friends was Mayrhofer, the poet. Tall and slight, with delicate features and a little sarcastic smile, he came and went, sometimes burning with generous emotions, at others silent and lethargic. He seemed to be swayed by conflicting passions, over which he had no control. He was constantly writing poetry, which Schubert was constantly setting to music. But as time went on, his nervous malady developed itself. He wrote less, and for hours gave himself up to the dreams of confirmed hypochondria. He held a small post under Government. One morning, going into his office as usual, he endeavoured in vain to fix his attention. He soon rose from his desk, and, after a few turns up and down the room, went up to the top of the house. A window on the landing stood wide open—he rushed to it, and sprang from a great height into the street below. He was found quite unconscious, and expired in a few moments.

Schubert could not have got on well without the brothers HÜTTENBRENNER; to the end of his life they fetched and carried for him in the most exemplary manner. They puffed him incessantly, at home and abroad; they bullied his publishers, abused his creditors, carried on much of his correspondence, and not unfrequently paid his debts; they were unwearied in acts of kindness and devotion to him, never frozen by his occasional moroseness—never soured or offended by the brusqueness of his manner. They have still in their possession many of his MSS., every scrap of which they have carefully preserved, with the exception of two of his early operas, which the housemaid unluckily used to light the fires with.

The last and most important of this little *coterie* was

Johann Michael Vogl, born in 1768. He was educated in a monastery, and although he sang for twenty years in the Viennese opera, he never lost his habits of meditation and study, and might often be met with a volume of the New Testament, Marcus Aurelius, or Thomas à Kempis in his hand. Twenty-nine years older than Schubert, and possessed of a certain breadth and nobleness of character in which his friend was somewhat deficient, he very soon acquired a great ascendancy over him. They became fast friends, and Vogl was the first to introduce Schubert to the Viennese public. He could hardly have been more fortunate in his interpreter. Vogl not only possessed a remarkably fine voice, perfect intonation, and true musical feeling, but he was universally respected and admired; and as he had ample means of studying the real spirit of Schubert's songs, so he had frequent opportunities of extending their popularity.

Schubert himself was now about twenty years old. His outward appearance was not prepossessing; he was short, with a slight stoop; his face was puffy, and his hair grizzled; he was fleshy without strength, and pale without delicacy. These unpleasant characteristics did not improve with years. They were partly, no doubt, constitutional, but confirmed by sedentary, perhaps irregular habits; and we are not surprised to find his doctors, some years later, recommending him to take fresh air and exercise. Schubert, though a warm-hearted, was not always a genial friend, and his occasional fits of depression would sometimes pass into sullenness and apathy; but music was a never-failing remedy, and Gahy used to say that, however unsympathizing and cross he might be, playing a duet always seemed to warm him up, so that, towards the close, he became quite a pleasant companion. Hüttenbrenner, it is true, called him a tyrant, because he was in the habit of getting snubbed for his excessive admiration. "The fellow," growled out Schubert, "likes everything I do!" Schubert did not shine in general society. He possessed neither the political sympathies of Beethoven, nor the wide culture of Mendelssohn and Schumann. Almost always the greatest man present, he was frequently the least noticed; and whilst drawing-room plaudits were often freely lavished upon some gifted singer, few thought of thanking the stout, awkward, and silent figure who sat at the piano and accompanied the thrilling melodies which had sprung from his own heart. Only when music was the subject of discussion would he occasionally speak like one who had a right to be heard. At such times his face would seem to lose all that was coarse or repulsive, his eyes would sparkle with the hidden fire of genius, and his voice grow tremulous with emotion.

In 1818, Count Esterhazy, a Hungarian nobleman, with his wife Rosine, and his two daughters, Marie and Caroline, aged respectively fourteen and eleven, passed the winter at Vienna. Schubert, who as a rule refused to give music lessons, was induced in this one instance to waive his objections, and entered this nobleman's house in the capacity of music master. He found the whole family passionately devoted to the art. Marie had a beautiful soprano voice, Caroline and her mother sang contralto, Baron Schönstein took the tenor, and the Count completed the quartet by singing bass. Many of Schubert's most beautiful quartets were written for the Esterhazy family; amongst them, "The Prayer before the Battle," on the words of La Motte Fouqué, and numbers of his songs (such as "Abendlied," "Morgengruss," "Blondel zu Marien," and "Ungeduld") were inspired by the charms of their society, and the scenes which he visited with them.

At the close of the season the family thought of leaving Vienna, but Schubert had become necessary to them, and they could not bear to part with him, so he went back with them to Hungary. Count Esterhazy's estate was situated at the foot of the Styrian Hills, and here it was that Schubert fell in love with the youngest daughter, Caroline Esterhazy. As his affectionate intercourse with the family was never interrupted, we may suppose that Schubert kept his own counsel at first, and was never indiscreet enough to press his suit. The little girl was far too young to be embarrassed by his attentions, and when she grew older, and may have begun to understand the nature of his sentiments, she was still so fond of him and his music that, although she never reciprocated his love, there was no open rupture between them. Caroline played at platonic affection with great success, and afterwards married comfortably. She could, however, sometimes be a little cruel, and once she reproached her lover with never having dedicated anything to her. "What's the use," cried poor Schubert, "when you have already got all!"

Had not art been his real mistress, he would probably have been still more inconsolable. Perhaps no one ever knew what he suffered from this disappointment in early love. Even with his most intimate friends he was always very reserved on these subjects. That he was not insensible to the charms of other women is certain, and in the matter of passing intrigues, he was perhaps neither better nor worse than many other young men. But it is also certain that no time or absence ever changed his feelings towards Caroline Esterhazy, for whom he entertained to the last day of his life the same hopeless and unrequited passion. In Baron Schönstein, the family tenor, he found another powerful and appreciative admirer, and a vocalist second only to Vogl. "Dans les salons," writes Liszt in 1838, "j'entends avec un plaisir très vif, et souvent avec une émotion qui allait jusqu'aux larmes, un amateur, le Baron Schönstein, dire les lieder de Schubert—Schubert, le musicien, le plus poète qui fut jamais!"

Schubert was not a happy man, and as he advanced in life he lost more and more of his natural gaiety and flow of spirits, and at times would even sink into fits of the deepest despondency. He writes to a dear friend in 1824,—

"You are so good and kind that you will forgive me much which others would take ill of me—in a word, I feel myself the most wretched and unhappy being in the world! Imagine a man whose health will never come right again, and who in his despair grows restless and makes things worse,—a man whose brilliant hopes have all come to nought, to whom the happiness of love and friendship offers nothing but sorrow and bitterness, whom the feeling—the inspiring feeling, at least of the beautiful, threatens to abandon for ever, and ask yourself whether such an one must not be miserable? Every night when I go to sleep I hope that I may never wake again, and every morning renews the grief of yesterday; my affairs are going badly—we have never any money."

No doubt Schubert suffered from the exhaustion and relapse which is the torment of all highly sensitive and imaginative temperaments. But his troubles after all were far from imaginary. Step by step life was turning out for him a detailed and irremediable failure. Crossed in early love, he devoted himself the more passionately to art, and with what results? He had, indeed, a small knot of admirers, but to the public at large he was comparatively unknown. He set about fifty of Goethe's songs to music, and sent some of them to the poet, but never got any acknowledgment, nor was it until after his death that Goethe paid him the compliment of a tardy recognition. Although many of his airs were treasured up in the monasteries, when Weber came to Vienna in 1823, he was unacquainted with any of his music, and called him a dolt; and in 1826, when Schubert humbly applied for the place of vice-organist at the Imperial Chapel,

Chapel-master Eybler had never heard of him as a composer, and recommended Weigl, who was accordingly chosen instead. Although the publishers accepted a few of his songs, he constantly saw the works of men like Kalkbrenner and Romberg preferred to his own. Of his two great operas, *Alfonso and Estrella* was practically a failure, *Fierrabras* was neither paid for nor performed. Public singers not unfrequently refused to sing his music, and his last and greatest symphony, the Ninth (see Mr. Grove's appendix to Schubert's life), was pronounced to be too hard for the band, and cast aside. Much of this failure may be attributed, no doubt, to his constant refusal to modify his compositions, or write them down to the public taste. His behaviour towards patrons and publishers was not conciliatory—he was born without the "get on" faculty in him, and was eminently deficient in what a modern preacher has called the "divine quality of tact." In the midst of all these disappointments, although Schubert was never deterred from expressing his opinion, his judgment of his rivals was never embittered or unjust. He was absolutely without malice or envy, and a warm eulogist of Weber and even Rossini, although both of these favourites were flaunting their plumage in the sunshine whilst he was withering in the shade.

In 1824 he revisited the Esterhazys, in Hungary. His little love was now sixteen, but with her dawning womanhood there was no dawn of hope for him. And yet he was not unhappy in her society. His many troubles had made him so accustomed to pain—it was so natural for joy to be bitter, and life to be "mixed with death," "and now," he writes, "I am more capable of finding peace and happiness in myself." All through the bright summer months, far into the autumn, he stayed there. Many must have been the quiet country rambles he enjoyed with this beloved family. Marie seems now to have become his confidante, and from the tender sympathy she gave him, and the care she took of every scrap of his handwriting, we may well believe that a softer feeling than that of mere friendship may have arisen in her breast as they wandered together amongst the Styrian Hills, or listened to the woodland notes which seem to be still ringing through some of his inspired melodies. Gentle hearts!—where are they now?—the honest Count and Rosine—the laughing, affectionate girls—the simple-hearted, the gifted, the neglected Schubert?—not one of them survives, only these memories—like those sad garlands of Immortelles, which are even now from year to year laid upon the tomb of Germany's greatest song-writer.

There remains little more to be told of Schubert's life —yet one scene before the last must not be passed by.

For thirty years Schubert and Beethoven had lived in the same town and had never met. Schubert worshipped at a distance. "Who," he exclaimed, "could hope to do anything after Beethoven?" On their first meeting, Beethoven treated Schubert kindly, but without much appreciation, and contented himself with pointing out to him one or two mistakes in harmony. Being quite deaf, he requested Schubert to write his answers; but the young man's hand shook so from nervousness that he could do and say nothing, and left in the greatest vexation and disappointment. It was only during his last illness that Beethoven learned with surprise that Schubert had composed more than five hundred songs, and from that time till his death he passed many hours over them. His favourites were, "Iphigenia," "The Bounds of Humanity," "Omnipotence," "The Young Nun," "Viola," and "The Miller's Songs." Between the intervals of his suffering he would read them over and over, and was repeatedly heard to exclaim with enthusiasm, "There is, indeed, a divine spark in Schubert. I, too, should have set this to music." But the days of Beethoven were numbered, and in March of the year 1827 he was overtaken by his last illness. Several of his friends, hearing of his dangerous state, came to visit him—amongst them came Schubert, with his friend Hüttenbrenner. Beethoven was lying almost insensible, but as they approached the bed he appeared to rally for a moment—looked fixedly at them, and muttered something unintelligible. Schubert stood gazing at him for some moments in silence, and then suddenly burst into tears and left the room. On the day of the funeral, Schubert and two of his friends were sitting together in a tavern, and after the German fashion, they drank to the soul of the great man whom they had so lately borne to the tomb. It was then proposed to drink to that one of them who should be the first to follow him—and hastily filling up the cup, Schubert drank to himself!

In the following year (1828) he finished his ninth and last great Symphony in C, and produced amongst other works the Quintet in C, the Mass in E flat, and the Sonata No. 10 (Hallé edit.), B flat major. His health had been failing for some time past, but although he now suffered from constant headache and exhaustion, we do not find that he ever relaxed his labours in composition. In the spring, he gave his first and last concert. The programme was composed entirely of his own music. The hall was crowded to overflowing—the enthusiasm of Vienna was at length fairly awakened, and the crown of popularity and success seemed at last within his reach; but the hand which should have grasped it was already growing feeble. He thought of going to the hills in July; but when July came he had not sufficient money. He still looked forward to visiting Hungary in the autumn, but was attacked with fever in September, and expired November 19th, 1828, not having yet completed his thirty-second year.

He lies near Beethoven, in the crowded cemetery of Währing. On the pediment beneath his bust is the following inscription:—

> " 'Music buried here a rich possession,
> and yet fairer hopes.'
> Here lies FRANZ SCHUBERT; born Jan. 31, 1797; died Nov. 19, 1828,
> aged 31 years."

We pass from the composer to his works. Works belonging to the highest order of genius depend upon the rare combination of three distinct qualities,—(1) Invention, (2) Expression, (3) Concentration. Speaking generally, we may say that Beethoven and Mozart possessed all three. Mendelssohn,* the second and third in the highest degree; Schumann,† the first and third; Schubert, the first and second. As fast as his ideas arose they were poured forth on paper. He was like a gardener bewildered with the luxuriant growth springing up around him. He was too rich for himself,—his fancy outgrew his powers of arrangement. Beethoven will often take one dry subject, and by force of mere labour and concentration, kindle it into life and beauty. Schubert will shower a dozen upon you, and hardly stop to elaborate one. His music is more the work of a gifted dreamer, of one carried along irresistibly by the current of his thoughts, than of one who, like Beethoven, worked at his idea until its expression was without a flaw. His thought possesses Schubert—Beethoven labours till he has possessed his thought.

Schubert has left compositions in every style,—

* The *quality*, at once delicate, tender, and sublime, of Mendelssohn's creations is not questioned; but the endless though bewitching repetitions, or inversions of the same phrase, and an identity of form which amounts to more than mere mannerism, compel us to admit that the range of his musical ideas was limited.

† Again, extraordinary powers of expression are not denied to Schumann. He sometimes hits you, like Robert Browning, with the force of a sledge-hammer, but you often feel that, like that poet, he is labouring with some thought for which he can find and for which there is no adequate verbal expression.

operas, church music, symphonies, songs, and unexplored masses of pianoforte music. His operas were uniformly unsuccessful, with the exception of "War in the Household," which is on a very small scale, and has the advantage over all the others of an experienced librettist, Castelli. The truth is that Schubert was probably deficient in the qualities which are necessary to the success of an opera. Besides melody, harmony, facility, and learning, an attention to stage effect, a certain tact of arrangement, and above all things (what Schubert never possessed) the faculty of coming to an end, are necessary. Anything like diffuseness is a fault. A successful opera must have definite points to work up to, and a good crisis. How many Italian operas depend upon three situations, one quartet, and a good murder! And how many of them are worth a page of Schubert's music?

Some of his Masses and Psalms are still unpublished; the few we have had the good fortune to hear possess all the breadth and sweetness of his secular works. The twenty-third Psalm, for women's voices, might be sung by a chorus of angels.

Schubert wrote in all seven complete symphonies. Of these the sixth, in C, is interesting, as showing the transition from the forms of Mozart and Beethoven to true Schubertian. The seventh and last (1828) is a masterpiece, and tastes of nothing but Schubert from beginning to end. Comparisons of merit are usually senseless or unjust, but different qualities are often best observed by the light of contrast. In Schubert's pianoforte music and symphonic writing for strings or full orchestra, we miss the firm grip of Beethoven, the masterful art-weaving completeness of Mendelssohn, the learning of Spohr, or even the pure melodic flow of Mozart;—grip there is, but it is oftener the grip of Phaëton than the calm might of Apollo,—a weaving there is, no doubt, but like the weaving of the Indian loom—beautiful in its very irregularity,—learning there is, and that of the highest order, because instinctive, but how often do we find a neglect of its use in the direction of curtailment or finish!—melodies there are in abundance, but they are frequently so crowded upon each other with a destructive exuberance of fancy, that we fail to trace their musical connection or affinity. In speaking thus, we are dealing of course with characteristics and tendencies, not with invariable qualities. Movements of Schubert might be pointed out as rounded and complete, as connected in thought and perfect in expression, as the highest standard of art could require; but these will be found more often amongst his pianoforte four-hand and vocal music than in his larger works. We must, however, admit that the exceptions to this rule are triumphant ones, and criticism stands disarmed before such works as the Quintet in C, the Sonata in A minor, and the Seventh Symphony.

In describing this symphony, Schumann has not fallen into the shallow mistake of explaining to us the particular thought which the author had in his mind: but whilst admitting that probably he had none, and that the music was open to different interpretations, he neither there nor elsewhere in the mass of his criticism, explains how the same piece of music can mean different things, or why people are so apt to insist upon its meaning something. The fact is, when we say a piece of music is like the sea or the moon, what we really mean is, that it excites in us an emotion like that created by the sea or the moon; but the same music will be the fit expression of any other idea which is calculated to rouse in us the same sort of feeling. As far as music is concerned, it matters not whether your imagination deals with a storm gradually subsiding into calm—passionate sorrow passing into resignation—or silence and night descending upon a battle-field—in each of the above cases the kind of emotion excited is the same, and will find a sort of expression in any one of these different conceptions. In illustration of the number of similar ideas which will produce the same emotion, and of the different ways in which the same emotion will find an utterance, see an article in the *Argosy*, II., by Matthew Browne, —"It has seemed to me that no note of pain, shriek of agony or shout of joy—*for either would do*,—could be strong enough to express sympathy with a meadow of buttercups tossed and retossed by the wind."

How often in Beethoven is it impossible to decide whether he is bantering or scolding, and in Mendelssohn, whether he is restless with joy or anxiety!

Thus a very little reflection will show us that music is not necessarily connected with any definite conception. Emotion, not thought, is the sphere of music; and emotion quite as often precedes as follows thought. Although a thought will often, perhaps always, produce an emotion of some kind, it requires a distinct effort of the mind to fit an emotion with its appropriate thought. Emotion is the atmosphere in which thought is steeped, —that which lends to thought its tone or temperature, —that to which thought is often indebted for half its power. In listening to music we are like those who gaze through different coloured lenses. Now the air is dyed with a fiery hue, but presently a wave of rainbow green, or blue, or orange, floats by, and varied tints melt down through infinite gradations, or again rise into eddying contrasts, with such alternations as fitly mirror in the clear deeps of harmony the ever-changeful and subtle emotions of the soul. Can any words express these? No! Words are but poor interpreters in the realms of emotion. Where all words end, music begins; where they suggest, it realizes; and hence the secret of its strange, ineffable power. It reveals us to ourselves—it represents those modulations and temperamental changes which escape all verbal analysis—it utters what must else for ever remain unuttered and unutterable—it feeds that deep, ineradicable instinct within us of which all art is only the reverberated echo, that craving to express, through the medium of the senses, the spiritual and eternal realities which underlie them! Of course, this language of the emotions has to be studied like any other. To the inapt or uncultured, music seems but the graceful or forcible union of sounds with words, or a pleasant meaningless vibration of sound alone. But to him who has read the open secret aright, it is a language for the expression of the soul's life beyond all others. The true musician cares very little for your definite ideas, or things which can be expressed by words—he knows you can give him these; what he sighs for is the expression of the immaterial, the impalpable, the great "imponderables" of our nature, and he turns from a world of painted forms and oppressive substances to find the vague and yet perfect rapture of his dream in the wild, invisible beauty of his divine mistress!

Although music appeals simply to the emotions, and represents no definite images in itself, we are justified in using any language which may serve to convey to others our musical impressions. Words will often pave the way for the more subtle operations of music, and unlock the treasures which sound alone can rifle; and hence the eternal popularity of song. Into the region of song Schubert found himself forced almost against his will. He could get himself heard in no other, and this, after all, proved to be the sphere in which he was destined to reign supreme. His inspirations came to him in electric flashes of short and overwhelming brilliancy. The white-heat of a song like the "Erl King," or "Ungeduld," must have cooled if carried beyond the limits of a song. Nowhere is Schubert so great as in the act of rendering some sudden phase of passion. Songs like "Mignon" and "Marguerite Spinning" remind one of those miracles of photography where the cloud is caught in actual motion—the wave upon the very curl. Schubert was always singing. The Midas of music, everything dissolved itself into a stream of golden melody beneath his touch. All his instrumental works are full of melodies piled on melodies. We need not wonder at the number of his songs. He began by turning every poem he could get hold of into a song, and had he lived long enough he would have set the whole German literature to music. But he who, like Coleridge, is always talking, is not always equally well worth listening to. Schubert composed with enormous rapidity, but seldom condensed or pruned sufficiently, and his music sometimes suffers from a certain slipper-and-dressing-gown style, suggestive of a man who was in the habit of rising late, and finishing his breakfast and half-a-dozen songs together. His warmest admirers cannot be quite blind to an occasional slovenliness in his accompaniments; but, like Shelley, he is so rich in his atmospheric effects that we hardly care to look too nearly at the mechanism. His songs may be divided into seven classes. We can do no more at present than barely enumerate them, pointing out specimens of perfect beauty in illustration of each. We quote the "Wolfenbüttel" Edition, in five vols., edited by Sattler. The first number refers to the volume, the second to the page.

I. *Religious*—"Ave Maria," ii. 248; "The Young Nun," ii. 222.
II. *Supernatural*—"The Double," v. 183; "The Ghost's Greeting," iii. 431.
III. *Symbolical*—"The Crow," ii. 409; "The Erl King," i. 2.

IV. *Classical*—"Philoctetes," iv. 97; Æschylus," iv. 125.
V. *Descriptive*—"The Post," ii. 406; "A Group in Tartarus," i. 112.
VI. *Songs of Meditation*—"The Wanderer," i. 20; "Night and Dreams," ii. 225.
VII. *Songs of Passion*—"Mignon," iv. 176; "Thine is my Heart," i. 132; "By the Sea," v. 181; "Anne Lyle," ii. 348.

Notwithstanding the opinion of an illustrious critic to the contrary, we must be allowed to doubt whether Schubert ever reached his climax. Those works of his latest period not manifestly darkened by the shadow of approaching death—*e.g.* "Seventh Symphony" and "A minor Sonata"—bear the most distinct marks of progress; and during the last year of his life he had applied himself with vigour to the study of Bach, Handel, and the stricter forms of fugue and counterpoint. What the result of such severe studies might have been upon a mind so discursive, we can only conjecture. He might have added to his own richness more of Beethoven's power and of Mendelssohn's finish; but in the words of Schumann, "He has done enough;" and as we take a last glance at the vast and beautiful array of his compositions, we can only exclaim again with Liszt, "Schubert!—Schubert, le musicien, le plus poète qui fut jamais!"

CHOPIN.

Born 1810, Died 1849.

VI

WHAT SCHUBERT was to Song, CHOPIN was to the Piano; but whilst the genius of Schubert ranged freely over every field of musical composition, that of Chopin was confined within certain narrow limits. Borne into the mid-current of that great wave of Romanticism first set in motion by Schubert, he was destined, with the aid of Liszt and Berlioz, to establish its influence permanently in Paris. Paris—at once so superficially brilliant and so profoundly acute—the same in theology, philosophy, and the arts—always slow to receive German influences, and always sure to adopt them in the long-run—Paris became in reality the great foreign depôt of the Romantic school. But political events had something to do with this. About 1832, the effervescence of the first years of the July Revolution seemed to pass naturally into questions of art and literature, and as the French are occasionally tired of blood but never of glory, the great battle of the Romantic and Classical schools was fought out in the bloodless arena of the arts.

It was the old contest, with which in so many other forms we have grown familiar—what Mr. Mill calls "the struggle between liberty and authority,"*—or as Mr. Carlyle once said at Edinburgh, "the question of whether we should be led by the old formalities of use and wont, or by something that had been conceived of new in the souls of men." Dead fruit has to be shaken periodically from every branch of the tree of knowledge. But if any good is to be done, the shaking must be severe and thorough. The constantly recurring question between the new wine and the old bottles admits of no compromise. "What compromise,"† asks Liszt, "could there be between those who would not admit the possibility of writing in any other than the established manner, and those who thought

* Mill on "Liberty," chap. i.

† Liszt's fifth chapter, "Life of Chopin," contains a statement of the points at issue.

that the artist should be allowed to choose such forms as he deemed best suited for the expression of his own ideas?" We know how the question was settled. We know how Mendelssohn saved the movement from suicidal extravagance in its early stages — whilst Schumann, and later still Wagner, have done something towards sanctioning its very excesses. The cause of freedom, in music as elsewhere, is now very nearly triumphant; but at a time when its adversaries were many and powerful, we can hardly imagine the sacred bridge of liberty kept by a more stalwart trio than Schubert the Armourer, Chopin the Refiner, and Liszt the Thunderer.

FREDERIC FRANCIS CHOPIN was born in 1810, at Zelazowa-Wola, near Warsaw. His family was of French extraction, and though gifted with a certain native distinction, seems to have been neither rich nor prosperous. Frederic was a frail and delicate child, and a source of constant anxiety to his parents. He was petted and coaxed on from year to year, and seemed to gain strength very slowly. He was a quiet and thoughtful child, with the sweetest of dispositions—always suffering and never complaining. At the age of nine he began to learn music from Ziwna, a passionate disciple of Sebastien Bach; but it does not appear that either he himself or his friends were at that time aware of his remarkable powers. In 1820 he was introduced to Madame Catalani, who for some reason gave him a watch,—whether merely as a woman she was attracted towards the pale and delicate boy, or as an artist, with a certain prophetic instinct, when his life was yet in the bud,—

> "She too foretold the perfect rose,"—

we cannot say. At any rate, the bud soon began to open. Through the kindness of Prince Radziwill, a liberal patron of rising talent, Chopin was sent to the Warsaw College, where he received the best education, and where his musical powers began to make themselves felt. At the age of sixteen he became the favourite pupil of Joseph Elsner, Director of the Conservatory at Warsaw, and from him he learned those habits of severe study, and that practical science, which gave him in later years so complete a mastery over his subtle and dreamy creations. At college he made many friends, more especially amongst the young nobility, and upon being introduced to their families, he assumed without an effort that position in society which he ever after retained, and for which nature had so peculiarly fitted him. "Gentle, sensitive, and very lovely, he united the charm of adolescence with the suavity of a more mature age—through the want of muscular development he retained a peculiar beauty, an exceptional physiognomy, which, if we may venture so to speak, belonged to neither age nor sex. . . It was more like the ideal creations with which the poetry of the Middle Ages adorned the Christian temples. The delicacy of his constitution rendered him interesting in the eyes of women. The full yet grateful cultivation of his mind, the sweet and captivating originality of his conversation, gained for him the attention of the most enlightened men, whilst those less highly cultivated liked him for the exquisite courtesy of his manners."*

The manners of Chopin seem to have impressed every one with the same sense of refinement. Tinged with a certain melancholy which was never obtrusive, and which exhaled itself freely in his music alone, he was nevertheless a most charming companion. Only those who knew him well knew how reserved he really was. He received every one with the same facile courtesy, and was so ready to be absorbed by others, that few noticed how little he ever gave in return. He was unmoved by praise, but not always unmortified by failure; yet he never lost that quiet and affable dignity which some may have thought a little cold and satirical, but which to others seemed at once natural and charming. He was usually cheerful, but seldom showed deep feeling. He was not, however, deficient in impulse, nor wanting in depth, and beneath a somewhat placid exterior lay concealed the warmest family affections, a burning patriotism, a passionate love, and a stern, unalterable devotion to the true principles of his art.

Soon after completing his education at Warsaw, he visited Vienna, where he played frequently in public;

* George Sand.

but Liszt had been before him, and he found those large audiences whose ears had been so lately stunned with the thunder of cascades and hurricanes, wholly unprepared to listen to the murmuring of the waterfall, or the sighing of the midnight wind. The genius of Chopin could never cope with the masses. "I am not suited for concert-giving," he said to Liszt. "The public intimidate me,—their breath stifles me. You are destined for it, for when you do not gain your public, you have the force to assault, to overwhelm, to compel them." But he found some compensation for the indifferentism of the many in the enthusiastic admiration of the few. A little circle of friends, consisting of several distinguished amateurs, and some of the first artists of the day, began to gather round the new pianist, and the public prints soon took the hint, and described him as "a master of the first rank," and the most remarkable meteor then shining in the musical firmament, and so forth.*

After the revolution of 1830, the position of Poland seemed more hopeless than ever, and Chopin, like so many of his compatriots, determined to leave his country, and seek a temporary asylum in England. But unforeseen events delayed the accomplishment of this plan. On his way to England, he often said, with a sad and satirical smile, "he passed through Paris;" but when he left Paris it was not for London, but for an island in the Mediterranean. Great was the

* *Leipsic Gazette*, 1829, No. 46.

curiosity in some French circles when Chopin's visit was announced. All the first musicians and connoisseurs, including Liszt, M. Pleyel, Kalkbrenner, Field, and others, assembled in M. Pleyel's concert-rooms to hear him. Chopin played his First Concerto and several of his detached pieces, and the sensation which he produced is still fresh in the memory of Liszt and others who were present on that occasion. But whilst all were astonished, some were not convinced, and sober pianists like Kalkbrenner took exception to such unconstitutional effects as the new *virtuose* was in the habit of producing by using his third finger for his thumb, etc. Chopin was at once received into the best society, and here he breathed the atmosphere most congenial to him. Unlike Schubert, he was not averse to giving lessons, but chose only pupils of the highest natural endowments, and when we add that the most distinguished and beautiful women in Paris eagerly sought his instructions on any terms, we can imagine him engaged in a more unpalatable occupation. Chopin, in a word, became the rage: he was *fêted* in the salons, and sought after by the highest circles. There he formed many admirable pupils, who closely imitated his style, and generally played nothing but his music.

Meanwhile he lived quietly in the Chaussée d'Antin —shunned the celebrities, literary and philosophical —seldom entertained, and objected to the invasion of his privacy. But his friends and admirers would sometimes take no refusal, and occasionally invaded his apartments in a body. Through the kindness of Dr. Liszt, who was usually the ringleader in such disturbances, we can easily transport ourselves in imagination to one of these impromptu *levées*. It is about nine o'clock in the evening. Chopin is seated at the piano, the room is dimly lighted by a few wax candles. Several men of brilliant renown are grouped in the luminous zone immediately around the piano.

HEINE, the sad humorist, leans over his shoulder, and as the tapering fingers wander meditatively over the ivory keys, asks "if the trees at moonlight sang always so harmoniously?"

MEYERBEER is seated by his side: his grave and thoughtful head moves at times with a tacit acquiescence and delight, and he almost forgets the ring of his own Cyclopæan harmonies in listening to the delicate Arabesque-woven mazourkas of his friend.

ADOLPHE NOURRIT, the noble and ascetic artist, stands apart. He has something of the grandeur of the Middle Ages about him. In his later years he refused to paint any subject which was wanting in true dignity. Like Chopin, he served art with a severe exclusiveness and a passionate devotion.

EUGENE DELACROIX leans against the piano, absorbed in meditation,—developing, it may be, in his own mind, some form of beauty, or some splendid tint, suggested by the strange analogies which exist between sound and colour.

"Buried in a *fauteuil*, with her arms resting on a

table, sat Madame Sand, curiously attentive, gracefully subdued" (Liszt). She was listening to the language of the emotions,—fascinated by the subtle gradations of thought and feeling which she herself delighted to express, she may have there learned that wondrous melody of language which so often reminds one of a meditation by Chopin. It is in memory of some such golden hours that she writes,—"There is no mightier art than this, to awaken in man the sublime consciousness of his own humanity; to paint before his mind's eye the rich splendours of nature; the joy of meditation; the national character of a people; the passionate tumult of their hopes and fears; the languor and despondency of their sufferings. Remorse, violence, terror, control, despair, enthusiasm, faith, disquietude, glory, calm,—these and a thousand other nameless emotions belong to music. Without stooping to a puerile imitation of noises and effects, she transports us in the spirit to strange and distant scenes. There we wander to and fro in the dim air, and, like Æneas in the Elysian fields, all we behold is greater than on earth, godlike, changed, idealized!"*

It was soon after the extraordinary creation of "Lelia," in which all the phials of her passionate scorn are poured out upon man, whilst everything, except "the Eternal Feminine,"† is exalted in woman, that Madame Sand first met Chopin. She was then suffering from that exhaustion and lassitude which generally follow the attempt to realize an impossible

* "Consuelo."

† "Das ewig Weibliche."—*Goethe.*

ideal. Her creation was still before her, but it did not satisfy her,—like the statue of Pygmalion, it wanted life. What was, after all, the world of dreams to her, if there were no realities to correspond to them? She would not ask for a perfect realization, but, woman-like, something she must have. She who "had surprised such ineffable smiles on the faces of the dead,"* —she who "had dreamed of scenes which must exist somewhere, either on the earth or in some of the planets, whose light we love to gaze upon in the forests when the moon has set,"†—seemed to find for the time an outward reflection of her ideal world in the mind and music of Chopin. Her strong, energetic personality at once absorbed the fragile musician. She drew him as a magnet draws steel. He was necessary to her. She felt that one side of her nature had never been adequately expressed. She was many-sided. She would have everything in turn. She would lay heaven and earth under contribution. The passing moment was her eternity. Nothing seemed to her limited which filled the present phase. For a time, in the course of her imperious self-development, the part represented to her the whole, and thus it happened that Chopin, whose whole was only a part, was offered up, amongst others, upon the altar of her comprehensive and insatiable originality.

In his twenty-seventh year (1837) Chopin was attacked with the lung disease which had threatened

* "Spiridion." † "Lettres d'un Voyageur."

him from his earliest childhood. Madame Sand had now become his constant and devoted companion, and with her he was induced to leave the heated drawing-rooms and perfumed *boudoirs* of Paris for the soft and balmy breezes of the south. They finally settled in the island of Majorca, and for the events which followed we must refer the reader to the pages of "Lucrezia Floriani," where Madame Sand is "La Floriani," Chopin the "Prince Karol," and Liszt the "Count Salvator Albani." Those who have lingered in feeble health by the shores of the Mediterranean, know how from those sunny waters and cloudless skies a sweet, new life seems to pass into the veins, whilst, as it were, Nature herself arises to tend her sickly children. The grounds of the Villa Floriani were bounded only by the sand of the sea-shore—here and there the foliage dipped into the water. Can we wonder if, in this momentary and delusive rest, health returned to the overtasked and exhausted musician, or that some of his loveliest inspirations arose as he lingered by the blooming coast, gazed upon the summer sea, or floated out into its moonlit waters?

He returned to Paris with a show of health which was soon to disappear beneath the shocks of passion and disappointment which now awaited him. The dream of Chopin's life was union with Madame Sand in marriage. He had not followed her in her speculations—he did not agree with her conclusions—he only prayed that what had become dearer to him than life itself might be secured to him for ever, and he asked the woman he loved to sacrifice her philosophical opinions to his passionate devotion. But unfortunately marriage found no place in Madame Sand's system of morals. She considered it a snare to a man, and a delusion to a woman. This controversy first brought out the glaring differences of character which had always existed between them, and from the hour of Madame Sand's deliberate refusal, Chopin was seized with a restless and inextinguishable jealousy. Although Madame Sand had been considerate and consistent enough to remove every cause, yet Chopin was never satisfied, and in his misery and impatience he began to attack her philosophy and religion. It was a fatal step! Off his own peculiar ground, he was not able to meet her. The "Floriani" confesses that at last she grew tired of his endless reproaches, and the knell of their separation at length sounded. It could not be otherwise. They met and parted in dreamland, and it is the keenest satire on Madame Sand's philosophy of passion, that an intimacy, begun with the conviction that here at last were all the elements of a deep and enduring union, should end with the mournful confession that "two natures, the one rich in its exuberance, the other in its exclusiveness, could never really mingle, and that a whole world separated them!"*

But the love that was only an episode in the life of Madame Sand proved to be the whole life of Chopin. "All the cords," he would frequently say, "that bound me to life are broken." From this time his health

* "Lucrezia Floriani."

visibly declined. He was soon seized with another severe attack of his old complaint; but he was now no longer tended by his incomparable nurse. Her place was supplied by his favourite pupil, M. Gutman, "whose presence," he said, "was dearer to him than that of any other person." Contrary to expectation, he rallied; but a great change had passed over him; he had lost much of his outward equanimity, and looked so pale and cadaverous, that his friends hardly recognised him. He soon began to resume his former occupations, but with an ever-growing restlessness which announced too surely the beginning of the end. He seemed utterly careless about his health: "Why should he care?" he would sometimes ask; there was nothing to live for now; "no second friend." He had "passed through Paris,"—Paris could never be the same to him again,—he had best leave it, and go anywhere—to London. So his friends and disciples assembled once more in M. Pleyel's rooms, and there they heard him for the last time. In vain they besought him to delay his visit; Chopin was bent upon leaving Paris immediately, and although threatened with a relapse, at the most inclement season of the year he started for England.

His fame had preceded him, and the highest circles opened their ranks to receive him. He was presented to the Queen by the Duchess of Sutherland; played twice in public at Willis's Rooms, and at many private concerts. He went much into society, sat up late at night, and exposed himself to constant fatigues. Against the advice of his physicians, he next visited Scotland, and returned to London in the last stage of consumption. One more concert, the last he ever played at—in aid of his exiled countrymen, the Poles—and then he hurried back to Paris. But his favourite physician, Dr. Molin, who had saved his life more than once, was dead, and Chopin had no confidence in any other. His unnatural energy was now succeeded by the deepest lassitude and dejection. He scarcely ever left his bed, and seldom spoke. M. Gutman, Louise, his own sister, and the beautiful and accomplished Countess Delphine Potocka, were his constant attendants.

One evening towards sunset, Chopin, who had lain insensible for many hours, suddenly rallied. He observed the Countess draped in white standing at the foot of the bed. She was weeping bitterly. "Sing!" murmured the dying man. She had a lovely voice. It was a strange request, but so earnest a one that his friends wheeled the piano from the adjoining parlour to his bedroom door, and there, as the twilight deepened, with the last rays of the setting sun streaming into the room, the Countess sang that famous canticle to the Virgin, which it is said once saved the life of Stradella. "How beautiful it is!" he exclaimed. "My God, how beautiful!—Again, again!" In another moment he swooned away.

On the 17th of October, 1849, having entered upon his fortieth year, Chopin breathed his last in the arms of his devoted pupil, M. Gutman. Many of his intimate friends came to see him; his love of flowers was well known, and the next day they were brought in such quantities, that the bed on which he lay, and indeed the whole room, disappeared beneath a variegated covering of a thousand bright tints. The pale face seemed to have regained in death all its early beauty! there was no more unrest,—no signs of care,—he lay sleeping tranquilly amongst the flowers.

On the 30th day of October his requiem was sung at the Madeleine Church in Paris,—Signor Lablache, Madame Viardot, and Madame Castellan claiming the principal solos, and M. Wély presiding at the organ. He lies in the cemetery of Père la Chaise, between Cherubini and Bellini.

Chopin was essentially a national musician. Although he lived much in France, his music is never French. "He sings to one clear harp in divers tones," the swan-song of his people's nationality. His genius was elegiac. He is more often tender than strong, and even his occasional bursts of vigour soon give way to the prevailing undertone of a deep melancholy. His country is ever uppermost in his thoughts. His Polonaises reflect the national ardour of a noble but unhappy patriotism. His mazourkas and scherzos are full of the subtle coquetry and passionate sensibility of his gifted countrywomen, whilst his ballads* are

* There are sixteen published. They are very little known. No. 12, "My Joy," and 10, "Riding Home from the Fight," are quite remarkable.

nothing but the free, wild songs of his native land, transcribed for the first time by himself.

He, first of all musicians, understood the dignity of manners and the language of deportment, and with varied utterance he seems to be continually reminding us that—

> "Manners are not idle, but the fruit
> Of noble nature and of loyal mind."

His dance music has added a strange and fascinating solemnity to the graces of the ball-room,—elevating a mere pastime into what may almost be called a philosophy.

As a romance writer for the pianoforte, he had no models, and will have no rivals. He was original without extravagance, and polished without affectation. It is to him we owe the extension of chords struck together in *arpeggio*, the little groups of superadded notes, "falling like light drops of pearly dew upon the melodic figure;" he also invented those admirable harmonic progressions which lend importance to many a slender subject, and redeem its slightest efforts from triviality. Of Schubert he once remarked, that "the sublime is desecrated when followed by the trivial or commonplace." A certain rollicking fun, and vulgar though powerful energy, that frequently peeps out in Schubert's marches, was abhorrent to him. Perhaps he hardly appreciated the enormous range of men like Beethoven or even Schubert. His own range was limited, but within it he has probably never been equalled in absolute perfection of finish. His works are marked by a complete absence of commonplace, and you will search throughout them in vain for a slovenly chord or an unskilful combination. His boldness is always justified by success, and his repetition by a certain weird and singular pathos.

He was great in small things, but small in great ones. His two concertos with orchestral accompaniments are more ambitious than successful. The other instruments, like the general public (thin as are his orchestral scores), seem to stifle and embarrass him, and we long to have Chopin alone again at the pianoforte.

Thus much in general. Volumes more might doubtless be written about these men and their music, but they had better be left to speak for themselves to the listening ear and the loving heart. We lay down the pen of the critic,—we look up once more at the familiar features of Franz Schubert and Frederic Chopin. They have long been to us a running commentary upon all nature, and the gentle companions of our solitude; May never comes with its glittering freshness and myriad bloom, but the songs of Schubert are ringing in our ears,—nor June with its glowing tints and tender twilights, but the melodies of Chopin seem to haunt the air.

> "For the stars and the winds are unto them
> As raiment, as songs of the harp-player;
> For the risen stars and the fallen cling to them,
> And the south-west wind and the west wind sing!"

THE LETTERS OF

MOZART.

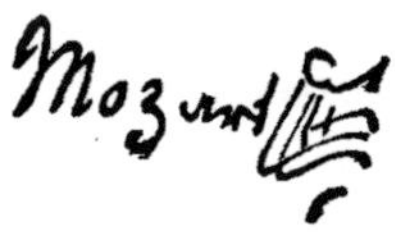

VII.

A GROUP of musical biographies without two such central figures as Mozart and Beethoven, is like a collection of the British Poets without Shakspeare and Milton; but we must remind our reader that, in this book, there is a third great name that has only been mentioned incidentally, the name of Sebastien Bach; whilst an illustrious group of nineteenth-century composers, in France, Italy, and Germany, have not been touched.

Mozart and Beethoven may be hereafter treated in two separate volumes. The position of Sebastien Bach would, according to our method, be most aptly considered whenever a detailed biography of Mendelssohn comes to be written. The modern Italian and French schools may also form an interesting subject for future consideration, whilst the germs of musical art in England should not be neglected as hopeless or trivial.

The present volume should be taken, not as a complete survey of musical art, but merely as a serious tribute to its importance combined with a group of biographies, suggestive of a few great landmarks in the rise and development of modern music.

I have felt it impossible to close this second book without trying to give the reader a passing glimpse of Mozart, Beethoven, and Mendelssohn. The study on *Elijah* will, I trust, not be considered *de trop*.

To open Mozart's letters is like opening a painted tomb. We are surrounded by people long dead,—we read the once familiar names, forgotten now,—we look curiously at the busy every-day life of a century ago,—we almost catch the ringing laugh and the sound of voices. The colours are all fresh, the figures are all distinct. Let us select one group. There is Leopold Mozart, the father, with his old threadbare coat, and oaken stick, a God-fearing, sensible, but somewhat narrow-minded man; his wife—the very model of a thrifty housewife. There is pretty little

Nannerl, now about fifteen, who "looks like an angel in her new clothes," and plays the clavier to the astonishment of Herr von Mölk, the stupid lover, and the other Court musicians who frequent the worthy Capellmeister's house at Salzburg. There is Bimberl the dog, who gets so many kisses, and the canary that sings in G sharp; and last there is the glorious boy Wolfgang Amadeus Mozart, now about thirteen, in his little puce-brown coat, velvet hose, and buckled shoes, and long flowing curly hair, tied behind after the fashion of the day. He has already visited Paris, London, and Rome, and is no less famous for uproarious merriment than for music. At the age of four he wrote tunes, at twelve he could not find his equal on the harpsichord, and the professors of Europe stood aghast at one who improvised fugues on a given theme, and then took a ride a cock-horse on his father's stick.

The first two sections of Letters, which carry us up to his twenty-second year, reach from 1769 to 1778, and are dated variously from Verona, Milan, Rome, Bologna, and Venice. We have also an account of a professional tour in Germany with his mother, in the fruitless search after some settled employment. He seems to have met with many friends, much praise, some jealousy, but so little money that he charged only four ducats for twelve lessons, and could write to Martini, the old Italian Nestor of music, "We live in a country where music has very little success." Meanwhile, he has excellent spirits, and laughs at everything and everybody—at the ascetic friar who ate so enormously—at Nannerl's lover, poor Herr von Mölk, whimpering behind his pocket-handkerchief—at the violin professor, who was always saying, "I beg your pardon, but I am out again," and was always consoled by Mozart's invariable reply, "It doesn't in the least signify"—at the Italian singer who had "*una rugged voce e canta sempre* about a quarter of a note too *hardi o troppo o buon ora!*" Contrasted with these lighter moods, it is striking to observe a deep undertone of seriousness, as when he assures his father of his regularity at Confession, and exclaims, "I have always had God before my eyes. Friends who have no religion cannot long be my friends;" "I have such a sense of religion that I shall never do anything that I would not do before the whole world:" and we recognise the loving, unspoiled heart of a boy in the young man's words, "Next to God comes papa." This period was marked by the composition of the greater number of his masses, most of which were written before his twenty-third year.

The years 1778 and 1779, which he spent in Paris, were probably the most uncongenial of his life. He found the people coarse and intriguing, the musicians stupid and intractable, the nobles poor and stingy, the women unconversable and dissolute. The whole tone of the French mind displeased him. "The ungodly arch-villain Voltaire has died like a dog," he writes. But upon the French music he pours all the vials of his wrath. "The French are, and always will be, downright donkeys." "They cannot sing, they scream." "The devil himself invented their language." In 1779, he came back to Germany, resolved to abandon for ever both the French and Italian styles, and devote himself to the cultivation of a real German opera school. The *Idomeneo* was the first-fruits. It was produced at Munich for the carnival of 1780—a date for ever memorable in the annals of music as the dawn of the great classical period in Mozart's history. From 1781 to 1782, all his letters are dated from Vienna, where he finally settled down. Money is still scarce. "I have only one small room," he writes: "it is quite crammed with a piano, a table, a bed, and a chest of drawers;" but combined with his almost austere poverty, we notice the same regularity in his religious duties, the same purity in his private life; of this, such letters as Vol. II., No. 180—182, afford the strongest circumstantial evidence. In 1781 his reasons for marrying, though quaintly put, are quite unanswerable—viz., because he had no one to take care of his linen; because he could not live like the dissolute young men around him; and lastly, because he was in love with Constance Weber. The marriage took place in 1782, Mozart being then twenty-six, and his bride eighteen. The same year witnessed the production of *Il Seraglio*, and shortly afterwards we find him dining pleasantly with the veteran composer Gluck, who, although of quite another school, and in some sense a rival, was always cordial in his praises of Mozart. So thoroughly indeed had the spirit of the new music begun to revolutionize the public mind, that popular Italian composers engaged Mozart to write arias for them, in order to insure the success of their operas.

The rest of Mozart's life can be compared to nothing but a torch burning out rapidly in the wind. Unwearied alike as a composer and an artist, he kept pouring forth symphonies, sonatas, and operas, whilst disease could not shake his nerve as an executant, and the hand of death found him unwilling to relinquish the pen of the ready writer. In April, 1783, we find him playing at no less than twenty concerts. The year 1785 is marked by the six celebrated quartets dedicated to Haydn. "I declare to you," exclaimed the old man, upon hearing them, to Mozart's father, "before God and on the faith of an honest man, that your son is the greatest composer who ever lived." In 1786 *Figaro* was produced; and in 1787 *Don Giovanni* was written for his favourite public at Prague. It will hardly be believed that all this time Mozart was in the greatest want of money. His works were miserably paid for. He visited Berlin, Dresden, and Leipzic to recruit his fortunes: the nobles gave him watches and snuff-boxes, but very little coin, and in 1790 we find Mozart, at the zenith of his fame and popularity, standing dinnerless and "in a state of destitution," at the door of his old friend Puchberg. It is difficult to account for this, as he certainly made more money than many musicians. His purse, indeed, was always open to his friends; he was obliged to mix on equal

On a stormy December morning, through the deserted streets of Vienna, amidst snow and hail, and unaccompanied by a single friend, the body of Mozart was hastily borne, with fifteen others, to the common burial-ground of the poor. In 1808, some foreigners, passing through the town, wished to visit the grave; but they were told that the ashes of the poor were frequently exhumed to make room for others, and no stone then remained to mark the spot where once had rested the body of JOHANN CHRYSOSTOM WOLFGANG AMADEUS MOZART.

These letters in great measure supply the want of material noticeable in every biography of Mozart between the years 1785—90, and are further valuable as correcting several hasty and ill-advised statements in the otherwise learned and elaborate narrative of M. Oulibicheff, such as, that Mozart had a passion for travelling, when he declares that he could never sleep in his carriage, and hated being from home—or that he was fond of wine and women, when throughout his life he was scoffed at for being chaste and sober—or that he was extravagant, when he continually sent large sums to his father, wore the coarsest linen, and devoted everything else to the comfort of an invalid wife—or that his talents were not recognised at Vienna, where many of his most successful concerts were given—or that *Figaro* was received coldly there, when he writes, "There were seven encores."

The following passages will be perused with interest, as specimens of Mozart's style of letter-writing.

On a journey in 1778, from Paris to Strasburg, he writes:—

"I submitted to this conveyance for eight days, but longer I could not stand it—not on account of the fatigue, for the carriage was well hung, but from want of sleep. We were off every morning at four o'clock, and thus obliged to rise at three. Twice I had the satisfaction of being forced to get up at one o'clock in the morning, as we were to set off at two. You know that I cannot sleep in a carriage, so I really could not continue this without the risk of being ill. I would have taken the post, but it was not necessary, for I had the good fortune to meet with a person who quite suited me—a German merchant who resides in Paris and deals in English wares. Before getting into the carriage we exchanged a few words, and from that moment we remained together. We did not take our meals with the other passengers, but in our own room, where we also slept. I was glad to meet this man, for, being a great traveller, he understands it well."

The following passage may be safely commended to persons about to marry. Mozart writes to the reluctant parent of the period; it is the old story. Papa thinks it unwise to marry without means, and again it is the old story,—son, of a contrary opinion:—

"You can have no possible objection to offer, nor can there be any, and this you admit in your letters. Constanze is a well-conducted, good girl, of respectable parentage, and I am in a position to earn at least *daily bread* for her. We love each other, and we are resolved to marry. All that you have written, or may possibly write, on this subject, can be nothing but well-meant advice, which, however good and sensible, can no longer apply to a man who has gone so far with a girl. There can, therefore, be no question of further delay. Honesty is the best policy, and cannot fail to ensure the blessing of Providence. I am resolved to have no cause for self-reproach. Now farewell!"

Just after the wedding he writes:—

"My darling is now a hundred times more joyful at the idea of going to Salzburg, and I am willing to stake—ay, my very life, that you will rejoice still more in my happiness when you know her; if, indeed, in your estimation, as in mine, a high-principled, honest, virtuous, and pleasing wife ought to make a man happy."

Late in his short life he writes the following characteristic note to a friend, whose life does not appear to have been one of the most regular :—

"Now tell me, my dear friend, how you are. I hope you are all as well as we are. You cannot fail to be happy, for you possess everything that you can wish for at your age and in your position—especially as you now seem to have entirely given up your former excited mode of life. Do you not every day become more convinced of the truth of the little lectures I used to inflict on you? Are not the pleasures of a transient, capricious passion widely different from the happiness produced by rational and true love? I feel sure that you often in your heart thank me for my admonitions. I shall feel quite proud if you do. But, jesting apart, you do really owe me some little gratitude if you are become worthy of Fraulein N——, for I certainly played no insignificant part in your improvement or reform.

"My great grandfather used to say to his wife, my great grandmother, who in turn told it to her daughter, my mother,* who repeated it to her daughter, my own sister, that it was a very great art to talk eloquently and well, but an equally great one to know the right moment to stop. I therefore shall follow the advice of my sister, thanks to our mother, grandmother, and great grandmother, and thus end, not only my moral ebullition, but my letter."

---

* Mozart has here made a slip. His great grandmother's daughter was probably his *grandmother*, not his *mother*.

THE LETTERS OF

BEETHOVEN.

Born 1770—2, Died 1827.

VIII.

THE person of Beethoven, like his music, seems to have left its vivid and colossal impress upon the age. "The square Cyclopean figure attired in a shabby coat, with torn sleeves," described by

Weber, is familiar to all, and the face too,—the rough hair brushed impatiently off the forehead, the boldly arched eyebrows, resolute nose, and firmly set mouth—truly a noble face, with a certain severe integrity, and passionate power, and lofty sadness about it, seeming in its elevation and wideness of expression to claim kindred with a world of ideas out of all proportion to our own. The face at the beginning of Vol. I. of Beethoven's published letters is better than anything in the book.

We open these letters with the greatest eagerness; we close them with a feeling of almost unmingled pain and disappointment. Unlike Mozart's, they are not a sparkling commentary on a many-coloured life. Beethoven's outward life was all one colour, and his letters are mainly occupied with unimportant, vexatious, or melancholy details. His inward life has long since been given to the world, but not in words, only in—

> "The tides of music's golden sea,
> Setting toward eternity."

Born in 1770 or 1772,* Ludwig Van Beethoven early showed a strong dislike to music. His father had to beat him before he would sit down at the piano. At the age of eleven, however, he declares that for several years music had been his favourite pursuit. His compositions were always abundant, and from the first met with the approval of the publishers. His early compositions were at once understood. And no

* See Fétis, "Biographie Universelle des Musiciens;" art. "Beethoven."

wonder, for in him the bereaved public found Mozart *redivivus* with variations. "Mind, you will hear that boy talked of!" whispered the great composer when he first heard Beethoven play. Did he foresee with what firm and gigantic strides the "boy," as he entered manhood, would lead the way to fresh woods and pastures new? ever triumphant and successful,—amidst what trials and disasters!

On the very threshold of his career, he was met by two gloomy companions—Poverty and Disease—who accompanied him to the grave. In 1800, he lost his patron, the Elector of Cologne, and with him a small salary, and in 1801 he became partially deaf. Both evils were lightened by success; but what is success without health or spirits? "Oh, blissful moment! how happy do I esteem myself!" and in the same letter, "I cannot fail to be the most unhappy of God's creatures!" About this time occur those strange letters to his "immortal beloved," the Countess Giulietta Guicciardi; and in the still more immortal song of "Adelaide," written then, we can almost hear the refrain of "My angel! my all! my life!" (15), and such-like passionate utterances. The Countess married some one else, and Beethoven does not seem to have broken his heart. His relations with women were always severely honourable. This is the only burst of love he ever permitted himself, and if we except his unhappy love for Marie Pachler, and the wild fancy which that strange little being, Bettina Brentano, seems to have inspired in Goethe, Beethoven, and every one who came near her, we must suppose that the myth of Platonic affection became for once real history. He was not, however, at all insensible to the charms of female society. The ladies might knit him comforters, make him light puddings, he would even condescend to lie on their sofas after dinner, and pick his teeth with the snuffers, while they played his sonatas. Madame Breuning and Frau Von Streicher especially seem to have been invaluable friends and advisers. He told them all his petty troubles: "Nany is not strictly honest;" "I have a cough and severe headache." Then follow details about servants' clothes and wages. If, however, his relations with women were unromantic, they were proportionably constant. His correspondence was limited in range, but the same names, both male and female, recur to the end of his life. This fact speaks volumes. It is more to retain than to win. The head may win; the heart alone can keep.

Walking one day in the woods with his devoted friend, Ferdinand Ries, he disclosed to him the sad secret of his increasing deafness—this was as early as 1800. From this time his patience and money were vainly lavished on doctors without success. The world of sweet sounds and pleasant voices was gradually closing up for him. "I wander about here with music paper among the hills, and dales, and valleys, and scribble a great deal. No man on earth can love the country as I do." But he could not hear the birds sing. No one was naturally a more intelligent converser, but he could hardly hear the voices of his friends. Early in life he writes, "I must tell you my extraordinary deafness is such that in the theatre I am obliged to lean close up against the orchestra; a little way off, I lose the high notes of both instruments and singers;" and latterly no sound from the thunder of a full orchestra, whilst he stood in the midst of it with his back to the audience, could reach him. He had to be turned round at the end of one of his symphonies, that he might see the enthusiasm which his music had created. Thus, in 1802, he bids farewell to his hearing, in one of those bitter heart-cries which remind us of that other immortal plaint,—

> "When I consider how my life is spent,
> Ere half my days in this dark world and wide:"

"As autumn leaves fall and wither, so are my hopes blighted. Almost as I came I depart. Even the lofty courage which so often animated me in the lovely days of summer is gone for ever. Oh, Providence! vouchsafe me one day of pure felicity! How long have I been estranged from the glad echo of true joy! When, O my God! when shall I feel it again in the temple of nature and man?—never!"

When we hear it recorded of Beethoven that he was a morose, churlish, and ill-tempered man, "full of caprice, and devoid of all complaisance," let us rather remember one who, in the midst of sufferings which we cannot estimate, and trials which we have not known, never lost his reverence for God, his deep and tender devotion to all that was highest in man, his patient forbearance with the weak and selfish, and a certain indomitable courage, wideness of vision, and power of will, which has raised him, the lonely worker, to one of the most solitary pinnacles of Fame.

The years from 1805 to 1808 witnessed the production of "The Mount of Olives," "Leonora," "Pastorale," and "Eroica," besides a host of concertos, songs, and sonatas. In 1809 his affectionate patron, the Archduke Rudolf, settled a small pension on him for life, and henceforth Beethoven hardly ever moved from Vienna, except to go to Baden in the summer months.

In 1816 he writes in better spirits to his comical friend, Zmeskall, "For the sake of various scamps in this world I should like to live a little longer." His general health had improved, a new and sudden interest in life had come to him with the guardianship of his nephew Carl, who, upon his father's death, was rescued by his uncle from the clutches of a most abandoned mother.

His love for this young rascal is the most affecting thing in his whole life. He put him to school—had him home for the holidays—gave him every indulgence, and lavished upon him all the love which was never destined to flow through happier channels. He had a natural horror of business and detail, but nothing could be small or vexatious which concerned Carl. The size of his boots—the cut of his coat—his physic—his food—and above all, his pianoforte playing, were subjects of unfailing interest to Beethoven. By the way, here is a valuable hint to teachers, from the great master to the pianist Czerny: "When sufficiently advanced do not stop his (Carl's) playing on account of little mistakes, but only point them out at the end of the piece. I have always followed this system, which quickly forms a *musician.*" But unfortunately Carl was not a musician, but an idle fellow who cared for nothing but pleasure, and nobody but himself. It was the last bitter drop in the poor uncle's cup—a drop which he refused to taste until his hair began to get grey—that he, who had been father, mother, servant, nurse, everything to Carl, was only looked upon by him in the light of the "relieving officer." The saddest letters are those from 435 to 450, addressed to this miserable nephew:—

"Dear son, I still feel very weak and solitary—my weakness often amounts to a swoon. Oh, do not further grieve me! Farewell, dearest boy, deserve this name; anything you want shall be purchased. If it is too hard a task for you to come and see me, give it up, but if you can by any possibility come, &c., let us not refer to the past. If you had any depth of feeling, you would have acted differently. Be my own dear precious son! imitate my virtues, not my faults."

The "precious son" seems to have met all this affection with coldness, ingratitude, and the meanest lying. At last the whole truth breaks upon the unhappy old man, and he exclaims, we can almost fancy with tears, "I know now you have no pleasure in coming to see me—which is only natural, for my atmosphere is too pure for you. God has never yet forsaken me, and no doubt some one will be found to close my eyes." Carl, after attempting suicide, gambling, and commerce, and failing signally in each, finally enlisted, and so disappears from these letters; but we read his last forgiveness in the brief codicil of Beethoven's will,—"I appoint my nephew Carl my sole heir."

Beethoven's external life presents us with the familiar picture of the man of genius and misfortune struggling with the world. "*Miser e pauper sum*," he would often say. He was wretched because deaf and solitary and disappointed in the deepest and most sensitive parts of a nature singularly tender and profound. He was poor because the best pay in those days was bad, and because the men who could have helped him hung back until the life that might have been prolonged and cheered by their kindly support was closed abruptly without it. George IV., then Prince Regent, never acknowledged the dedication of the battle symphony, or took the slightest notice of its composer. Neither the Imperial family nor the Austrian Government ever showed the smallest interest in either Haydn, Mozart, or Beethoven. They left them to the mercy of private patrons. Beethoven was always very poor, but in his poverty he never forgot to be generous. At a concert given in aid of the soldiers wounded at Hanau, he supplied music and conducted. Schuppanzigh, Spohr, and Mayseder were amongst the violins, and old Salieri played the drums and cymbals (Meyerbeer, Moscheles, and Hummel also assisted). When some offer of payment was made, he writes, "Say

Beethoven never accepts anything where humanity is concerned."

On another occasion, when the concert was for poor Ursuline nuns,—"I promise you an entirely new symphony—my joy will be beyond bounds if the concert prove a success." But his charity was not merely for show—it began at home. His friends never applied in vain for money as long as he had any to give, and his purse-strings were often loosed for those who had injured him deeply.

Beethoven's relations with his London publishers were satisfactory. The Philharmonic paid liberally for his works, honoured him with appreciation during his life, and sent him a present of £100 when he was lying on his death-bed.

Beethoven's domestic life was one of singular discomfort. He was always changing his lodgings—getting into worse ones and falling amongst thieves. He no sooner got into new rooms than the chimneys began to smoke, or the rain came in through the roof, or the chairs came down when sat upon, or the doors came off their hinges. He was no more fortunate with his servants. "Nancy is too uneducated for a housekeeper—indeed, quite a beast." "My precious servants were occupied from seven o'clock till ten trying to heat the stove." "The cook's off again." "I shied half a dozen books at her head." They made his dinner so nasty that he could not eat it. "No soup to-day, no beef, no eggs again—got something from the inn at last."

From a life of public neglect and private suffering and trial, he turned to the ideal life in art. In all his earthly strivings he might well say with Goethe, "I have ever looked up to the highest." To him art was no mere recreation or luxury, but the expression of all that was conceivable and most worthy of being expressed in things Divine and human. It was a call, a mission, an inspiration; and the ear so early closed to the discords of earth seemed all the more intently open to the voice of the informing Spirit:—

> "Lo, I have given thee
> To understand my presence and to feel
> My fulness: I have filled thy lips with power.
> I have raised thee nigher to the spheres of heaven,
> Man's first, last home; and thou with ravished sense
> Listenest the lordly music flowing from
> Th' illimitable years."

"Nothing can be more sublime," he writes, "than to draw nearer to the Godhead than other men, and to diffuse here on earth these God-like rays among mortals." But none understood better than he that "the excellency of the power was not of him:"—

"What is all this compared to the grandest of all Masters of harmony—above, above!" And so this mighty spirit seemed always reaching forward with the glorious "not as though I had attained" for ever on his lips. "I feel," he writes in 1824, "as though I had written scarcely more than a few notes of music!" for to him—

> "All experience seemed an arch, wherethro'
> Gleamed that untravell'd world whose margin fades
> For ever and for ever as we move."

Beethoven had worked too hard. In 1823 his eyes gave way; for several years before his death he had been spitting blood, and his digestion was nearly gone. In December of the year 1826 he found himself upon a sick bed, in great poverty, and unable to compose a line of music. There are a few more letters, written in a tremulous hand; others only signed still more illegibly; letters to Moscheles, to Sir George Smart, and to Baron Pasqualati, an old friend, who sent him fruit, wine, and other delicacies during his illness.

On the 18th of March, 1827, all hopes of Beethoven's recovery were abandoned. On the 23rd, they read him his will. It was suggested that the words "natural heirs" should be put in the place of "heirs of my body," as he had no children, and the words might provoke disputes. He replied that the one term was as good as the other, and that it should remain just as it was. "This was his last contradiction."

In the afternoon of March 26th, 1827, Beethoven was seized with his last mortal faintness. Thick clouds were hanging about the sky; outside, the snow lay upon the ground; towards evening the wind rose; at nightfall a terrific thunderstorm burst over the city of Vienna, and whilst the storm was still raging, the spirit of the sublime master departed.

Ludwig Van Beethoven died in his fifty-seventh year, and is buried in the cemetery of Wahring, near Vienna.

The passages which I am about to quote from Beethoven's Will, are likely to tell the reader more of Beethoven's inner life than almost any of his letters :—

"O ye, who consider or declare me to be hostile, obstinate, or misanthropic, what injustice ye do me! ye know not the secret causes of that which to you wears such an appearance. My heart and my mind were from childhood prone to the tender feelings of affection. Nay, I was always disposed even to perform great actions. But only consider that, for the last six years, I have been attacked by an incurable complaint, aggravated by the unskilful treatment of medical men, disappointed from year to year in the hope of relief, and at last obliged to submit to the endurance of an evil the cure of which may last perhaps for years, if it is practicable at all. Born with a lively, ardent disposition, susceptible to the diversions of society, I was forced at an early age to renounce them, and to pass my life in seclusion. If I strove at any time to set myself above all this, O how cruelly was I driven back by the doubly painful experience of my defective hearing! and yet it was not possible for me to say to people, 'Speak louder—bawl—for I am deaf!' Ah, how could I proclaim the defect of a sense that I once possessed in the highest perfection, in a perfection in which few of my colleagues possess or ever did possess it? Indeed, I cannot! Forgive me, then, if ye see me draw back when I would gladly mingle among you. Doubly mortifying is my misfortune to me, as it must tend to cause me to be misconceived. From recreation in the society of my fellow-creatures, from the pleasures of conversation, from the effusions of friendship, I am cut off. Almost alone in the world, I dare not venture into society more than absolute necessity requires. I am obliged to live as an exile. If I go into company a painful anxiety comes over me, since I am apprehensive of being exposed to the danger of betraying my situation. Such has been my state, too, during this half year that I have spent in the country. Enjoined by my intelligent physician to spare my hearing as much as possible, I have been almost encouraged by him in my present natural disposition; though, hurried away by my fondness for society, I sometimes suffered myself to be enticed into it. But what a humiliation when any one standing beside me could hear at a distance the flute that I could not hear, or any one heard the shepherd singing, and I could not distinguish a sound! Such circumstances brought me to the brink of despair, and had well-nigh made me put an end to my life: nothing but my art held my hand. Ah! it seemed to me impossible to quit the world before I had produced all that I felt myself called to accomplish. And so I endured this wretched life—so truly wretched, that a somewhat speedy change is capable of transporting me from the best into the worst condition. Patience—so I am told—I must choose for my guide. Steadfast, I hope, will be my resolution to persevere, till it shall please the inexorable Fates to cut the thread.

"Perhaps there may be an amendment—perhaps not; I am prepared for the worst—I, who so early as my twenty-eighth year was forced to become a philosopher—it is not easy—for the artist more difficult than for any other. O God! thou lookest down upon my misery; thou knowest that it is accompanied with love of my fellow-creatures, and a disposition to do good! O men! when ye shall read this, think that ye have wronged me: and let the child of affliction take comfort on finding one like himself who, in spite of all the impediments of nature, yet did all that lay in his power to obtain admittance into the rank of worthy artists and men.

* * * * *

"I go to meet death with joy. If he comes before I have had occasion to develop all my professional abilities, he will come too soon for me, in spite of my hard fate, and I should wish that he had delayed his arrival. But even then I am content, for he will release me from a state of endless suffering. Come when thou wilt, I shall meet thee with firmness. Farewell, and do not quite forget me after I am dead; I have deserved that you should think of me, for in my lifetime I have often thought of you to make you happy. May you ever be so!

"LUDWIG VAN BEETHOVEN.

"M.P. (L. S.)

"HEILIGENSTADT, *October* 6*th*, 1802."

MENDELSSOHN.

IX.

A BIOGRAPHY of Mendelssohn has yet to be written, but before presenting the reader with an analysis of the *Elijah*, I propose to transfer to these pages a slight sketch not of Mendelssohn's life, but of Mendelssohn himself, drawn almost entirely from a volume of Reminiscences, published by his intimate friend Edward Devrient. The book is neither a biography nor a book of scattered notes; but it is a kind of narrative, giving a connected and vivid impression of Mendelssohn as he appeared to one of his most intimate friends, from a very early age to the time of his death. Nothing so real and life-like about him has yet come before the public. "Lampadius" only professes to give a sketch. Mr. Benedict's charming little work is but the shadow of an affectionate sketch. The two volumes of Mendelssohn's own letters are, of course, priceless; but Elise Polko's anecdotes are almost disfigured by enthusiasm. Edward Devrient is content to draw very fully, as far as he could see it, the picture of one who was more than a brother to him, —whose genius he profoundly reverenced, whose character he understood perhaps better than anybody now living, whose virtues he never ceased to extol, but whose faults he never attempted to conceal. Some will doubtless consider that the additional letters of Mendelssohn, there published for the first time, are the most valuable portion of the book; and indeed they possess in the highest degree all those qualities which drew the public towards the first two volumes of Mendelssohn's letters. The little vivid touches of description betray the same poetic heart and facile pen:—

* I send you this from Styria. The convent is quite enclosed by green wooded hills—there is a rushing and murmuring on every side, and the consequence is trout for supper. It is now only seven o'clock, and already quite dark. This reminds one of autumn, no less than by

day do the thousand tinted hills, where the red of the cherry trees and the pale green of the winter corn gleam gaily through each other. I went in the twilight to the convent, and made acquaintance with the organ."

Educated with an almost Spartan rigour—early brought into contact with every department of human knowledge, and associating constantly with his elders, Mendelssohn nevertheless retained throughout his life the simplicity and impulsiveness of a child; yet his career is full of manly energy, enlightened enthusiasm, and the severest devotion to the highest forms of art. He had a passion for cake and sweetmeats, and a detestation of every kind of meanness and hypocrisy. He could romp like a child, but shrunk from anything like dissipation or excess. Nothing can be more genuine than his indignation upon one occasion when his anxious friend Devrient, hearing of the adulation lavished upon him in London, wrote to warn him of the dangers and seductions of London society. Mendelssohn was then a very young man, and his older friend might well be excused some little anxiety on his account.

"If you were here I might walk up and down your room, and vent my vexation about many things, but it will be some time till we meet, and if you have not full reliance in one whom you should know, you will have cause enough hereafter to feel uncomfortable about him. Now I should be sorry for this, and very sorry if anything again were to be useful or hurtful to me in your good opinion, or that you thought I could ever change. Upon my word, Devrient, when I improve or deteriorate I shall let you know by express. Till then believe it not. Of course I mean as to certain things usually called sentiments."

Mendelssohn's very weaknesses were lovable. If

he was sometimes sharp with his friends, it was because he could not bear the shadow of suspicion; if he was sometimes suspicious himself, it was because his sensitive nature was too open to sudden and often one-sided impressions; if he could not pardon jealousy or meanness in lower natures than his own, it was because he was incapable of understanding them. His want of resolution is sometimes charming. When Devrient had persuaded him to go to old Zelter, his beloved master, in order to try and win him over to the production of Bach's *Passions Musik*, Mendelssohn characteristically says at the door—

"'If he is abusive I shall go. I cannot squabble with him.' 'He is sure to be abusive,' said I, 'but I will take the squabbling in hand myself.'

What delicate little touches of character are these!—

"He came to us at twilight to say good-bye, anxious and cast down. I went with him across the court, and we walked up and down a long time under the projecting eaves by the summer drawing-room, as there was a gentle rain. Felix poured himself out in almost infantile lamentations; he wept, nor was I able to comfort him."

He had little coaxing ways with his friends, which made them love him with something like a child's love. When in company with Devrient, he would sometimes pronounce his name with an affectionate and lingering drawl, "Edeward," *àpropos* of nothing in particular, and gently stroke his head or lean confidingly upon his arm. Devrient tells us with emotion how, years later, when much had passed between them, many things had changed, and he sometimes fancied his friend was not the same Mendelssohn of old times, the old word, pronounced in the old loving way, recalled him to himself and almost brought tears to his eyes.

Mendelssohn's brain was from the first over-stimulated. But nature had prepared remedies for him—remedies which could not prevent premature decay, but which no doubt lengthened out his short life. Trifles sometimes excited him almost to frenzy; he could not bear disappointment or opposition. On one occasion when there was some likelihood of a royal summons interfering with a little domestic *fête*—

> "His excitement increased so fearfully that when the family was assembled for the evening, he began to talk incoherently and in English, to the great terror of them all . . . . they took him to bed, and a profound sleep of twelve hours restored him to his normal state."

It was by these sleeps, often almost like death in their silent torpor, that nature recreated a frame constantly overtaxed to the extreme limits of endurance by nervous excitement. His appetite also never failed him; he could eat almost at any time, and, according to his own playful admission, to any extent.

With such a temperament there was keen joy, much work, and great suffering for him in life; and deeply he drank of each cup until one by one he put them down empty, and composed himself for his last deep sleep. It has been the fashion to say in England that Mendelssohn was not a good conductor; that he was too irritable and exacting. The same was said in

Berlin; but this was never said at Leipsic. No doubt when out of a sympathetic atmosphere, when contending at his desk with the obstinacy of the Berliners, who looked upon him as an interloper, and the stupidity of the English players, many of whom thought him an upstart, he failed sometimes to conciliate the orchestra or to conquer its defects. Yet it is allowed that with the most stubborn materials he wrought wonders in England; and although he was never appreciated at Berlin, he always had the greatest difficulty in escaping. Devrient is probably right when, admitting his excessive irritability at times, he speaks of his conducting when surrounded by those who loved to play as quite perfect. He declares that the way in which he was able to infuse himself into the band was little short of magical, and at times he would leave off in a kind of trance, and listen with his head a little on one side quite rapt with delight at the band itself having become Mendelssohn, and therefore hardly needing Mendelssohn's bâton for the time.

But there are pages in Mendelssohn's life which have never been filled up, and points of interrogation which have never been answered. His relations with his wife Cecile *née* Jean-Renaud appear to have been tender and satisfactory, and yet her name is hardly ever mentioned in any letter or book of reminiscences which has yet appeared. She seems before her own death to have destroyed all his letters to herself, and with the exception of a few casual, but affectionate remarks in some letters written very soon after their marriage, Mendelssohn does not allude to her in his published correspondence.

A change, which Devrient himself can only partially account for, seems to have passed over Mendelssohn on his return from England in 1846.

"I became clearly conscious of a change that had come over the sources of his inner life. His blooming youthful joyousness had given place to a fretfulness, a satiety of all earthly things, which reflected everything back from the spirit of former days. Conducting concerts, everything that savoured of business, was an intolerable annoyance to him; he took no longer any pleasure in the conservatorium; he gave over his pianoforte pupils; not one of the young people inspired him with any sympathy; he could not bear to see any of their compositions."

If there is any explanation of this change beyond disease of the brain, which seems to have been hereditary in the Mendelssohn family, we shall probably not know yet awhile, or indeed until some of his contemporaries, who may have the keys of the enigma in their hands, have passed away.

He never got over the death of his favourite sister Fanny. He went to Interlachen with his family, and worked hard at the education of his children, the unfinished *Lorelei* and the unfinished *Christus*. Soon after at Leipsic, working with ever more and more application as he felt the night approaching, he was seized with a fatal pain in his head. A relapse followed.

"On the 5th, I went in the evening to Bendemann, where I hoped to learn the latest tidings from Leipsic. There came Clara Schumann with a letter, weeping; Felix had died yesterday evening, Nov. 4th."

We must conclude with a few more of Devrient's own touching words :—

"Hensel led me to the corpse, which he had thoughtfully decorated. There lay my beloved friend in a costly coffin, upon cushions of satin, embroidered in tall growing shrubs, and covered with wreaths of flowers and laurels. He looked much aged, but recalled to me the expression of the boy as I had first seen him. Where my hand had so often stroked the long brown locks, and the burning brow of the boy, I now touched the marble forehead of the man. This span of time in my remembrance encloses the whole of happy youth in one perfect and indelible thought."

ORATORIO OF ELIJAH.

First Part.

Next to the Messiah, the Elijah is the most popular oratorio in England. It is shorter and more dramatic than Handel's masterpiece, less theological than Spohr's *Last Judgment*, and less didactic than the wondrous *Passion Music* of Sebastien Bach. Thus, whilst the subject-matter of the *Elijah* is full of the most stirring incidents, its artistic form is sufficiently brief to rivet the attention of even an uncultivated audience from the first recitative down to the last chorus. No man ever wrote more in the presence of his public and less in the seclusion of his study than Mendelssohn, and in no other work has he so finely calculated the capacities of the ordinary music-loving mind, and so richly poured forth treasures which the most experienced musician will find, if not inexhaustible, yet always perfect.

The strange and majestic figure of the "Prodigiosus Thesbites," as he is called in the *Acta Sanctorum*, is ushered in by four solemn but not violent trumpet blasts—a mode of appeal to the imagination of the audience which a second time accompanies the appearance of Elijah.

The northern kingdom of Israel under Ahab, in the luxury of its magnificent cities of Jezreel and Samaria, had forgotten the God who had led the wandering tribes like sheep through the deserts of Sinai. Jezebel, the Sidonian queen, had not only persecuted the prophets of the true God, but had superseded the Jewish worship of holiness and purity with the seductive idolatry of power and passion. On every high hill flamed the pagan sacrifices, and wild, licentious orgies had penetrated even into the sanctuary of Israel and taken the place of Jehovah's pure and elevating ritual. The harvest of sin seemed ripe, the time was near at hand, the hearts of the seven thousand who had not bowed the knee to Baal cried aloud from the dens and caves of the earth, and the God of righteousness at last arose to confound the rebellious nation with famine and drought. Alone, the man of the desert, clothed in a rough sheepskin and wearing a leathern girdle about his loins, with the suddenness of an apparition confronted the idolatrous Ahab, and pronounced the curse of drought upon the streams and valleys of the land.

The opening prelude indicates the gradual awakening of the nation to the sense of a new calamity. Less and less water, the wells fast drying up, the routine of life gradually affected, the cattle fainting on the highways, the people vainly seeking for relief, the impatient and irritable chafing of the sufferers at the consequences of a curse as yet but half realized; such is the purport of the first subject. The second begins with a *crescendo* of semiquavers, indicating very powerfully the approach of a more intense anguish. Still the first phrase of impatience is woven into this new subject as an under-current, and the movement is then carried on with increasing vehemence until impatience rising to fury, fury sinks at last into the wild impotence of despair, which culminates in the desperate cry of "Help, Lord!" wrung from the whole body of the apostate people.

After the first three passionate shouts the solid business of the first chorus begins, with a chromatic phrase of mournful and tender beauty taken up gently and distinctly by each part—"The harvest is over, the summer days are gone, no power cometh to help!" The sorrow goes on rocking itself into a calm and almost pensive mood, when suddenly a change of emotion occurs with the words, "Will then the Lord be no more God in Zion?" It is one of those abrupt and magical inspirations which Mendelssohn often employs to bind together the different sections of his choruses; anon the old plaintive phrase is woven in with a newly-developed meaning; the heavy grief is rapidly yielding to a stern and bitter feeling in the contemplation of certain special incidents of the drought, such as "the suckling's tongue cleaving to the roof of his mouth" and "the children crying for bread."

Another chorus full of heavy affliction follows, but its tone is more chastened, and it is not until all irritation has died away, and the hearts of the people have been brought low by the Divine judgments, that Obadiah, the king's servant, in the character of a minor prophet, comes forth to speak of a God who is slow to anger and of great kindness, and repenteth him of the evil. With the immortal tenor song, "If with all your hearts ye truly seek me," the hearer now enjoys a short respite from the dreary and hopeless anguish of the afflicted people.

But the rest is of short duration, for no sooner have the last echoes of the tenor solo died away than the chorus breaks out again into wild lamentations, mingled this time with a consciousness of sin as well as of suffering, and with that sense of sin comes terror. This last emotion is almost immediately suspended by a chorale of calm and severe beauty worthy of Sebastien Bach, as a vision of God's holiness dawns upon the sensual and idolatrous heart. The mourners seem to forget their sorrow for awhile and become rapt in the contemplation, not so much of a jealous God who visits the sins of the fathers upon the children, as of one "whose mercies fall upon thousands." In this wider and more consolatory view of the Divine nature we are again lifted above the harrowing scene of a great national calamity, and soon afterwards we find ourselves transported with Elijah to a solitary place by the brook Cherith, to await in the hollow of the torrent's bed the further unfolding of the Divine purposes.

It is here, beyond the cries of a distracted nation—beyond the reach of Ahab and the wrath of Jezebel, that Elijah listens in a dream to a double chorus of angels. These quartets are managed with two trebles, two altos, two tenors, and two basses, and anything more truly ethereal than the effect produced can hardly be conceived than "He shall give his angels charge over thee." The waves of high, clear melody break upon the stillness of the desert, and float joyously through the air. The veil of heaven itself seems rent, and in the clear blue sky the faces and forms of the angels are ranged in calm and beautiful ranks, as in the pictures of Fra Angelico, smitten with the eternal brightness and filled with Divine harmony, as when "the morning stars sang together, and all the sons of God shouted for joy."

No wonder that the prophet who had listened to such music and received the promise of Divine protection "in all his ways," returned with more than mortal strength to minister among men. Armed with angelic might, nothing was now impossible to him. The passionate appeal of the widow woman of Sarepta is answered by the calm words—"Give me thy son,"—and as the blood begins to course again through the veins of the dead child, and the breath in faint rushes comes and goes, the infinite love of God seems to break upon the poor woman's soul for the first time, and the chorus, "Blessed are the men who fear Him," at once suggests the meaning of Elijah's miracle, and confirms in the mother's heart a new emotion of adoration and trust.

Once more the trumpets peal forth as Elijah reappears, after three years, in the presence of the king, and announces the close of the drought. A short choral burst interrupts his recitative—it is the clamouring of the fickle people, now rebellious, now penitent, then again ready to rend in pieces the prophet of the Lord as they shout aloud the words of the angry king: "Thou art he that troubleth Israel." But the solemn conclusion of all doubt is at hand, and both the multitude and the priests of Baal become strangely docile beneath the attractive power of a great impending catastrophe. Every word of Elijah is now caught up as readily by the chorus as were but lately the words of Ahab. The crowds sweep on at the bidding of the prophet, who, from this time forth throughout the scene on Carmel, never for one moment loses his ascendancy over them. They catch from his lips the inspiration of their brief chorus—"And then we shall see whose God is the Lord," as he gathers them together and summons the four hundred and fifty prophets of Baal to meet him upon the mountain promontory.

At the command of Elijah, the first heathen chorus

breaks forth. It is of a severe and formal character, very simple in construction, consisting of a hard, short melody, repeated again and again, with a kind of dogged abruptness. Indeed, the second phrase is sufficiently bare and ancient in form to remind one forcibly of the Macbeth music, commonly though falsely attributed to Matthew Locke.

The second Baal chorus begins with greater earnestness. It is full of misgivings, and at last loses every vestige of ritualistic stiffness in the wild cries of "Baal, hear us!" followed by death-like pauses, in which the whole assembly waits for the reply of Baal. "Call him louder!" shouts the prophet of Jehovah, as he stands apart and views with derision the scene of idolatrous fanaticism.

The trumpets peal forth derisively, as though to herald in the answer of Baal, and his prophets spend themselves in frantic efforts to awaken their sleeping god, but in vain. Then, maddened by the exulting sarcasm of Elijah, they pour forth their last wild chorus, leaping upon the altar and cutting themselves with knives, fainting at times from sheer exhaustion and loss of blood; then starting up with shrieks of frenzy and despair, they fall back upon the ground, and their plaint relapses into a protracted monotone of pain, succeeded by an awful stillness.

Wounded and bleeding around their unconsumed sacrifice crouch the false prophets. The shadows begin to darken in the mountain hollows, and the sun dips slowly in the western sea.

In the deepening twilight the voice of Elijah is heard, and the strong, calm prayer of the true prophet ascends to God. The meditative quartet, "Cast thy burden upon the Lord," follows. It is exactly what is needed to prepare the mind for the violence and tumult of the next terrible scene.

Once more Elijah speaks, but no longer in prayer. He has transcended all ordinary forms of communion, and his mind seems rapt in the contemplation of a spirit-world out of all proportion to ours; he is conversing with none other than the flaming ministers of heaven; and at the words, "Let them now descend," the fire falls from the skies with the hurtling crash of thunder, and the immense chorus of the people, thrilled with mingled ecstasy and terror, closes in round the blazing altar of victorious Jehovah.

The pent-up excitement of a long day finds a splendid and appropriate utterance in the passionate adoration of the crowd, and they fall upon their faces with one mighty and prolonged cry of, "God the Lord is our God: we will have none other God but Him." In another moment the religious emotion has passed into a murderous frenzy, and the prophets of Baal are hewn down like corn beneath a pelting hailstorm. The carnage is over and the vengeance done ere night descends upon the tumultuous throng and the smoking altar of the true God.

With a really splendid temerity characteristic of him, Mendelssohn dares after this climax return to the subject with a bass *solo,* descriptive of Elijah's prophetic majesty upon that memorable day, and a quiet *alto* song, full of solemn pathos, pronouncing woe upon all those who forsake God. It is here that, were it not for the exquisite beauty of what we may call this didactic episode, the action of the first part might be in danger of dragging a little. But the composer is still master of the situation. He knew that the mind would be exhausted by the prolonged vigil and sustained excitement of the scene upon Mount Carmel, and the needful repose is provided.

The way in which a second great climax is rendered effective so soon after the first is worthy of some attention.

After the two didactic pieces alluded to above, which are intended to recreate the emotions, the action becomes exceedingly rapid. Two short recitatives, then the brief cry for rain, followed by the thrilling dialogue between the prophet who prays on Carmel and the youth who watches the sky for the first filmy shadow of a rain-cloud. "There is nothing!" and the music is suspended on a long note of intense anticipation. "Hearest thou no sound?" and a growing agitation in the accompaniment makes us feel the distant stirring of the wind. Then the little cloud appears like a man's hand, and in a moment, as the prophet rises abruptly from his knees, with the rapidity of an Eastern tempest, the deluge of rain is upon us, drenching the parched valleys of

Carmel, and dashing into the empty pools. We are but one step from the grand conclusion of the first part; but that conclusion is not to be in the storm, as we should have expected. No temptation can hurry Mendelssohn from his artistic purpose; not a point is to be lost, not a touch of perfection omitted. A brief shout of mad delight rises from the people; in the pauses of the tempest, the dominant voice of the mighty Tishbite is once more heard, uttering the phrase, "Thanks be to God!" which is in another moment reiterated by the whole multitude; and the last and greatest chorus of the first part then commences, and thunders on with uninterrupted splendour to its magnificent close.

SECOND PART.

The second part of the *Elijah* is in some respects finer than the first. It contains at least as many immortal fragments, whilst the great danger of monotony is avoided by a variety of new and startling incidents, woven into an elaborate whole, which, if it does not exceed the first part in beauty of arrangement, has evidently made greater demands upon the composer, and astonishes the listener by its sustained power and completeness.

The *Messiah* is composed in three parts; but we may fairly say that although Mendelssohn found it possible to produce a second part in many respects more powerful than the first, the unique splendour of that second part rendered the very notion of a third simply out of the question.

Resuming the subject, we find that the action is not immediately recommenced. It would indeed be hard if we could not put up with some moral comment upon the events which have just occurred, especially when the moral is conveyed by one of the most thrilling soprano songs ever written. The clear freshness of the key of five sharps breaks upon us with an impetuous rush of words, "I, I am he that comforteth; be not afraid; I am thy God." The highest pitch of exultation is reached when the voice sweeps up from C to the high A, to descend through a splendid sequence and rest upon the lower A in the words, "I the Lord will strengthen thee." In the course of the song, all the most brilliant soprano effects which are calculated to express the confidence of a burning impetuosity seem to have been well-nigh exhausted. The same phrase from C to A has apparently brought things to a climax towards the end; but in the next line a completely new and still more startling effect is attained by sweeping up from B to A natural (instead of the normal A sharp of the key) and descending through a long G to the close of the song in B.

But we have not yet done with the exulting sentiment started by the soprano, for we are now close upon what has been not unjustly considered the greatest of Mendelssohn's choruses. After a silence of about half a bar, the mighty "Be not afraid," with the whole power of the chorus, orchestra, and organ, bursts with a crash upon the audience, already filled with the emotion of triumph in its more simple song-form. Now it is not one shrill angel only, but, as it were, all the battalions of heaven, with joyous shouting and glad thunder marching onwards, and chiming as they go the glorious deliverance which God has prepared for his people.

The languishing of thousands is then described in a *minor* phrase of contrast taken up by each part in succession, whilst the accompaniment expresses the fainting of those who rise and fall and gasp for breath; and the old scene of the wide land smitten with drought and inexorable suffering of thirst-stricken people, comes back to us like a dim memory in the midst of this glorious atmosphere of redemptive joy, when, with a suddenness and imperious decision that nothing can check, the dream is arrested, and vanishes for ever before the recurrence of the first colossal subject, which now proceeds for some time with a steady swing and a kind of white heat at once resistless and sublime. The rapid march of the chorus now so fastens the listener that he almost pants for an enlarged sense, or rather longs to take in the sound with more senses than one. There are no pages more utterly satisfactory, even to the ordinary hearer, than the closing pages of "Be not afraid." The satisfaction is shared by the orchestra; every instrument has to play what it can play so well; the first violin parts, especially, make the heart of a violinist leap to look at them. Who does not remember the richness of the accompaniments in that striking passage towards the close, where the musical phrase rises on a series of melodic steps, supported by the richest harmonic suspensions, from B, B to A, from D, D to C, from C, C to B, until the long D is reached in the word "afraid," and the violins in serried ranks, with all the power of the most grinding *stretto,* scale to upper E once, with a shrill scream that pierces high through the orchestral tempest, and then draw down to the long-expected D which ends the phrase? This consummate passage is repeated *in extenso,* without pause or interlude, and brings us to the two last shouts of "Be not afraid," accompanied by the significant silences which usher in the close of the chorus; and then, in the simplest and broadest form, come the eight bars of thundering chorale, "Thy help is near, be not afraid, saith the Lord." The chorus is well weighted. Those bars rendering their three massive choruses are felt to be sufficient balance without any extra page of musical peroration. Anything more simple can hardly be imagined; but nothing more complicated would produce so complete and majestic an effect. Mendelssohn is not less great because he knows when to be simple.

The enthusiasm of the people, for the worship of the true God and his prophet, proves short-lived enough, and a new figure is now brought before us in connection with the popular disaffection. A few words of scathing rebuke addressed to Ahab, in some of those matchless recitatives which knit together so many portions of the oratorio as with links of pure gold, a lofty proclamation of the outraged sovereignty of God, and a sharp condemnation of Baal worship, are sufficient to bring out the Sidonian queen with powerful dramatic effect. The type at once of heathen pride, beauty, and insolence, this great pagan figure, in the might of her haughty and indomitable will, towers high above the wretched vacillation of King Ahab on the one hand, and the miserable irresolution of the populace on the other. In all Israel she was the only worthy rival of Elijah, for she alone seems to have thoroughly known her own mind. Not for one moment did she confuse the points at issue. It was human passion and human power pitted against the righteousness of Jehovah; it was the licentious orgies of Ashtoreth and the splendid rites of the Sidonian Baal against the worship of holiness and the severe purity of the Jewish ritual. But in the moment of her supreme rage Jezebel did not forget her cunning, and she sums up her case before the people in the most effective possible manner, when in her remarkable recitative she exclaims, "Doth Ahab govern the kingdom of Israel while Elijah's power is greater than the king's?" For popular purposes it was not so much Jehovah against Baal as Elijah against Ahab; and the populace now side with the queen as readily as they had before sided with Ahab and Elijah. Shouts of "He shall perish!" rend the air; and in the pauses the voice of Jezebel is heard lashing the multitude into savagery with her scorpion tongue. The popular wrath settles at length into the powerful but somewhat unattractive chorus of "Woe to him!" rounded off with a brief orchestral close, in the course of which the last *forte* is toned down into *pianissimo*, and the much-needed rest comes in the shape of a beautiful and tender recitative and melody, in which Obadiah bids the prophet hide himself in the wilderness, assuring him, in a phrase of singular purity and elevation, that the Lord God shall go with him, "and will never fail him nor forsake him." And yet Elijah was destined shortly afterwards to feel himself most forsaken.

Sheltered only by the scanty boughs of a solitary bush in the wilderness, alone amidst the inhospitable rocks of Southern Palestine, we can scarcely picture to ourselves a figure more utterly forlorn. Faint and weary, his steadfast spirit for once sinks within him. A great reaction, physical as well as mental, now sets in. Flesh and blood can stand only a certain amount of pressure, and Elijah's power of endurance had been fairly over-wrought. The long watch upon the mountain, the intense emotion of that silent prayer for rain in which the prophet seemed to bear in his heart to God the sins and the sorrows of a whole nation—the stupendous answer to his petition, followed by the almost immediate apostacy of those to whom it was granted—the wrath of Jezebel, and the rapid flight for life—all this seems to have broken down for a moment even the noble courage and endurance of Elijah. The first and the last feeble plaint now escapes him, "It is enough, O Lord, now take away my life." We are filled with reverent sympathy at the sight of the prophet's utter dejection. Never, surely, was there anything conceived in the language of sound more pathetic than the melody to which these words are set. We follow every graduated expression of the almost monotonous emotion until we perceive how largely due to mere physical causes is this apparent spiritual lapse. Elijah prays for the sleep of death, but the recreative sleep of the body is all that he really needs; and presently, in spite of himself, overcome with intense weariness and exhaustion, whilst his lips have hardly ceased to falter out the words, "It is enough!" he falls asleep under the juniper tree.

It is a sight for angels to look upon, and with the silence of the wilderness and the sore need of the prophet, the celestial ministry recommences.

Not less exquisite, though more brief and, if possible, more perfect, than the angelic chorus in the first part ("He shall give his angels") is the soprano trio, "Lift thine eyes unto the hills." Happy prophet! to pass from the arid wilderness to such a dream of heaven, and to exchange suddenly the valley of the shadow of death for the bright morning hills, "Whence cometh thy help." No other vocal trio with which we are acquainted equals this one in perfection of form and in the silver-toned ripple of its unbroken harmony.

It was doubtless hard to follow such an inspiration; and with supreme skill, ere the prophet awakes, we are gently let down to earth by a chorus only a little less heavenly than the matchless trio itself. "He, watching over Israel," moves along with a certain quiet weaving of sweet rhythm and sound which indicates marvellously the steady and tireless vigil of the heavenly Father over his frail children during the hours of their helplessness.

Very softly at last comes the voice, mingling with, but as yet hardly dissipating, the prophet's slumber, "Arise, Elijah!" and very touching is the answer, "I have spent my strength for nought, O that I might now die!"

The heavenly music was reserved for his dreams, but true to nature, with his first waking moments the melody reproduces the feeling of profound dejection in which he fell asleep praying that his life might be taken away. Listless, without hope or fear, the disheartened prophet, in passive obedience to the Divine commands, starts upon his long lonely journey of forty days unto Horeb, the Mount of God; and some of the thoughts which in that pilgrimage may have sustained and cheered him are embodied in the contralto song, "O rest in the Lord," and the quiet chorus, "He that shall endure unto the end."

The hearer is frequently so entranced by the full richness of the melody, that he may have failed to notice the art-concealing art of one of the loveliest of all sacred songs. The delicate and minute changes in a perfectly unlaboured and simple accompaniment—the fragments of tender counter-melody which, without being obtrusive, prevent the least monotony—the gentle continuity, so expressive of sustained and chastened devotion, which requires less than one whole bar of rest from the time the voice begins to the time it leaves off—the perfectly original and characteristic *coda* where, in the last two utterances of the phrase, "O rest in the Lord," the voice ascends unexpectedly to G instead of descending to C, and where the accompaniment contains a thrilling surprise in the slurred G to C in octaves above the line; and finally the long "wait" drawn out through a semibreve of time, with an aspiration of unbounded confidence, presently to be resolved into a deep and happy repose of patience—all this, and much more, will come back to the memory of those who have once studied this matchless song.

We pass over the grave and somewhat severe chorus, "He that shall endure to the end," simply remarking that at this point the interest of the oratorio seems to be intentionally diminished, so that we are tempted to think the action is again beginning to drag, at the very moment we are about to be restored to the society of the leading character, and to assist at one of the most stupendous effects of dramatic music that has ever yet been realized.

A soft prolonged chord forms a prelude to the reappearance of Elijah among the rocky and cavernous clefts of Mount Horeb. The night is falling around him—his mood is changed, his deep depression has vanished. He is now filled with a passionate desire, not to die, but to feel the presence of his God and be assured of His protection. In such an aspiring and expectant state of mind he hears the voice of a strong angel,—no murmur as of the night wind, but distinct, loud, and decisive: "Arise now!"—then a trembling in the accompaniment and a kind of agitation immediately suppressed into a whisper full of awe, with the words, "Thy face must be veiled," prepares us for the dread announcement in a single bar of unaccompanied recitative—"For He draweth nigh!" With a burst like that of a sudden earthquake the chorus, "Behold, God the Lord passed by," comes upon us; but the *forte* is almost instantly suppressed, like fire that tries to escape. As when we watch the almost silent working of some monstrous engine whose force is nevertheless sufficient to crush the strongest fabric to atoms, we feel the presence of a power in all that immense repression, —something latent in the noiseless motion of the wheel which makes the inexorable swiftness of its revolutions all the more imposing, so the same kind of emotional effect is produced by Mendelssohn's use of *pp's* in such words as "A mighty wind rent the mountains!" Great and glorious gusts of sound burst forth almost directly afterwards, and the *crescendo* increases with the throes of the earthquake until shock after shock subsides with a *diminuendo*, leaving us each time breathless with the anticipation of what is about to follow.

What follows is so unexpected in the elevation of its harmonic temperature that we have known persons in a state of rapt excitement upon hearing this chorus for the first time, break out into a cold sweat at the words, smitten like tongues of fire from the rocks, "But the Lord was not in the tempest!"

The mere excitement of watching for the recurrence of this thrilling major phrase makes each stormy interval full of new interest. Every time it recurs on a different note—"But the Lord was not in the earthquake,"—"But the Lord was not in the fire"—which last major, before it brings the series to a close, is carried on with a reiteration so urgent and absorbing as to impress the mind with the thought of a soul seized with a Divine frenzy to see God, and in almost a terror of anguish at finding the wind, and the earthquake, and the fire, pass without any definite discovery of the Divine Presence. So near the absolute beatific vision, and yet no vision! The earthquake and the tempest, and the blaze of the lightning, and yet no voice, for "The Lord was not in the fire!"

As the last wild and nearly distracted cry dies away there comes very softly one of those magic changes in which the whole of the emotional atmosphere shifts—the cry of the spirit is going to be answered with a gentleness and a power above all that it could ask or think. The key changes from one to four sharps, and the words, "After the fire, there came a still, small voice," then follow, with a peace and majesty of the most ineffable sweetness, "And in that still, small voice onward came the Lord." The melody flows on in the clear and silvery key of E major: it passes like the sweeping by of a soft and balmy wind, never rising, never falling, but gentle, and strong, and pulseless, coming we know not whence, and passing with the "tides of music's golden sea" into eternity. And as the last delicate strains of the accompaniment die away, we are left still looking up to heaven with senses enraptured and purified like those who have stood beside the gates of pearl and seen the King "in His beauty."

The recitative and chorus following, "Above Him stood the Seraphim," and "Holy, holy," develop the memory of this blessed vision, whilst the outburst of earthly praise at the close prepares us for the more commonplace scenery of this lower world, where we are allowed to rest awhile before the final scene of the sacred drama.

Once more, and for the last time, Elijah sets out upon his solitary way, but now he is sustained by an unfaltering trust. No more suffering, no more persecution, no more faintness or weariness; he is filled through and through with a sense of the Divine presence, and bears the light of God's splendour upon his countenance. The quiet *arioso andante*, "For the mountains shall depart," is thrown in skilfully, to recreate the mind after the extreme tension to which it has so lately been held, and to prepare it for a second climax of equal greatness and solemnity.

Nothing can be finer than what we may call the transfiguration of Elijah before his departure.

When we come upon him for the last time, he is more imposing than ever—more terrible than when he first met Ahab in the way, more majestic than when he stood upon Carmel alone before the altar of the true God.

We are permitted to see him thus only for a few moments in the chorus, "Then did Elijah the prophet break forth like a fire." Not in vain had he been upon the Holy Mount and seen the Lord pass by; not in vain had the earthquake rent the rocks at his feet and the sky been changed into a sheet of living flame; the tempest and the flame seem in a manner to have passed into his being; and the whole man was growing almost elemental as he was about to enter into the presence of his God. Those who met with him were stricken with awe at his appearance, and marked how "his words appeared like burning torches;" then remembered they how he had "heard the judgments of the future and seen the vengeance of God in Horeb."

The action from this point becomes almost intolerably rapid; indeed, it is wonderful how the mind has been enabled to bear another climax in so short a time.

But it was doubtless impossible to put off the last

scene any longer. We feel that the beloved but terrible prophet is already breathing the atmosphere of another world, and has well-nigh done with this earth.

Abruptly, in a moment, the phrase, "And when the Lord would take him away to heaven," is heard; first from a solitary bass voice, then from a rushing and impetuous chorus, as of a multitude who see the heavens opened before them, and answer with a frantic shout of mingled terror and adoration. A brief pause, and the chariot and horses of fire are there, and black clouds hurled about by a whirlwind, and flashes of intolerable radiance and mighty thunderings—and Elijah has passed.

"He went up by a whirlwind into heaven."

All through this rending of sky, and cloud, and terror of blinding flame, the tension on the mind, produced by the accompaniment of incessant triplets in semiquavers, supported by a magnificent pedal bass of chords and octaves, is so great that we lose all account of the time taken by the whirlwind. It is, however, very considerable, as a glance at the score will show us, and accordingly produces an adequate and massive impression, suitable to the august and miraculous nature of the event. The last long "Whirl—wind" on a minim, is but one more instance of Mendelssohn's inexhaustible command of effects at the moment when he seems to have strained our powers of endurance to the utmost, and exhausted every combination of sound.

Few composers would have attempted to produce at no great distance from each other in one and the same part, two such crises as the scene on Horeb and the Fiery Ascension; but surely none but the very finest genius would have resisted the temptation of closing the oratorio with this last scene. But Mendelssohn has had the courage to despise mere sensation for the sake of perfection, and has thus here, as elsewhere, asserted his claim to join hands with Handel, Mozart, and Beethoven.

Steadily through the glare of light which at once transports and dazzles us, does this great Oratorio "orb into the perfect star we saw not when we moved therein." The bad art of leaving off with a shock finds no favour with so complete an artist as Mendelssohn, and his greatness is never more felt than in the incomparable richness of the music from the time when all scenic effect is over, and all dramatic action has ceased.

At the close of some refulgent summer day, when the sun has set, darkness does not immediately take possession of the earth—the sky still pulses with pale light, and long crimson streaks incarnadine the west. Then, as we watch, the colours change and flicker, thin spikes of almost impalpable radiance shoot upwards through the after-glow, and with celestial alchemy turn many a grey cloud to gold. The rising mists are caught and melted capriciously into violet and ruby flame—and as the eye, still dazzled with the sun, traverses the deserted heavens, the prospect is no doubt more peaceful than when the fiery globe was there—more peaceful, for the cold twilight grows apace, and the eye is gradually cooled as it gazes upon the fading fires, until at last the subtle essences of the night have toned all down into a calm monotint of grey and passionless repose.

The conclusion of the *Elijah* is like the splendour and the peace of such a sunset. The day-star is indeed gone, but all things are still impregnated with his glory, and not until every gradation of colour has been traversed are we suffered to rest from our contemplations and drink deep, as it were, from the cool cisterns of the silent night.

From the time of Elijah's departure we notice a preponderance of clear refreshing majors, which make us feel aware that we are coming to the end of our journey—just as the odour of brine from the ocean tells the traveller that he is approaching the sea-shore. The great tenor song, "Then shall the righteous shine," which falls as out of high heaven, like the clarion shout of an angel, is in the major; so is the chorus, "But the Lord;" so is the delicious quartet, "O come every one that thirsteth, come to the waters;" and so also is the final chorus, "And then shall your light break forth as the light of the morning!"

The one recitative which occurs gives a curious theological twist to the close by working in an allusion to Elijah's second advent as the forerunner of Messiah; indeed, we may call the quartet, "O come every one," strictly Messianic. It is as if Mendelssohn felt the incompleteness of the grandest revelation in the Old Testament apart from the New, and wished to give his hearers at least a hint of the Christian dispensation, a subject which he would, no doubt, have developed, had he lived to complete his unfinished oratorio of *Christus*. Some people complain of the last chorus as dull and needlessly protracted. But the more we study the *Elijah*, the more we perceive that this chorus is necessary, and in its place at the end. It is quite regular, and even somewhat mechanical, and it leaves the mind in an atmosphere at once severe and tranquil. That is a very high level of conception for the closing treatment of so majestic a subject, and it would be difficult to improve upon it without fatally destroying the musical morality as well as the artistic beauty of the work.

The *Elijah* destroyed Mendelssohn. It was produced for the first time at the Birmingham Festival in 1846, when Mendelssohn himself conducted; and there can be little doubt that the excitement and incessant toil incident upon so great an undertaking, largely helped to shatter a frame already enfeebled by excessive mental exertion.

On the 4th of November, 1847, Felix Mendelssohn Bartholdy died at Leipsic, before he had completed his thirty-ninth year.

END OF THE SECOND BOOK.

Third Book.

INSTRUMENTAL.

VIOLINS, PIANOFORTES, BELLS, AND CARILLONS.

Third Book.

VIOLINS.

I.

I HAVE never been able to class violins with other instruments. They seem to possess a quality and character of their own. Indeed, it is difficult to contemplate a fine old violin without something like awe: to think of the scenes it has passed through long before we were born, and the triumphs it will win long after we are dead. To think of the numbers who have played on it, and loved it as a kind of second soul of their own; of all who have been thrilled by its sensitive vibrations; the great works of genius which have found in it a willing interpreter; the brilliant festivals it has celebrated; the solitary hours it has beguiled; the pure and exalted emotions it has been kindling for perhaps two hundred years: and then to reflect upon its comparative indestructibility! Organs are broken up, their pipes are redistributed, and their identity destroyed; horns are battered and broken, and get out of date; flutes have undergone all kinds of modifications; clarionets are things of yesterday; harps warp and rot; pianofortes are essentially short-lived; but the sturdy violin outlasts them all. If it gets cracked, you can glue it up; if it gets bruised, you can patch it almost without injury; you can take it to pieces from time to time, strengthen and put it together again, and even if it gets smashed it can often be repaired without losing its individuality, and not unfrequently comes home from the workshop better than ever, and prepared to take a new lease of life for at least ninety-nine years.

These and similar thoughts forced themselves upon me as I found myself some time ago in the quaint old workshop of one of the most gifted violin-makers of the age. It might have been the house of Stradiuarius at Cremona, in 1720. Violins lay around us in every possible stage of composition and decomposition—new violins made with loving care by the keen workman who would never hear them in their maturity; old violins that had somehow got wrong, and which had to be kept like watches until they went right; violins suffering from the "wolf," others bruised and dilapidated; sick violins with their bellies* off, others, equally indisposed, waiting to have their backs put on, a vast number without any heads, several waiting for ribs, and piles and piles of what we may call violin-bones, con-

* Technical term for the front of the instrument.

sisting of various pieces of hundreds of instruments of all ages, waiting to be made up at the discretion of the artificer into violins of no particular age. The dim light came in through one window upon those relics of the past. The sun seemed to have subdued himself for the occasion. A stronger glare, I felt, would have affronted the dusky browns and sober tints of that old-fashioned workshop.

Rome was not built in a day; nor was the violin the invention of any one man or age. Like the piano, its elements may be said to have come together from the four quarters of the globe. They appear to have been combined in every possible proportion, until endless experiments and the most grotesque forms resulted at length in the singularly perfect and exquisitely simple instrument known as the Cremona violin, which no time seems likely to impair, and no art seems able to improve. As we look with a certain interest at the earliest daubs of a great painter, or compare the wooden huts of a barbarous age with the stately edifices of our own, so we may be allowed to recall for a moment those rough early forms which have contributed their several elements to the violin.

If I were writing a treatise in the German style, I should be prepared to show how, at some remote period before the dawn of history, the great European races migrated from India, passing through Bactria, Persia, Arabia, and Armenia, and crossing the Hellespont, overflowed Roumelia, Wallachia, Croatia, Styria, and

Bohemia, then stretching away to the Danube and the Rhine, proceeded to people all Gaul under the name of Celt, from whence, as we all know, they crossed over to Britain; and then, after proving that the *Chrotta Britanna* was an instrument common to both Gaul and Britain, I should show, by a comparison between the instruments now in use in India and those played on by the ancient Europeans, that the Indo-Celtic race must certainly have transported the first rough model westward from the East. But perhaps it would be more true, if not quite so learned, to say that the principle of a string stretched on wood and set in vibration by horsehair or some kind of fibre has been known time out of mind by almost every nation in the world; and as we are now concerned only with the modern violin, I must beg leave to make short work with the *savants*, and confine the reader's attention to what I may call its three roots, *e.g.* :—

The *Rebek*, or lute-shaped instrument, with one or three strings; the *Crouth*, or long box-shaped instrument, with six or more strings (in both these the strings are supported by bridges and played with bows as in the violin); and lastly, the *Rotta*, or kind of guitar, without a bridge or bow, and played by the fingers.

In a MS. of the ninth century we have a drawing of the rebek, although it was probably known as early as the sixth. The crouth is somewhat later; we have no representation of it earlier than the eleventh century. It was an improved form of the rebek, but it does not appear to have superseded it for many centuries. The last player on the crouth was a Welshman, whose name was, of course, Morgan—John Morgan. He lived in the Isle of Anglesea, and died about 1720. The rebek was by far the ruder instrument of the two, and became extinct at a somewhat earlier date. It was the instrument of the people, and was rasped at every fair and tournament. It found little favour with either monks or nobles, who are usually represented playing on the more aristocratic crouth. It stood in somewhat the same relation to the latter as the accordion does to the concertina. The rotta may be thought of simply as a form of guitar. But it must be remembered that all these three instruments were constantly undergoing modifications in size and shape; that some rebeks had but one string, some crouths three or six, some rottas as many as seventeen.

And now, if the reader wishes to know how the violin arose out of this medley, adopting various items in the composition of each of the above instruments, and adding a something of its own which bound these scattered hints of substance and shape and sound into a higher unity, we advise him to take a good look at Figs. 1, 2, and 3, and then accompany us through the following brief analysis.

In the rebek (Fig. 1, p. 375) we get the rounded form pierced with two slits to let the sound out, which we also find in the upper part of the front of a violin. We have a bridge, a tail-piece, and screws, with doubtless a sound-post inside to resist the thrust of the bridge upon the front or belly. We also note that a box for the screws and the shape of the head come from the rebek, and not from the crouth.

From the crouth (Fig. 2) we get the important detail of the back and the belly joined by sides. This principle of two vibrating surfaces joined by what we call ribs or sides was an immense step forwards, as will be presently seen. The shape of the tail-piece was nearly the same as in our violins.

From the rotta, or, speaking more generally, from the guitar tribe, came the suggestion of the two curves inwards in the sides, and the semicircular curve of lower part to correspond with the top. From the guitar tribe we also get the elongated neck made separate from the body of the instrument, and ultimately the six frets on the finger-board, now happily abolished, which for a hundred and fifty years marred the perfection of the violin.

We have now an instrument of the viol tribe something like this (Fig. 3), which we may place roughly in the twelfth century. Although to the inexperienced it may look something like a violin, the most that can be said of it is that it contains only those elements of the violin which that instrument has borrowed from the rebek, crouth, and rotta, and still lacks the characteristics which constitute the violin proper, and raise it above the whole race of the old viols.

About the end of the fourteenth century, at the dawn of scientific music, viols were made in great profusion: the number of strings does not appear to have been fixed, and ranged from three to six or more. About this time it was noticed that human voices might be divided into four classes—soprano, contralto, tenor, and bass—and in the light of this discovery we soon find viols divided into the quartet, *e.g.* violette, alto, tenor, and bass. We shall probably never know all the curious shapes and sizes of viols which were made between the twelfth and sixteenth centuries. Large quantities have perished, others have been used up for violins. The lute-makers were constantly trying experiments. We find instruments which it is difficult to class at all, others that early went out of fashion, whilst the most recognised forms were hardly fixed, and were continually being modified, altered, or added to. As music grew, so did the rage for viols, and it is owing partly to the quantities made and partly to the caprice of the makers, partly to the waste and ruin of time, that it becomes difficult to trace in detail the steps from the rough viol to the violin, until we suddenly find this latter about the middle of the sixteenth century occupying a modest position in the midst of that host of viols which it was destined to supersede for ever. But the violin, with four strings, and tuned as at present, continued for a few years in obscurity.

In a concise Italian catalogue (printed 1601) of viols then in use, it is not once mentioned; and in 1607, when two were certainly used in Monteverde's opera of *Orfeo,* played at Mantua, they are alluded to as "two little French violins," which seems to indicate that the French makers first discovered this modification of the viol. In 1620, Michael Prætorius, in his *Theatrum Instrumentorum*, published at Wolfenbüttel, gives us an undoubted picture of an instrument which is none other than the violin. And, now, if the reader will glance from Fig. 3 to 4, he will at once see how the mongrel of the twelfth century was transformed through a course of successive developments into the violin of the sixteenth. The flat guitar-front is changed for the raised belly, the smooth curves of the sides are broken into four corners,*—a form which was found better to resist the strain of the bridge, and also allows a freer action of the bow. The slits in the shape of ƒ ƒ 's take the place of the C Ↄ's; the handle, instead of being flat and wide, is narrow and rounded; the finger-board is raised and reaches over the curve of the belly, instead of being in the same plane with the flat guitar front; and the guitar frets are abolished. Soon after we meet with the tenor viol and double bass, all built on the same model; and the constellation of "The Violin," suddenly detaching itself from the confused nebulæ of the violas, shines out brightly in the musical firmament.

The violin has four strings tuned in fifths; the first is E between the lines, the second A between the lines, the third D under the lines, and the fourth string G under the lines. The natural compass is from G under the lines to B above the lines; but by shifting the

* Since writing the above I have seen a drawing of a capital in the Abbey S. George de Boscherville, near Rouen, containing a viol with *sides broken into four corners*. 1066 is the date. I believe this to be a singular curiosity.

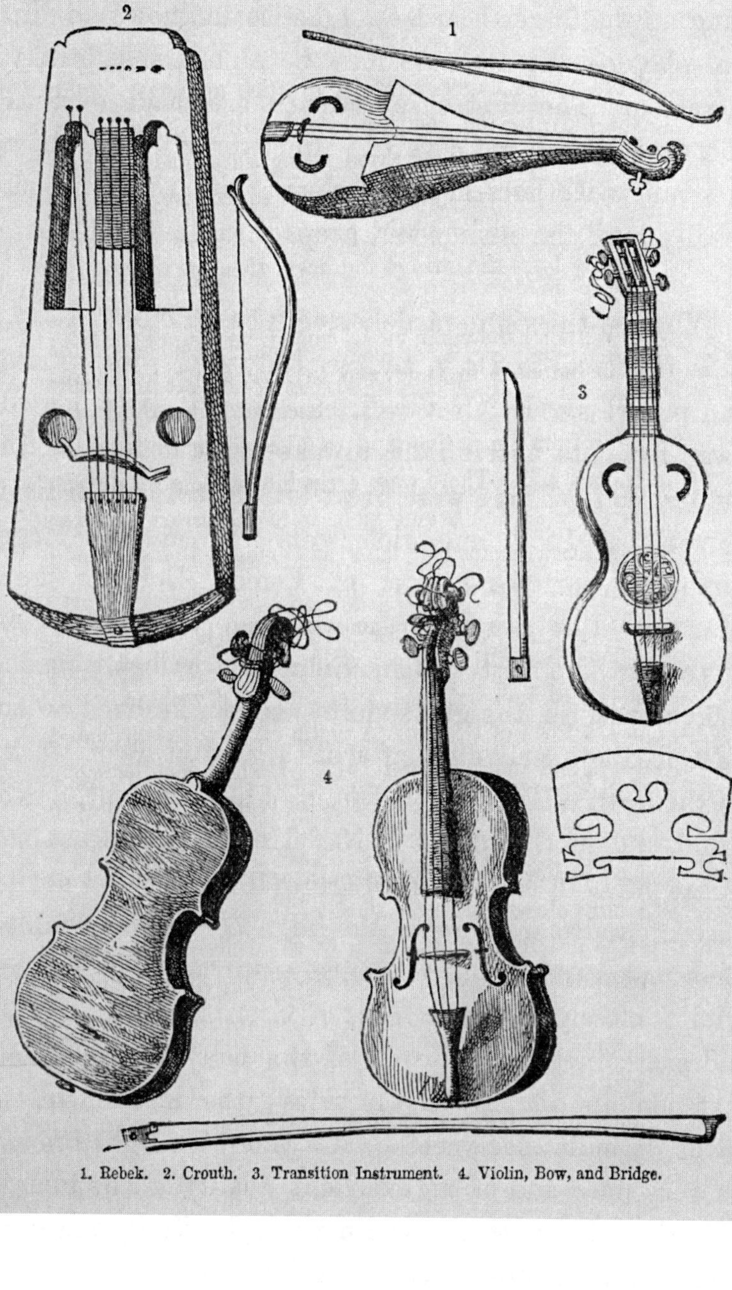

1. Rebek. 2. Crouth. 3. Transition Instrument. 4. Violin, Bow, and Bridge.

hand up the finger-board—a practice unknown to the viol-player—the compass may be almost indefinitely increased. The first three strings are made of thin gut, the fourth of gut covered with silver wire. The bow is strung with horsehair, powdered with rosin, which readily bites the strings and keeps them in vibration.

Whether the violin model came from France or Italy, it is indebted to Italy, and to Italy alone, for its rise and progress. If it was a French seed, it early floated away from its native land to take root and flourish in Italian soil. There were great lute schools at Brescia as early as 1450, and viols were fabricated in large quantities somewhat later at Venice, Bologna, and Mantua. But it was in the workshop of GASPARO DI SALO that the first Italian violin was probably made. Like almost all the great violin-makers, he lived to an advanced age, and died, after fifty good years of work, in the town of Brescia. A violin of his is extant, dated 1566, and another dated 1613. He found at least one great pupil in Jean Paul Magini (1590—1640): not to be confounded with *Santo* Magini, a celebrated double-bass maker in the seventeenth century. The Magini violins closely resemble those of Gasparo di Salo. The sides are narrow, the arch of the belly is high, and extends almost up to the sides; the instrument is strongly built; the varnish, of a yellowish light brown, is very pure and of an excellent quality. The tone is like that of a powerful violin muffled. It is, however, much more sonorous than the older viols.

Passing by such inferior makers as Antonio Mariani, Juvietta Budiana and Matteo Bente, both of Brescia, we come to the illustrious founder of the Cremona School, ANDREUS AMATI. When and where he was born, and who were his masters, we cannot say with certainty. What is certain is, that he worked in the first half of the sixteenth century, and set up a manufactory of his own at Cremona—some say, after having studied in the old Brescia school of Magini. A large number of his finest violins disappeared from Versailles after the 5th and 6th of October, 1790. These instruments had been the property of Charles IX., who seems to have been a great fiddler.

Like all the cabinet instruments of the day, spinets, lutes, theorbos, mandores, and guitars, the violins of Andrew Amati are not loud—a loud violin would have killed the other instruments, and grated on ears only accustomed to the feeble twanging of old viols and faint tinkle of the ancestors of the harpsichord and pianoforte. The Andrew Amatis are usually a little smaller than the Maginis, much raised towards the centre, finely worked throughout, and thickly varnished light brown; the sound is soft and clear.

His two sons, JEROME and ANTONIUS AMATI, inherited their father's workshop in 1580. They seem to have worked together, and those instruments which were the results of their united efforts are the finest. They are highly vaulted in front, deeply scooped out on either side of the vaults, the wood is chosen with great care, the workmanship is exquisitely smooth, they have not much power, the first and second strings are sweet and delicate, the third a little dull, and the fourth disproportionately weak. About 1635 Antonius died. Jerome married, and, although some of his instruments are equal in workmanship to the earlier ones made conjointly with his brother, those made after the death of Antonius are, as a rule, inferior.

Nicolas, son of Jerome, born 1596, was the greatest of the Amatis. The superior grace and elegance of his forms at once strike the practised eye. The curves are less abrupt and more carefully studied, the proportions more subtle and harmonious, the varnish is plentiful, soft, and glossy. A few extant violins, which have been worked out with a truly astonishing labour of love, are of indescribable beauty and finish. M. Allard, the eminent French violinist, possesses one of them. Another perfect gem, bearing date 1668, belonged to Count Cozio. With great sweetness and evenness of tone they unite a certain clear unmuffled brilliancy prophetic of the last achievements of the art.

The second Jerome, the last of this great family, is in nowise remarkable, except for the mediocrity of the instruments which he has labelled with the great name of Amati. To the school of Nicolas Amati belongs the illustrious Joseph Guarnerius, whose genius and originality might well entitle him to a separate biographical notice; but the Amatis and all their successors pale before the one great name which is for ever associated with Cremona, Antonius Stradiuarius. We have now traversed just one hundred years from Gasparo di Salo to Stradiuarius. One after another, quality after quality had been discovered. Gasparo and Magini determined the main outline and build, and produced a new tone essentially superior to that of the old viols, though still somewhat dull and muffled. The Amatis and J. Guarnerius brought the workmanship near to perfection, improved the proportions, and produced a clear soft tone of silvery sweetness. It remained for one master mind at this propitious crisis to step in and unite to the softness and brilliancy of his predecessors a powerful depth and body of sound entirely his own.

The rise of music in Italy and the perfection of the great violin schools closely followed the rise and perfection of Italian painting. It was at the beginning of the sixteenth century that all the elements of the art which had existed apart from each other began to come together: the study of anatomy and chiaroscuro, from Florence and Padua, richness of colour from Venice, reverence for ideal beauty from Umbria. It was towards the end of the seventeenth century that one great maker gathered up in himself the perfections of all his predecessors, and bequeathed to modern ears, in tonal splendour, delights analogous to those which the noblest painters have left us in form and colours. Like the rapid perfection of Greek sculpture under Pericles, or the sudden blossoming of Italian art under Pope Julius II., so, at the close of one short century, broke into perfect bloom the flower of the Cremonese school. Antonius Stradiuarius stands crowned the monarch of his art, the Phidias or the Raphael of the violin.

This remarkable man was born in 1644. There could be but one master for Stradiuarius—the great Nicolas Amati. The highest genius is often the most impressionable in its early stages, and we should never be surprised to find it engaged for a time simply in reflecting with utter devotion and the most perfect fidelity the highest known types. The early pictures of Raphael are scarcely distinguished from the later productions of Perugino; Beethoven's first strains remind us forcibly of Mozart; and the first violins made by Stradiuarius are not only exact copies of Amati, but are actually labelled with his name. Little is known about the great pupil, but that little exhibits to us a man who never had but one ambition—who without haste, but also without rest, laboured for the perfection of the violin. He took his time to watch, to listen, to test, and to ponder, waiting frequently years for his results, and accounting failure oftentimes as precious as success. To him the world was nothing but one vast workshop. On the western slopes of the Swiss mountains there were fair forests of maple and willow. It may be doubted whether he ever saw them, but they grew good wood for violins. The sun of Lombardy beat fiercely down on the white marble dust of the Italian roads, and made Cremona in the dog days little better than an oven; but the heat was good to dry the wood for violins. The fruit of the vine was refreshing, but the most precious ingredient was, after all, the spirit which mixed the varnish for the wood of violins. Sheep, oxen, and horses were, no doubt, valuable for food and labour, but the best parts of them were the intestines, which made strings for violins; the mane or tail, which provided hair for the bow; and the gelatinous hoofs, which yielded good glue for the manufacture of violins. After his first essays, in which he may be supposed to have completely mastered the forms of the old makers, and sounded their shortcomings, Stradiuarius appears to have passed almost twenty years in profound absorption and study. He was trying to solve those problems in sound which previous makers had only suggested. Why were some violins sweet and others harsh, or some clear whilst others were muffled? What were the peculiar forms and proportions which made Nicolas Amati superior to his predecessors? Was it possible by deviating from these forms to gain an increase of power without a loss of sweetness? Some such speculations as these no doubt occupied Antonius from 1670 to 1690. They were his years of meditation, theory, and experiment. We have few violins of this period, but these few bear his own name, and still bear a strong resemblance to the Amatis. It seems almost as if, in what he gave to the world, he had been unwilling to depart from the finest model he knew until he had discovered a finer. After all, it is only the second-rate minds that are for ever explaining their methods, and bringing the paraphernalia of the workshop before the public; the first-class men have a passion for the perfect work, and can afford to suppress many beautiful failures which seem to them merely steps in the ladder of progress.

No doubt, then, the sudden change we notice in 1690 was not the result of a momentary inspiration, so much as the embodiment of twenty years of thought and experiment.

Stradiuarius had discovered a *better model,* and his work henceforth ceases to be a close copy of his masters. His violins are now somewhat wider, the arch of the belly is less abrupt, the thicknesses of the wood are fixed according to more rigorous experiments, the varnish has a tinge of red in it, yet the maker has not reached his climax. The violins up to this period, from 1690 to 1700, are called Stradiuarius Amati. The great artist had now reached his fiftieth year—his hand and eye had at length attained supreme skill and freedom. The violins from 1700 to 1725 have all the grace and boldness of a Greek frieze drawn by a master's hand. The curves are perfectly graceful—the arch of the belly, not too flat or too much raised, is the true natural curve of beauty. On each side the undulating lines, as from the bosom of a wave, flow down and seem to eddy up into the four corners, where they are caught and refined away into those little angles with that exquisite finish which rejoices the heart of a connoisseur. When the instrument is held sideways against the light, the curve of the back, without being exactly similar, is seen to form a sweep in delicious harmony with the upper arch. The details have lost all the old cut-and-dried stiffness; the two *f*'s are carved with a symmetry and elegance of pattern which later makers have copied closely, but have not ventured to modify. The Stradiuarius is throughout a thing of beauty, and, it may be added, almost a joy for ever. When opened for repairs, the interior is no less perfect. The little blocks, and ribs, and slips of wood to strengthen the sides, all are without a scratch or shadow of roughness; the weight and size of each are carefully adjusted to the proportion of the whole; and as great poets are said to spend days over a line, so Stradiuarius may well have spent as long over the size, position, and finish of many a tiny block; and as the great architects of the thirteenth century lavished exquisite work on little details of their cathedrals, in lofty pinnacles and hidden nooks, so did this great maker finish as carefully interior angles and surfaces that were, perhaps, never to be seen but once in a hundred years, if so often, and then only by the eye of some skilful artificer.

It is in this way that many plausible forgeries are detected. Early in the present century the French makers began to copy the Stradiuarius violins so closely that to the eye there seemed little difference between the originals and the copies; but when the forgeries were taken to pieces to improve their dull tone, or to be cleaned and mended, the dead men's bones, in the shape of rough blocks, lumps of glue, and rugged work of all kinds, were disclosed, and it became quite clear that these miserable whited sepulchres had never imprisoned the soul of a Cremona. And thus the labour of love, which might have seemed in vain to the master's contemporaries, has had its reward at last, and lives for ever to testify to the cunning hand and the devoted heart. And by a singular accident, which the old makers could not have foreseen, all their violins have been opened, and the faithfulness of their work made manifest, for the bar which runs down the middle of the inside of the arch, to support the strain of the bridge, has had to be replaced in each case by a stronger bar, as the pitch has risen through successive years, and the tension of the strings increased in proportion.

Stradiuarius made, besides violins, tenors, violoncellos, and basses, a great quantity of lutes, guitars, and viols, which are still celebrated. His tenors are few in number, but very fine, and his basses have all the characteristic qualities of the violins. In a few instruments belonging to his fine period (1700—1725) we notice a departure from his most perfect forms—some are elongated, and others bulge like the older models—and both are proportionately inferior in quality.

From 1725 to 1730 the violins are still fine, but fewer in number, and of more doubtful authenticity. Some are begun by him and finished by pupils; others made under his direction merely bear his name. About 1730 the master's name begins to disappear; yet after this date there are several violins known to be by his hand: the execution is uncertain, the designs are drawn with less vigour, and a want of finish generally attests the dim eye and feeble hand of old age.

In 1736, Stradiuarius being then ninety-two years old, took up his keen chisel and completed with his own hand his last violin. The old man had been waiting for death ever since 1729, the year in which he had his tomb made ready; he died in 1737.* His last years were employed in forming such pupils as Bergonzi and Peter Guarnerius. He was quite aware that his creative period was long past, and although he no longer labelled his instruments, in his last years he made an incredible number of sketches and models for violins, which were afterwards finished by his numerous pupils, and sold as genuine products.

Lute-maker Antonius was probably little moved by the political convulsions of his age. In 1702 Cremona was taken during the War of Succession by the French Marshal Villeroy, recovered by Prince Eugenius, and taken again by the French. After that time for many years Italy continued in a state of profound and fatal tranquillity. But peace no doubt suited the absorbed workman better than any patriotic war.

If, before we take leave of the personal history of this great man, we are to try and see him as he appeared in his green old age to the inhabitants of

* "In pulling down the church of San Domenico, at Cremona, the tomb of Antonio Stradivari, the great violin-maker, has been discovered. His remains have been transported to the cemetery, where a monument will be erected to him."—*Musical Standard.*

Cremona, we must transport ourselves to the house No. 1239, in the Piazza S. Domenico, at Cremona, and imagine that (now) carpet warehouse changed into an old workshop like that described at the commencement of this chapter. There lived and died Antonius Stradiuarius, known to all men, respected as one of the oldest inhabitants, and envied by not a few as the most celebrated lute-maker in Italy. We cannot join hands with him through any living person who has seen him, but we can almost. Bergonzi, grandson of the great Carlo Bergonzi, who died only a few years ago, at the age of eighty, used to point out the house of his grandfather's contemporary. And old Polledro, late chapel-master at Turin, describes Antonius as an intimate friend of his master, and we shall get no nearer to Antonius than the description he has left of him. He was high and thin, and looked like one worn with much thought and incessant industry. In summer he wore a white cotton nightcap, and in winter a white one made of some woollen material. He was never seen without his apron of white leather, and every day was to him exactly like every other day. His mind was always riveted upon his one pursuit, and he seemed neither to know nor to desire the least change of occupation. His violins sold for four golden livres a piece, and were considered the best in Italy, and as he never spent anything except upon the necessaries of life and his own trade, he saved a good deal of money, and the simple-minded Cremonese used to make jokes about his thriftiness, and not perhaps without a little touch of envy, until the favourite proverb applied to a prosperous fellow-citizen used to be "*As rich as Stradiuarius!*" *

And now it may be thought that enough has been said concerning violins and their makers, but in truth we have only come to the threshold of the subject, and the mysteries of the manufacture remain to be expounded. This it would be exceedingly difficult to do without the aid of a great many diagrams, and indeed without presupposing the reader to have acquired some practical knowledge of the art. I must here confine myself to a few leading points.

It has been sometimes said that the merit of a violin is not so much in the make as (I.) in the age, and (II.) the quality of vibration produced in the wood by incessant use. It may be answered, first, that no doubt age improves violins, but age will never make a good violin out of a bad one; witness the host of violins that were made in the time of Stradiuarius by makers whose names are either known as greatly inferior to his, or forgotten altogether. Again, that using a violin keeps it in good condition is no doubt true; but, that much using a bad one will make it good, is not certainly the case: for, how many bad fiddles are there that have been scraped assiduously for ages, and are still as bad as can be?

* Fig. 4 is copied from a very perfect and powerful instrument in the writer's possession, bearing a label with the master's seal: "Antonius Stradiuarius Cremonensis faciebat anno 1712."

Thus it would appear that the secret of excellence lies neither in age nor use, but must be sought elsewhere.

The excellence of a violin depends, roughly speaking, upon two ranges of qualities—1. The thickness, density, and collocation of the various woods. 2. On the nature and direction of the curves.

1. The front of a violin is of soft deal, the back and sides are of maple. Now it is well known that a piece of wood, like a string in tension, can be set in vibration, and will then yield a certain musical note—the pitch of that note will depend upon the length, thickness, and density of the wood—and that note will be generated by a certain number of sound-waves or vibrations. Now, when the back or front of a violin is covered with fine sand, and struck, or otherwise caused to vibrate, the sand will arrange itself in certain lines, corresponding to the waves of sound which generate the note belonging to the back or front, as the case may be. M. Savart maintains that after testing a great many of Stradiuarius's violins in this way, he found that all the finest gave the same note, but that in no case was the note of the front the same as the note of the back. Further experiment showed that in the finest violins there was a whole note between the back and the front, and that any departure from this rule was accompanied with injury to the tone. There is probably a general kind of truth at the bottom of these remarks, although suspicion has been thrown on the worth and extent

of M. Savart's experiments by some of our experienced makers; however, the following facts, stated necessarily with considerable roughness, may be relied upon:—

For the front of the violin you must choose a very light, soft, and porous wood—there is nothing better in this way than common deal. When dry, if you cut a section and look at it through the microscope, you will see it to be full of little hollow cells, once filled with the sap; the more of such cells there are, the more quickly will the wood vibrate to sound. Of such wood, then, we make the table of harmony, or sound-board, or belly of our violin. But in proportion to the quickness will be the thinness and evanescence of the sound, and if the back vibrated as quickly as the front, the sound would be very poor. Accordingly we take maple wood for the back. It is a harder wood, containing less sap, and consequently fewer hollow cells when dry. It therefore vibrates more slowly than deal: the effect of this is to detain the waves of sound radiating from the deal, and to mix them with slower vibrations of the back in the hollow of the instrument. The ribs or sides of the violin, which are also made of maple, serve to connect the quickly vibrating belly with the slowly vibrating back, and hold them until both throb together with full pulsation and body of sound. But we must not omit to mention a little bit of stick called the sound-post, which is stuck upright inside the violin, just under the bridge, and helps the front to support the strain put upon it by the strings. This insignificant little post, connecting as it does the inside roof of the belly directly with the back, is so important in helping to communicate and mix the vibrations, that the French have called it the "soul of the violin;" indeed, by moving it only a hair's breadth a sensible difference in the quality of the tone is produced, and a whole morning may be sometimes wasted in putting it up and shifting it about from one side to the other. The best possible advice to all amateurs is, when your sound-post is up, leave it alone; but if it is evidently in the wrong place, don't attempt to alter it yourself, but have it set right by some first-rate violin doctor.

But we have not quite done with the vibratory qualities of the wood. Great skill must be exercised in the choice of woods. You might cut up a dozen maple trees without finding a piece of wood so smooth and regular in grain, and of such even density as some of the Stradiuarius backs; and then, although deal is more porous than maple, yet all deal has not the same porousness, nor is all maple equally close-grained. Consequently, two pieces of deal of equal dimensions will not give the same note.

How did Stradiuarius find out the notes of his wood?—how did he measure its vibration?—was he aware of the interval between the notes of his fronts and his backs? How much he knew we shall perhaps never be able to ascertain. His experiments in sound have not been handed down to us, any more than his way of mixing that crystal varnish into which you can look as into the warm shadows of sun-lit water. The best authorities believe that *he did not know* the reason of what he did—did not determine at all scientifically the various densities of his woods, or intentionally place a whole tone between the back and the belly; and for this reason, that had he once discovered these laws, neither he nor his pupils would have deviated from them, and we know that he *did* so deviate; for out of the immense number of his instruments only the finest of his finest period obey the test of these natural laws of acoustics.

The eminent violin maker, Mr. Hill, of Wardour Street, assured me that he could, after years of familiarity with violins and their woods, tell the different densities of wood by the feel, just as blind people can tell certain colours; and it is possible that Stradiuarius, in his choice of woods and their tonal relations, was guided by a certain instinct insensibly founded upon the immense range of his experience. I am assured by an eminent maker that he can tell by the *feel* the kind of wood likely to form the right front to get on well with a certain back, and *vice versâ.*

2. But we must not forget to say a word about the curves. We have seen that the general shape of the violin has been fixed, after years of varied experiment. It is not shaped so for convenience (although its last most perfect shape happens to be also the most convenient), but because its final shape is acoustically

proved to be the best. The most important curves are the longitudinal and latitudinal lines of the belly and the back. At first viols were made flat, like guitars, then in all sorts of fanciful curves; the older ones are thick and bulgy, like pumpkins. The curve gradually subsided, until we get the exquisite wavy lines of Stradiuarius. That curve is so graceful, because it is the curve of nature. Set a string in vibration, and you will get the curve in the rise of a Stradiuarius back. And I am told that it is one of the most modern discoveries that this curve itself—as it were distilled from a vibration—is the only one which is found perfectly to conduct the vibratory waves of sound. If Stradiuarius had known this, would he ever have departed from it? As a fact, we have some of his instruments whose curves are as far removed from nature as those of Amati or Magini. We are bound almost to infer that he did not know *for a certainty*, but got at last to know the kind of curves which, in conjunction with other qualities, went to produce the finest tone.

But the sides or ribs also call for special notice. The height of these determines, of course, the air-bearing capacity of the instrument. It is found by experiment that all the best violins contain about the same amount of air, and that a certain fixed relation between their air-bearing capacity and the thickness of the wood is always adhered to. And any departure from this rule is found to injure the intensity of the sound. If there is too much air the deep tones are dull and feeble, the high notes thin and screamy; if too little air, the deep tones are harsh and the first string loses its brilliancy.

Again, if the sounding-board or belly is too thin, the sonority will be poor and weak; if too thick, the vibrations will be slow and stiff, or, as violin-players say, the instrument will not "speak." Arch the belly too much, or make it too flat, in either case the equilibrium of the mass of air will be disturbed, and the sound will be muffled and nasal.

The shape and proportions of the two ƒƒ's cannot safely be departed from; no more can the model and the various incisions of the bridge. Immense numbers of holes, of all shapes and sizes, were tried, and also every possible description of bridge, before Stradiuarius fixed the pattern, which no good violin-maker has since ventured to alter or modify in the least degree.

The Stradiuarius varnish, which has a warm reddish tinge in it, preserves the wood from damp, and prevents it from rotting; it lies upon the wood like a thin sheet of the most transparent agate. The inside of the violin is not varnished; the hard outer coat of varnish serves to drive the sound inward, where it mixes and vibrates before escaping through from the two ƒƒ's.

We have now done with our historical and technical description of the violin; and perhaps we have said enough to show why it is, and must ever remain, the most fascinating of instruments, not only to the hearer and the player, but even to the collector. There seems to be a strangely sensitive, almost human element about it, which exists in no other instrument, and which goes far to explain the enormous prices paid for some of the fine violins; 300, and even 400 guineas are not unfrequently paid down cheerfully for a single one. No doubt there is often some "fancy" in the price. You meet with a violin that suits you, and it is simply worth anything that you can afford to pay. Different instruments, equally fine in their way, have separate qualities and peculiar characters; and the violin, which in some hands will prove unmanageable, will yield up to others all its hidden and mysterious sweetness. No instrument is so capricious or so absorbing. If one string chances to be a little too thick, the others will rebel; it will take to some particular bridge, and reject others; it will have its bridge in one place, and only one; it feels every change in the weather, like a barometer, and has to be rubbed and coaxed and warmed into good humour, like a child. Sometimes after being caressed, and, above all, played into splendid condition, the sensitive way in which it responds to each tiny variation of the touch will entrance and astonish the player himself. Thus it will often seem as if the player found quite as much power as he brought; and if at times he dictates to the violin, the violin, at others, seems to subdue him, and carry him away with its own sweetness until he forgets his own mind, and follows the lead and suggestion of his marvellous companion.

We have no room left for hints to amateur violinists, but we may as well close with two practical remarks:—

Firstly. Do not take up the violin unless you mean to work hard at it. Any other instrument may be more safely trifled with.

Secondly. It is almost hopeless to attempt to learn the violin after the age of ten.

PIANOFORTES.

II.

BEFORE the Pianoforte came the Harpsichord, and before the Harpsichord came the Spinet, and before the Spinet came the Virginal, and before the Virginal came the Clavichord and Monochord, before these the Clavicytherium, before that the Citole, before that the Dulcimer and Psaltery, and before them all the Egyptian, Grecian, and Roman harps, and lyres innumerable.

Some of the harps of antiquity were struck with a quill or "plectrum,"—we know very little more about them except that some were round and some angular, some with three corners, some with more, some had ten strings, some thirteen; and modifications of these varieties formed the staple of stringed instruments in the Middle Ages. The Middle Ages then had harps of all kinds, and out of the harp grew the psaltery, the dulcimer, and citole. The Psaltery was a box with metal strings stretched over it; it was plucked with a quill. The Dulcimer* was also a box with strings stretched over it; but it was *struck* with two crooked sticks. The Citole, or "little chest," was another box with strings stretched over it; but it was played with the fingers. And now if we roll all these into one, we shall get the first glimmering notion or embryo of a piano. A piano involves three fundamental ideas—*Percussion* (hammer), *Vibration on sonorous box* (sounding-board), and *Finger-touch through mechanical action* (keyboard). From the dulcimer, sometimes called *hacbret*, or hack-board (alas, how many young ladies go back to the dark ages and turn their pianos into hack-boards!)—from the dulcimer, we get *percussion with a hammer*, and from all three we get *the sonorous box*, or sounding-board; but no one had yet thought of that crowning glory—that now, at length, so perfect and subtle a minister of touch, the *keyboard*. As early as the eleventh century the keyboard was applied to the organ, and some time afterwards an unknown Italian (perhaps Guido of Arezzo) adapted it to stringed instruments, and hence arose the Clavicytherium or Keyed-lyre. For many reasons the Clavicytherium was not extensively popular, and for centuries after we read that at the feasts there was "Cytolyng and eke harping, y[e] fydle dovcemere, y[e] psaltery and voices sweet as bell." But little mention is made of the Clavicytherium, the "dark horse" which was, after all, to be the winner. The fact is, in those days people

* Dulcimer, "dulce melos," sweet sound.

seem sometimes to have progressed backwards: *e.g.* the Clavicytherium was fitted with *catgut* strings and *plucked with quills*, called jacks; and so, incredible as it may seem, the instrument in gaining a keyboard, actually lost its *metal* strings and the *percussion* touch! The construction of the Clavicytherium was coarse and simple to a fault. I have no doubt that, like our first harmoniums, it was always getting out of order—keys sticking, catgut snapping, &c., and was, altogether, much less manageable and portable than hack-boards and citoles.

The Clavichord * (1500) was a real advance; it was in most respects like the Clavicytherium, with the restoration of metal strings and the addition of that *sine quâ non* of all delicate effects of harmony—the damper. The damper, as every one knows, is a piece of cloth which descends upon the strings after they have been struck, to check the vibration and so prevent the sounds from running into one another.

The Clavicymbal differed only from the Clavichord in shape; it bore the same relation to the Clavichord that a small square piano does to an upright semi-grand.

With the Clavichord and Clavicymbal we enter civilized regions; instead of having to fall back upon unknown dulcimer players, copied from old manuscripts, and ladies out of stained windows with citoles on their laps, we have the solemn figure of old Sebastien Bach,

* "Clavi," a key; "chorda," a string.

with his neat periwig and silk stockings, thrumming those wonderfully melodious jigs and sarabands on his favourite instrument the clavichord. "I find it," he says, "capable of expressing the most refined thoughts. I do not believe it possible to produce from any harpsichord or pianoforte (*i.e.* a pianoforte of the Bach period) such a variety in the gradations of tone as upon this instrument, which, I allow, is poor in quality and small in scale, but extremely flexible." In 1772 Dr. Burney visited C. P. E. Bach, and heard him play. "M. Bach," he writes, "was so obliging as to sit down to his *Silbermann clavichord*, on which he played three or four of his choicest compositions. In the pathetic and slow movements, whenever he had a long note, he absolutely contrived to produce from his instrument a cry of sorrow or complaint, such as can only be effected on the clavichord, and perhaps by himself."

The Virginal and Spinet were still nearer approaches to the pianoforte; they were an improved and more expensive kind of clavichord; they were much in vogue towards the end of the sixteenth century, and were found chiefly in the Elizabethan boudoirs of the fine ladies of that stirring and romantic epoch. Here, for instance, is a description of Mary Queen of Scots' virginal. "It was made of oak, inlaid with cedar, and richly ornamented with gold; the cover and sides were beautifully painted with figures of birds, flowers, and leaves, and the colours are still bright. On the lid is a grand procession of warriors, whom a bevy of fair dames are propitiating by presents of wine and fruit."

Some think virginal refers to Elizabeth, who liked to be called the virgin queen. Dr. Johnson says it was a compliment to young ladies in general, who all liked to strum on the virginal. But another writer, with better judgment, reminds us how in the pleasant twilights of convents and old halls it served to lead sweet voices singing hymns to the Virgin. The very sound of the word "*virginal*" reminds one of St. Cecilia sitting, as Raphael has painted her, in a general atmosphere of music, with angels listening; or else the light should fall through stained glass upon old impanelled wainscots of dark oak, or upon purple velvet cushions and rich tapestry. And there, in some retired nook of an ancient palace, at sunset, "my love doth sit," saith Spenser,

"Playing alone, careless, on her heavenlie virginals."

Or here is another picture drawn from life; it is to be found in the "Memoirs of Sir James Melvil," 1683, ambassador from Mary Queen of Scots to Queen Elizabeth: "After dinner my Lord of Hundsen drew me up to a quiet gallery, that I might hear some musick (but he said that he durst not avow it), where I might hear the Queen (Elizabeth) play upon the virginals. After I had hearkened awhile, I took up the tapestry that hung before the door of the chamber, and seeing her back was towards the door, I entered within the chamber and stood a pretty space, hearing her play excellently well; but she left off immediately she turned about and saw me. She appeared to be surprised to see me, and came forward, seeming to strike me with her hand, alledging she used not to play before men, but when she was solitary, to shun melancholy. She asked how I came there. I answered, as I was walking with my Lord Hundsen, as we passed by the chamber door I heard such a melody as ravished me, whereby I was drawn in ere I knew how—excusing my fault of homeliness as being brought up at the court of France, where such freedom is allowed. Then she sate down low upon a cushion, and I upon my knees by her. She inquired whether my queen or she played best. In that I found myself obliged to give her the praise."

Again he writes—"She (Elizabeth) asked me if she (Mary Queen of Scots) played well? I said, 'Reasonably, for a queen.'" This reminds us of Handel's reply to his royal patron, who asked him how he liked his playing on the violoncello. "Vy, sir, your highness plays like a Prince!"

Shakspeare was fully alive to the sentimental side of the "heavenlie virginal," as the following sonnet proves:—

"How oft when thou, my music, music playst
  Upon that blessed wood whose motion sounds
With thy sweet fingers, when thou gently swayst
  The wiry concord that mine ear confounds,
Do I envy those jacks that nimbly leap
  To kiss the tender inward of thy hand,
Whilst my poor lips that should that harvest reap
  At the wood's boldness by thee blushing stand?

To be so tickled, they would change their state
And situation with those dancing chips,
O'er whom thy fingers walk with gentle gait,
Making dead wood more blest than living lips!
Since saucy jacks so happy are in this,
Give them thy fingers—me thy lips to kiss!"

About the year 1700 the Virginal went out of fashion, and its place was finally taken up by the improved clavichord, called *Spinet,** and later on *harpsichord.* In 1760, a first-class harpsichord by Rücker, the most celebrated maker, cost one hundred guineas. A grand harpsichord looked precisely like a grand piano, only it was provided with two key-boards, one above the other, the top one being to the bottom one very much what the swell keyboard of the organ is to the main keyboard. To every note there were four strings, three in unison, the fourth tuned an octave higher, and there were stops capable of shutting off or coupling any of these together. The *quality* of the sound depended upon the material of which the jack was made—whether, that is, the string was struck with cloth, quill, metal, or buff leather; the *quantity* did not depend, as in the piano, upon the finger touch, but upon the number of strings coupled together by the stops. It now at last occurred to admirers of the harp and violin that all refinement of musical expression depended upon touch, and that whereas you could only pluck a string by machinery in one way, you might hit it in a hundred different ways.

* From "spina," a thorn—hence "quill."

The long-abandoned notion of striking the strings with a hammer was at length revived, and by the addition of this third and last element, the harpsichord emerged into the Pianoforte. The idea occurred to three men at the same time, about the beginning of the eighteenth century—Cristofali, an Italian, Marius, a Frenchman, and Schröter, a German; the palm probably rests with the Italian, although, so clumsy were the first attempts, that little success attended them, and good harpsichords on the wrong principle were still preferred to bad pianos on the right one: but the key-note of the new instrument had been struck in more senses than one—the object of centuries was, in fact, accomplished—the age of the quill, pig's bristle, thorn, ivory tongue, &c., was rapidly drawing to its close. A small hammer was made to strike the string and awake a clear, precise, and delicate tone unheard before, and the "scratch with a sound at the end of it," was about to be consigned after a long reign, to an eternal oblivion.

We cannot wonder at the old harpsichord and clavichord lovers, even the greatest of them, not taking kindly at first to the pianoforte; the keys required a greater delicacy of treatment, it became necessary for professionals and amateurs to change their style of playing, and this alone was enough to hand over the new instrument to the rising generation. Silbermann showed two of his pianofortes to Sebastien Bach, who praised them as ingenious pieces of mechanism, but complained of their feebleness of tone. Silbermann, nothing disconcerted, retired into his workshop, and, after some years of study, during which no expense was spared, he at last produced an instrument which even Bach, wedded as he was to the clavichord, pronounced to be "without fault." From that moment a rapid demand for Silbermann's pianos rose throughout Germany, they could not be made fast enough.

Frederick the Great, who indulged in a variety of the most improbable pursuits, had several of them about his palace; and having the finest pianos, he was naturally anxious to hear the finest player in the world upon them. But Sebastien Bach, like other great "spirits of the vasty deep," would not always come when called for. At last, one night in the year 1747, as the king took up his flute to perform a concerto at a private concert in the palace, a messenger came in with a list of the guests already arrived. With his flute in his hand, the king ran over the names, and turning suddenly to the musicians, in a most excited manner, said, "Gentlemen, old Bach is come!" The great man had indeed alighted, after his long journey, at his son's house; but by express orders from the king he was hurried to the palace. The concert was suspended; no doubt the courtiers, in little groups, began eagerly discussing the new event; and the king's enthusiasm speedily spread through the assembly. Presently the door opens, and "old Bach," in his dusty travelling coat, his eyes somewhat dazzled with the sudden glare of light, steps into the midst of this lordly company of powdered wigs and doublets, and diamonded tiaras and sword hilts. His Majesty, after a warm and unceremonious greeting, besought the great contrapuntist to improvise to the company; and Bach passed the remainder of the evening going from room to room, followed by troops of admiring court ladies and musicians, and trying "*forte pianos, made by Silbermann.*"

But the man who, more than any other, made the piano and pianoforte music popular in England and all over the Continent, was Muzio Clementi, born at Rome, 1752. At eighteen, he composed his Op. II., which forms the basis of all modern pianoforte sonatas, and which required very considerable powers of execution. Clementi was educated in England, by the kindness of Mr. Beckford, and soon rivalled Bach as a popular teacher. In 1780 he went to Paris, and was perfectly astounded at his reception. He was dubbed the greatest player of the age, Mozart perhaps excepted, and soon afterwards left for Vienna, where he became acquainted with Mozart, the reigning star, father Haydn, and old Salieri, who was decidedly going off, and hated the new music, new pianos, and everything new. What right, forsooth, had these young upstarts to write music which the old men could not play? And such music too! Mozart was a charlatan, Beethoven an impostor, and even Schubert, the dear little choir boy, who might have carried on the glorious old Italian traditions, was becoming tainted, and writing music like Mozart! Poor Salieri! if he could only have heard the Schubert Symphony in C, and the A minor Sonata, what would have become of him?

One evening, Mozart and Clementi met in the drawing-room of the Emperor Joseph II., the Emperor and Empress of Russia were the only others present. The royal trio were longing for a little music; but how could one great master take precedence of the other? At last, Clementi, the elder of the two, consented to begin, which he did with a long improvization, winding up with a sonata. "Allons," says the Emperor, turning to Mozart, "d'rauf los!" (now fire away!), and Mozart, after a short prelude, played one of his own sonatas. The royal audience were delighted, although Mozart observed of Clementi, "He is a good player, and that is all; he has great facility with his right hand, but not an atom of taste or feeling!" We know, however, that this faint praise was only addressed to Mozart *père* in order to set his mind at ease about Clementi, who was in reality a formidable rival to Mozart *fils*.

The pianos used by Mozart and Clementi were the last improved pianos of Stein, the successor of Silbermann, with an extended compass of five octaves; yet in comparison with the commonest pianos now in use, these were but miserable machines. The genius, however, was even then alive who was destined to sweep away every imperfection in the working of the piano, and place it once and for ever on its present proud pedestal.

Sebastian Erard was born at Strasburg, April 5th, 1752. His extraordinary mechanical genius early attracted the attention of all the scientific mechanics in France; every problem was brought to him and generally solved by him as speedily as incomprehensible sums in arithmetic used to be by the Calculating Boy. His manners were refined, and the force of his amiable and versatile character gained him admission into the highest circles. He lived in the homes of the French nobility, and amused them by the uninterrupted flow of brand-new inventions and extraordinary mechanical contrivances. Nothing was too hard for him to accomplish, and nothing so good but what he could find means to improve upon it. In 1796 he made his first horizontal grand pianos, and Dussek played on one with great *éclat* in Paris in 1808. But the touch was still heavy and somewhat slow. It was not until 1823 that Erard produced an instrument susceptible of the finest gradations in touch; and thus, after laying down all the new principles which have since made his name so illustrious, he breathed his last at his country house, "La Muette," near Passy, on the 5th of August, 1831, at the age of seventy-nine.

The greatest manufacturing firms in Europe are those of Erard, Broadwood, Collard, and Pleyel.

Touch and *tone* are the two great tests of a piano's excellence; speaking roughly, Erard will bear the palm for touch and Broadwood for tone. Collard's flat Semi-grands and upright Trichords may be especially recommended as brilliant and good for wear and tear. It would be hazardous to pronounce in favour of any one of these great firms, as almost every player has his own opinion, and so far we have merely given ours. There are about two hundred well-known pianoforte makers, and each one has his own peculiar keyboard action, most of them being very slight modifications of those used by the four great firms. The strings of a Grand pull between eleven and twelve tons, or about twenty-five thousand pounds. There are forty-eight different materials used in constructing a piano, laying no less than sixteen different countries under contribution, and employing forty-two different hands. The finest piano may be obtained for about one hundred and twenty guineas. In the Great Exhibition of 1851, Erard's grand was valued at one thousand, Broadwood's at one thousand two hundred, and Collard's at five hundred guineas; but the extra money was to pay for the gorgeous cases. About twenty thousand pianos are annually fabricated.

The following simple rules are more commonly known than observed. Keep your piano out of damp rooms; never place it too near the fire or the window, or between them, or in a draught, but place it at least a foot from the wall, or in the middle of the room. Do not load the top of it with books; and if it is a cottage, don't turn the bottom—as I have known some people do—into a cupboard for wine and dessert. Keep the keys carefully dusted, and always shut down the lid when you have done playing.

BELLS.

III.

THE long, winding staircase seems to have no end. Two hundred steps are already below us. The higher we go the more broken and rugged are the stairs. Suddenly it grows very dark, and clutching the rope more firmly we struggle upwards. Light dawns again, through a narrow Gothic slit in the tower—let us pause and look out for a moment. The glare is blinding, but from the deep, cool recess a wondrous spectacle unfolds itself. We are almost on a level with the roof of a noble cathedral. We have come close upon a fearful dragon. He seems to spring straight out of the wall. We have often seen his lean, gaunt form from below—he passed almost unnoticed with a hundred brother gurgoyles—but now we are so close to him our feelings are different; we seem like intruders in his lawful domains. His face is horribly grotesque and earnest. His proportions, which seemed so diminutive in the distance, are really colossal—but here everything is colossal. This huge scroll, this clump of stone cannon-balls, are, in fact, the little vine tendrils and grapes that looked so frail and delicately carven from below. Amongst the petals of yonder mighty rose a couple of pigeons are busy building their nest; seeds of grasses and wild flowers have been blown up, and here and there a tiny garden has been laid out by the capricious winds on certain wide stone hemlock leaves; the fringe of yonder cornice is a waste of lilies. As we try to realize detail after detail the heart is almost pained by the excessive beauty of all this petrified bloom, stretching away over flying buttresses, and breaking out upon column and architrave, and the eye at last turns away weary with wonder. A few more steps up the dark tower, and we are in a large dim space, illuminated only by the feeblest glimmer. Around us and overhead rise huge timbers, inclining towards each other at every possible angle, and hewn, centuries ago, from the neighbouring forests, which have long since disappeared. They support the roof of the building. Just glancing through a trap-door at our feet we seem to look some miles down into another world. A few foreshortened, but moving specks, we are told are people on the floor of the cathedral, and a bunch of tiny tubes, about the size of a pan-pipe, really belong to an organ of immense size and power.

At this moment a noise like a powerful engine in motion recalls our attention to the tower. The great clock is about to strike, and begins to prepare by winding itself up five minutes before the hour. Groping amongst the wilderness of cross beams and timbers, we reach another staircase, which leads to a vast square but lofty fabric, filled with the same mighty scaffolding. Are not these most dull and dreary solitudes—the dust of ages lies everywhere around us, and the place which now receives the print of our feet has, perhaps, not been touched for five hundred years? And yet these ancient towers and the inner heights and recesses of these old roofs and belfries soon acquire a strong hold over the few who care to explore them. Lonely and deserted as they may appear, there are hardly five minutes of the day or the night up there that do not see strange sights or hear strange sounds.

As the eye gets accustomed to the twilight, we may watch the large bats flit by. Every now and then a poor lost bird darts about, screaming wildly, like a soul in Purgatory that cannot find its way out. Then we may come upon an ancient rat, who seems as much at home there as if he had taken a lease of the roof for ninety-nine years. We have been assured by the carillonneur at Louvain that both rats and mice are not uncommon at such considerable elevations.

Overhead hang the huge bells, several of which are devoted to the clock—others are rung by hand from below, whilst somewhere near, besides the clock machinery, there will be a room fitted up, like a vast musical box, containing a barrel, which acts upon thirty or forty of the bells up in the tower, and plays tunes every hour of the day and night.

You cannot pass many minutes in such a place without the clicking of machinery, and the chiming of some bell—even the quarters are divided by two or three notes, or half-quarter bells. Double the number are rung for the quarter, four times as many for the half-hour, whilst at the hour, a storm of music breaks from such towers as Mechlin and Antwerp, and continues for three or four minutes to float for miles over the surrounding country.

The bells, with their elaborate and complicated striking apparatus, are the life of these old towers—a life that goes on from century to century, undisturbed by many a convulsion in the streets below. These patriarchs, in their tower, hold constant converse with man, but they are not of him; they call him to his duties, they vibrate to his woes and joys, his perils and victories, but they are at once sympathetic and passionless; chiming at his will, but hanging far above him; ringing out the old generation, and ringing in the new, with a mechanical, almost oppressive, regularity, and an iron constancy which often makes them and their grey towers the most revered and ancient things in a large city.

The great clock strikes—it is the only music, except the thunder, that can fill the air. Indeed, there is something almost elemental in the sound of these colossal and many-centuried bells. As the wind howls at night through their belfries, the great beams seem to groan with delight, the heavy wheels, which sway the bells, begin to move and creak: and the enormous clappers swing slowly, as though longing to respond before the time.

At Tournay there is a famous old belfry. It dates from the twelfth century, and is said to be built on a Roman base. It now possesses forty bells. It commands the town and the country round, and from its summit is obtained a near view of the largest and finest cathedral in Belgium, with its five magnificent towers. Four brothers guard the summit of the belfry at Tournay, and relieve each other day and night, at intervals of ten hours. All through the night a light is seen burning in the topmost gallery, and when a fire breaks out the tocsin, or big bell, is tolled up aloft by the watchman. He is never allowed to sleep—indeed, as he informed us, showing us his scanty accommodation, it would be difficult to sleep up there. On stormy nights, a whirlwind seems to select that watchman and his tower for its most violent attacks; the darkness is often so great that nothing of the town below can be seen. The tower rocks to and fro, and startled birds dash themselves upon the shaking light, like sea-birds upon a lighthouse lanthorn.

Such seasons are not without real danger—more than once the lightning has melted and twisted the iron hasps about the tower, and within the memory of man the masonry itself has been struck. During the long peals of thunder that come rolling with the black rain-clouds over the level plains of Belgium the belfry begins to vibrate like a huge musical instrument, as it is; the bells peal out, and seem to claim affinity with the deep bass of the thunder, whilst the shrill wind shrieks a demoniac treble to the wild and stormy music.

All through the still summer night the belfry lamp burns like a star. It is the only point of yellow light that can be seen up so high, and when the moon is bright it looks almost red in the silvery atmosphere. Then it is that the music of the bells floats farthest over the plains, and the postillion hears the sound as he hurries along the high road from Brussels or Lille, and, smacking his whip loudly, he shouts to his weary steed as he sees the light of the old tower of Tournay come in sight.

Bells are heard best when they are rung upon a slope or in a valley, especially a water valley. The traveller may well wonder at the distinctness with which he can hear the monastery bells on the Lake of Lugano or the church bells over some of the long reaches of the Rhine. Next to valleys, plains carry the sound farthest. Fortunately, many of the finest bell-towers in existence are so situated. It is well known how freely the sound of the bells travels over Salisbury Plain. Why is there no proper peal, and why are the bells not attended to there? The same music steals far and wide over the Lombard Plain from Milan Cathedral; over the Campagna from St. Peter's at Rome; over the flats of Alsatia to the Vosges Mountains and the Black Forest from the Strasburg spire; and, lastly, over the plain of Belgium from the towers of Tournay, Ghent, Brussels, Louvain, and Antwerp. The belfry at Bruges lies in a hollow, and can only be seen and heard along the line of its own valley.

To take one's stand at the summit of Strasburg

Cathedral at the ringing of the sunset bell, just at the close of some refulgent summer's day, is to witness one of the finest sights in the world. The moment is one of brief but ineffable splendour, when, between the mountains and the plain, just as the sun is setting, the mists rise suddenly in strange sweeps and spirals, and are smitten through with the golden fire which, melting down through a thousand tints, passes, with the rapidity of a dream, into the cold purples of the night.

Pass for a moment, in imagination, from such a scene to the summit of Antwerp Cathedral at sunrise. Delicately tall, and not dissimilar in character, the Antwerp spire exceeds in height its sister at Strasburg, which is commonly supposed to be the highest in the world. The Antwerp spire is 403 feet high from the foot of the tower. Strasburg measures 468 feet from the level of the sea: but less than 403 feet from the level of the plain.

By the clear morning light, the panorama from the steeple of Notre Dame at Antwerp can hardly be surpassed. One hundred and twenty-six steeples may be counted, far and near. Facing northward, the Scheldt winds away until it loses itself in a white line, which is none other than the North Sea. By the aid of a telescope ships can be distinguished out on the horizon, and the captains declare they can see the lofty spire at one hundred and fifty miles distant. Middleburg at seventy-five, and Flessing at sixty-five miles, are also visible from the steeple. Looking towards

Holland, we can distinguish Breda and Walladuc, each about fifty-four miles off.

Turning southward, we cannot help being struck by the fact that almost all the great Belgian towers are within sight of each other. The two lordly and massive towers of St. Gudule's Church at Brussels, the noble fragment at Mechlin, that has stood for centuries awaiting its companion, besides many others, with carillons of less importance, can be seen from Antwerp. So these mighty spires, grey and changeless in the high air, seem to hold converse together over the heads of puny mortals, and their language is rolled from tower to tower by the music of the bells.

"Non sunt loquellæ neque sermones audiantur voces eorum."

("There is neither speech nor language, but their voices are heard among them.")

Such is the inscription we copied from one bell in the tower at Antwerp, signed "F. Hemouy, Amstelodamia (Amsterdam), 1658."

Bells have been sadly neglected by antiquaries. There are too few churches or cathedrals in England concerning whose bells anything definite is known, and the current rumours about their size, weight, and date are seldom accurate. In Belgium even, where far more attention is paid to the subject, it is difficult to find in the archives of the towns and public libraries any account of the bells. The great folios at Louvain, Antwerp, and Mechlin, containing what is generally supposed to be an exhaustive transcript of all the monumental and funereal inscriptions in Belgium, will often bestow but a couple of dates and one inscription upon a richly-decorated and inscribed carillon of thirty or forty bells. The reason of this is not far to seek. The fact is, it is no easy matter to get at the bells when they are once hung, and many an antiquarian, who will haunt tombs and pore over illegible brasses with commendable patience, will decline to risk his neck in the most interesting of belfries. The pursuit, too, is often a disappointing one. Perhaps it is possible to get half way round a bell, and then be prevented by a thick beam, or the bell's own wheel, from seeing the other half, which by a perverse chance generally contains the date and name of the founder. Perhaps the oldest bell is quite inaccessible, or, after half an hour's climbing amid the utmost dust and difficulty, we reach a perfectly blank or common-place bell. To any one who intends to prosecute his studies in belfries, we should recommend the practice of patience, an acquaintance with the Gothic type, and a preliminary course of appropriate gymnastics. These last might consist in trying to get through apertures too small to admit the human body, hanging from the ceiling of a dark room by one hand whilst trying to read an illegible inscription by the light of a lucifer match held in the other, attempting to stand on a large wheel whilst in gentle rotation, without losing your equilibrium, and employing the bell-ropes as a means of ascent and descent without ringing the bells.

It may be worth while to mention that as it is often possible to pass the arm round a bell and *feel* the dates and letters which it may be impossible either to see or in any way illuminate, a little practice with raised inscriptions will soon enable the bell-hunter to read as the blind read—with his fingers.

The antiquary will note with satisfaction the incontestable antiquity of bells. We read in Exodus xxviii. 34, a description of the high-priest's dress at the celebration of the high sacrifices. He was to wear a "golden bell and a pomegranate upon the hem of his robe round about:" and to show that no mere ornament is intended, in the next verse (35) we read, "It shall be upon Aaron to minister, and his sound shall be heard when he goeth in unto the holy place before the Lord, and when he cometh out." This ancient use of bells in the old Hebrew services irresistibly reminds us of the bell which is introduced into the Roman ritual at the celebration of the mass, for a very different purpose.

It is unnecessary here to trace the history of bells before the Christian era. It is certain that they were early used in the Christian Church for devotional purposes. The first large bells for this purpose were probably cast in Italy: they were soon afterwards introduced into this island.

Ingulphus, who died in the year 870, mentions a chime of six bells given by the Abbot Turketulus to the Abbey of Croyland, and he adds, with much satisfaction, as the sound of those famous old bells came back upon him, with memories perchance of goodly refections at the abbey, and noble fasts on fish, and long abstinence tempered with dried raisins from Italy and the British oyster,—"Non erat tunc tanta consonantia campanarum in tota Anglia." ("There wasn't such a peal of bells in all England.") *

We believe there is no bell extant of so early a date as 800. Bad bells have a habit of cracking, and the best will be worn out by the clapper in time, and have to be recast. There are, however, some wondrous bells in different parts of the world, which deserve to be mentioned even in so informal a treatise as the present. Father Le Comte, the Jesuit missionary, speaks of seven enormous bells at Pekin, each of which was said to weigh nine tons. They proved too heavy for the Chinese tower, and one day they rang it into ruins. Indeed, a Chinese tower never looks as if it could bear a good storm of wind, much less the strain and heavy rhythmic vibration of a peal of bells.

The largest bell in the world is the great bell at Moscow—if it has not been broken up. It was cast in 1653, by order of the Empress Sophia, and has never been raised—not because it is too heavy, but because it is cracked. All was going on well at the foundry, when a fire broke out in Moscow—streams of water were dashed in upon the houses and factories, and a little stream found its way into the bell metal at the very moment when it was rushing in a state of fusion

* This document is now considered unauthentic.

into the colossal bell-mould, and so, to the disappointment of the Russian people and all posterity, the big bell came out cracked. It may be as well to mention that a gentleman lately returned from Moscow throws discredit upon this generally accepted statement, and maintains that the bell was originally hung and that the crack was caused by its subsequent fall. It is said to weigh no less than 198 tons. The second Moscow bell is probably the largest in the world in actual use, and is reported to weigh 128 tons. The following extract from Chambers's "Encyclopædia," a work of unusual accuracy, will illustrate the great difficulty of arriving at anything like facts and figures: "The largest bell in the world is the great bell or monarch of Moscow, about 21 feet high, and weighing 193 tons (*sic*). It was cast in 1734, but fell down during a fire in 1737, was injured and remained sunk in the earth till 1837, when it was raised, and now forms the dome of a chapel made by excavating the space below it. Another Moscow bell cast in 1819 weighs 80 tons (*sic*)." Our first account of the great Moscow bell is derived from M. Severin van Aerschodt, the celebrated bell founder at Louvain.

There are not many English bells worth noticing. In 1845 a bell of 10¾ tons was hung in York Minster. The great Tom at Lincoln weighs 5½ tons. His namesake at Oxford seven tons.

We have to allude by-and-by to the bells at St. Paul's Cathedral and at Westminster, but for the present we return to Belgium, the "classic land of bells," as it has been well called by the Chevalier van Elewyck.

About 1620, whilst the Amatis in Italy were feeling their way to the manufacture of the finest violins, the family of the Van den Gheyns, in Belgium, were bringing to perfection the science of bell-founding. The last Van den Gheyn who made bells flourished only a few years later than Stradiuarius, and died towards the beginning of this century. The incessant civil wars in which Belgium for centuries had been engaged—at one time the mere battle-field of rival cities, at another the sturdy defender of patriotic rights against France, Germany, and, lastly, against her old mistress, Spain—gave to the bells of Belgium a strange and deep significance. The first necessity in a fortified town like Ghent or Bruges was a tower to see the enemy from, and a bell to ring together the citizens. Hence the tower and bells in some cathedrals are half civil property. The tower was usually built first, although the spire was seldom finished until centuries afterwards. A bell was put up as soon as possible, which belonged to the town, not to the cathedral chapter. Thus the Curfew, the Carolus, and the St. Mary bells in the Antwerp tower belong to the town, whilst the rest are the property of the cathedral chapter.

It is with no ordinary emotion that the lover of bells ascends these ancient towers, not knowing what he shall find there. He may be suddenly brought into contact with some relic of the past which will revive the historical life of a people or a period in a way in which hardly anything else could. He hears the very sound they heard. The inscriptions on the bell, in their solemn earnestness or their fresh forebodings, are often like drops of blood still warm from the veins of the past. None but those who have experienced it can understand the thrill of joy, as of treasure-trove, which strikes through the seeker upon catching sight of the peculiar elongated kind of bell which proclaims an antiquity of perhaps four hundred years. How eagerly he climbs up to it! how tenderly he removes the green bloom over the heavy rust which has settled in between the narrow Gothic letters! how he rubs away at their raised surfaces, in order to induce them to yield up their precious secret! How the first thing he always looks for is a bell without a D or 500 in it —*e.g.* MCCCXX.—and how often he is disappointed by deciphering MCCCCCXX., where MDXX. might have been written, and put an end at once to his hopes of a thirteenth or fourteenth century bell. Then the first bell he will seek on reaching a famous tower will be the "bourdon," or big bell, which has probably proved too large for the enemy to carry away, or which by some lucky chance has escaped the sacrilegious melting down, and been left to the town, perhaps at the intercession of its fairest women, or its most noble citizens. Ascending into the open belfry, his eye will rest with something like awe upon the very moderate-sized bell, hanging high up in the dusk by itself—the oldest in the tower, which from its awkward position and small value, has escaped the spoliation and rapine of centuries.

We can hardly wonder at the reverence with which the inhabitants of Mechlin, Ghent, and Antwerp regard their ancient bells, and the intelligent enthusiasm with which they speak of them. Certain bells which we shall have to mention are renowned, not only throughout Belgium, but throughout the civilized world. Most people have heard of the Carolus Bells at Antwerp, and there is not a respectable citizen in any town of Belgium who would not be proud to tell you its date and history.

Will the reader now have patience to go back a century or two, and assist at the founding of some of these bells? It is no light matter, but a subject of thought and toil and wakeful nights, and often ruinous expense. Let us enter the town of Mechlin in the year 1638. We may well linger by the clear and rapid river Senne. The old wooden bridge, which has since been replaced by a stone one, unites two banks full of the most picturesque elements. To this day the elaborately-carved façades of the old houses close on the water are of an incomparable richness of design. The peculiar ascent of steps leading up to the angle of the roof, in a style of architecture which the Flemish borrowed from the Spaniards, is still everywhere to be met with. Several houses bear dates from 1605 and upwards, and are still in habitable repair. The river line is gracefully broken by trees and gardens which doubtless in the earlier times were still more numerous within the precincts of the rough city wall, and afforded fruits, vegetables, and scanty pasturage in time of siege. The noblest of square florid Gothic towers, the tower of the cathedral church dedicated to St. Rumboldt, and finished up to three hundred and forty-eight feet, guides us to what is now called the Grande Place, where stands still, just as it stood then, the "Halles," with a turret of 1340, and the Hôtel de Ville of the fifteenth century.

But our business is with an obscure hut-like building in the neighbourhood of the cathedral: it is the workshop and furnaces adjoining the abode of Peter van den Gheyn, the most renowned bell-founder of the seventeenth century, born in 1605. In company with his associate, Deklerk, arrangements are being made for the founding of a big bell. Let us suppose it to be the celebrated "Salvator," for the cathedral tower hard by.

Before the cast was made there was no doubt great controversy between the mighty smiths, Deklerk and Van den Gheyn; plans had to be drawn out on parchment, measurements and calculations made, little proportions weighed by a fine instinct, and the defects and merits of ever so many bells canvassed. The ordinary measurements which now hold good for a large bell are, roughly, one-fifteenth of the diameter in thickness and twelve times the thickness in height.

We may now repair to the outhouses, divided into two principal compartments. The first is occupied by the furnaces, in whose centre is the vast caldron for the fusion of the metal; and the second is a kind of shallow well, where the bell would have to be modelled in clay. Let us watch the men at their work. The object to be first attained is a hollow mould of the exact size and shape of the intended bell, into which the liquid metal will then be poured through a tube from the adjacent furnace, and this mould is constructed in the following simple but ingenious manner:—Suppose the bell is to be six feet high, a brick column of about that height is built something in the shape of a bell, round which clay has to be moulded until the shape produced is exactly the shape of the outside of a bell. Upon the smooth surface of this solid bell-shaped mass can now be laid figures, decorations, and inscriptions in wax. A large quantity of the most delicately prepared clay is then produced; the model is slightly washed with some kind of oil to prevent the fine clay from sticking to it, and three or four coats of the fine clay in an almost liquid state are daubed carefully all over the model; next, a coating of common clay is added to strengthen the mould to the thickness of some inches; and thus the model stands with its great bell-shaped cover closely fitting over it.

A fire is now lighted underneath. The brickwork in the interior is heated through, then the clay, then the wax ornaments and oils, which steam out in vapour through two holes at the top, leaving their impressions on the inside of the cover. When everything is baked thoroughly hard, the cover is raised bodily into the air by a rope, and held suspended some feet exactly above the model. In the interior of the cover thus raised will of course be found the exact impression in hollow of the outside of the bell. The model of clay and masonry is then broken up, and its place is taken by another perfectly smooth model, only smaller and exactly the size of the *inside* of the bell. On this the great cover now descends, and is stopped in time to leave a hollow space between the new model and itself. This is effected simply by the bottom rim of the new model forming a base, at the proper distance upon which the rim of the clay cover may rest in its descent. The hollow space between the clay cover and the second clay mould is now the exact shape of the required bell, and only waits to be filled with metal.

So far all has been comparatively easy, but the critical moment has now arrived. The furnaces have long been smoking; the brickwork containing the caldron is almost glowing with red heat; a vast draught-passage underneath the floor keeps the fire rapid; from time to time it leaps up with a hundred angry tongues, or, rising higher, sweeps in one sheet of flame over the furnace-embedded caldron. Then the cunning artificer brings forth his heaps of choice metal —large cakes of red coruscated copper from Drontheim, called "Rosette," owing to a certain rare pink bloom that seems to lie all over it, like the purple on a plum; then a quantity of tin, so highly refined that it shines and glistens like pure silver: these are thrown into the caldron, and melted down together. Kings and nobles have stood beside these famous caldrons, and looked with reverence on the making of these old bells; nay, they have brought gold and silver, and pronouncing the holy name of some saint or apostle which the bell was hereafter to bear, they have flung in precious metals, rings, bracelets, and even bullion. But for a moment or two before the pipe which is to convey the metal to the mould is opened, the smith stands and stirs the molten mass to see if all is melted. Then he casts in certain proportions of zinc and other metals which belong to the secrets of the trade; he knows how much depends upon these little refinements, which he has acquired by experience, and which perhaps he could not impart even if he would—so true is it that in every art that which constitutes success is a matter of instinct, and not of rule, or even science. He knows, too, that almost everything depends upon the moment chosen for flooding the mould. Standing in the intense heat, and calling loudly for a still more raging fire, he stirs the metal once more. At a given signal the pipe is opened, and with a long smothered rush the molten fluid fills the mould to the brim. Nothing now remains but to let the metal cool, and then to break up the clay and brickwork, and extract the bell, which is then finished, for better for worse.

A good bell, when struck, yields one note, so that any person with an ear for music can say what it is. This note is called the consonant, and when it is distinctly heard the bell is said to be "true." Any bell of moderate size (little bells are too small to be experimented upon) may be tested in the following manner. Tap the bell just on the curve of the top, and it will yield a note one octave above the *consonant*. Tap the bell about one quarter's distance from the top, and it should yield a note which is the *quint*, or fifth of the octave. Tap it two quarters and a half lower, and it will yield a *tierce*, or third of the octave. Tap it strongly above the rim, where the clapper strikes, and the quint, the tierce, and the octave will now sound simultaneously, yielding the consonant or keynote of the bell.

If the tierce is too sharp, the bell's note (*i.e.* the consonant) wavers between a tone and a half-tone above it; if the tierce is flat the note wavers between a tone and a half-tone below it; in either case the bell is said to be "false." A sharp tierce can be flattened by filing away the inside of the bell just where the tierce is struck; but if the bell, when cast, is found to have a flat tierce, there is no remedy. The consonant or keynote of a bell can be slightly sharpened by cutting away the inner rim of the bell, or flattened by filing it a little higher up inside, just above the rim.

The greatest makers do not appear to be exempt from failure. In proportion to the size is the difficulty of casting a true bell, and one that will not crack; and the admirers of the great Westminster bell, which is cracked, may console themselves with the reflection that many a bell, by the finest Belgian makers, has cracked before our Big

Ben. The Salvator bell at Mechlin, renowned as was its maker, Peter van den Gheyn, cracked in 1696 —*i.e.* only fifty-eight years after it was made. It was recast by De Haze of Antwerp, and lasted till a few years ago. On the summit of Mechlin tower we fell in with the man who helped to break up the old Salvator, and although he admitted that it has now issued from Severin van Aerschodt's establishment, cast for the third time, as fine as ever, he shook his head gravely when he spoke of the grand old bell which had hung and rung so well for two hundred years. When a bell has been recast, the fact will usually be found recorded on it by some such inscription as that on the "St. Maria" bell at Cologne Cathedral:—"Fusa anno MCCCCXVIII.—refusa per Ionnem Bourlet anno MDCLXXXXIII." The name of Bourlet is still to be found in the neighbourhood of Cologne.

The names that most frequently occur in Belgium are those of the Van den Gheyns, Dumery, and Hemony. We have come across many others of whom we can learn nothing. "Claude & Joseph Plumere nous ont faict," and underneath, regardless of grammar, "me dissonam *refundit*, 1664." "Claes Noorden Johan Albert de Grave me fecerunt Amstelodamia, 1714."

The above were copied in the belfry of St. Peter's at Louvain. The name of Bartholomeus Goethale, 1680, is found in St. Stephen's belfry at Ghent, and that of one Andrew Steiliert, 1563, at Mechlin. Other obscure names occur here and there in the numberless belfries of this land of bells, but the carillon of Bruges (which, by the way, is a facsimile of the Antwerp carillon, and consists of forty bells and one large Bourdon, or *Cloche de Triomphe*), bears the name of Dumery. Sixteen bells at Sottighen, several at Ghent, and many other places, bear the same name. Perhaps, however, the most prolific of all the founders was Petrus Hemony. He was a good musician, and only took to bell-founding late in life. His small bells are exceedingly fine, but his larger bells are seldom true. It is to be regretted that the same charge may be brought against several of Dumery's bells in the celebrated carillon at Bruges.

"Petrus Hemony me fecit," 1658 to '68, is the motto most familiar to the bell-seeker in Belgium. The magnificent Mechlin chimes, and most of the Antwerp bells, are by him.

Besides the forty bells which form the carillon at Antwerp, there are five ancient bells of special interest in that tower. These five are rung from the same loft at an elevation of 274 feet.

The oldest is called "Horrida;" it is the ancient tocsin, and dates from 1316. It is a queer, long-shaped bell, and out of consideration for its age and infirmities, has of late been left unrung.

Next comes the "Curfew," which hangs somewhat apart, and is rung every day, at five, twelve, and eight o'clock.

The third is the "St. Maria" bell, which is said to weigh 4½ tons; it rang for the first time when Carl the

Bold entered Antwerp in 1467, and is still in excellent condition.

The fourth is "St. Antoine."

The last, but greatest and best-beloved of all, is the "Carolus." It was given by Charles V. (Charles Quint), takes sixteen men to swing it, and is said to weigh 7½ tons. It is actually composed of copper, silver, and gold, and is estimated at £20,000. The clapper, from always striking in the same place, has much worn the two sides, although now it is rung only about twice a year. The Antwerpians are fonder of this than of all the other bells; yet it must be confessed, notwithstanding the incomparable richness of its tone, it is not a *true* bell. I had considerable difficulty, during the greater part of a day spent in the Antwerp belfry, in gaining access to this monarch amongst bells, for it is guarded with some jealousy by the good Anversois.

After some trouble I got into the loft below it, where the rope hangs with its sixteen ends for the ringers; but I seemed as far as ever from the bell. It appears that the loft where the Carolus and its four companions hang is seldom visited, and then only by special order. At length I found a man who, for a consideration, procured the keys, and led the way to the closed door.

In another moment I stood beside the Carolus. It was not without emotion that I walked all round it, and then climbing up on the huge segment of the wheel that swings it, endeavoured in vain to read either the inscription or the date, so thickly lay the green rust of ages about the long thin letters. Creeping underneath its brazen dome, I found myself close to the enormous clapper, and was seized with an irrepressible desire to hear the sound of the mighty bell.

But, alas! where were the sixteen men? It might take that number to move the bell; but it immediately struck me that much less was required to swing the clapper as it hung. Seizing it with all my might, I found with joy that it began to move, and I swung it backwards and forwards until it began to near the sides. At last, with a bang like that of the most appalling but melodious thunder, the clapper struck one side and rushed back; once and twice and thrice the blow was repeated. Deaf to the entreaties of my guide, who was outside the bell, and did not care to come in at the risk of being stunned by the vibration, not to say smashed by the clapper, I felt it was a chance that comes but once in a lifetime, and so I rang the Carolus until I was out of breath, and emerged at last, quite deaf, but triumphant.

The decorations worked in bas-relief around some of the old bells are extremely beautiful, whilst the inscriptions are often highly suggestive, and even touching. These decorations are usually confined to the top and bottom rims of the bell, and are in low relief, so as to impede the vibration as little as possible. At Mechlin, on a bell bearing date "1697, Antwerp," there is an amazingly vigorous hunt through a forest with dogs and all kinds of wild animals. It is carried right round the bell, and has all the grace and freedom of a spirited sketch. On one of Hemony's bells, dated 1674, and bearing the inscription "Laudate Domini omnes Gentes," we noticed a long procession of cherub boys dancing and ringing flat hand-bells, such as are now rung before the Host in street processions.

On some of the older bells the Latin grammar has not always been properly attended to, and P. van den Gheyn has a curious affectation of printing his inscriptions in type of all sizes, so that one word will often contain letters from three or four different alphabets. The old inscriptions are frequently illegible, from the extreme narrowness of the Gothic type and the absence of any space between the words. One of the Ghent bells bears an inscription which, in one form or other, is frequently found in the Low Countries:—

"Mynem naem is Roelant;
Als ick clippe dan ist brandt,
Als ick luyde dan is storm in Vlænderland."

(*Anglice*—"My name is Roelant;
When I toll, then it is for a fire;
When I swing, then there is stormy weather in Flanders.")

The famous Strasburg tower, although, unlike the Belgian towers, it possesses no carillon and but nine bells in all, is remarkably rich in inscriptions, and has been richer. Its bells are interesting enough to warrant a short digression.

The first, or "Holy Ghost" bell, dated "1375,

3 nonas Augusti," weighs about eight tons, and bears the beautiful motto—

> "O Rex Gloriæ Christæ veni cum Pace."

It is only rung when two fires are seen in the town at once.

The second bell, recast 1774, is named "the Recall," or the Storm-bell. In past times, when the plain of Alsatia was covered with forests and marsh land, this bell was intended to warn the traveller of the approaching storm-cloud as it was seen driving from the Vosges Mountains towards the plain. It was also rung at night to guide him to the gates of the city. It is fitted with two hammers, and is constantly used.

The third, the "Thor," or Gate-bell, is rung at the shutting and opening of the city gates. It was cast in 1618, and originally bore the following quaint inscription :—

> "Dieses Thor Glocke das erst mal schallt
> Als man 1618 sahlt
> Dass Mgte jahr regnet man
> Nach doctor Luther Jubal jahr
> Das Bös hinaus das Gut hinein
> Zu läuten soll igr arbeit seyn."

Did Mr. Tennyson, I wonder, read this inscription before he took up the burden of the old bell's song, and wrote :—

> "Ring out the old, ring in the new,
> * * * *
> Ring out the false, ring in the true?"

In 1641 the Thor bell cracked, and was recast. It broke and was recast again in 1651.

The "Mittags," or twelve-o'clock bell, is rung at midday and at midnight. The old bell was removed at the time of the French revolution, and bore the inscription—

> "Vox ego sum vitæ
> Voco vos—orate—venite!"

The hanging of most of the Strasburg bells almost outside the delicate network of the tower is highly to be commended. They can be well heard and seen. The same remark applies to Antwerp, and it is to be regretted that in such towers as Mechlin and St. Peter's at Louvain many of the bells are so smothered up as to sound almost muffled. Almost all the bells which are open to public inspection, and which can be reached, bear white chalk inscriptions to the effect that our illustrious countryman, Jones of London, has thought it worth while to visit the bells on such and such a day, that his Christian name is Tom or Harry, and his age is, &c., &c. However, on the stone walls inside the Strasburg tower there are some more interesting records. I copied the following:—I. M. H. S., 1587; Klopstock, 1777; Goethe, 1780; Lavater, 1776; Montalembert, 1834; and Voltaire—the *Vo* was struck away from the wall by lightning in 1821, but has been carefully replaced in stucco.

In Mechlin tower I noticed the initials J. R. in the deep sill of the staircase-window; underneath is a slight design of a rose window, apparently sketched with the point of a compass.

Close inside the clock-tower of Antwerp Cathedral, and sheltered by the skeleton clock dial, although exposed to the weather, is scratched the name Darden, 1670. It is strange, but true, that what we condemn in tourists is regarded by us with interest when the tourist happens to be eminent, or even when he happens to have been dead for two or three hundred years.

For the sake of contrast, it may now be worth while to look into one or two English belfries before I close this paper. I will select St. Paul's, Westminster Abbey, and the Clock Tower.

The bells of St. Paul's Cathedral are four in number; three belong to the clock, and hang in the south-west tower; one small one hangs alone in the north-west tower, and is rung for service. The largest bell weighs over five tons, and is commonly supposed to have been recast from the metal of "Great Tom" of Westminster. The truth seems to be as follows. "Great Tom" was no doubt at one time conveyed from Westminster to St. Paul's, but having cracked, it became necessary either to recast it or to procure a new one. The bell-metal was considered so bad, that by the advice of Richard Phelps, the bell-founder, a new one was made for £627. He allowed $9\frac{1}{2}d.$ a pound for the old bell, but did not work up any of this metal for the present bell. This is quite certain, as I have the best authority for saying that the old bell was not removed until the new bell was delivered at the cathedral. The inscription is perfectly legible, and, as copied on a particularly bright morning by me, runs thus :—

"Richard Phelps made me, 1716."

A common fleur-de-lis pattern runs round the top, varied only by the arms of the Dean and Chapter, whilst the bottom is decorated by a few straight lines.* There is absolutely nothing to be said about the other bells, except that R. Phelps made them, and that they are all more or less out of tune in themselves and with each other—a fact which that truly musical people whose metropolis they adorn will probably be prepared to deny with a vehemence equally patriotic and superfluous.

On ascending the Westminster Abbey tower, with note-book and candle, after being told that the bells were all rather modern, I was agreeably surprised to find at least one or two interesting specimens. There are in all seven bells. Each is rung by a rope and wheel, and has a clapper inside; and in addition to this, each is acted upon by an external hammer, worked by the striking apparatus of the clock. They are, as a rule, in quite as good condition as the Belgian bells of an equal age. The largest bears this inscription :—

"Remember John Whitmell, Isabel his wife, and William Rus, who first gave this bell, 1430.

"New cast in July, 1599, and in April, 1738. Richard Phelps, T. Lester, fecit."

The oldest bell, somewhat smaller, dates from 1583.

* This bell has a very fine tone, and is rung at the hour.

The next oldest is the second largest bell, date 1598. It bears an inscription—"Timpanis patrem laudate sonantibus altum. Gabriel Goodman, Decanus, 1598." Gabriel Goodman was dean 1561 to 1601. A smaller bell bears this inscription:—

"Thomas Lester, London, made me,
And with the rest I will agree,
Seventeen hundred and forty-three."

Another small bell by T. Lester bears the same date, whilst the smallest of all, hung at an almost inaccessible height, is by Richard Lester, in 1738. One bell bears no date. It is inscribed "+ Christe : audi : nos." The Rev. Mr. Ellacombe, of Clyst St. George, a well-known writer on Bells, has been good enough to send me an extract from *Notes and Queries* by Mr. Thomas Walesby, giving a more accurate and detailed account of the Westminster bells than I obtained on my first visit to the tower.

The Westminster bells fail to inspire us with much interest. They are products of manufacture, not works of art. Unlike almost all the Belgian bells, they are one + excepted without symbols or ornamentation of any kind. There has been no labour of love thrown away upon them—not a spray or a branch relieves the monotony of the metal surface. Not even a monogram, or a crown, or an ecclesiastical coat-of-arms, is bestowed upon any of them. The Latin, like a great deal of bell Latin already quoted, is very bad; the spelling is equally indifferent. The type is poor, and devoid of fancy, and the wax in which the letters were originally moulded has been so carelessly laid on, that the tops of T's are often twisted down upon the letter, and the dots of the full stops have got displaced. It is interesting to notice that all the dates, even the earliest, 1583, are in the Arabic, and not, as we should naturally expect, in the Roman numerals.

By an easy transition we may pass from the grey majestic towers of the old Abbey to the big square-sided pillar with the tall nightcap, commonly known as the Westminster Clock Tower.

This top-heavy edifice contains some of the latest specimens of English bell-founding in the nineteenth century, and I must do it the justice to say that it is better inside than out. On a close inspection the massiveness of the structure is imposing, and it is really surprising that such a huge amount of stone-work should be so wanting in external dignity. The walls are of an uniform thickness of between five and six feet, and are little likely ever to be shaken down, like the Pekin tower, by the vibration of the bells. There is a wide passage all round the top of the tower between the white enamelled glass clock-face and its illuminating apparatus. The proportions of the four discs are truly colossal, measuring each over 70 feet in circumference. Each is illuminated by a blazing wall of light behind it, composed of five horizontal gas tubes, full of jets, of an average length of 17 feet apiece. Thus the four clock discs that can be seen so well from all parts of London at night, owe their lighthouse radiance to a furnace composed of no less than 340 feet of gas pipes. Outside, the mighty minute-hand swings visibly round, travelling at the pace of a foot a minute. The machinery of the clock, to which a large room is devoted, being on a colossal scale, looks extremely simple. It bears the inscription—"This clock was made in the year of our Lord, 1854, by Frederick Dent, from the designs of Edmund Becket Denison, Q.C." Telegraph wires from Greenwich are introduced into the interior of the works, in order to regulate the time. We may select a quarter to twelve o'clock to enter the immense belfry, containing the five bells. The iron framework in which they are swung is at once neat and massive, and contrasts with the rough and ponderous timbers of the older belfries very much as a modern iron-clad might contrast with an ancient man-of-war. We feel in the presence of these modern structures that we have gained much and lost something. The mechanical element preponderates over the human, and in the presence of these cast-iron columns, symmetrical girders, and neat bolts, we experience a sense of power, but without the particular dignity which belongs to the heavy and cumbrous rafters of the more ancient towers. The very same feeling is inspired by the massive modern iron-work in the belfry of Cologne Cathedral.

Big Ben hangs in the middle, and the four quarter-bells at the four corners. The original big bell was cast by Warner, of Clerkenwell, who is also the founder of the four quarter-bells. This bell, having cracked, was replaced by Ben, from the foundry of George Mears. It bears the following inscription :—

> "This bell, weighing 13 tons 10 cwt. 3 qrs. 15 lbs., was cast by George Mears, at Whitechapel, for the clock of the Houses of Parliament, under the direction of Edmund Becket Denison, Q.C., in the 21st year of the reign of Queen Victoria, and in the year of our Lord MDCCCLVIII."

The decorations round the top are of the hard Gothic type of the Houses of Parliament. On one side of the bell is the ordinary raised heraldic grating, and on the other are the arms of England. The letters are of the worst possible kind of that narrow Gothic type which makes the despair of the antiquarian. In a couple of hundred years, when the rust and mould, which have already begun to accumulate in our wretched English atmosphere, has clotted the letters together and confused the tops, we may safely predict that this inscription will be entirely illegible.

The largest of the four quarter-bells, cast in 1856 by Warner, weighs 3 tons 17 cwt. 2 qrs.; the second weighs 1 ton 13 cwt. 2 qrs.; the third, 1 ton 5 cwt. 1 qr.; the fourth, 1 ton 1 cwt.

After seeking for some quaint text, or solemn dedication, which should convey to posterity some idea of the founder's reverence for his work or taste for his art, I discovered the following noble and original inscription :—" John Warner and Sons, Crescent Foundry, 1857," then follows her Britannic Majesty's arms, and, underneath, the striking word "Patent."

I could not help thinking of the Belgian bells, on which the founder—half poet, half artist—has printed the fair forms that seemed for ever rising in his free and fertile imagination. How often do we feel as we note the graceful tracery, and the infinitely varied groups, just sufficiently unstudied to be full of feeling, that the artist has been tracing memories of netted branches, beloved faces, or nature's own hieroglyphics written upon flowers and sea-shells! There is one bell in a dark corner of a Louvain belfry, nearly plain, only against the side of it a forest leaf has, as it were, been blown and changed to iron, with every web-like vein perfect—but, of course, a forest leaf is a poor thing compared to a "Patent."

Neither in the Abbey, nor St. Paul's, nor the Clock Tower do we find the bells have any higher vocation than that of beating the tom-tom. They do not call the citizens "to work and pray." They remind them of no One above the toiling and moiling crowd; of no changeless and eternal sympathy with man, his joys and his sorrows. They give no warning note of fire, of pestilence, of battle, or any other peril. There are no Peals of Triumph, no Storm-bells, no Salvators—merely Old Toms and Big Bens.

Big Ben is cracked; and his tone grows sensibly worse every year—I might almost say every month. Yet, considering he is 8½ inches thick, we can hardly be surprised that the crack does not go right through him (1871). It is said that the designer of the bell insisted upon the metals being mixed on scientific principles, and in certain proportions; and it is rumoured that had the advice of the founder been followed, and the metals mixed as only a practical founder knows how, the bell would not have cracked. On this subject I cannot pretend to have even an opinion. Big Ben is not a true bell. He suffers from a flat third. His unhappy brother Patent, who is, nevertheless, so far in his right mind as to be still uncracked (we allude to the next largest bell, which hangs at one of the corners), is no more true than his magnified relative. If I am not very much mistaken, he is afflicted with a sharp third. To crown all, I fear it must be confessed (but on this subject I would willingly bow to the decision of Sir Sterndale Bennett or Sir Michael Costa) that none of the bells are in tune with each other. The intended intervals are, indeed, suggested; but it can scarcely be maintained by any musician that the dissonant clangour, which is heard a quarter before each hour, is anything more than a vague approach to the intended sequence.

The excited citizens of Mechlin or Antwerp would have had these bells down after their first tuneless attempt to play the quarter; but the strength of Old England lies more in patents than tuning-forks—So we must still cry, "Vive le mauvais quart-d'heure!"

I have before mentioned that one bell in the neighbouring tower of the Abbey, on which is inscribed "John Lester made me," &c., expresses a laudable desire "with the rest" to "agree." We may regret that its aspiration rose no higher; and, still more, that modest as it is, it was not destined to be realized. But if both the Clock Tower and the Abbey Tower bells are thus discordant in themselves, and with each other, it must be admitted that they agree excellently well in disagreeing.

I do not wish to be hard upon English bells, and I confess that I have seen more of foreign than of English ones, although since writing the above I have inspected a great many English towers, amongst them Peterborough, York, Lichfield, and Durham; yet such specimens as I have seen have not inspired me with much enthusiasm, and it is with a feeling of relief that I turn even from such celebrated belfries as St. Paul's and Westminster Abbey to the old cathedrals of Belgium, with their musical chimes and their splendid carillons.

CARILLONS.

IV.

THE foot sinks into black dust at least an inch thick. A startled owl sweeps out of the old belfry window; the shutters are broken, and let in some light, and plenty of wind and rain in winter. The cement inside the steeple has rotted away, and the soft stone is crumbling unheeded. Some day the noble old tower will be proclaimed unsafe, and if no funds are forthcoming, twenty feet will be taken off it, and the peal of bells will have to come down. It requires no prophet to foretell this, one glance is sufficient. Everything is already rotting and rusting. The inscriptions on the six or eight great bells are almost illegible; the beams which support them have lost their rivets' heads, and are all loose, probably unsafe; the unpainted wheels are cracked, and every time the bells ring the friction about the pivots from the dust and dirt which has accumulated and worked into them, is very great.

We may well ask Builders, Architects, Deans and

Chapters in general, in these days of church restoration, how they can account for such a state of things in so many otherwise well-restored churches? Why are mighty dust-heaps and vagrant owls almost invariably to be found in the belfry? Alas! because the belfry is the one spot in the church which is hardly ever visited. When a rope breaks, or a wheel gets out of order, some one climbs up and mends it. When an antiquarian wishes to see some famous peal, or copy the legend upon some bell, he gets permission to ascend the tower—perhaps this may happen once in a year. Yet the bells are often the most interesting things about the church. They have their histories, and the few words inscribed upon them are not unfrequently very quaint and suggestive. But who is to stumble up the old decayed stairs, or plunge into the dust and filth of centuries, at the risk of breaking his neck? Only a few enthusiasts, who are powerless to help the poor bells in their corrosion, and the poor towers in their rottenness.

The notion that there is nothing to do up in the belfry after the bells are hung, but to let them swing and everything else rot, seems to be a very prevalent one. This natural process is at all events going on in many cathedral towers in England at this moment. Thousands are spent annually upon the outward decorations; every Gothic detail is carefully replaced, every mullion repaired; the interior is rehabilitated by the best architects; all is scrupulously clean above the nave and chancel, and side aisles and sacristy, and not even an organ pipe is allowed to get out of tune; but there is nevertheless a skeleton in the house—we need not descend into the vaults to find it—our skeleton is in the belfry. His bones are the rotten timbers, his dust is the indescribable accumulations of ages—the vaults are clean in comparison with the belfry. Open yonder little door at the corner of the nave, and begin the dark ascent; before you have gone far you will sigh for the trim staircase that leads down to the vaults. Enter the windy, dirty, rotten room where the poor old bells that cannot die are allowed to mildew and crack for want of a little attention, until they ring the tower down in the angry resonance of their revenge. You will think of the well-kept monuments in the quiet vaults below, where the dead lie decently covered in, and where the carefully-swept floor (a trifle damp, maybe) reveals many a well-worn, but still legible, epitaph or funereal symbol.

If the care of belfries and tower walls were a mere affair of sentiment, there might be room for regret, but hardly matter for protest. But, indeed, thousands of pounds might be annually saved if the anything but silent ruin going on inside our church towers all over the land were occasionally arrested by a few pounds' worth of timely cement, or a new beam or rivet, just enough to check the tremendously increased friction caused by loose bell machinery. Every antiquarian has had to mourn the loss of church towers that have literally been rung to pieces by the bells.

Let me here protest against the senseless practice of trying to tighten the loose bell-works by ramming beams, bricks, and wedges between the loose works and the wall of the tower—many a belfry has been cracked by the cruel thrust of such extemporized repairs. This is perhaps the commonest and most disastrous trick which ignorant carpenters are in the habit of playing in church towers. The great Bell of Time will no doubt ring down every tower in the land sooner or later, but at present, instead of arresting his action, we assist him as much as possible, by pretending not to see the ravages he is making, or by helping with our own brutal and clumsy wedges.

The other day I ascended the tower of one of the most beautifully restored cathedrals in England. It was by no means as badly kept as many; I therefore select it as a good average specimen to describe.

The tower and spire are of red sandstone, massive, but soft, and therefore specially dependent upon good cement and protection from the weather. The shutters were, as usual, old and rotting; large gaps admitted the rain and wind, whose action was abundantly manifest upon the flakes of soft stone which lined the interior of the spire: in places the old cement had completely fallen out, but the spire may still stand for another hundred years or more, after which it will have to be taken down or replaced at enormous cost. The bell machinery, like every machinery intended for mere peals (not carillons), was of course of the roughest kind—the old primitive wheel, and nothing more. This simple, and at the same time cumbrous, apparatus never can work smoothly on a large scale, and more complicated works, which would save half the friction, might easily be devised; but then who cares what the works up in the belfry are like? The tower may indeed come down by-and-by, but it will last our time, and the piety of posterity will doubtless build another.

There are ten bells in L—— Cathedral, of which I am speaking, the largest weighing 1¾ tons. These bells are in pretty constant use. On examining the wheels, I found them all to be more or less rough, rotten, and split. Each wheel, of course, swung between two stout beams. There was a rest for the axle of the wheel provided upon the surface of each beam, whilst a piece of wood kept fast by a movable rivet was fitted over the indentation in which the axletree worked, so as to prevent the wheel from rising and jolting in the beams when swung. I had the curiosity to go round and examine each socket. In every case the rivet was out, lying on the beam, or on the floor, or lost; consequently, whenever the peal is rung, the jolting and creaking alone must, in the long-run, greatly injure the tower. Indeed, I feel convinced that, in nine cases out of ten, it is not the sound of the bells so much as the unnecessary friction of the neglected bell machinery with its fatal wedges which ruins our towers and shakes down our church spires.

But, it may fairly be asked, What ought to be done? I profess no deep architectural knowledge, but a few obvious improvements will, no doubt, have already suggested themselves to the reader's mind. First, let architects remember that the towers are not only good for bells, but also for lovers of scenery; and let them repair the staircases. This might be done at little cost by casing the worn-out tower steps with good elm boards, which I am told on good authority, would last as long as any surface of stone, and would certainly be more easily as well as more cheaply repaired. Unless the staircase is decent, safe, and clean, the neighbouring panorama of hill and dale, land and water, will be lost to all but a few adventurous climbers. Then, the better the ascent, the more chance there is of the belfry being visited and cared for. And lastly, if the stairs are mended, perhaps the walls of the staircase—in other words, the fabric of the tower itself—might claim a little more frequent attention. But here are the bells: why should they be eaten up with corrosion and covered with filth and mildew? The Belgian bell-founders take a pride in sending out their bells smooth and clean. The English bell-founders send them out sometimes with bits of rough metal sticking to them from the mould, and full of pits and flaws. Well they know that none will care for the bells, or notice their condition, until they finally crack or tumble down. Why turn them out clean when they are never to be clean again?

But the bells should have their official, like the

clock. He should be called the Bell-stoker. He should rub his bells at least once a week, so as to keep them clean and prevent corrosion, and then the inscriptions would be preserved, and the surface of the bells being protected from disintegration, the sound would be improved, and the bells would be less liable to crack. The stoker should keep every rivet in its place; the wheels and beams should all be varnished or painted regularly. I have visited many belfries at home and abroad, but never have I seen a bit of paint or varnish in one yet. The shutters should be kept from swinging, with their flanges sloping downwards, so as to keep the wet from driving in, whilst allowing the sound to float freely out and down upon the town. But a far more radical change is required in the machinery of the bells. In these days of advanced mechanical appliances, it is strange to reflect that exactly the same machinery is now used to swing bells as was used in China thousands of years ago. A wheel with a rope round it—that and nothing more. The bell-works might occupy much less room, and the friction, by some of the simplest mechanical appliances, might be reduced to almost nothing. An eye for the belfry is a thing to be cultivated. The belfry should look like a fine engine-room in a first-class factory. It should be a pleasure, as well as an instructive lesson to go into it. When all was in motion, everything should be so neatly fitted and thoroughly oiled that we should hear no sound save only the melodious booming of the bells themselves. At present, when the bells are rung the belfry appears to go into several violent convulsions, corresponding too often to the efforts of the poor ringers below. At last the wheel is induced to move enough for the clapper to hit the bell an indefinite kind of bang—an arduous operation, which may or may not be repeated in some kind of rhythm, according as the ringer may or may not succeed in hitting it off with the eccentric machinery up aloft. I do not wish to disparage the skill of our bell-ringing clubs, though when their bells are out of tune, and their machinery bad, their labour is, to a great extent, wasted. Change-ringing—"triple majors" or "firing" is, as the *Church Times* (which ought to know) remarks, about the extent which the art has reached amongst us. "Hark! the merry Christ Church bells," and such like, may also on some occasions be heard, and little more.

Bells were not made for towers, but towers for bells. Towers were originally nothing but low lanterns, but when bells came into common use the lantern was hoisted up and grew into a spire supported by the bell-room or tower. One would have thought that this fact alone, that so many noble structures owe their existence to bells, might have invested bells with a superior dignity, and given them an honourable place in the affection of a church-and-chapel-going nation like our own. But probably the only influence which will ever be searching and powerful enough to get the wrongs of our bells and belfries righted is the influence of a more diffused musical taste. No one in England really associates the bells in our towers with musical progressions and musical notation. The roughest possible attempt at an octave is thought sufficient, and the most discordant sequences are considered sweet and lovely. The English people do not seem to be aware that a bell is, or ought to be, a musical note; that consequently a peal of bells is, under any circumstances, a kind of musical instrument, and under some circumstances a very fine kind. With all the musical agencies, and the concerts, and the money, and the enthusiasm which are annually devoted to music in England, we have yet much to learn—so much that at times the prospect seems hopeless. What shall we say to a nation that tolerates with scarcely a protest German bands in every possible state of decay? Bands made out of a sort of Ginx's Babies with bugles, horrid clarionets, and battered brass tubes blown by asthmatic refugees. We are not alluding to some really good German bands which condescend to the use of music-desks and the kettle-drum; but to those fiendish nomads who congregate together in our streets without any other principle of cohesion except what may be found in a dogged conviction that although each one is incapable of playing alone, yet all together may have the power of creating such a brazen pandemonium that sooner or later men must pay them to leave off. What shall we say to a people who will hear without remorse their favourite tunes on the barrel-organs of the period? Legislation has indeed been directed against every form of street-music because it is *noisy*, but never because it is *unmusical.* In Italy the government stops street organs which are out of tune. In England no distinction whatever is drawn between street noise and street music. As long as multitudes are content to have pianofortes without having them in tune, as long as clergy and congregations are content to put up with the most squeaky form of the harmonium, as long as organists can be found to play upon organs as much out of tune as those portable barrels of madness and distraction carried about our great country by the wandering minstrels of Italy, as long as tunes are allowed to be performed for Punch and Judy upon the discordant pipe of Pan, whilst negro melodists thrum the parchment and scratch the violin with more than demoniac energy, so long it is unreasonable to expect people to care for the tonal properties of their bells.

Great bells in London are generally considered insufferable nuisances. One church with daily service materially injures house property in the adjoining streets. But if instead of one or two bells cracked or false, or at any rate representing no true melodic progression, there were a dozen musically tuned and musically played, the public ear would soon appreciate the sound as an agreeable strain of aërial music, instead of being driven mad with the hoarse gong-like roar of some incurably sick bell. I question whether there is a musically true chime of bells in the whole of

England, and if it exists, I doubt whether any one knows or cares for its musical superiority. Many chimes are respectable, with the exception of one or two bells, which, being flat or sharp, completely destroy every change that is rung upon them, yet it never occurs to anybody to have the offenders down, and either made right or re-cast. The Romsey Abbey bells, for instance, an octave peal of eight, are respectably in tune with the exception of the seventh, which is too sharp, but which has hung there and been rung there ever since 1791 without (as far as we are aware) creating any unpleasant sensation in the neighbourhood. Similar charges might be brought against most of our cathedral and metropolitan chimes. This being the case, it can hardly be wondered at if our clock-chimes are found equally out of tune. I have before expressed my conviction that Big Ben with his four quarter-bells and the Westminster Abbey chimes would not be tolerated for twenty-four hours by any town in Belgium. As bells individually they may be good, bad, or indifferent; but as musical notes combined for musical purposes they are simply abominable. Yet the British citizen knows it not; nay, he prides himself upon the colossal Ben though cracked, he plumes himself upon the romantic chimes in the grey towers of the old Abbey, whereof the explanation is that the bells are to him as Time and Noise. But they are something worse than mere noise, they are rank discords and corrupters of the public ear. To hear a dozen or so of quarters struck out of tune every day must have a disastrous effect upon musical taste. It makes people indifferent to tune, which is the first essential of music. I have heard the street boys whistling Big Ben's quarters deliberately out of tune. The government would no doubt smile at the notion that it ought to prohibit such chimes and all such public discords as public offences against taste. Can there be any more lamentable proof of the truth of the much-contested sentence, "The English are not a musical people," than the fact that of all the lords and commons, the *élite* of the land, who sit at Westminster not a stone's throw from Big Ben, perhaps not half-a-dozen are aware that Big Ben and his four attendant quarter-bells are hideously out of tune?

Willingly do I escape from the din and discord of English belfries to Belgium, loving and beloved of bells.

The wind that sweeps over her campagnas and fertile levels is full of broken but melodious whispers.

In Belgium day and night are set to music, music on a scale more colossal than that of the largest orchestra ever yet heard; music more penetrating than the loudest trumpet or organ blast. For however loud the chorus and orchestra, it would scarcely be possible in the east end of London to hear a concert at Westminster, yet, on still nights, with a gentle wind blowing, we have often at that distance distinctly heard Big Ben. Well, in Belgium every seven minutes there is bell-music, not only for the whole town, but for the country miles round. Those carillons, playing the same cheerful air every hour throughout the year, at last acquire a strange fascination over one who lives within sight and hearing of some such grey old church as St. Rombaud, at Mechlin. The listener has heard them at moments when, elated with hope, he was looking forward to the almost immediate realization of some long-desired joy, and the melody of the bells has filled him with exultation. He has heard the same strain rung out in seasons of depression, and his heart has leapt up at the sound so filled with memories. The bells may have again smitten upon his ear at the moment when some tragic news has reached him; or out in the fields, steeped in yellow sunshine, above the hum of insect life, the same tune has come to him between the pauses of the summer wind; or deep in his dreams through sleep, without awakening him, the bells have somehow mingled their old rhythm with his dormant fancies, until at last their sound becomes so charged with the incidents and emotions of his life that they are almost as much a part of him as his memory. When he comes to leave a town where he has dwelt for some time, he feels as if he had lost a whole side of life; he misses the sound of the friendly bells, which always had the power by force of association to call up some emotion congenial to the moment, —the sympathetic bells which seemed always equally ready to weep or to rejoice with him—the unobtrusive bells so familiar as never to be a disturbance—the gentle bells that could, as it were, ring aside to themselves when not wanted, and yet never failed to minister to the listening spirit whenever it stood in need of their companionship or sympathy.

There is no greater mistake than to suppose that bell-music every seven minutes is an unpleasant disturbance or interruption; its very frequency enables it to become completely assimilated to our everyday life. Are we not surrounded by natural changes and effects quite as marked in their way as bell-music, and yet which have no tendency to unsettle, distract, or weary us? How loud at times does the wind blow; how suddenly on a dark day will the sun burst into our room; how shrill is the voice of our canary, which at last we hardly heed at all; how often does a rumbling vehicle pass along in the streets; and yet we cease neither reading nor writing for any of these!

The bells musically arranged never irritate or annoy one in Belgium. Instead of time floating by in blank and melancholy silence, or being marked by harsh and brazen clashes, time floats on there upon the pulses of sweet and solemn music. To return from a town like Mechlin to chimeless and gong-like England, is like coming from a festival to a funeral.

M. Victor Hugo stayed at Mechlin in 1837, and the novelty of the almost incessant carillon chimes in the neighbouring tower of St. Rombaud appears, not unnaturally, to have driven sleep from his eyelids; yet he was not irritated or angry so much as fascinated, and at last the creative instinct awoke in the poet, and rising from his bed he inscribed by moonlight the following charming lines with a diamond-ring upon the window-pane:—

> "J'aime le carillon dans tes cités antiques,
> O vieux pays, gardien de tes mœurs domestiques,
> Noble Flandre, où le Nord se réchauffe engourdi
> Au soleil de Castille et s'accouple au Midi!
> Le carillon, c'est l'heure inattendue et folle
> Que l'œil croit voir, vêtue en danseuse espagnole
> Apparaître soudain par le trou vif et clair
> Que ferait, en s'ouvrant, une porte de l'air.
> Elle vient, secouant sur les toits léthargiques
> Son tablier d'argent, plein de notes magiques,
> Réveillant sans pitié les dormeurs ennuyeux,
> Sautant à petits pas comme un oiseau joyeux,
> Vibrant, ainsi qu'un dard qui tremble dans la cible;
> Par un frêle escalier de cristal invisible,
> Effarée et dansante, elle descend des cieux;
> Et l'esprit, ce veilleur, fait d'oreilles et d'yeux,
> Tandis qu'elle va, vient, monte et descend encore,
> Entend de marche en marche errer son pied sonore!"

To Belgium belongs the honour of having first understood and felt bells as musical notes, and devised that aërial and colossal musical instrument known as the carillon.

"Carillon" is derived from the Italian word quadriglio or quadrille. A dreary kind of dance music, of which many specimens still survive, seems under this name to have come from Italy, and been widely popular throughout Europe in the sixteenth century. People hummed the quadriglio in the streets, and as town bells, whether in the cathedral or in the town belfry, were regarded as popular institutions, it is not to be wondered at that the quadriglio was the first kind of musical tune ever arranged for a peal of bells, and that these peals of time-playing bells became widely famous under the name of Carillons.

The rise of bell-music in Belgium was sudden and rapid. In the sixteenth century the use of several bells in connection with town clocks was common enough. Even little tunes were played at the quarters and half hours. The addition of a second octave was clearly only a matter of time. In the seventeenth century carillons were found in all the principal towns of Belgium, and between the seventeenth and eighteenth centuries all the finest carillons now in use, including those of Malines, Antwerp, Bruges, Ghent, and Louvain, were set up. There seems to have been no limit to the number of bells, except the space and strength of the belfry. Antwerp Cathedral has sixty-five bells; St. Rombaud, Mechlin, forty-four bells; Bruges, forty bells and one bourdon, or heavy bass bell; Ghent, thirty-nine; Tournay, forty; Ste. Gertrude, at Louvain, forty.

The great passion and genius for bells which called these noble carillons into existence can no longer be said to be at its height. The Van Aerschodts, descendants of the great bell-founding family of the Van den Gheyns, probably make as good bells as their forefathers, or better ones; and certainly the younger brother, Severin van Aerschodt, retains much of the artistic feeling and genuine pride in his bells so distinctive of the old founders. M. Severin is a good sculptor, and works easily and with real enthusiasm both in marble and in bronze. All bell-machinery can be infinitely better made now than ever; but notwithstanding the love of the Belgians for their chimes and carillons, and the many modern improvements that have been recently made, we cannot help feeling that the great bell period ended in 1785 with the death of the greatest organist and carillonneur Belgium has ever produced, Matthias van den Gheyn.

No one who has not taken the trouble to examine the machinery used for ringing these enormous suites of bells, many of which weigh singly several tons, can well appreciate all that is implied in the words, "Carillons aux clavecins et aux tambours," or, in plain English, musical chimes played by a barrel, and played from a key-board.

Up in every well-stored belfry in Belgium there is a small room devoted to a large revolving barrel, exactly similar in principle to that of a musical box; it is fitted all over with little spikes, each of which in its turn lifts a tongue, the extremity of which pulls a wire, which raises a hammer, which, lastly, falls upon a bell and strikes the required note of a tune. We have only to imagine a barrel-organ of the period, in which the revolving barrel, instead of opening a succession of tubes, pulls a succession of wires communicating with bell-hammers, and we have roughly the conception of the tambour-carillon.

But up in that windy quarter there is another far more important chamber, the room of the *clavecin*, or key-board. We found even in Belgium that these rooms, once the constant resort of choice musical spirits, and a great centre of interest to the whole town, were now but seldom visited. Some of the *clavecins*, like that in Tournay belfry, for instance, we regret to say, are shockingly out of repair; we could not ascertain that there was any one in the town capable of playing it, or that it had been played upon recently at all. Imagine, instead of spikes on a revolving barrel being set to lift wire-pulling tongues, the hand of man performing this operation by simply striking the wire-pulling key, or tongue, and we have the rough conception of the *carillon-clavecin*, or bells played from a key-board. The usual apparatus of the *carillon-clavecin* in Belgium, we are bound to say, is extremely rough. It presents the simple spectacle of a number of jutting handles, of about the size and look of small rolling-pins, each of which communicates most obviously and directly with a wire which pulls the bell-smiting hammer overhead. The performer has this rough key-board arranged before him in semitones, and can play upon it just as a piano or organ is played upon, only that instead of striking the keys, or pegs, with his finger, he has to administer a sharp blow to each with his gloved fist.

How with such a machine intricate pieces of music, and even organ voluntaries, were played, as we know they were, is a mystery to us. The best living carillonneurs sometimes attempt a rough outline of some Italian overture, or a tune with variations, which is, after all, played more accurately by the barrel; but the great masterpieces of Matthias van den Gheyn, which have lately been unearthed from their long repose, are declared to be quite beyond the skill of any player now living. The inference we must draw is sad and obvious. The age of carillons is past, the art of playing them is rapidly becoming a lost art, and the love and the popular passion that once was lavished upon them has died out, and left but a pale flame in the breasts of the worthy citizens who are still proud of their traditions, but vastly prefer the mechanical performance of the tambour to the skill of any carillonneur now living.

The supply of high-class carillonneurs ceased with the demand; but why did the demand cease? The only explanation which occurs to us is this:—the carillonneur was once the popular music-maker of the people, at a time when good music was scarce, just as the preacher was once the popular instructor of the people when good books were scarce. Now the people can get music, and good music, in a hundred other forms. It is the bands, and pianos, and the immense multiplication of cheap editions of music, and the generally increased facilities of making music, which have combined to kill the carillonneurs and depose carillons from their once lordly position of popular favour to the subordinate office of playing tunes to the clock.

When *Peter* van den Gheyn, the bell-founder, put up his modest octave of bells in 1562, at Louvain, his carillon was, doubtless, thought a miracle of tune-playing. But at that time German music did not exist. Palestrina, then just emerging from obscurity, was hardly understood outside Italy. Monteverde and Lulli were not yet born. But when *Matthias* van den Gheyn, the carillonneur, died, Handel and Bach had already passed away, Haydn was still living, Mozart was at his zenith, Beethoven was fifteen years old, and every form of modern music was created, and already widely spread throughout Europe. These facts seem to us to explain the decreasing attention paid to carillon music in Belgium. The public ear has now become glutted with every possible form of music. People have also become fastidious about tune and harmony, and many fine carillons which satisfied our forefathers are now voted well enough for clock chimes, but not for serious musical performances.

There is no reason whatever why the taste for carillon music should not be revived. Bells can be cast in perfect tune, and the exquisite English machinery for playing them ought to tempt our bell-founders to emulate their Belgian brothers in the fine-toned qualities of their bells.

Let us now try and form some conception of what has actually been realized by skilled players on the carillon key-board, by glancing at some of the carillon music still extant, and assisting in imagination at one of those famous carillon *séances* which were once looked forward to by the Belgians as our Handel festivals are now looked forward to by the lovers of music in England.

In the middle of the last century there was probably no town in Belgium more frequented than the ancient and honourable collegiate town of Louvain. Its university has always had a splendid reputation, and at this day can boast of some of the most learned men in Europe. Its town-hall, a miracle of the thirteenth-century Gothic, is one of the most remarkable buildings of that age. The oak carving in its churches, especially that of Ste. Gertrude, is of unsurpassed richness, and attests the enormous wealth formerly lavished by the Louvainiers upon their churches. The library is the best kept and most interesting in Belgium, and the set of bells in St. Peter's Church, if not the finest, can at least boast of having for many years been presided over by the greatest carillonneur and one of the most truly illustrious composers of the eighteenth century, Matthias van den Gheyn.

On the 1st July, 1745, the town of Louvain was astir at an early hour: the worthy citizens might be seen chatting eagerly at their shop doors, and the crowds of visitors who had been pouring into the town the day before were gathering in busy groups in the great square of Louvain, which is bounded on one side by the town-hall, and on the other by the church of St. Peter's. Amongst the crowd might be observed not only many of the most eminent musicians in Belgium, but nobles, connoisseurs, and musical amateurs, who had assembled from all parts of the country to hear the great competition for the important post of carillonneur to the town of Louvain.

All the principal organists of the place were to compete: and amongst them a young man aged twenty-four, the organist of St. Peter's, who was descended from the great family of bell-founders in Belgium, and whose name was already well known throughout the country, Matthias van den Gheyn.

The nobility, the clergy, the magistrates, the burgomasters, in short, the powers civil and ecclesiastical, had assembled in force to give weight to the proceedings. As the hour approached, not only the great square but all the streets leading to it became densely thronged, and no doubt the demand for windows at Louvain, over against St. Peter's tower, was as great as the demand for balconies in the city of London on Lord Mayor's day.

Each competitor was to play at sight the airs which were to be given to him at the time, and the same pieces were to be given to each in turn. To prevent all possible collusion between the jury and the players, no preludes whatever were to be permitted before the performance of the pieces, nor were the judges to know who was playing at any given moment. Lots were to be cast in the strictest secrecy, and the players were to take their seats as the lots fell upon them. The names of the trial pieces have been preserved, and the curiosity of posterity may derive some satisfaction from the perusal of the following list, highly characteristic of the musical taste of that epoch (1745) in Belgium.

"La Folie d'Hispanie," "La Bergerie," "Caprice," and one "Andante."

M. Loret got through his task very creditably. Next to him came M. Leblancq, who completely broke down in "La Bergerie," being unable to read the music. M. van Driessche came third and gave general satisfaction. M. de Laet was fourth, but he too found the difficulties of "La Bergerie" insuperable, and gave it up in despair. Lastly came Matthias van den Gheyn, but before he had got through his task the judges and the great assembly besides had probably made up their minds; there was no comparison between him and his predecessors. Loret and Van Driessche, both eminent professors, were indeed placed second, and the rest were not worth placing, but beyond all shadow of a doubt the last competitor was the only man worthy to make carillon music for the town and neighbourhood of Louvain, and accordingly Van den Gheyn was duly installed in the honourable post of carillonneur, which he held conjointly with that of organist at the church of St. Peter's. His duties consisted in playing the bells every Sunday for the people, also on all the regular festivals of the Church, on the municipal feast days, besides a variety of special occasions, in short, whenever the town thought fit. He was bound to have his bells in tune, and forbidden to allow any one to take his place as deputy on the great occasions. His salary was small, but there were extra fees awarded him upon great occasions, and on the whole he doubtless found his post tolerably lucrative, without being by any means a sinecure.

It is a comfort to think that this great genius was not destined always to spend himself upon the trivially popular airs of the period, such as appear to have been chosen for his ordeal.

The indefatigable efforts of the Chevalier van Elewyck have resulted in the discovery and restoration to the world of more than fifty compositions belonging to this great master, who has indeed had a narrow escape of being lost to posterity. We quite agree with MM. Lemmens and Fétis that some of the "Morceaux Fugués" (now for the first time published, by Schott et Cie., Brussels, and Regent Street, London) are quite equal, as far as they go, to similar compositions by Handel and Bach; at the same time they have a striking individuality and almost wild tenderness and poetry peculiarly their own. As there is no reason why these splendid compositions should any longer be forgotten, we shall make no apology for alluding to some of their prominent characteristics. And, in the first place, let us say that they are wonderful examples of what may be inspired by bells, and of the kind of music which is alone capable of making an effect upon the carillon.

The "Morceaux Fugués," though quite elaborate enough for the piano and organ, were actually played by Van den Gheyn upon the bells. They are bell-like in the extreme, full of the most plaintive melody, and marked by peculiar effects, which nothing but bells can render adequately. If ever we are to have effective carillon music, these compositions and their general laws must be closely studied. The difficulty of arranging and harmonizing tunes for bells seems to baffle ali attempts hitherto made in England. The resonance of the bell renders so much impracticable that upon piano or organ is highly effective. The sounds run into each other and horrid discords result unless the harmonies are skilfully adapted to the peculiarities of bell sound.

In this adaptation Van den Gheyn, as we might suppose, is a master, but such a master as it is quite impossible for any one to conceive who has not closely studied his carillon music. One great secret of bell-playing, overlooked in the setting of all our barrels, is to avoid ever striking even the two notes of a simple third quite simultaneously. Let any one take two small bells, or even two wine-glasses tuned to a third. Let him strike them exactly at the same time, and he will hardly get the sound of a third at all; he will only get a confused medley of vibrations: but let him strike one ever so little before or after the other, and the ear will instantly receive so definite an impression of a third, that however the sounds may mix afterwards, the musical sense will rest satisfied. We are not now concerned with the reasons of this, it is simply a fact; and of course the same rule holds good in a still greater degree with reference to sixths and chords of three or more notes, when struck upon bells.

The simultaneous striking, and hence confusion of vibrations, cannot of course be always avoided, but whenever it can be, we shall find that it is avoided by Van den Gheyn. It is true that he is not always at the pains of writing his thirds with a quaver and a crochet, to indicate the non-simultaneity of the stroke, but we are more and more convinced that whenever it was possible, his bells were struck, often with great rapidity, no doubt, but one *after* the other. Indeed, any one who has sat and played as the writer of this article has done, upon Van den Gheyn's own carillon in St. Peter's belfry, will see how next to impossible it would be with the rough and heavy machinery there provided to strike three notes simultaneously in a passage of considerable length, such as the brilliant passage, for instance, in sixths, with a pedal bass, which occurs at the close of the first Morceau Fugué.

Again, the use of one long pedal note running through three or four bars in harmony with a running treble, may have been suggested originally by bells. It is a well-known favourite effect of S. Bach, in his great pedal fugues, and has been transferred to orchestral and chamber music by Mendelssohn—conspicuously in one of his violoncello sonatas; but it is the peculiar property of the carillonneur, and has been used over and over again by Van den Gheyn with thrilling interest.

In the second Morceau Fugué we see how magnificently deep bells may be made to take the place of pedal pipes. In this massive and solemn movement, a subject of remarkable breadth and power, a truly colossal subject, suitable to its colossal instrument, is given out and carried through with bass pedal bells, and a running accompaniment in the treble. The use of smaller shrill bells, to pick out what we may call little definite sound-specks, is a pleasant relief to the ear towards the close, and prevents our experiencing the slightest effect of monotonous din throughout this wonderfully sustained and majestic piece. The way in which the final cadenza is led up to is masterly. That cadenza is, in fact, a bravura passage of great rapidity, the treble part of which it might tax a respectable violinist to get through creditably, and how it was ever played upon a Belgian clavecin passes our comprehension.

The whole of this second Morceau is so fresh and so prophetic in its anticipation of modern musical effects, that it might have been written by Mendelssohn; indeed, in many places, it forcibly reminds us of passages in his organ sonatas.

But we must not be tempted any longer to discourse upon what baffles all description; let us turn for a moment from the music to the man, and see him as he lived and moved a hundred years ago before the eyes of the worthy Louvainiers. Old men at Louvain remember well the descriptions of him still current in the days of their youth. It is Sunday afternoon, the great square of Louvain is full of gay loungers. The citizens, who have hardly had time to speak to each other during the week, now meet and discuss the latest news from France, the market prices, the state of trade. There are plenty of young students there from the university, and as they promenade up and down the Grande Place, we may well believe that they are not wholly insensible to the charms of the wealthy burghers' daughters, who then (as now throughout Belgium) considered Sunday as their especial *fête* day. We cannot do better than enter the Place and mingle in the crowd. Presently there is a sudden movement in the little knot of stragglers just where the Rue de Bruxelles leads into the Grande Place. People turn round to look, and the crowd makes way, as an elderly-looking man, wearing a three-cornered hat, and carrying a heavy stick with a large wooden knob at the top, comes smiling towards us. On all sides he is greeted with friendly and respectful recognition, and presently he stops to chat with one of the town council, and, taking a pinch of snuff, inquires if any important persons have newly arrived in town.

The appearance of Matthias van den Gheyn, for that is our elderly gentleman, is altogether distinguished. He wears a warm and glossy black coat of the period, his voluminous white cravat is fastidiously clean, his waistcoat and knee-breeches are of the finest black silk, and his shoes are set off with handsome gold buckles. His deportment is that of a man of the world accustomed to good society; and there is a certain good-natured, but self-reliant *aplomb* about him which seems to indicate that he is quite aware of his own importance, and expects as a matter of course the consideration which he receives.

After chatting for twenty minutes or so, during which time his quick eye has discovered most of the strangers in the crowd who may have come to Louvain to hear him play, he turns into the church of St. Peter, and having doffed his holiday costume and dressed himself in light flannels, ascends the winding staircase, and is soon seated at his clavecin. His performances, almost always improvisations on those Sunday afternoons, are said to have been quite unique. Fantasias, airs, fugues in four parts, were tossed about on the bells, and streamed out in truly wild and magic music over the town. The sound was audible far out in the fields around Louvain; and people at Everley might stand still to listen as the music rose and fell between the pauses of the wind.

The performance usually lasted about half an hour, after which time Van den Gheyn would resume his best suit, three-cornered hat, and massive walking-stick, and come down to mingle freely in the throng and receive the hearty congratulations and compliments of his friends and admirers.

Matthias van den Gheyn married young, and had a numerous family. His wife was a sensible woman, and did a thriving business in the cloth trade. Madame van den Gheyn had many customers, and her husband had many pupils, and thus this worthy couple supported themselves and their children in comfort and prosperity, deserving and receiving the respect and friendship of the good Louvainiers.

Matthias van den Gheyn was born in 1721; at the age of twenty-four (the same year that he was appointed carillonneur of Louvain) he married Marie Catherine Lintz, a Louvain girl aged twenty-one, by whom he had seventeen children. He died at the age of sixty-four in 1785.

The present famous Belgian bell-founders, André Louis van Aerschodt and Severin van Aerschodt, are the sons of Anne Maximiliane, the granddaughter of the great carillonneur, Matthias van den Gheyn. These gentlemen cast all the best bells that are made in Belgium.

And now in conclusion let us speak a good word for England.

The English bell-founders, it is true, do not at present seem to have the right feeling about bells, or any great sense of the importance of tune; but the English bell mechanism is beyond comparison the first in the world. We should order our bells in Belgium, and get them fitted with clavecin and carillon machinery in England.

The new carillon machinery invented by Gillet and Bland, of Croydon, and applied to a set of Belgian bells at Boston, Lincolnshire, occupies about a third of the room used by the Belgian works, avoiding the immense strain upon the barrel, and the immense resistance offered by the clavecin keys to the performer under the old system. In the old system the little spikes on the revolving barrel had to lift tongues communicating by wires *directly* with the heavy hammers which had thus to be raised and let fall on the outside of the bell. In the new system the spikes have nothing to do with lifting the hammers. The hammers are always *kept lifted* or *set* by a system of machinery devised specially for this heavy work. All the little spikes have to do is to lift tongues communicating with wires which have no longer the heavy task of raising the hammers, but merely of letting them slide off on to the bells.

The force required for this is comparatively slight; and if we substitute for the barrel with spikes a key-board played by human fingers, thus making the fingers through pressure on the keys perform the task of the barrel-spike in letting off the hammer, any lady acquainted with the nature of a pianoforte or organ key-board will be found equal to the task of playing on the carillon. This was a result probably never contemplated by the old carillonneurs, who used to strip and go in for a sort of pugilistic encounter with a vast row of obdurate pegs in front of them. The pegs have vanished, and in their place we have a small and tempting row of keys, which occupies about the same space, and is almost as easy to play upon, as a small organ key-board.

The Croydon carillon machine which we have lately examined plays hymn tunes on eight bells. The largest of these bells weighs 31 cwt., and the others are in proportion. Yet the machine (which stands under a glass case) is only 3 feet long, 2 feet wide, and 3 feet 9 inches in height. The musical barrel, made of hazel-wood (there is no key-board), is 10 inches in diameter and 14 inches long; the spikes on the barrel for letting off the heavy hammers are only 1-16 of an inch square. When we compare the delicacy of this machinery, which looks like the magnified works of a musical box, with the prodigious effects it is calculated to produce, one cannot help feeling convinced that the time is at hand when every tuneful peal in the kingdom will be fitted with this beautiful apparatus.

Meanwhile we cannot help repeating in more detail a suggestion made at the commencement of this article, and which occurs to us whenever we enter a dilapidated belfry full of creaking wheels and rotten timbers. Before we think of key-boards and barrels, let us supply some simple machinery for the common ringing of the bells. Great Peter at York has never yet been rung, and the friction caused by any attempt to ring him is very great. This is, no doubt, due to a defect in the hanging. We hear about towers being rung down by the vibrations of the bells; but it would be truer to say that they are rocked down by the friction of coarse and unscientific machinery. If all the bellowing of the Prussian guns failed to make any material impression upon the fragile stone filigree work of the Strasburg tower, it is not likely that the sound of bells has much to do with the ruin of brickwork and masonry.

In connection with the swinging of a heavy bell there always must be considerable strain upon the tower. But the friction might be indefinitely diminished if the bell machinery worked smoothly, and the labour, often at present herculean, of the poor bell-ringer might be reduced to almost zero were that machinery a little more scientific. When it is once understood that an improved system of ringing the bells would save Deans and Chapters all over the country enormous sums of money by suspending the wear and tear which now goes on in so many of our cathedral towers, we cannot help thinking that little opposition will be raised by those who have to pay for the damages. Bell-ringers are doubtless a most obstinate set of men; but if they were paid the same for working machinery which produced twice as much effect with less than half the labour, they too would soon give in to a better system. That ungrateful and barbarous rope and wheel, whose action upon the bell is now so uncertain, would probably disappear, and give place to something like a handle, a piston, or even a key-board and a set of wheels and pulleys. There is no reason whatever why, with a better ringing mechanism, one man might not ring half a dozen bells, instead of, as at present, half a dozen men being often set to ring a single big bell. I make these suggestions with the more confidence because they have been favourably entertained by the heads of one of the most eminent firms of horology in England. I am glad to say that in accordance with my suggestions these gentlemen have promised to give their attention to the development of a better mechanism for the ringing of bells. They write as follows:—"Although bells have never been rung by machinery, we believe it would be possible to accomplish this, although it might be expensive."

A little ordinary thought and common sense, not to speak of a little mechanical science, would work wonders in our belfries. There is hardly a cathedral tower in England where the hanging of one or more bells, or the oscillation of the tower, is not justly complained of. As a rule, the reason is not far to seek. In both York and Durham, for instance, the bells are hung too high up. In York there are twelve bells besides Great Peter, which hangs in a separate tower. They are all crowded together on one floor, instead of being distributed properly in an upper and a lower floor.

In Durham the two lower side towers, and not the high centre one, ought to have been fitted for the bells. When a bell is hard to ring, it is almost always not on account of its weight, but on account of its "hanging." The woodwork and hasps at the top of the bell are not in the right place. In nine cases out of ten when a bell works heavily, this is the reason, and it is the business of mechanicians to see to it. Large bells should have, if possible, a separate tower. Large bells, for the sake of the tower, should be hung as low as possible; the little bells can be hung even up in the steeple. But when there are a number of bells they ought always to be hung, according to their weights, in two or more layers.

All this has been known and practised in Belgium for two hundred years and more; why do not our bell-hangers visit the Antwerp or Mechlin towers? one glance would often be sufficient. When we extol English bell works we do not allude to the way in which English bells are hung, but rather to English carillon and clavecin and clock works. Let us hope that the time is coming when our bell-hangers will get some good mathematician to tell them a few of the ordinary laws of mechanics. Until then, Deans and Chapters may sigh and seek in vain to make their bells work and keep their towers from rocking to pieces.

Fourth Book.

CRITICAL.

MUSIC IN ENGLAND.

Fourth Book.

MUSIC IN ENGLAND.

I.

THE English are not a musical people, and the English are not an artistic people. But the English are more artistic than musical; that is to say, they have produced better artists than musicians. A country is not musical or artistic when you can get its people to look at pictures or listen to music, but when its people are themselves composers and artists. It cannot be affirmed that Englishmen are, or ever were, either one or the other. Let us explain.

Painting is older, and has had a longer time to develop, than music. There have been great English painters, who have painted in the Dutch, Italian, and Spanish styles—there has even been a really original school of English portrait and landscape painters—

and these later years have witnessed some very remarkable and original developments of the art in England; but the spirit of it is not in the people for all that, and the appreciation of good art is not in the public. No one mourns over this more than our painters themselves. There is want of enthusiasm and want of knowledge. The art of our common workmen is stereotyped, not spontaneous. When our architects cease to copy they become dull. Our houses are all under an Act of Uniformity.

Music in England has always been an exotic, and whenever the exotic seed has escaped and grown wild on English soil, the result has not been a stable and continuous growth. The Reformation music was all French and Italian; the Restoration music (1650), half French and half German. No one will deny that Tallis, Farrant, Byrd, in church music—Morley, Ward, Wilbye in the madrigal, made a most original use of their materials; but the materials were foreign, for all that. At the Restoration, Pelham Humphreys, called by Pepys "an absolute monsieur," is as really French as Sir Sterndale Bennett is really German. Purcell, the Mozart of his time, was largely French, although he seemed to strike great tap-roots into the old Elizabethan period, just as Mendelssohn struck them deep into S. Bach. But all these men have one thing in common,—they were composers in England, they were not English composers. They did not write for the people, the people did not care for their music. The music of the people was ballads—the music of the people is still ballads. Our national music vibrates between "When other lips" and "Champagne Charley."

These ballads of all kinds are not exotic: they represent the national music of the English people. The people understand music to be a pleasant noise and a jingling rhythm; hence their passion for loudness and for the most vulgar and pronounced melody. That music should be to language what language is to thought, a kind of subtle expression and counterpart of it; that it should range over the wordless region of the emotions, and become in turn the lord and minister of feeling—sometimes calling up images of beauty and power, at others giving an inexpressible relief to the heart by clothing its aspirations with a certain harmonious form;—of all this the English people know nothing. And as English music is jingle and noise, so the musician is the noisemaker for the people, and nothing more. Even amongst the upper classes, except in some few cases, it has been too much the fashion to regard the musician as a kind of servile appendage to polite society; and no doubt this treatment has reacted disastrously upon musicians in England, so that many of them are or become what society assumes them to be—uncultivated men, in any true sense of the word. And this will be so until music is felt here, as it is felt in Germany, to be a kind of necessity—to be a thing without which the heart pines and the emotions wither—a need, as of light, and air, and fire.

Things are improving, no doubt. When genius, both creative and executive, has been recognised over and over again as devoted to music, even a British public has had thoughts of patting the gods on the back. There is a growing tendency to give illustrious musicians the same position which has been granted in almost every age and country to illustrious poets and painters. Let us hope that refined musicians, even though not of the highest genius, may ere long meet with a like honourable reception. Why has this not been the case hitherto? I reply, because England is not a musical country. The first step is to awaken in her, or force upon her, the appreciation of music as an art. That is the stage we are now at. The second stage is to create a national school of composers—this is what we hope to arrive at.

The contrast between indigenous art and exotic art is always marked. When the people love spontaneously, there is enthusiasm and reverence for the artist and his work. Where or when in this country will ever be seen a multitude like the crowd which followed Cimabue's picture of the Madonna through the streets of Florence, or the mournful procession that accompanied Mendelssohn to his grave?

When art has to be grafted on to a nation, it is received fastidiously at first—the old tree likes not the taste of the new sap. When the graft succeeds, and the tree brings forth good fruit, the people pluck it and eat it admiringly, but ages sometimes elapse before it becomes a staff of life to them. But let art be indigenous, as in Greece of old, in modern Italy, in Germany, even in France, and every mechanic will carve and sculpt, every boor will sing and listen to real music, every shopman will have an intuitive taste and arrange his wares to the best possible advantage. In India the commonest workman will set colours for the loom in such a manner as to ravish the eye of the most cultivated European artist. In the German refreshment rooms of the great Paris Exhibition, there were rough bands working steadily through the symphonies of Mozart and Haydn, whilst the public were never found so intent on *sauer kraut* and sausages as not to applaud vociferously at the end, and sometimes even encore an adagio. Fancy the frequenters of Cremorne encoring a symphony by Mozart!

However, the people have their music, and it is of no use to deny it; and the marks of patronage bestowed upon ballad-mongers, one-eyed harpers, asthmatic flutes, grinders and bands from "Vaterland," are sufficient to inspire the sanguine observer with hopes for the future.

When a man cannot feed himself, the next best thing is to get a friend to do it for him. It cannot be denied that the English of all classes have shown great liberality in importing and paying for all kinds of foreign music as well as in cherishing such scanty germs as there happen to be around them. A musician of any kind is less likely to starve in England than in any other country, from the organ-grinder who lounges with his lazy imperturbable smile before the area railings, as who should say, "If I don't get a copper here I shall round the corner, and no matter," to the sublime maestro (Beethoven) who, abandoned in the hour of sickness and poverty by his own countrymen, received upon his death-bed an honorarium of £100 from the London Philharmonic Society.

English managers were the first who introduced the scale of exorbitant salaries now paid to opera singers and a few of the best instrumentalists. We believe the system began with Malibran, and on Paganini's arrival in England an attempt was made to double the prices of admission whenever he played at the Opera House. It is the old story—humming-birds at the North Pole and ice in the tropics will be found equally expensive.

We have now said the worst that can be said about music in England; all the rest shall be in mitigation of the above criticism. "May it please your highness," says Griffith, in *Henry VIII.*, "to hear me speak his good now."

II.

It is certainly true that if we do not sow the seed we provide an admirable soil. Let the English people once receive an impression, and it will be held with a surprising tenacity. When the now young and fair Madame or Mademoiselle Prima Donna of the period, at the age of one hundred—beautiful for ever but perfectly inaudible—shall advance to the footlights to take her farewell benefit, those of us who are still alive will flock to see her, and strew her path with flowers as fadeless as herself.

Amongst the most hopeful signs of the times, we may enumerate the success of Mr. Hullah's system, the recent introduction of the Tonic Sol-fa method, and the immense increase of musical societies throughout the country.

Fifty-five years ago the old Philharmonic was without a rival. Every year some new *chef-d'œuvre* was produced, and the English public was taught to expect at each concert two long symphonies, besides classical concertos, relieved only by a song or two as a kind of musical salts to prevent downright collapse. This discipline was thought by some to be too severe; but a little knot of connoisseurs maintained that in the symphonies of Haydn and Mozart were to be found the most precious treasures of music, and people hitherto only accustomed to instrumental music as an accompaniment to vocal, began to listen with a growing interest to purely orchestral performances. Haydn and Mozart soon became popular, but Beethoven was long a stumbling-block, and although held in great veneration, and at all times most liberally treated by the Philharmonic Society, yet even that advanced body took some time to unravel the mysteries of the great C minor, and for years after Beethoven's death his greatest orchestral works were, to a large majority of English ears, as sounding brass and tinkling cymbal.

It is impossible to overrate the influence of the old Philharmonic upon musical taste in England, but it did not long stand alone. A gold mine may be opened by a solitary band of diggers, but the road leading to it soon becomes crowded; a thousand other breaches are speedily made. We have seen during the last few years the swarms of daily papers which have sprung up round the *Times;* the same remark applies to the crop of quarterlies round the *Edinburgh;* the cheap magazines round the *Cornhill;* exhibitions round that of 1851; and, we may add, orchestral societies round the old Philharmonic.

We may fairly date the present wave of musical progress in this country from the advent of Mendelssohn. It is now more than thirty years ago since he appeared at the Philharmonic, and, both as conductor and pianist, literally carried all before him. He brought with him that reverence for art, and that high sense of the artist's calling, without which art is likely to degenerate into a mere pastime, and the artist himself into a charlatan. The young composer read our native bands some useful lessons. Himself the chevalier of music,—*sans peur et sans reproche,*—sensitive indeed to criticism, but still more alive to the honour of art, he could not brook the slightest insult or slur put upon music. Gifted with a rare breadth and sweetness of disposition, his ire began to be dreaded as much as he himself was admired and beloved.

At a time when Schubert was known here only by a few songs, Mendelssohn brought over the magnificent symphony in C (lately performed at the Crystal Palace), together with his own *Ruy Blas* overture in MS. The parts of Schubert's symphony were distributed to the band. Mendelssohn was ready at his desk—the bâton rose,—the romantic opening was taken,—but after the first few lines, signs of levity caught the master's eye. He closed the score;—certain gentlemen of the band evidently considered the music rubbish, and amidst some tittering, the parts were collected and again deposited in the portfolio.

"Now for your overture, Mendelssohn!" was the cry.

"Pardon me!" replied the indignant composer; and, taking up his hat, he walked out of the room.

Ruy Blas went back to Germany, but the lesson was not soon forgotten.

After living amongst us just long enough to complete and produce his masterpiece, the *Elijah*, at Birmingham, he died (1847), leaving behind him an illustrious school of disciples, of whom Sir Sterndale Bennett may be named chief, and to that new school, as well as to the old-established Philharmonic Society, may be traced the rapid increase of orchestral societies and orchestral concerts in England. In looking back through the last fifteen years, the difficulty is to choose one's examples.

The growing popularity of the orchestra is a sure sign of the popular progress in music. Ballad singing and solo playing, in dealing with distinct ideas and accentuated melodies, and by infusing into the subject a kind of personal interest in the performance, depend upon many quite unmusical adjuncts for their success; but orchestral playing, in dealing chiefly with harmony, brings us directly into the abstract region of musical ideas. The applause which follows "Coming through the rye," is just as often given to a pretty face or a graceful figure as to the music itself; and when people encore Bottesini, Wieniawski, or Rubinstein, it is often only to have another stare at the big fiddle, the romantic locks, or the dramatic sang-froid of these incomparable artists; but the man who applauds a symphony, applauds no words or individuals,—he is come into the region of abstract emotion, and if he does not understand its sovereign language, he will hear about as much as a colour-blind man will see by looking into a prism. It is a hopeful sign when the people listen to good German bands in the streets. A taste for penny ices proves that the common people have a glimmering of the strawberry creams which Mr. Gunter prepares for sixpence; and the frequent consumption of ginger-pop and calves' head broth, indicates a confirmed, though it may be hopeless, passion for champagne and turtle-soup. No one will say that the old Philharmonic in any sense supplied music for the people, but the people heard of it, and clamoured for it, and in obedience to the spirit of the age the man arose who was able to give them as near an approach to the loftier departments of music as the masses could appreciate.

The immortal Mons. Jullien, who certainly wielded a most magical white bâton, and was generally understood to wear the largest white waistcoat ever seen, attracted immense, enthusiastic, and truly popular crowds to his truly popular concerts. Knowing little about the science of music, and glad, says rumour, to avail himself of more learned scribes in arranging his own matchless polkas and quadrilles, he had the singular merit of finding himself on all occasions inspired with the most appropriate emotions. From the instant he appeared before a grateful public to the moment when, exhausted by more than human efforts, he sank into his golden fauteuil, Mons. Jullien was a sight! The very drops upon his Parian brow were so many tributary gems of enthusiasm to the cause of art. Not that Mons. Jullien ever lost his personality, or forgot himself in that great cause. The wave of his silken pocket handkerchief, with the glittering diamond rings, seemed to say, "There, there, my public! the fire of genius consumes me—but I am yours!"

But without further pleasantry, it must be acknowledged that the irresistible Jullien took the English public by storm, and having won, he made an admirable use of his victory. Besides his band in London, detachments travelled all over the country, and spread far and wide currents of the great central fire that blazed in the metropolis.

Those grand triumphs at the Surrey Gardens, when the Jullien orchestra, overlooking the artificial lake, rang through the summer evenings, and sent its echoes reverberating through the mimic fortress of Gibraltar, or the magic caves presently to be lit up by forty thousand additional lamps! Happy hours! many of us, since grown to years of discretion, may remember them in the days of our early youth! No summer evenings in the open air seem now so full of ecstasy; no fireworks explode with such regal and unprecedented splendour; must it be confessed? no music can come again with such a weird charm as that which filled the child's ear and ravished the child's heart with a new and ineffable tremor of delight. But it was the music, not the scenery, not the fireworks alone. It was hardly a display of fireworks, assisted by Mons. Jullien's band,—it was Mons. Jullien's band accompanied by fireworks! It would be wrong, however, to imply that these concerts were supported merely by big drums and skyrockets.

I do not think Mons. Jullien ever got due credit for the large mass of good classical music he was in the habit of introducing. Besides the finest German overtures, were heard movements from Haydn, Mozart, and Beethoven's symphonies admirably executed; of course without the repose and intellect of a classical conductor, but without offensive sensationalism, and with perfect accuracy.

Upon the shoulders of the late Mr. MELLON descended the mantle of Mons. Jullien. If Mellon's concerts lacked the romance and unapproachable fire that went out with the brilliant Frenchman, they retained all that could be retained of his system, and gave it additions which his perseverance had made possible, but which he had probably never contemplated. There was also the same care in providing the first soloists.

BOTTESINI, whose melodies floated in the open air over the Surrey Gardens, and filled the world with a new wonder and delight, was again heard under the dome of Covent Garden.

M. SIVORI—the favourite pupil of Paganini, who seems to have inherited all the flowing sweetness of the great magician without a spark of his demoniac fury—appeared, and filled those who remembered the master with a strange feeling, as though at length,

"Above all pain, yet pitying all distress,"

the master's soul still flung to earth faint fragments from the choirs that chime

"After the chiming of the eternal spheres."

Mons. LEVY, on the cornet, and Mons. WIENIAWSKI, on the violin, are the only other real instrumental sensations that have been produced at these concerts.

At any time instrumental genius is rare, and of the numbers who are first-rate, only a few feel equal to stilling the noisy, half-trained audiences usually found at promenade concerts. When we have mentioned

Chopin, Liszt, Thalberg, Mendelssohn, Madame Schumann, Madame Goddard, Rubinstein, and Hallé, on the piano; De Beriot, Paganini, Ernst, Vieuxtemps, Wieniawski, and Joachim, on the violin; Linley and Piatti on the violoncello; Dragonetti and Bottesini on the contra-basso; König and Levy on the cornet, the roll of solo-instrumentalists during the last fifty years may very nearly be closed. And of the above men, some, like Chopin, Hallé, and Joachim, never cared to face, strictly speaking, popular audiences; but those who did were usually secured by the popular orchestras of Jullien and Mellon, and by the givers of those intolerable bores called monster concerts,—which begin early in the afternoon and never seem to end.

III.

The immense advance of the popular mind is remarkably illustrated by the change in the ordinary orchestral programme. We have now Mozart nights, and Beethoven nights, and Mendelssohn nights. Not bits of symphonies, but entire works are now listened to, and movements of them are encored by audiences at Covent Garden. We have heard the Scotch symphony and the "Power (Consecration?) of Sound" received with discrimination and applause. A certain critical spirit is creeping into these audiences, owing to the large infusion of really musical people who are on the look-out for good programmes, and invariably support them.

The old and new Philharmonics, the London Musical Society, the performances under Mr. Hullah at St. Martin's Hall, the Sacred Harmonic under Sir W. M. Costa, the Birmingham Festival and the Cathedral Festivals, Jullien, Mellon, Arditi, Rivière, Mr. Barnby's Oratorio Concerts, Mr. Henry Leslie's wonderful choir, and last—and greatest of all—the Crystal Palace band, have no doubt supplied a want, but they have also created one. They have taught thousands to care about good music. They have taught those who did care to be more critical. The time is gone by when the Philharmonic had it all its own way, or when only the wealthy could hear fine music, or when the public generally was thankful for small mercies. The ears of the public have grown sharp. When musical amateurs now go to hear a symphony, they know what they go for, and they know, too, whether they get it. They hear the Italian Symphony by the Crystal Palace band on Saturday afternoon, and not long afterwards at the Philharmonic, and there is no possibility of evading a comparison. The members of the Crystal Palace band, from playing every day all the year round together under the same admirable conductor, have achieved an excellence hitherto unknown in England.

I might here be expected to notice the Opera, but I purposely omit an incomplete disquisition upon this subject which appeared in the First Edition of "Music and Morals," and for a more complete treatment I have no space in the present volume. I might also be expected to refer to the various societies of sacred music, but the subject is too wide, embracing as it does ecclesiastical music generally, and I must postpone its further treatment. I may, however, observe, in passing, the popular progress made in this department. The people of London in 1868 listened to shilling oratorios for the first time at the Agricultural Hall in the East, and St. George's Hall in the West End of London. And who cannot bear joyful witness to the change that has passed over the choirs of churches and chapels during the last twenty years?

Music thus promises to become in England what it has long been in Germany,—a running commentary upon all life, the solace of a nation's cares, the companion of its revelry, the minister of its pleasure, and the inspired aid to its devotion.

IV.

If we now enter for a moment the music-halls of the metropolis, we shall notice that the happy change is extending downwards. The members of our cathedral choirs do not disdain to produce before these once despised, and it must be confessed, sometimes equivocal audiences, the part-songs of Mendelssohn and the ballads of Schubert.

In the better class establishments whole evenings pass without anything occurring on the stage to offend the delicacy of a lady; whilst, if we go lower, we shall find the penny gaffs, and public-house concerts, coarse, it may be, but on the whole moral, and contrasting most favourably with anything of the kind in France.* It must be understood that I am alluding merely to the musical portion of these entertainments. Of late years the general increase of ballets and vulgar clap-trap comic songs has not tended to elevate the tone of our music-halls.

There is one other branch of strictly popular music which seems to be considered beneath the attention of serious critics; but nothing popular should be held beneath the attention of thoughtful people—we allude to the Negro Melodists now best represented by the Christy Minstrels. About twenty years ago a band of enthusiasts, some black by nature, others by art, invaded our shores, bringing with them what certainly were nigger bones and banjos, and what professed to be negro melodies. The sensation which they produced was legitimate, and their success was well deserved. The first melodies were no doubt curious and original; they were the offspring of the naturally musical organization of the negro as it came in contact with the forms of European melody. The negro mind, at work upon civilized music, produces the same kind of thing as the negro mind at work upon Christian theology. The product is not to be despised. The negro's religion is singularly childlike, plaintive, and emotional. It is also singularly distinct and characteristic. Both his religion and his music arise partly from his

* See two admirable essays on "Art and Popular Amusement," in "Views and Opinions," by that ingenious writer, Matthew Browne.

impulsive nature, and partly from his servile condition. The negro is more really musical than the Englishman. If he has a nation emerging into civilization, his music is national. Until very lately, as his people are one in colour, so were they one in calamity, and singing often merrily with the tears wet upon his ebony cheek, no record of his joy or sorrow passed unaccompanied by a cry of melody or a wail of plaintive and harmonious melancholy. If we could divest ourselves of prejudice, the songs that float down the Ohio river are one in feeling and character with the songs of the Hebrew captives by the waters of Babylon. We find in them the same tale of bereavement and separation, the same irreparable sorrow, the same simple faith and childlike adoration, the same wild tenderness and passionate sweetness, like music in the night. As might have been supposed, the parody of all this, gone through at St. James's Hall, does not convey much of the spirit of genuine negro melody, and the manufacture of national music carried on briskly by sham niggers in England is as much like the original article as a penny woodcut is like a line engraving. Still, such as it is, the entertainment is popular, and yet bears some impress of its peculiar and romantic origin. The scent of the roses may be said to hang round it still. We cherish no malignant feeling towards those amiable gentlemen at St. James's Hall, whose ingenious fancy has painted them so much blacker than they really are, and who not unfrequently betray their lily-white nationality through a thin though sudorific disguise; we admit both their popularity and their skill; but we are bound to say that we miss even in such pretty tunes as "Beautiful Star," the distinctive charm and original pathos which characterized "Mary Blane" and "Lucy Neal."

I cannot close without alluding to a very different class of music.

The true musician enters as it were the domestic sanctuary of music, when he sits down to listen to, or to take part in a string quartet. The time has gone by when men like Lord Chesterfield could speak of a fiddler with contempt. Few people would now inquire with the languid fop, what fun there could be in four fellows sitting opposite each other for hours and scraping catgut; most people understand that in this same process the cultivated musician finds the most precious opportunities for quiet mental analysis and subtle emotional meditation.

The greatest masters wrote their choicest thoughts in this form—it is one so easily commanded and so satisfying. The three varieties of the same instrument —violin, viola, and violoncello—all possessing common properties of sound, but each with its own peculiar quality, embrace an almost unlimited compass, and an equally wide sphere of musical expression.

The quartet is a musical microcosm, and is to the symphony what a vignette in water-colours is to a large oil-painting. The great quartet writers are certainly

Haydn, Mozart, and Beethoven. Haydn is the true model. He attempts nothing which four violins cannot do; the parts are exquisitely distributed, scrupulous justice is done to each instrument, and the form is perfect. Mozart's quartet is equally perfect, as such, but much bolder and more spontaneous. Beethoven carried quartet writing, as he did every other branch of music, into hitherto untrodden regions, but, with the sure instinct of the most balanced of all geniuses, never into inappropriate ones. Fascinating as are the quartets of Spohr and Mendelssohn, as quartets I am bound to place them below the above great models. Spohr seldom distributed his parts fairly; it is usually first violin with string accompaniment. Mendelssohn frequently forgets the limits of the legitimate quartet; orchestral effects are constantly being attempted, and we pine at intervals for a note on the horn, whilst the kettledrum is occasionally suggested. Schubert can wander on for ever with four instruments, or with anything else—mellifluous, light-hearted, melancholy, fanciful by turns. When he gets half-way through, there is no reason why he should not leave off, and when he gets to the end there is no reason why he should not go on. But in this process form and unity are often both lost.

The characteristics of Schumann require separate attention. Under the general heading of cabinet music would be comprised the addition of the pianoforte in trios, quartets, and quintets; as also the addition of a horn, a flute, or a clarionet, in sestets and octets. Variety is always pleasant, but none of these combinations equal the string quartet in beauty of form or real power and balance of expression. The piano in a trio will eke out a good deal, but it usually results in the strings accompanying the piano, or the piano accompanying the strings. Mendelssohn's two trios are small orchestral whirlwinds, and quite unique, but the trio form might be seriously demurred to as inappropriate.

On the other hand, one feels the pianoforte in a quartet, or even a quintet, as a kind of interloper—a sort of wasp in a bee-hive—a sort of cuckoo in a hedge-sparrow's nest. One would rather see the natural bird there; one would rather have the second violin in its place. Again, in octets and sestets, splendid as are some of these compositions, we feel the orchestral form is the one aimed at, and consequently the poverty of the adopted one is constantly making itself felt. Space compels us to speak most generally and without even necessary qualification on these points, and we pass on to the quartet playing that has of late years come before the public.

Mysterious quartets in back rooms and retired country-houses becoming more and more frequent, the experiment of public performances was at last made; but they were to be for the few. The Musical Union under Mr. Ella's direction was one of the first societies which provided this luxury every season. There is no one man who has done more for good music in England than Professor Ella. He soon, however, met with a formidable rival in the quartet concerts at Willis's Rooms, under Messrs. Sainton, Hill, Piatti, and Cooper. But the man and the hour were still to come. The concerts were too select and too expensive. Mr. Chappell flew to the rescue with a chosen band of heroes, foremost amongst whom must always stand M. Joachim.

M. Joachim is the greatest living violinist; no man is so nearly to the execution of music what Beethoven was to its composition. There is something massive, complete, and unerring about M. Joachim that lifts him out of the list of great living players, and places him on a pedestal apart. Other men have their specialities; he has none. Others rise above or fall below themselves; he is always himself, neither less nor more. He wields the sceptre of his bow with the easy royalty of one born to reign; he plays Beethoven's concerto with the rapt infallible power of a seer delivering his oracle, and he takes his seat at a quartet very much like Apollo entering his chariot to drive the horses of the sun.

Mr. Henry Holmes' quartets at Hanover Square Rooms deserve honourable mention. They afford one more proof of the increasing popularity of such high class music. Mr. Holmes is a violinist who does honour to our country, and whose reputation is increasing every year. He has for some years been a favourite abroad.

The crowded and attentive audience which assembles every Monday night throughout the season at St.

James's Hall is the latest and most decisive proof of the progress of music in England. When an audience numbering some thousands is so easily and frequently found, it matters little where it comes from. No doubt many connoisseurs are there, but many others also attend who have cultivated, and are cultivating, a general taste for certain higher forms of music, hitherto almost unknown in England.

V.

No survey of music in England, however cursory, should fail to give some account of so pronounced a character as the MUSICAL AMATEUR. He may be a depressing subject for contemplation, but he is the best possible index to the musical taste of a people. Given the musical amateurs of a country, and the music they like, and it is easy to say where the nation is in the scale of musical progress. We place Italy and France below Germany when we see that the ordinary Italian is satisfied with melody and a little noise, the ordinary Frenchman with less melody and more noise, while the German insists upon melody, harmony, and thematic treatment combined.

Who are the English amateurs? What do they like? How do they play and sing? In the following pages these questions will receive some definite answers, and these answers may furnish us with a new clue to the state of music in England.

The first obvious description of musical amateurs is, PEOPLE WHO PLAY THE PIANOFORTE. In twenty years Mr. Broadwood has sold 45,863 pianos; Mr. Collard, 42,000. About 20,000 are annually issued from the manufactories of Great Britain, whilst about 10,000 foreign pianos are annually imported. From these figures, I believe, it would not be difficult to show that over 400,000 pianos are at present in use in the British Islands, and that more than one million persons at least answer to the description of PEOPLE WHO PLAY THE PIANOFORTE.

All these are not amateurs, but most of them are, and the exceptions exist chiefly for their benefit.

Most young ladies play the piano as an accomplishment. A girl's education is as much based on the pianoforte as a boy's is on the Latin grammar, and too often with similar results. A girl without musical tastes objects to Mozart, as a boy without a classical turn hates Cæsar. Meanwhile it is pleaded that the education of the sexes must be carried on; that some routine must be adopted; that what need not be pursued as an end is nevertheless good as a means; that the Latin grammar strengthens a boy's memory, and teaches him to study the meaning of words; that the piano makes a girl sit upright and pay attention to details; and against the schoolroom view of music as training for mind and body we have nothing to say. But the other prevalent view of music as a necessary accomplishment, is more open to objection.

In Germany no girl is ashamed to say she cannot

play or sing; but in England such an ill-bred admission would be instantly checked by mamma. The consequence is that young ladies whose honest ambition would naturally begin and end with Cramer's exercises in the schoolroom, are encouraged to trundle through Beethoven's sonatas in the drawing-room, and perhaps pass their lives under the impression that they are able to play the "Lieder ohne Wörte."

By all means let every girl begin by learning the piano. Such a chance of gaining a sympathetic companion for life should never be thrown away. Even to the unmusical girl it is valuable as a training, but to the musical girl its value is beyond price. As a woman's life is often a life of feeling rather than of action, and if society, whilst it limits her sphere of action, frequently calls upon her to repress her feelings, we should not deny her the high, the recreative, the healthy outlet for emotion which music supplies. Joy flows naturally into ringing harmonies, while music has the subtle power to soften melancholy by presenting it with its fine emotional counterpart. A good play on the piano has not unfrequently taken the place of a good cry up-stairs, and a cloud of ill-temper has often been dispersed by a timely practice. One of Schubert's friends used to say, that although often very cross before sitting down to his piano, a long scramble-duet through a symphony, or through one of his own delicious and erratic pianoforte duets, always restored him to good-humour.

But if a person is not musical, pianoforte instruction

after a certain point is only waste of time. It may be said, "Suppose there is latent talent?" To this we reply that, as a general rule, musical talent develops early or not at all. It sometimes, though very seldom, happens that a musical organization exists with a naturally imperfect ear. In this case it may be worth while to cultivate the ear. But when the ear is bad, and there is no natural taste for music, we may conclude that the soil is sterile, and will not repay cultivation.

If a boy has no taste for classics, when he goes to the university his tutor tells him to study something else for his degree. Why should not a girl try drawing or painting or literary composition? Why should the money be spent on her music when she has perhaps shown some other gift? Many a girl with real literary or artistic taste has achieved excellence in nothing because her energies have been concentrated upon the piano, which she will never be able to play, or upon songs which are just as well left unsung. But such performances are otherwise inconvenient. Why am I expected to ask a young lady to play, although I know she cannot play, is nervous, dislikes playing before people, and so forth? How many are there who would fain be spared the humiliation of exposing their weak points! The piano is a source of trouble to them and to their friends. If they cry over their music lesson, their friends groan over the result, and it is difficult to say which is the worst off, the professor who has to teach, the pupil who has to learn, or the people who have to listen. But the cause of music suffers most of all. We have no hesitation in saying that the rubbish heaps that accumulate every year under the title of pianoforte music, and which do more than anything to vulgarize musical taste in England, owe their existence to the unmusical people who are expected to play the piano. If such are to play at all, then indeed it is better that they should play anything rather than Beethoven and Mendelssohn; but why should they play at all?

The piano is a noble instrument, less scientifically perfect than the violin and less extensive than the organ; it has more resource than the first, and infinitely more delicacy than the second. With the aid of a piano we can realize for ourselves and for others the most complicated orchestral scores, as well as the simplest vocal melody: intricate harmonies lie beneath our ten fingers, and can be struck out as rapidly as the mind conceives them. There is not a single great work in oratorio, in opera, in quartet, in concerto, or in song, which cannot be readily arranged for two or four hands, and be rendered, if not always with the real instrumental or vocal impressiveness, at least with unerring polyphonal accuracy. And lastly, there has been written expressly for the piano a mass of music which, for sublimity, pathos, variety, and gradation, is equal to anything in the whole realm of musical conception, whilst in extent it probably surpasses the music written for all other instruments put together.

And now, what are some of the uses to which we apply this noble instrument, this long-suffering piano? When the gentlemen in the dining-room hear that familiar sound up-stairs, they know it is time to have tea in the drawing-room. Let us enter the drawing-room after dinner. The daughter of our hostess is rattling away at the keys, and quite ready for a chat at the same time; if conversation comes her way, she can leave the bass out, or invent one, as it is only the "Sonate Pathétique." She has long passed the conscientious stage, when an indifferent or careless performance caused her the least anxiety. She plays her fantasia now as lightly as she rings the bell, not for its own sake, but because it is time for the gentlemen to come up, or for the ladies to begin a little small talk, or for somebody to make love. When she gets up, another sits down, and continues to provide that indispensable stimulant to conversation called "a little music."

It must be admitted, that to be a good player is no distinction in English society. It has its reward, no doubt, in the quiet happiness of long hours—hours of loving application; hours of absorption; hours lived in a world of subtle and delicate emotion, such as musical dreamers alone realize; and, above all, real musicians have the luxury of meeting occasionally those who can listen to and understand them. They give, but they also receive. Good players and good listeners are equally happy in each other's society. How seldom they meet in England! how few, even fine amateur pianists, have anything like a musical circle! It is very seldom that a neighbourhood can muster the materials for a Mozart or a Beethoven trio, not to say quartet; and seldom that an amateur has the opportunity of playing a concerto of Mendelssohn's with string accompaniments, or any other accompaniment than that of noisy children or general conversation. But no. Late years have witnessed some remarkable combinations, which, however indifferent, are often respectfully listened to.

The harmonium and concertina force themselves upon our attention. There are certain perfect forms and perfect players of both these instruments; but we deal not now with the master workmen, the Regondis, the Blagroves, the Tamplins, and the Engels. The same instrument which in the hands of these men is a thing of beauty and delight, is capable of tempting the musical amateur into wild and tuneless excesses! We will put it to any impartial person, was there ever found in the house of an amateur, a concertina or harmonium in tune with the piano? Was there ever an amateur who could be deterred from playing these instruments together, however discordant the result? When there is a chance of having a duet, people seem to lose all sense of tune. If the concertina is only about a half-semitone flat, the lady thinks she can manage. A little nerve is required to face the first few bars, but before "Il Balen" is over, not a scruple remains, and the increasing consternation of the audience is only equalled by the growing complacency of the performers.

The same indifference to tune may be observed in the amateur flute and cornet. Each player has his method of treating the piano, which, as he tells you, is only the accompaniment, and must follow him. If the piano is more than a semitone flat or sharp, the flute inquires whether it cannot be tuned to his instrument. The piano replies that the tuner has just been, and asks whether the flute cannot alter his pitch. This ends in the flute trying to unscrew himself a little. Then he sounds a C with the piano—thinks it is a little better, unscrews a little more, and asks the piano whether that will do. The piano does not know. Cannot flute get a bit flatter? Not a bit. The heat of the room will make it all right, and then they begin!

The cornet is not much better, with this exception, that the cornet is generally ready to play alone, anywhere. For there is this peculiarity about him—he is never tired of playing, as some people are of hearing, the same tunes over and over again, and, after playing them next door for six months every day, if you ask him to your house, he will play them after dinner in your conservatory, with the same touching expression and crack exactly in the same place. There is a composure about the flute and the cornet, an unruffled temperament, a philosophical calm, and an absolute satisfaction in their respective efforts, which other musicians may envy, but cannot hope to rival. Other musicians feel annoyed at not accomplishing what they attempt; the cornet and the flute tell you at once they attempt what cannot be done.

The organist is disturbed if his organ begins to cipher, the violinist if his string breaks, the pianist if the pedal squeaks; but if the flute is out of tune, or plays octaves by mistake, our friend is easily satisfied after unscrewing and screwing up again; and the cornet, however prone to crack, feels quite happy after putting in a new crook, and fidgeting a little with the pistons.

The amateur violin is seldom heard in mixed society. If good, as he usually is, he is fastidious about accompanyists, still more sensitive about conversation, and won't play. If bad, nobody cares to ask him. However, most of us have come across a fine violin amateur, and enjoyed his playing as much as, perhaps more than, that of many professional artists. It is difficult to speak of the bad violin player without being thought censorious; but we all know the shriek of a slate pencil on a slate, and how bad and wanton little boys use it to torment governesses. Better that than the scratch of a greasy bow on a bad fiddle; and better, too, the boy than the man, for the boy knows he is bad and can be stopped, but the absorbed violinist knows not, neither can he be told, neither can he be stopped!

It is difficult to explain the ascendancy which the violin gains over the minds of its votaries for good or or evil. It can boast of two distinct types of admirers,

—between which, as between two poles, all the others may be said to vibrate. There is the man with one bad fiddle who plays much and miserably, and there is the man who cannot play a note, but has collected a room full of splendid violins, most of which remain unstrung. But we must not dwell on this tempting subject. We proceed to notice the lowest form of the solo instrumentalist.

It is the amateur who plays by ear. Ladies will often gratify you by playing a little of Chopin "by ear"—that means as much as they can recollect of the tune with any kind of bass. It would be well for all young musicians to remember that it is never safe to attempt Chopin, Mendelssohn, and above all Schumann, by heart, without a most careful previous study of the notes, and the regular process of committing a piece to memory: even when once learned the notes should be occasionally used to refresh the memory and ensure accuracy.

The difficulty of expressing or reproducing in notes a given musical idea is greater than at first sight appears. A piece of music is heard, it rings in your ears, you try to learn it, or you sit down and try to play it. If you have little musical culture, merely natural taste and a good ear, you will soon satisfy yourself, and you will say, "That is exactly the tune I heard." Probably it is only an imperfect suggestion of what you have heard. There is sure to exist a gap between it and the original piece. When the subject happens to be good music, even small deviations are fatal to the composer's thought, and a slight change will suffice to vulgarize a theme, just as in poetry a word transposed may destroy the power of a fine line. Who does not see that a note transposed, or left out, or altered, is as fatal to a phrase as the following re-arrangement lately made in our hearing, of one of Mrs. Browning's lines, is to the beauty of that line. The verse stands—

> "O *supreme love!* chief misery,
> The sharp regalia are for thee."

As improved in quotation—

> "O *love supreme!* chief misery,
> The sharp regalia are for thee."

Of course, there can be no harm in a general way of singing and playing by ear to amuse one's self; but how troublesome it is on some occasions to hear people sing and play for your entertainment their so-called reproductions of the opera or classical music, most musicians know very well. But it is not easy to convince them of this; and the poor critic has generally to retire sad and wounded; in short, he is voted a rude, ill-natured, or eccentric kind of person, and is hummed and strummed out of court.

VI.

Let us now turn to the second great class of musical amateurs: The People who sing.

It is thought almost as rude to interrupt a lady

when she is speaking as to talk aloud when she sings. Accordingly the advantages of being able to sing in society are obvious. The lady can at any moment fasten the attention of the room on herself. If a girl has a voice, the piano is too soon suppressed in favour of it, and the only chance of her becoming a musician is thrown away. It is true she usually accompanies herself; that is, she dabbles about on the keys, and strikes a chord at the end of her song, always cutting out the closing bars as not of the "voice voicy," but the room listens, and the room applauds. The maiden is happy; and mamma thinks she requires no more singing lessons.

Every one likes to understand and talk a little about music, and a very slender knowledge will enable an unmusical person to occupy a very creditable position in most musical parties. The following hints may prove useful. Perhaps a chorus is got up. If you are asked to sing bass, first make sure that all the parts are doubled. Then stand behind the piano with the others. You need not sing if you don't like, but you won't do much harm if you sing. If you sing loud, the other bass will think he is wrong; if you sing low, he will think that you are reading the music; if you don't sing at all, he will only think you have lost your place; and as the chances are he has never found his own, he will take no notice. The piece is almost sure to be "All among the Barley," and you can say at the end, "All Mendelssohn's part songs are so good." Perhaps some one will say, "'All among the

Barley' is not Mendelssohn's." Then you can answer, "Of course not!" Very likely, however, the piece may be Mendelssohn's. Then it is sure to be "O Hills and Vales of Pleasure," and at the end you can say, "Do you know another part song called, 'All among the Barley?'" Then some one is sure to say, "Yes, but I like Mendelssohn best;" and then you can answer appreciatively, "Oh, yes, of course!" When a soprano duet is sung, the name of it is sure to be, "I would that my Love," by Mendelssohn. When a contralto sings alone, the song is usually, "In questa tomba," by Beethoven. When a soprano sings, it is more difficult to speak with certainty. However, you can always, if you are at a loss, ask, "Which do you like best, the ballads of Virginia Gabriel or Claribel?" Then, if the singer says, "Virginia Gabriel," it is quite open to you to say, "Claribel," or *vice versâ*. If a tenor sings, you will not be far wrong in supposing the song to be "Spirito Gentil." If, however, it is neither that nor "Martha," nor "Ah! che la morte," you may justly compliment him upon his original and extensive repertory. You must speak of Beethoven as "sublime, but occasionally obscure;" of Spohr, as "scientific, but too sickly and chromatic;" of Mendelssohn, as "fascinating;" of Schumann, as "a man of some genius;" and you may say of Gounod, that "he is very charming, but that you doubt whether he will last;" and it will always be safe, except in the presence of really good musicians, to sniff at Wagner and the music of the future.

And now, if we seem to have conveyed a somewhat harsh estimate of drawing-room music and drawing-room criticism under the form of mock counsel to the reader, let us ask whether the blots of amateur music may not be pointed out as effectually in this way as in any other? Is it not true that a person following the above advice will be able to conceal his ignorance of music in almost any "at home" in England? And why? Simply because so few English people know the difference between the good and the bad in music, or rightly estimate its value. So many regard it as the most frivolous of pastimes, as a tea-bell, as a cloak for scandal, to drown or to promote conversation, to attract to self, or to outbid a rival. There is nothing wrong in being without ear and in caring nothing for music; it is a misfortune, but it is no fault. If a man has no taste for conchology, he is not ashamed to say so. In Germany people never pretend to play; in Italy they never pretend to sing; and if they know nothing about it, they can afford to be silent. Why should not some of us do likewise?

We have dwelt on a somewhat gloomy side of drawing-room music, because few people seem to realize its serious defects; and until this is done improvement is impossible. But light dawns as we think of the noble amateur singers and fine professional performers, which it is more and more our privilege to hear in private society. Power makes its own terms, and professional singers and players, beginning to assume a position and dignity which they ought never to have lost, refuse any longer to promote conversation, or to be turned on like machines. Let amateurs who can, follow their example. If it were considered *hors de règle* for people to sing and play in company unless they happened to have both talent and cultivation, and equally objectionable in others to interrupt th[illegible] who had, or fancied they had, the necessary quali[illegible] bad playing and bad taste in music, would sc[illegible] of fashion.

VII.

We pass on to a more encouraging phase of amateur music. We find ourselves in a quiet cheerful room, at the back of a good house; it is morning; there are only four people present; they are all intent upon playing; they can all play, and there is no one present to molest with praise or blame. Two violins, viola, and violoncello, and the quartet is complete. The first violin is a gifted amateur, the second violin is a thoughtful gentleman, perhaps an art critic, not a brilliant player, but steady, and never tired. Viola is a rather testy, but thoroughly good-natured professional, who never can quite get over the fact of somebody else playing first fiddle, and occasionally has to be called to order for putting in little bits which belong to some one of the other instruments. Violoncello is a good amateur, or perhaps a semi-professional, who plays a little of every instrument under the sun. However, these men can really make music. Let us begin with a light Haydn quartet—No. 63.

It begins with seven-bars rest for the first violin, and seems to glide off the bows—facile, easy, rippling along like a summer rivulet. Every one knows it, every one likes it: the smart *allegro moderato,* the *cantabile adagio,* just long enough, the rousing minuet and trio, and the smart *vivace staccato,* which invariably runs all the fiddlers off their legs, and ends with "Bravo, first fiddle!" and a good laugh at violoncello and tenor, who have too often been dancing through the movement with the light and airy gait of elephants. But now all four have whetted their swords—rosined their bows, we mean—and feel eager for more serious work. Beethoven is put up on the desks. Let us choose the first of the set in F. What an opening movement! Good, broad music, nothing laboured or obscure, but inspiration everywhere flowing from a full fount. It is phrased like a symphony, and yet all is fairly within the compass of the four instruments. The slow movement — than which nothing more tender and lofty was ever invented—tries the first violin; and our professional tenor, who is much dissatisfied with Primo Violino's reading of the closing bars, kindly fiddles them over in the right way, to the disgust of first fiddle. But in the trio that presumptuous fiddle is fairly beaten. He is a good player, but a scramble is all he can make of it. He masters, however, the not difficult bravura passage at the end of the closing movement, and comes in for a compliment from his friend and mentor the cantankerous tenor. Then there is a general motion in favour of Mozart. It must be one of those six perfect works dedicated to "Papa Haydn." After this, as a complete contrast, we select a solo quartet of Spohr, not very hard, although so showy; and then, every one having got into full swing, we may be able to rattle through Mendelssohn's *canzonet* before the lunch-bell rings.

Four hours of it in the morning might seem enough; but that is nothing to the quartet player. After lunch those four men will begin again, and work away till dusk. Then they will go out for a turn in the park or by the sea before dinner, and will very likely set to again after dinner, and play from nine till twelve o'clock. In musical country-houses it is not uncommon to have a quartet party staying in the house; and then woe to the unmusical! The best quartet work is no doubt done in the morning; but the quartet is irrepressible, it may break out at all times, and anywhere—suddenly on the lawn, in summer; in the dining-room, after dinner; in very hot weather, in some sonorous housekeeper's room; even in the pantry, all over the drawing-room, in the library, on the balcony, or up-stairs in any of the bed-rooms.

But we must not linger. Converse with these exceptionably fine amateurs spoils us for the kind of performance which it is now our painful duty to describe, and which we may call THE SCRATCH QUARTET.

Our friend Harmonics, who is rather a good player, has invited three worse than himself. They come with their wives, and a musical friend is perhaps asked in to listen. The ladies are not to talk, and the friend is not to talk; they are to listen. Harmonics leads off with a Haydn. Our heavy friend, with greasy bow and inferior violin, stumbles after him, tenor scrapes placidly—flat, of course, but not unhappy, for he has a bad ear. The neighbouring organist, rather glad of a little violoncello practice, grins at the noise, but goes on. It seems a point of honour with these men not to stop. They are all wrong, and they know it. But first fiddle pretends he has never got out, second fiddle declares he was beating time (which he certainly was, with his foot loud enough to be heard all over the room), and therefore couldn't be wrong (which does not follow). Tenor smiles, and has no opinion. 'Cello thought they would get right somehow if they pulled on through the breakers into the smooth water, commonly known as "the place where the subject begins again." After each double bar there is a regular discussion, in which each performer defends himself, and brings counter-charges, and then the *Adagio* begins. Second violin now has a chance, the theme has come his way at last. He plays the *pp's* fortissimo —he rasps the accompaniment, so that Harmonics cannot hear himself; but, of course, No. 2 *will* hack and hew, he *must* play out. The violoncello will not be outdone—even the tenor is roused at last—and all seem to rush headlong upon the music with screams of discordant sound, until, apparently maddened by their own scraping, they finish in a sort of wild *scrunch*, which they call "coming in all right in the end." The ladies exclaim, "How beautiful!" Musical friend says it's delightful, and, remembering another engagement, is off in a hurry, and then these infatuated men begin again. At last outraged nature herself protests. Even Harmonics is exhausted. No. 2 thinks they have done enough. Tenor is simply sleepy and pensive. Violoncello can hardly lift what he calls "his *strad.*" It is late—a glass of wine and a sandwich—a couple of cabs. The reader heaves a sigh of relief. They are gone, and may they ne'er come back again!

Out of *Quartet Societies*, good, bad, and indifferent, comes the Orchestral Musical Society, or, as it is sometimes called, the Symphony Society. The theory of these societies seems to be that of some street bands, that a good many who cannot play by themselves can play very well all together. The amateurs of the band usually supply a few violins, violoncellos, a flute, perhaps two, let us hope but one cornet, and any number of volunteers for the drums. The rest are professionals, who supply a leader on the violin, brass, clarionet, oboë, as required, and an excellent professional gentleman, who conducts with a bâton. How ever the public performances are got through is a wonder, for the rehearsals cannot be said to be got through at all.

Impelled by the noblest aspirations, nothing will daunt our devoted band: not Beethoven's C minor, not Mendelssohn's Italian Symphony, not Weber's overtures. Haydn's symphonies, which they might play, are soon voted slow; Handel's music is out of date; even Mozart is too easy a triumph. A few Italian overtures they could perhaps manage, but then they are classical players, and cannot stoop to that sort of thing.

"Seven o'clock punctually, if you please, gentlemen, for the next rehearsal!" says Mr. Amadeus Le Bâton, at the end of the practice; and at seven punctually Amadeus enters a perfectly empty room. There are about twenty or thirty music desks waiting. The conductor's desk stands facing him. Presently in comes a man with a violin case. Then another, dragging a double bass. In about a quarter of an hour the leader and one first fiddle have arrived, but as first fiddle is above playing second, nothing can be done. Le Bâton pulls out his watch, and upbraids those who have not arrived to those who have. Perhaps by a quarter to eight they are ready to begin; but to begin what? Tuning, of course. Some people admire the tuning of the Handel Orchestra, others have been known to appreciate the tuning at Exeter Hall more than the performance. But for a dreadful orgie in sound—the very memory of which is calculated to make you start in your dreams for months afterwards, under the impression that all the cats and dogs which have ever been drowned in the Thames have come to life again, and are howling round your pillow—for a row compared with which the noise of a menagerie about feeding time is positively agreeable—commend me to the tuning of an amateur orchestra. But we have more to hear than that. In the midst of it all, some violin will play the *Carnival de Venise*, the flute will practise his bits, the violoncello tries to do fiddle passages up high on his finger-board, the cornet has the effrontery to add to the confusion by playing a waltz, some one behind him is imitating the howl of a dog or the squeak of a rat on the reed of his clarionet. Kettledrums is pretending to tune, by alternately thumping the parchment and screwing at the side with a key. Triangle, when pulled up, solemnly declares he is practising his part in Q flat!

At last they *do* seem to be off. Every one playing as if his were the only instrument in the world, for *piano* is the last word the amateur learns. Still the conductor does not complain, until Drums (who has two hundred bars rest and then two little notes very soft) comes down half a bar too soon with an absolutely deafening roll. The flute is thrown completely out; the cornet seems much excited by that noble "rataplan," and keeps on his note a bar too long. The violin bows are literally at sixes and sevens, like the pendulums in a watchmaker's window. Amadeus may stamp, Amadeus may shout, Amadeus may beat his poor little bâton to bits against the desk, no one heeds him, or ever thinks of looking at him—the band took some time to get ready, but now they are off for better for worse, and who can stop them? Even if half the band stops, the other half will go on. Poor Amadeus Le Bâton! what can he do? It is obvious that he can do nothing, and after shouting himself hoarse, and gesticulating wildly, he gives it up, claps both hands to his ears, and gazes despondingly at the "score" before him.

The VOCAL ASSOCIATION or SINGING CLASS, in its various forms, is a more popular and generally a more successful affair. All over the country such societies are now being established, sometimes on Mr. Hullah's, sometimes on the Tonic-Sol-Fa system, both of which enable a very moderate professor to teach the general principles of part-singing to large numbers with comparative ease. As a part of parochial machinery the singing class is most valuable. Since young people will have amusement, what more delightful pursuit could be found for them than music? And since they persist in taking a peculiar delight in each other's society, where could they better meet than at the music class in the schoolroom, or town-hall, when their minds are to some extent occupied, discipline maintained, and a healthy and exhilarating recreation provided for them?

The parochial aspect of singing societies has hardly been sufficiently recognised. Literary institutes, popular lectures, elocution, French, arithmetic, or drawing classes, will all grow naturally out of the musical fount. But of this we cannot speak here more particularly.

We have discussed instrumental and vocal societies separately, but perhaps amateurs succeed best when the two are combined. A piano, harmonium, or both, will very well eke out a small but by no means inefficient string band. The organist will conduct, choruses will be got up at separate rehearsals, the Prima Donna of the neighbourhood will consent to learn the principal solos, and an oratorio will be forthcoming about Christmas time. That oratorio is invariably "Judas Maccabæus," and indeed it is but another proof of the simple and sublime genius of Handel that he should be welcomed at Exeter Hall, and not out of place in a village schoolroom.

But we have already chatted too long about AMATEUR MUSIC IN ENGLAND. As we look back upon the foregoing pages truth forbids us to tone down some painful and unpalatable admissions, but whilst it cannot be said that we have omitted to point out blots in the existing state of things, we may be accused of gliding too lightly over much that is really hopeful and striking in English musical taste.

We seem, as a people, to be musically many-sided, unbalanced, and above all unschooled by the inexorable laws and conditions of true art. We deal in heights and depths—we abound in inconsistencies which admit of no reconciliation. We pay our shilling and rush to hear the "Messiah" at the Agricultural Palace or the Albert Hall, then we go home and sing Glover. We sit for two hours in St. James's Hall to hear Beethoven's or Spohr's quartets, and the next day we buy "God bless the Prince of Wales."

All this is simple fact. But it is fair to add that whilst for want of high national models, English musical taste falls below that of France or Italy, it rises higher than either in its honest enthusiasm for the great German masters.

It may be that we are on the eve of a creative period in the history of English music. This confusion of ideas may be nothing but the coming together of what will by-and-by develop into our national school. This eclectic taste, which at times looks much like chaos, may also be the ferment out of which a new and beautiful life is ready to be born.

As an original artist will be caught and absorbed by one influence after another, being possessed by his art long before he learns to possess himself,—as he will at times appear to be swayed to and fro by various distinct impulses, without being able to bring them into harmonious relationship,—as we may watch him year by year melting down one style after another in the crucible of his genius, until he has gained fine gold, and stamped it with his own image, even so we seem to see England now calling in the musical currencies of the world, which she may before long re-issue with the hall-mark of her own originality and genius.

VIII.

THE last sign of our musical times which we feel disposed here to dwell upon may be summed up in the ominous words "STREET MUSIC." There are many problems in connection with national music which have never been solved. It would be difficult to find any country without some kind of popular music; but why have some nations called in the aid of science, and developed national schools of music, like France, Italy, Germany, whilst others, like Russia, Spain, and, above all, Ireland, Scotland, and Wales, have never got beyond rude national ballads? Again, how strange it is to find the old popular forms running side by side with the new scientific forms of modern music without losing their distinctive features!

Mr. Ap Thomas tells us that the Welsh harper to this day preserves his ancient customs. "Now, as of old, he may be seen, as soon as the sun rises, in the large oak chair (which, as a fixture, stands at the entrance of every neat and tidy Welsh inn), welcoming, harp in hand, the weary traveller, or solacing the hours of friends never tired of listening to his national strains. Many of these harpists are blind and very old."

The primitive nature of the bagpipes would seem to need no comment; but, curiously enough, although the bagpipes play many of the old national tunes, they are not the old national instrument of Scotland, nor were the oldest tunes composed for the bagpipes, as is usually supposed. Up to the sixteenth century the harp was the national instrument of both Ireland and Scotland, and the national melodies of both countries were not dissimilar. The Irish and Scotch melodies, reduced to their simplest expressions, abound in thirds, fifths, and octaves. They were composed for the harp, which was strung with wire, and very resonant. To avoid discord, it became necessary that every note should form a concord with the last; and hence the peculiar and for ever pleasing character of Scotch and Irish melodies.

The abominable characteristics of the bagpipes are not really Scotch, but French. How the bagpipes superseded the harp in Scotland has always been considered a mystery. We believe it may be traced to French influence, and distinctly to the period of Mary Queen of Scots. At all events, about that time, toward the close of the sixteenth century, the harp went out of fashion, and the bagpipe came in. Is it unlikely that in the foreign train of Mary Stuart, there may have been players of the national *cornemuse*, or French bagpipes, who managed to set a fashion which, for some reason or other, took root and has lasted ever since? The attempt to graft on Scotland foreign customs, instead of adopting Scotch ones, is entirely consistent with what we know of the Queen of Scots' policy.

But the cornemuse of southern France is perhaps the most striking instance of the way in which primitive national music may continue wholly uninfluenced by modern culture. The cornemuse has struck the keynote of all really national French music, and cornemuse forms of melody are not only to be found in the modern popular French ballads, but abound in the operas of Auber and Gounod; yet the cornemuse itself remains unchanged, nor are its melodies ever varied in the direction of modern music. Madame Sand, in one of her amusing digressions, gives an account of a conversation she had with a cornemuse player at a French fair. He did not make his tunes—they were all made by the woodcutters in the great forest: if a man wished to excel, he must go into the woods and catch the melodies from these wild men. The tunes were handed down from generation to generation, and might be endlessly varied; but there was no development, no change in their structure, nor had there been, as far as she could ascertain, for centuries.

Now, speaking generally, the state of music in Scotland, Ireland, Wales, France, Germany, Italy, Russia, and Spain is not wholly unintelligible. Scotland, Ireland, and Wales have no schools, but they have national ballads: music there is a wild germ, that, for some reason or other, has remained undeveloped by civilization. The same thing may be said of Spain and Russia. In France a regular school of music has appropriated the rude popular elements (as a *point du départ*), which nevertheless remain alongside of the music-school in all their primitive simplicity. In Italy the same phenomenon has occurred, only the connection between the Abruzzi mountaineer with his pipe stuck into an inflated goatskin and the Italian opera, is less obvious than that between the cornemuse player and modern French song.

In Germany, however, where music has attained its highest and most truly national development, the rude element will soon have reached the vanishing point; hardly an old melody of mountain or vale but what has received a new setting—our idea of a *Volkslied* is something in two or three parts by Mendelssohn, or at all events a charming air with a graceful accompaniment. Even the wild airs of Poland have been remodelled by Chopin. The "yodelling" of the peasants is generally heard in combination with delicious harmonies unknown to their forefathers, and the Swiss "hurdy-gurdy" is probably the last remnant of barbarism to be found in the direction of Germany.

IX.

But what shall be said of England? We can imagine the nations passing before us, each represented by its popular form of street music. Germany comes with a band of singers, followed by a band of men playing on all kinds of musical instruments. France comes fresh from the woods with her cornemuse. Italy issues from the mountains with that tuneful and fascinating goatskin and pipe, so finely rendered by M. Gounod in *Mirella*. Spain comes with a mandoline; Scotland with the bagpipes; Ireland and Wales with harps of well-known national form and proportion. Even Russia sings a good bass tune, and blows a horn well; and England brings up the rear with—a policeman requesting an organ-grinder to move on!

Indeed, that man plays all the favourite tunes. It is true he is not English, but he represents the popular tastes in music. Does he play national melodies? Not many—chiefly the melodies of other countries, or what will pass for them with the million; but he does *grind* certain English ballads too, claptrap sort of jingles—not especially national, or especially anything; he cannot be said to *play* them; no fancy, or originality, or taste is displayed, except by the monkey who sits on his shoulder; the performance from first to last is a *grind*. In the streets of other countries you seldom meet with foreign musicians—at least not in France, Germany, and Italy; but who will deny that the staple of street music in England is organ-grinding? And the grinder is a foreigner, who only grinds a few English tunes under protest. In fact, "He's a Pal o' mine" and "Jolly Dogs," are used as gold leaf, to gild pills like "Casta Diva" and the "Carnival de Venise."

But as the organ-grinder is a *great fact*, and perhaps in a survey of street music in England the most prominent fact, he deserves a few moments' calm consideration. There are big organs drawn by a donkey, and little organs carried by boys; nondescript boxes with a cradle at the top and two babies, drawn by a woman;

uprights on a stick, with a little handle turned by a crazy old man; chest open in front and shut at the back, or shut in the front and open at the back. There are flute organs, with a wonderful system of wooden pipes, visible through glass; great magnified accordions, played somehow with a handle—horrid things, which grind only the Old Hundredth and a chant on metal pipes. There are tinkling cupboards, which remind one of Dickens' pianoforte with the works taken out, so irregular and uncertain is the effect of the handle upon the tune. There are illustrated organs, with Chinese mandarins performing conjuring tricks in a row, or Nebuchadnezzar's band; and there are organs with a monkey, triangle, bones, tambourine, or whistle obligato. Every man has probably had moments in his life when he has not been sane upon the question of barrel organs. He has perhaps been placed in difficult circumstances. Let us say he occupies a corner house. On one side, at the bottom of the street, commences the "Chickaleary Bloke;" on the other side, at the bottom of another street, is faintly heard "Polly Perkins:" both are working steadily up to a point—that point is his corner house—let us say your own corner house. You are in your study writing poetry; nearer and nearer draw the minstrels, regardless of each other, and probably out of each other's hearing, but both heard by you in your favourable position. As they near the point the discord becomes wild and terrible; you rush into the back study, but the *tom-tom* man is in the yard; you rush out of the front door to look for a policeman—there is none; you use any Italian words you can recollect; at the same time, pointing to your head, you explain that your father lies dangerously ill up-stairs, and that several ladies are dying in the neighbourhood; you implore the Italian to move on, and the scene ends in No. 1 slowly grinding down the street which No. 2 came up, and No. 2 grinding up the street which No. 1 has just come down. At such moments we are apt to speak recklessly on the great subject of barrel organs, and we sometimes—idle employment!—write letters to the newspapers, which are pardonably one-sided. The fact is, the organ question, like all other great questions, has two sides to it, although we seldom hear but one.

Let not those who write abusive letters to the newspapers, and bring in bills to abolish street music, think they will be able to loosen the firm hold which the barrel-organist has over the British public. Your cook is his friend, your housemaid is his admirer; the policeman and the baker's young man look on him in the light of a formidable rival.

But, for once, let us speak a good word for him. We know all that can be said against him, let us now plead his cause a little. His sphere is large; he conquers more worlds than one; his popularity is not only wide, but varied—he enters many clean and spacious squares, and little chubby faces, well-born and rosy, look out from high-railed nursery-windows, and as they look out he looks up, and baby is danced at the bars and stops crying directly, and Tommy forgets his quarrel with Johnny, and runs to the window too, and tears are wiped and harmony is restored in many and many a nursery, and nurse herself finds the penny and smiles, and "organ-man" pockets the penny and smiles, and plays five more tunes in for the money, and lifts his hat, and waves "ta-ta!" in Italian, and walks off to "fresh fields and pastures new,"—and isn't it worth the penny?

And where does he wander to now—that happy, easy-tempered son of the South? Ah, he has no proud looks, and though he has just played to members of the aristocracy, he is willing to turn as merrily for the lowest of the people.

I meet him in the dingy alleys of the great city—I meet him in the regions of garbage and filth, where the atmosphere inhaled seems to be an impartial mixture of smoke and decomposition, and where the diet of the people seems to consist of fried herrings and potato parings: there is our organ-man—and there, at least, we may bless him—grinding away to the miserable, sunken, and degraded denizens of Pigmire Lane or Fish Alley. Let him stay always there—let him grind ever thus. I confess it does my heart good to see those slatternly women come to their doors and stand and listen, and the heavy, frowning, coal-besmeared men, lean out of the windows with their pipes, and forgetting hunger and grinding poverty, hushing also the loud oath and blasphemy for a little season, smile with the pleasure of the sweet sounds. Through that little black window with the cracked panes, you can see the lame shoemaker look up for a moment, and, as he resumes the long-drawn-out stitches with both hands, it is with countenance relaxed, and almost pleasurable energy. The pale-faced tailor looks out from the top story (yes! like a beam of sunshine the music has struck through him), he forgets the rent, and the work, and the wages, and the wretchedness of life. It is the end of the day, it is lawful to rest for a moment and listen, and they do listen—the men and women clustering in groups on their doorsteps, and leaning from the windows above, and the children—oh! the children! I look down the alley, and suddenly it is flooded with the light of the low sun; it smites the murky atmosphere into purple shades, and broad, warm, yellow light upon the pathway, and glitters like gold leaf upon the window-panes; and the children—the children are dancing all down the alley, dancing in long vistas far down into the sunny mist, two and two, three and three, but all dancing, and dancing in time; and their faces—many poor pale faces, and some rosy ones too—their faces are so happy, and the whole alley is hushed, save only for the music and the dancing of the children.

I bless that organ-man—a very Orpheus in hell! I bless his music. I stand in that foul street where the blessed sun shines, and where the music is playing, I give the man a penny to prolong the happiness of those poor people, of those hungry, pale, and ragged children, and, as I retire, I am saluted as a public benefactor; and was ever pleasure bought so cheap and so pure?

X.

Towards evening we find the organ-grinder fairly expelled from some quarters of the town—from the better streets and the more respectable squares. What we may have striven in vain to accomplish, what there was no policeman at hand to do, has been triumphantly effected by *the second great fact* of street music,—The German Band. The full-blown brass band, with drums, plays fine music, and is patronised in high places. The men wear uniforms, and are from six to twelve in number. The head man leads on the clarionet, arranges the music, and is generally a capital theoretical and practical musician. Every man carries his own stand of music, and, by an arrangement of strings and weights, can set it up and play through any moderate hurricane. The hardiness of these men is astonishing. They stand in cutting draughts at the corners of the streets; they will play through any ordinary shower. The cornet executes variations in the snow, the drum keeps himself warm in frosty weather by a close application to business, the flute chirps and twitters with the thermometer at zero, when other people cannot even whistle. The men with the great brass tubes and serpents pour forth volumes of breath on tropical nights, when other people can hardly breathe; the triangle man has the lightest time of it, but then he is expected to walk about and sue for coppers; indeed, that appears to be his real business—the triangle is only his pastime.

As we sit with our windows open in the summer evenings, we can hear them playing at the corner of the street. Now it is *Masaniello*, dashed off with great fire, and generally taken too fast; then a selection from *Faust*, or the last new opera chopped up, sometimes very cleverly, for street use. On these occasions the principal instruments play the "arias," and one often regrets that men who play so well have not had more opportunities of hearing the songs which they are the means of making so widely popular. The airs are constantly taken at a pace or in a style which proves that the player has never heard them on the stage, nor has the faintest notion of what they mean.

Although forced to play chiefly Italian and French overtures, opera selections, firework quadrilles, cataract waltzes, &c., to catch the public, the German feeling will creep out, and is not unkindly received. Homœopathic doses of Haydn, Mozart, or Beethoven are administered in the shape of a slow movement, allegretto, or minuet and trio out of some symphony, and these, inserted sandwich-like, between a "Slap Bang" polka and "Fra Diavolo," go down very well. But as we contemplate the model German band, the scene changes, and we find ourselves as in some bad dream listening to a hideous parody. Four poor fellows have got together, the sport of a cruel destiny—none of their instruments are in tune, the public will not hear them nor pay them, their own ears have become vitiated, they have learned to regard any brass instruments blown together anyhow as a German band. Of course, they do not long hang together; some of them get happily drafted into bigger bands, others pair off, and we thus have that form of street music which may be called the *Brass Band dissolved.* This may mean one of two things; it may mean either the *Brass without the Band,* or the *Band without the Brass.*

The *Brass without the Band* means generally a cornet and a bass horn, who undertake to perform "Suoni la Tromba in trepido;" sometimes the bass horn does "Il Balen," or at least any part of it which happens to be within the compass of his instrument. On these occasions the cornet flourishes about wildly, and appears to be carrying on a kind of guerilla warfare with his panting antagonist, which ends in the successful demolition of the latter, who finally wheezes and puffs himself to death, whilst the cornet screams a pæan of victory. At other times the cornet leads off with "Ah! che la morte," whilst the bass horn, coming to life again, gasps in an explosive manner. Before long it usually happens that the bass horn, jealous of the cornet's supremacy, absorbs himself into a band again, and the cornet, if he does not go and do likewise, wanders away to enter into a fruitless competition with "organ-man" in Fish Alley, or tries to get a precarious living off "The Blue Bells of Scotland," in front of a third-rate public-house in a deserted quarter of the city.

If the *Brass without the Band* can fall to a lower depth still, it is when he seats himself on the top of a van full of tipsy Foresters, and after sharing their potations during the daytime, "joins in" frantically with the chorus of lunatics as they drive home through the streets of the city, making night hideous with bellow and blare. We may here take leave of the *Brass without the Band.*

The second part of the *Brass Band dissolved* is the *Band without the Brass,* which generally means a flute or a clarionet *solus.* Unlike the "brass," the "wood" never walk a road together. As they are both solo instruments, the rivalry would be too bitter; and finding a lonely life intolerable, they soon join themselves to, or go to make up, what may be called *the third great fact* of street music—THE STRING BAND.

The highest form of the string band is too seldom seen. It consists of from six to twelve performers,—two violins, tenor, violoncello, or double bass, flute, clarionet, or the above doubled, or in such other various proportions as time and circumstances may allow of. We have met with them at seaside places in fine weather, and occasionally in the more retired parts of the city in the afternoon. But as stringed instruments in any perfection are delicate things, the expense of keeping them together in any number and efficiency is great; and the German bands, both louder and hardier in organization, drive them out of the field. For some reason these large string bands are generally English, they play excellent music, but are not so popular or so well paid as their German rivals.

Another form of the string band, however, is the most popular and the best paid of any street music; but, from its very delicacy and excellence, its sphere of operation is restricted as to time and place, and few itinerant musicians seem to combine the necessary qualifications for success. Visitors to Brighton have all noticed the great rival to the excellent German band on the beach, in the shape of four Italian musicians. The leader, Signor Beneventano, is a fine violin-player out of doors, although the writer discovered that in a room he is somewhat coarse in tone and execution, which in great measure accounts for his success in the open air. He is accompanied by a harp, a second violin, and a flute. Each man is capital in his department, and each man knows his place. This little band of accomplished players forms the centre for a group of attentive listeners, who are regaled with charming versions of the modern opera, the *primo violino* occasionally playing solos with excellent pathos and effect. We have seen shillings, half-crowns, and even gold put into the cap, in return for which regular printed programmes are distributed. But at the first spot of rain or gust of wind—in the middle of a passage or "scena," however touching—Signor Beneventano signals to stop, packs up fiddle and bow, a cloth is hastily flung over the harp, the flute is unscrewed, the music folded up, all made "taut," and the artists retire. The brass band thinks them poor creatures.

But if we seldom hear either what we may call *the*

Orchestral String Band or *the Italian Miniature Band*, *the String Band dissolved* is, alas! always with us. It is a harp and a fiddle. The harpist is generally a man with an ear for time, but not for tune; the fiddler has an ear for tune, but none for time. The fiddler can afford to be in tune, because he has only four strings; but the harpist, who has forty, very naturally cannot. We have heard people wonder how the harpists can keep their strings from breaking;—they don't. Others ask how it is possible in the open air to have so many strings in any sort of tune;—they never are. The picked Italian band *is* fairly in tune, and that *is* a wonder. But though in the *String Band dissolved* there is much to regret, there is nothing to wonder at, except it be how such people ever get a living. The *sang-froid* of the harpist is great—one accompaniment does for all times and tunes; or, if he has different accompaniments, he never fits them on to their right tunes; and if for a couple of bars he blunders into the right measure, he does not notice it before he gets wrong again. A cat might walk over the strings with quite as much, probably a very similar, effect. But he is outdone by the determination of the violinist, who is superior to all accompaniment, and treats the harpist like a lackey. He does not tell him when he is going to begin, how long he is going on, or when he means to stop; indeed he is generally much the better man of the two, and might play a respectable fourth-rate second violin at a third-class theatre if he practised hard and did not show such overweening confidence in his variations on the "Carnival de Venise." Where will that man end? Cross the street, and we can show you. Yonder comes an old blind man with a knowing dog who is constantly persuading him that it is necessary to move on whenever he stops and begins to play a tune. He has thus got into the habit of playing and walking. He is weak and old with drink before his time, and does not play much now except on the open strings. Sometimes it is his wife who leads him; now he is blind she keeps the drink from him, and prolongs his life a little. One day she will sell his old fiddle, they will go into the workhouse together, and the *String Band* will be completely *dissolved.*

XI.

We must here notice a large class of nondescript street musicians—chiefly self-made men. We may call these the *fourth great fact* in street music, and treat them under the head of Miscellaneous Artists. Many of them are men of strong original powers, subjected to the most eccentric development. We remember one strange man who bore the appearance of a North American Indian armed to the teeth. He was hung round, saddled, propped up, sat upon, wedged in, and stuck all over generally with some two dozen or more instruments, and boasted that he could play most of them simultaneously. A drum, worked with a wire by one foot, rattled above his head—his mouth moved round a semicircle, blowing into such things as pan-pipes, flutes, clarionets, horns, and other tubes conveniently slung to his neck like an ox's cradle; one hand moved an accordion tied to his thigh, whilst a triangle jingled from his wrist; the other hand played the bones, whilst the elbow clapped a tambourine fixed to his side; on the inside of his knees were cymbals, which he kept knocking together. There was now only one foot and ancle left, and on that ancle he had bells, which rang with every motion. We describe from memory, and doubt whether we have detailed half the instruments. If Julius Cæsar had ever met that man, he would have felt quite ashamed of himself for not being able to do more than three things at a time.

Then we have, at the sea-side, the Bohemian dwarfs on little three-legged stools, with tiny mandolines, strumming away almost inaudibly, but apparently quite content, and remunerated out of pity.

Then there is the piano on wheels which goes about till one day it gets rained on unmercifully and bursts. And the harmonium on wheels which, in a very little time does nothing but "cipher," and has to retire into private life. There is the street Picco, who plays cleverly on the penny whistle, and the street Bonnay, who plays with hammers on a wooden instrument; another plays with hammers on bits of metal, another on bits of glass, another on regular musical glasses, another on bells, and another on strings; but the most original of this class is a man who produces singularly beautiful effects by using two balls of india-rubber to set in vibration a perfectly tuned system of musical glasses. The india-rubber is used to rub the edge of the glass as children rub finger-bowls with wet fingers, and the sound elicited is the same. This man plays pathetic tunes with great taste and extraordinary execution. He has lately substituted a series of glass tubes.

Having got thus far in my meditations, it occurred to me that it was time to pass from instrumental to vocal music, but the transition seemed abrupt—there must be a connecting link. I think I have discovered that missing link in the person of the "tom-tom" man. He is both vocal and instrumental. Many persons who have not studied the question may suppose that he only beats the tom-tom; but this is an error. On very hot days, if you go close up to him, you will perceive that he sings what are doubtless the national melodies of his native land. As far as we can make out, they are as simple as they are plaintive, and consist mainly in the constant repetition of

"Yow, yow, aie! yagger, yow, yow."

Here then we may be said to have a link between instrumental and vocal street music.

XII.

VOCAL street music divides itself naturally into ballad and chorus, or solo and part songs. The street ballads emanate from the music halls and penny gaffs. And, of all the encouraging facts in connection with popular music in England, this—our *fifth fact*—of BALLAD MUSIC is the least. This is the form in which whatever there is national in English music is uttered, and what utterances we have here! Every now and then, it is true, a really graceful ballad, such as, "When other lips," "Jeanette and Jeanot," gets into general vogue: but, as a rule, the really popular songs are those that minister to the lowest rollicking tastes, such as "Champagne Charley," or to the vulgar commonplaces of life, such as the "Postman's Knock," or to the feeblest sentimental fancies, such as "Sea Shells." About most of them there is a low affectation and a sense of unreality that pierces, and the people that troll them about the streets never sing them with earnestness or humour, like the Germans or the Italians, just because music is not to our lower orders a deep need, a means of expressing the pent-up and often oppressive emotions of the heart, but merely a noisy appendage to low pastimes. Even the less objectionable ballads which concern the most touching affections of our nature are full of vamped-up and artificial sentiment. What, for instance, can be more feeble in sentiment and false in taste than "Let me kiss him for his mother?" And yet, trash like this, which would be scouted in any other form by every national school-boy, is considered finely pathetic by the lower orders when it comes to them in the disguise of a ballad, for music to them is an artificial thing, having artificial and unreal standards of propriety, and too often unconnected with their real interests and genuine emotions. And the consequence is, that our street ballads last but from year to year, almost from month to month; they are constantly being replaced, not by songs that enrich the national stock, but by songs whose chief object seems to be to extinguish their predecessors, and when they have accomplished this, die themselves, like bees after discharging their sting. Who ever hears "Slap bang" now? Even "Old dog Tray," a really pathetic thing, seems dead at last, whilst the echoes of "Not for Joseph" seem finally to have died away.

There is a certain feeble prettiness about the Virginia Gabriel and Claribel school of ballads, but it is the "Baby asleep," "Papa, come to tea" style of thing, so eloquently condemned in the painting of the period, at the Royal Institution, by Mr. Ruskin; and when the ballad is not strictly social, spooney, or domestic, can we imagine any twaddle feebler than what is put forward to do duty for thought and feeling? In one ballad, for instance, the following ingenious conundrum is propounded, "What will to-morrow be?" the answer is, "Who can tell?" Of course nobody can, and this insult to our intelligence is repeated through several verses, to music nearly as exasperating. From the mud-heaps of ballads lying around us we may no doubt pick out some gold nuggets; but the finest ballads are sure to be the least popular. All honour to Madame Sainton Dolby, Mr. Santley, and a few others, for keeping some really good ballads before the public. Let us only trust that Mr. Sullivan, the brightest hope of the young English school, will keep before him the high ballad ideal of his Shakespeare songs, and those lyrics which Mr. Tennyson has written for him, and not be tempted into the "Ever of thee" style, by the tears of sopranos or the solemn warnings of publishers.

But if we have for a moment escaped from the streets, we are reminded by the shrill voice of a woman outside, that it is with these and not with the drawing-room, that we are now concerned. The poor creature, meanly clad, is singing, "We may be happy yet," or "My pretty Jane." The crying baby has at last fallen asleep, but the song is almost more piteous. But we have only to go down one of the back streets, until we come to a third-class public-house, and we reach at once the lowest depths to which the English ballad can descend. Two coarse and grimy ruffians, with greasy slips of thin paper, printed all over and adorned with villanous woodcuts, are tramping stoutly down the reeking alley, and chanting forth to admiring groups of the unwashed, some account of the latest murder, in rhyme, or the interesting contest between Champion Tommy and the Charcoal Pet. Let us draw a veil over their proceedings, as we pass with a sigh of relief to *the sixth fact* of street music, which consists of CHORUS and PART SONG in various forms.

The blind singers, who with the assistance of a concertina ply through the whole of London, are known to every one. They render their psalm tunes, soundly harmonized, in a hard *canto fermo* style, which has its legitimate attractions, and with that peculiar concentration and directness of purpose which characterizes blind people, and which has a pathos of its own. We fancy that regular bands of accomplished part singers are less common now than they were a few years ago. They may have been driven out of the field by the negro melodists, and have no doubt found a more congenial sphere in the various music-halls which have been lately opened in great numbers all over the country. We must, however, notice the Praeger family, who are unique in their excellent part-singing and improvisations: we hear that it is not an uncommon thing for them at the close of the Brighton or Folkestone season to deposit several hundred pounds in the bank previous to their departure for the Continent. Out of the season the young ladies receive an excellent general education in one of the first French schools, and every year the return of the family is anxiously awaited by many thousands of discriminating admirers.

But there is a foreign band of singers—foreign only in appearance—that never leaves our shores, the *Negro melodists*. The conquering nigger landed some years ago, and after capturing this small island, caught many of the aborigines, blacked them over, and sent them off to proclaim the glories of Niggerdom throughout the length and breadth of this benighted land. The princes of the art sit in royal council at St. James's Hall, and it is an affecting thing to see the poor white men who resort to their levées in crowds, welcomed by them as men and brethren. It is the fashion to smile at the "Christy (now Moore and Burgess) Minstrels," and indeed uninterrupted gravity would be somewhat out of place in their assemblies, but we must not forget that they furnish one of the most original elements of our street music. From St. James's Hall, and not from "Old Virginny," come constant supplies of new melodies. The original melodies, such as "Lucy Neal," "Uncle Ned," some of which were no doubt genuine American negro productions, are almost forgotten, but from that new source of negro pathos and humour, numbers of songs and choruses continue to flow, some of them good imitations, and many of them retaining the characteristic form of the negro melody, viz., nigger *solus*, niggers *tutti*, interludes and brilliant finale by Bones, accompanied by the whole band. The real negro is passionately attached to music—his sorrows and joys are both accompanied by the banjo—and slave-life, in which the present generation of negroes has been born and bred, is full of touching episodes and dramatic incidents. The English public were subdued by the power and beauty of these, as depicted, or as some say overdrawn, in Mrs. Stowe's book; and it is not too much to presume that the lasting popularity and deep appreciation of negro fun and pathos in

England is mainly due to the genius of "Uncle Tom's Cabin."

The gentlemen who nightly blacken their faces in order to portray to a sympathetic audience the life and manners of a hitherto oppressed race, have certainly a fair claim upon our indulgent interest. There is something pathetic even about these worthy Englishmen themselves; and it is not without emotion that we gaze at the portraits of the most successful "Bones" of the age, outside St. James's Hall—representing above the mighty W. P. Collins, black as to his face, and otherwise equipped for action; whilst underneath, the same face, only washed, looks appealingly at us, and seems to say, "You see the black all comes off. I am not so bad-looking either. You can hardly see me at night. But remember *P.* Collins is white, and although his initial is *P.*, he was not christened Pompey."

The street niggers are often excessively clever, but are forced to pander in a variety of ways to the popular taste. For the sake of an undiscerning public, English fun is mixed up with negro humour. Punch conducts with a bâton and a desk before him; light and flippant remarks are addressed to the crowd in good broad English; capers are cut in season and out of season to the dismay of cab horses and omnibus drivers; and even practical jokes are played off on any who come too near "bones" or "tambourine." But a state of chronic fun is not without its penalties: the chorus over, and the crowd dispersed, no faces look so downcast and woebegone as the faces of the minstrels. They walk silently, two and two, or follow each other, a string of lonely, dispirited men, down a back street into a public house. Not even there is rest. Two go in, and immediately recommence, and banjo consumes a solitary pint outside, whilst fiddle and bones strike up within to earn another.

CONCLUSION.

WE close our survey of music in England with mingled feelings of hope and discouragement. The influence of music is every day becoming more widespread; but is it an influence which soothes, relieves, recreates, and elevates the people? We believe it is so in part; but before the musical art accomplishes this its high mission amongst us, it must become a real, not an artificial, expression of the emotions as they work in English hearts and English homes. We must not be content with foreign models, grand as some of them are—with German music composed in England, or even with little bits of ballad-music, unlike that of any other country, and therefore supposed to be English, but we must aim at forming a real national school, with a tone and temper as expressive of, and as appropriate to England, as French music is to France, Italian to Italy, and German to Germany. And we must do this, first, by keeping alive and active that love for the art which really does exist; secondly, by believing in ourselves; and, lastly, by encouraging native talent wherever it can be found, not destroying its independence by any false system of protection or puffery, but allowing it the freest development under the salutary conditions of just criticism and liberal recognition.

When we have a national school of music, and not before, we shall have high popular standards, and the music of the people will then be as real an instrument of civilization in its way, and as happily under the control of public opinion, as the Press, the Parliament, or any other of our great national institutions.

APPENDIX.

THE Author desires to acknowledge in the fullest possible manner his obligations to those writers whose books he has made most use of. The following should be especially mentioned :—

The History of Modern Music. A Course of Lectures, delivered at the Royal Institution of Great Britain by John Hullah. Parker, Son, & Bourne, London. 1862.

A Course of Lectures on the Transition Period of Musical History, delivered at the Royal Institution of Great Britain by John Hullah. Longman, Green, Longman, London. 1865.

F. J. Fétis, "Biographie Universelle des Musiciens." Firmin-Didot Frères, Paris. 1862.

The Life of Handel. By Victor Schœlcher. Trübner & Co., London. 1857.

Gluck. F. Fleischer, Leipsic.

Biographie des Musiciens. Felix Clement. Hachette et Cie., Paris. 1868.

Haydn and Mozart. Translated from the French of L. H. C. Bombet. Second edition. John Murray, London. 1818.

Franz Schubert. H. Kreissle von Hellborn, Wien. W. R. Allen, London. 1865.

Life of Chopin. Liszt. New York. 1863.

Lucrezia Floriani. George Sand. Bruxelles. 1846.

Mozart's Letters. Translated from the collection of Ludwig Nohl. Longmans, Green, & Co., London. 1865.

Beethoven's Letters. Translated from the collection of Ludwig Nohl. Longmans, Green, & Co., London. 1866.

The Pianoforte. Edward F. Rimbault, LL.D. Robert Cocks & Co., London. 1860.

Antoine Stradivari. F. J. Fétis. Vuillaume, Paris.

Matthias van den Gheyn. Xavier van Elewyck. Ch. Peters, Louvain. 1862.

The author is also much indebted to Professor Tonnessin, who placed the Louvain University Library at his disposal; to the Chevalier van Elewyck, who kindly allowed him to examine many of Van den Gheyn's unpublished MSS.; and to M. Severin van Aerschodt, the eminent Belgian bell-founder, who permitted him to inspect every part of his manufactory, and offered the most valuable and copious information upon the manufacture of bells.

To Mr. George Grove and to Mr. Felix Moscheles I am also indebted for the use which they have allowed me to make of the composers' MS. music and signatures in their possession.

16, Welbeck Street,
London, 1871.

THE END.